D0867180

CATHOLICS IN THE VATICAN II ERA

Debates about the meaning of Vatican II and its role in modern Catholic and global history have largely focused on close theological study of its authoritative documents. This volume of newly commissioned essays contends that the historical significance of the Council is best examined where these messages encountered the particular circumstances of the modern world: in local dioceses. Each author examines the social, political, and domestic circumstances of a diocese, asking how it produced a distinctive lived experience of the Council and its aftermath. How did the Council change relationships and institutions? What was it like for laymen and laywomen, for clergy, for nuns, for powerful First-World dioceses, and for those in what we now know as the Global South? A comparative reading of these chapters affords insights into these dimensions of Vatican II and will spark a new generation of research into the history of twentieth-century Catholicism as both international and local.

Kathleen Sprows Cummings is Associate Professor of American Studies and History and Director of the Cushwa Center for the Study of American Catholicism at the University of Notre Dame. Her research focuses on the history of women and American religion, particularly U.S. Catholicism. She is the author of *New Women of the Old Faith: Gender and American Catholicism in the Progressive Era* (2009).

Timothy Matovina is Professor and Chair of Theology at the University of Notre Dame. He specializes in U.S. Catholic and U.S. Latino theology and religion. His most recent book is *Latino Catholicism: Transformation in America's Largest Church* (2012).

Robert A. Orsi is Professor of Religious Studies and History and Grace Craddock Nagle Chair in Catholic Studies at Northwestern University. He studies religion in the United States, with a focus on American Catholicism in both historical and ethnographic perspectives. Orsi's most recent book is *History and Presence* (2016).

CATHOLICS
IN THE VATICAN II ERA

Local Histories of a Global Event

Edited by

KATHLEEN SPROWS CUMMINGS
University of Notre Dame

TIMOTHY MATOVINA
University of Notre Dame

ROBERT A. ORSI
Northwestern University

CAMBRIDGE
UNIVERSITY PRESS

CAMBRIDGE
UNIVERSITY PRESS

University Printing House, Cambridge CB2 8BS, United Kingdom

One Liberty Plaza, 20th Floor, New York, NY 10006, USA

477 Williamstown Road, Port Melbourne, VC 3207, Australia

314–321, 3rd Floor, Plot 3, Splendor Forum, Jasola District Centre, New Delhi – 110025, India

79 Anson Road, #06–04/06, Singapore 079906

Cambridge University Press is part of the University of Cambridge.

It furthers the University's mission by disseminating knowledge in the pursuit of
education, learning, and research at the highest international levels of excellence.

www.cambridge.org
Information on this title: www.cambridge.org/9781107141162
DOI: 10.1017/9781316493380

© Cambridge University Press 2018

First published 2018

Printed in the United States of America by Sheridan Books, Inc.

A catalogue record for this publication is available from the British Library.

ISBN 978-1-107-14116-2 Hardback

CONTENTS

CONTRIBUTORS

Jeffrey M. Burns is Director of the Harpst Center for Catholic Thought and Culture at the University of San Diego and Director of the Academy of American Franciscan History at the Franciscan School of Theology. His publications include *Disturbing the Peace: A History of the Christian Family Movement, 1949–1974* (1999) and *Keeping Faith: European and Asian Catholic Immigrants* (2006).

Marjet Derks is a Cultural Historian at Radboud University in Nijmegen, the Netherlands. She holds a chair in Sports History and also specializes in religion and gender in modernity. Her most recent publications include the co-edited *Episcopacy, Authority, and Gender: Aspects of Religious Leadership in Europe, 1100–2000* (2015).

Massimo Faggioli is Professor in the Department of Theology and Religious Studies at Villanova University. He blogs for *Commonweal*, and his publications in English include *Vatican II: The Battle for Meaning* (2012) and *A Council for the Global Church: Receiving Vatican II in History* (2015).

Alana Harris is Lecturer in modern British history at King's College London. Her research interests span the transnational history of modern Catholicism, gender and sexuality, pilgrimage, migration, and material and devotional cultures. Her most recent monographs include *Faith in the Family* (2013) and the co-edited *Love and Romance in Britain* (2014).

Kathleen Holscher is Associate Professor of American Studies and Religious Studies and holds the endowed Chair in Roman Catholic Studies at the University of New Mexico. She is the author of *Religious Lessons: Catholic Sisters and the Captive Schools Crisis in New Mexico* (2012), and several recent journal articles.

Jennifer Scheper Hughes is Associate Professor at the University of California, Riverside. She studies the history of religion in Latin America with special consideration for the spiritual lives of Mexican and Mexican American

Catholics. Hughes explores themes of popular practice, material religion, and affective approaches to the study of religion.

Joseph A. Komonchak is Professor Emeritus at the Catholic University of America, where he held the John C. and Gertrude P. Hubbard Chair in Religious Studies. He studied at the Pontifical Gregorian University in Rome from 1960 to 1964 and specializes in the history and theology of the Second Vatican Council. He served as editor of the English edition of the five-volume *History of Vatican II* (1996–2005) as well as *The New Dictionary of Theology* (1987).

Andrew S. Moore is Professor of History at Saint Anselm College in Manchester, New Hampshire. He is the author of *The South's Tolerable Alien: Roman Catholics in Alabama and Georgia, 1945–1970* (2007), and several journal articles and book chapters.

Gilles Routhier holds doctorates in theology from the Catholic University of Paris and in history of religion and religious anthropology from the University of Paris-Sorbonne. His research focuses on the Second Vatican Council, its teaching, history, hermeneutics, and reception. He is currently the dean of the Faculty of Theology and Religious Studies at Laval University in Quebec City.

John C. Seitz is Associate Professor in the Department of Theology at Fordham University. He is Associate Director of the Curran Center for American Catholic Studies and co-edits a book series entitled *Catholic Practice in North America*. Seitz is the author of *No Closure: Catholic Practice and Boston's Parish Shutdowns* (2011).

Sol Serrano is Professor of History and Vice Provost for Research at the Pontificia Universidad Católica de Chile. Among recent books she has authored, coauthored, or edited are *Qué hacer con Dios en la República. Política y secularización en Chile 1845–1885* (2009) and *Historia de la Educación en Chile 1810–2010* (2013).

Leslie Woodcock Tentler is Professor Emerita of History at the Catholic University of America, where she specialized in the history of American Catholicism. Her most recent book is *Catholics and Contraception: An American History* (2004).

Brandon Vaidyanathan is an Associate Professor of Sociology at the Catholic University of America and is a Public Policy Fellow at the Center for Ethics and Culture at the University of Notre Dame. He holds a Ph.D. in Sociology from the University of Notre Dame.

Luz María Díaz de Valdés holds a master's degree in Latin American history from Tufts University and is pursuing a Ph.D. in Global History at Tufts. Her dissertation examines the emergence of leftist clergy in Chile during the late 1960s and early 1970s. She was a guest scholar at the Kellogg Institute for International Studies at the University of Notre Dame in the spring of 2012.

PREFACE

Elected to the Chair of Saint Peter on October 28, 1958, Angelo Giuseppe Roncalli, who took the name John XXIII, appears in photographs of the time as a gentle and benign Italian *nonno*, always smiling broadly. The new pope was an old man. The thinking in Rome among Vatican *cognoscenti*, including some of the cardinals who participated in the conclave that chose him, was that Roncalli's would be a sort of interim papacy, a breath-catching pause after the long and eventful pontificate of Pius XII (1939–1958). Things did not turn out this way, of course. On January 25, 1959, just three months after his election, John XXIII announced his plan to convoke an ecumenical council, "for the edification, enlightenment and joy of the entire Christian people." Looking ahead to the meeting, the pope extended "a renewed cordial invitation to the faithful of the separated communities to participate with us in this quest for unity and grace, for which so many souls long in all parts of the world." Three years later, after "arduous preparation," in the pope's words, the Council opened, on October 11, 1962. In his address to the assembly in Saint Peter's that fall morning, Pope John recalled with sly humor the initial reaction in the Roman Curia to the idea of an ecumenical council. "At first those present were unexpectedly struck silent, as if by a brilliant ray of light from above." Revolutions are not usually announced so quietly and clearly, or with such warm wit. But this one was.[1]

The pope had kept his plans secret. Skilled in the semiotics of power, the curial cardinals and even more so the members of their staffs, who had no idea that such a thing was on the horizon, would have noted the pope's positive and pastoral tone. They would also have grimly observed that instead of summoning "the faithful of separated communities" to Rome to submit to papal authority, the pope had asked Protestants to come share in the work of the future council, an invitation they accepted. This was at a time when barely tolerated "mixed marriages" required the consent of the non-Catholic partner to raise the couple's children Catholic. Curial listeners would also have discerned the pope's outward-looking attention to people – not only *Catholic* people – in all parts of the modern world, presumably including its communist and non-Christian parts, and his concern for the spiritual longing in modern men's and women's hearts.

The Second Vatican Council was an epochal event. The Council's enthusiastic and open engagement with the modern age in the hope of shaping a holier and more human future was said to be rooted in faithfulness to the past. This is how church reform has always been understood in Catholic history. The Council's word for its program of turning back to patristic theology and the ritual practices of the early Christian communities was *ressourcement*, an idea from *la nouvelle théologie*, the interwar European theological revival that had a profound influence on the intellectual orientation of the Council. As Pope John said on the Council's first day, its charge was "to restore the simple and pure lines that the face of the Church of Jesus Christ had at its birth." It was as if all the many ages of the church were in play during the years of the Council. Not until the tearing down of the Berlin Wall in 1989 would contemporary history again seem so fluid, so excitingly in motion. A sense of exhilarating optimism prevailed among many of the roughly 2,400 prelates in attendance on the opening day, especially after hearing the pope sternly admonish those who "see only ruin and calamity in the present conditions of human society . . . and act as if they have nothing to learn from history."[2]

"We must quite disagree," the pope continued, "with these prophets of doom who are always forecasting disaster, as if the end of the world were at hand." Everyone in Saint Peter's Basilica that first morning knew to whom the pope was speaking. While at all times the church has condemned error "with the greatest severity," the pope declared, "at present, the spouse of Christ prefers to use the medicine of mercy rather than the weapons of severity." Once again the pope had taken the curia by surprise, substituting this address for the one he had circulated earlier. The Council was put on notice: there would be change. The name Pope John XXIII gave to this change was "*aggiornamento*."[3]

★

Since the Council's closing session on December 8, 1965, presided over by Pope John's successor, Pope Paul VI, there has been an ongoing and often contentious debate around the Catholic world about what happened at the Council, whether anything happened, or anything new, and what it means to be Catholic in the Council's wake. Did Vatican II represent a rupture with the Catholic past or was it in continuity with "the twenty Ecumenical Councils and the innumerable and not insignificant provincial and regional Councils" that Pope John cited on the first day of its first session? What is the right ordering between the authority of an ecumenical council and the authority of the papacy – and of the Vatican bureaucracy? The stakes of such questions are very high. They cut to the heart of the identity of "the church that can and cannot change," in jurist and historian John T. Noonan Jr.'s phrase, and they have profound implications for how Catholics around the world in various social, cultural, and political contexts practice their faith, including their relationships with men and women of other religions.[4]

And what of the years after the Council? Is there anything in its documents that may guide contemporary Catholics through issues that were not only not on the Council's agenda but were still undreamt of in the early 1960s, principally what historian Stephen Schloesser, SJ, calls "biopolitics"? Schloesser means by this the revolution in sexual mores and identities that lay ahead, just over the horizon of the Council's final session, and the rapidly changing technologies of life and death. Or may such guidance be found in "the spirit of the Council," a controversial phrase that refers to what the prelates gathered in Rome intended and envisioned beyond what they inscribed in the official conciliar documents? Is there anything in the Council's theology or ecclesiology to help contemporary Catholics struggling with the causes and consequences of the clergy sexual abuse crisis, with the pain of having been abused by an *alter Christus* and the anger of having been betrayed by a bishop? The conciliar years were followed first by an ebullient period of experimentation within Catholicism, when Catholics explored new ways of worshipping, for example, and new forms of social and political engagement, and then by an era of constraint, when the more radical-seeming of the Council's implications were reframed in favor of stricter, more "traditionalist" interpretations, with secure lines of authority restored at all levels of the church. Has all this interpretation and reinterpretation of the Council turned Catholics into "a people adrift," as journalist Peter Steinfels argued in 2005, or into a people more prepared to contend in openness and faith with the challenges of the various worlds they inhabit, as Pope John had hoped? "I am certainly not alone in believing," wrote Georgetown's John O'Malley, author of *What Happened at Vatican II*, "that the best – indeed, the indispensable – approach to understanding Roman Catholicism today is through Vatican II." To understand the Second Vatican Council, in other words, is always to understand much more than the Second Vatican Council.[5]

Debates about the Council's meanings and more broadly about its role in modern Catholic and in global history have largely proceeded via close theological study of its authoritative documents. These consisted of four "constitutions" (*On the Sacred Liturgy, On the Church, On Divine Revelation,* and *On the Church in the Modern World*); nine "decrees" (*On the Media of Social Communications, On the Catholic Churches of the Eastern Rite, On Ecumenism, Concerning the Pastoral Office of Bishops, On the Adaptation and Renewal of Religious Life, On Priestly Training, On the Apostolate of the Laity, On the Missionary Activity of the Church,* and *On the Ministry and Life of Priests*); and three "declarations" (*On Christian Education, On the Relation of the Church to Non-Christian Religions,* and *On Religious Freedom*). Many who have engaged in this work, wherever they are on the spectrum of liberal/conservative Catholicism, have been heavily invested in one or the other interpretation of the Council as the sole correct one – rupture/continuity – and their readings have been influenced by extratextual considerations and commitments, among them political and cultural understandings and values and divergent attitudes toward the dangers and promise of what the Council referred to as "the modern world." Such theological hermeneutics are essential, and many of the contributors to this volume have contributed to the unfolding international debate.

Catholics in the Vatican II Era approaches the meanings and impact of the Council from a different perspective. Its core argument is that the historical significance of the Council, within but also outside specifically Catholic contexts, is best examined at the combustive points where the Council's messages, aspirations, and fears, explicit and implied, intended and unintended, met up most explosively with the particular circumstances of the modern world it was directed to engage in a new spirit of openness and humility by Pope John XXIII. The Second Vatican Council was among other things a global media event. By the Council's opening day, John O'Malley writes, the Vatican had issued more than a thousand press passes. This meant that the Council's deliberations and decisions were reported, in real time, in local and international media, both Catholic and secular. When they spoke up during debates on the floor, bishops did so not only from their theological positions but also from the perspective of the historical concerns, interests, and exigencies of their home dioceses. The decisions taken in Rome about the sacred liturgy, for instance, or about the vocations of priests and nuns, in turn got caught up in the minutia of local parish life back in the bishops' dioceses. Obviously the history of this era in Catholic history cannot be read out of the Council's documents as if these were scripts that Catholics wherever they were simply acted out. This was especially so given the Council's repeated emphasis on the dignity and freedom of individual conscience and its encouragement of an active laity, as well as the inevitable ambiguity and hermeneutical latitude of documents intended for the universal church but read in local contexts, as is usually the case in Catholic history. At the forefront of the chapters ahead are the ways that Catholics living in very different social, political, and domestic circumstances and within the particularities of different histories and memories embraced, resisted, and interpreted change in the church.[6]

In other words, while *something* certainly happened at the Council, not *everything* did. Moreover, not everything happened *at* the Council, but *between* the Council and the world. The Council was a global event and it took the whole world and many decades to work out its implications and meanings, a task that may never end. Think here of the roiling debates over the meaning of the framers of the U.S. Declaration of Independence in 1776 or of the 1945 Charter of the United Nations.

To take a particularly revealing example of what we mean, the Council's culminating document *Gaudium et Spes* (promulgated by Paul VI on December 7, 1965) boldly declared that "there must be made available to all men everything necessary for leading a truly human life ... the right to education, to employment ... to respect, to appropriate information, to activity in accord with the upright norm of one's conscience, to the protection of

privacy and rightful freedom, even in religious matters." This ringing statement
was heard differently in Santiago, Chile, amid the deepening political crisis
before and after the 1973 assassination of Salvador Allende in a coup sponsored
by the American Central Intelligence Agency (see the chapter by Sol Serrano
and Luz María Díaz de Valdés); in San Francisco, California, by the growing
gay community just finding its political and religious voices (as Jeffrey M. Burns
describes it); and in Detroit, Michigan, contending with the ever more perilous
racial and economic stratification of the city and the dreadful consequences of
the 1967 riot, with white ethnic Catholics and African Americans, including
African American Catholics, meeting on the front lines of urban change
(discussed by Leslie Woodcock Tentler).[7]

   This is what makes the history of the conciliar era global: not the fact that
Catholics are everywhere on the planet, but that the Council's meanings and
impact took shape globally, with influence moving in many directions at once, as
developments among Catholics within the circumstances of one part of the
world – as reported by the international media present in Rome for the duration –
resonated with Catholics elsewhere in different circumstances. The African
bishops at the Council, for instance, played a pivotal role in developing the
concept of "enculturation," according to which Catholic ritual and theology
would be reformulated in indigenous languages, conceptualizations, and aesthetics. This idea freed particular Catholic populations on other continents to
develop their own theologies grounded in local metaphors and experiences, to
redesign church art and architecture in accordance with specific aesthetic
traditions and histories, and to make the Eucharist a blessing on these cultural
inheritances. As several of the chapters make clear, such a seemingly affirmative
impulse could have explosive consequences at the intersection of the conciliar
vision of renewal with social worlds riven by long-standing linguistic, racial,
and economic divisions.

   In this way, a lived history approach to the Council and its global reception
restores a sense of contingency and immediacy to Catholic life and thought in
this era as it situates the Council more fully in the movement of time, which is to
say, in what preceded it and what came after. There was a tradition in Spanish-
speaking New Mexico, for example, of local lay leadership that long antedated
the Council, as Kathleen Holscher discusses in her chapter. The Council's
mandate for lay ministries in the church would have to build on this local
inheritance in the Southwest, and in the process both were changed. The
historiography of lived religion also recovers the ironies of which history always
consists, especially so in times of such profound change, when an old order is
inchoately giving way to a new one, as during the conciliar era.

   Andrew Moore shows in his account of the diocese of Atlanta, Georgia, that
the social interaction among parishioners encouraged by the new liturgy, during
the exchange of a sign of peace, for instance, made it more difficult to integrate
Southern parishes because now it was not only a matter of black and white

Catholics sitting alongside each other but of touching each other's hands during Mass. Conciliar liturgists emphasized that this seemingly novel innovation was actually "the reintroduction of a practice which has its roots in early Christian tradition," as American liturgist Father Joseph M. Champlin explained to irate readers of his popular column in the early 1970s, but in the simultaneity of the unsimultaneous characteristic of Catholic history and life, this is not how it felt in the pews.[8]

Such unpredictability and contingency were taken by some Catholics at the time of the Council and since as evidence that the church had lost the authority that comes from standing stock still above and outside history and culture, anchored in unchanging doctrine. Opening the windows of the churches in Atlanta, as Pope John wanted, had the unintended consequence of letting in from the raging streets the ugliness of American racism and the bitter controversy over the war in Vietnam. Yet as the authors in this volume show, at no moment was the Council free of its times, just as at no moment is Catholicism itself ever free of its times. What to some may seem the loss of sacred transcendence to others appears as the courage of taking on the tough challenges of the modern world in a spirit of faithfulness and humility. A lived history approach offers the tools for readers to think through this large question at the level of experience.

★

In the chapters ahead, the diocese is taken as the most relevant unit of historical study. Of the twelve dioceses discussed in this volume, seven are in North America; these make up Part I. Part II widens the volume's geographical and historical lenses to include dioceses in southern and northern Europe, in South America, and on the Indian subcontinent. But what does Santiago, Chile, or Detroit, Michigan, or Boston, Massachusetts – to name three of the dioceses studied here – have to do with the history of the Council itself? Diocesan history is the most resolutely local of all forms of Catholic historiography, whereas the Second Vatican Council was global in composition and vision. There seems to be a problem of scale here.

Governed by bishops, dioceses, or sees, are administrative districts of church governance mapped onto the coordinates of local geographies (e.g., counties, regions, states) usually headquartered in metropolitan areas. In canon law and Catholic theology, the diocese stands as a synecdoche for the universal church. A diocese is Catholicism in miniature. The decision to focus on dioceses rather than on national churches was made in part for the obvious reason that the individual dioceses in the Catholic world were represented at the Council by their bishops, who meditated between diocesan concerns (as the bishop understood them) and the conciliar agenda. Modern telecommunications made it possible for bishops to stay in everyday contact with the challenges arising at home, including the demand for new parishes in the expanding suburbs, decaying urban parish schools, dissatisfaction among priests and nuns, rumblings of civil unrest, and anti-colonial protests. Such absorption in local matters was a distraction for some; for others, it was a way of monitoring how the people in their care, lay and clerical, thought about what was happening in Rome, how anxious or excited, or both, they were about the future.

The local diocese is the major nexus of contact between church and world, and it was here, at this level, where the Council's decisions were experienced most intimately and unpredictably. It was in the diocese that the new ideas and practices coming from Rome were interpreted, implemented or not, or contested, by bishops who were overly cautious, too enthusiastic, or overtly hostile to the changes. These ordinaries served as lightning rods for dissent across the Catholic spectrum for laity and clergy alike. With its other characteristics, the conciliar era was a time of intense self-scrutiny among Catholics and insistent pulse taking.

Never before had Catholic psychologists, pollsters, and sociologists been so in demand for their expertise in understanding the times! It was most often at the diocesan level that the many studies of laypeople's attitudes toward the new liturgy, for example, or of the changing lives of priests and nuns were commissioned and conducted. The evidence they gathered circulated back around through the chancery to "nourish the archdiocese with material for analysis, reflection, and pastoral planning," as Luz María Díaz de Valdés and Sol Serrano write of such a circulation in Santiago.

Dioceses have their own histories and memories carried in the minds, hearts, and bodies of parishioners; of priests, nuns, and lay brothers; of elementary school and high school students and teachers; of the editors of diocesan papers; and of chancery staffs, as well as in the stones, smells, colors, and spaces of its architecture, shrines, cemeteries, and schools. The many new institutional forms that arose in the wake of the Council – social justice task forces, pastoral centers, commissions and offices for the concerns of particular groups of Catholics, new programs of seminary education, retreat centers, study groups, centers for theological and liturgical studies, senates of priests and nuns, unions of Catholic intellectuals, Latin Mass societies, and so on – proliferated at the level of the diocese. Each diocese around the world was a conciliar micro climate, a laboratory of change and resistance, and a school for understanding what the Council was about. Dioceses were not the only places where the local met the global in the Vatican II era, but diocesan-focused analyses are a necessary dimension of any history of the Council.

The potential of diocesan studies to shed new light on understanding Vatican II is illustrated in the examination of the dioceses of Detroit and s-Hertogenbosch, the Netherlands, as respectively discussed by Leslie Woodcock Tentler and Marjet Derks. To look across the Catholic world, as exemplified in these two locales, working-class Catholics often felt excluded by the lay middle-class elites who eagerly stepped into diocesan and parochial leadership positions during and after the Council and then claimed from these posts to speak for all local Catholics. "Less educated Catholics," Tentler writes, "might easily come to feel that the post-conciliar church was one that privileged qualities they themselves lacked." The Second Vatican Council coincided with Catholics' entry into the professional classes in greater numbers in many parts of the world. Historians of the Council may not have paid enough attention to the ways that conciliar mandates built on and even endorsed emergent structures of class, cultural capital, and privilege that were rapidly dividing Catholics into different strata in various places in this era, leading to a hermeneutics of social class in the interpretation and implementation of the Council's agenda or in resistance to it. Enculturation was not only a challenge for faraway congregations but also for the working-class parish down the street.

Such questions go to the heart of the place of the Second Vatican Council in history. They also contribute to the explication of its meanings. John O'Malley identifies two ways that Catholic history is written: in one, "the Church sails through the sea of history unaffected by it"; in the other, the church is understood as "a community of human beings living in time and space." For those who take the latter approach, as all the authors in this volume do, the Catholic tradition is "not an inert body of truths but an incarnated reality," a lived reality, which means a reality beset by all the vicissitudes, contingencies, ironies, possibilities, hopes, and failures of history. In his chapter on the intersection of the Council and Quebec's Quiet Revolution, Gilles Routhier calls this the "phenomenon of encounter." "As the Church converted the 'barbarians,'" O'Malley writes, "the barbarians influenced the church." It is difficult to see how one can possibly be true and not the other.[9]

Specific dioceses were chosen because we believed that each respectively offered an especially rich case study of some issue of particular importance for understanding the lived history of the Council. Alana Harris's chapter on English Catholics and the Diocese of Westminster, in London, for example, explores how the weight of the past in a diocese, as Catholics in a particular location remembered and cherished that past, might determine the fate of the Council's mandates. The introduction of the vernacular liturgy was one of the most popular of the era's changes among Catholics almost everywhere. But in London, the memory of the Elizabethan persecutions generated fierce resistance to the English Mass: for centuries, Latin had been the language of English Catholic identity and difference, sealed by the blood of Catholic martyrs, whereas English was the language of the executioner. In Cuernavaca, Mexico, a popular progressive bishop's efforts to uproot beloved but extra-liturgical devotions prompted many of the same poor people who had long revered him for his attacks on economic injustice to turn against him, as Jennifer Scheper Hughes describes. It was not the intention of the prelates and theologians who composed the *Constitution on the Sacred Liturgy* to intensify ethnic conflict and violence in the Archdiocese of Bangalore, but as Brandon Vaidyanathan shows, they did.

Everywhere in the Catholic world, the Council got entangled in stories that had been underway long before its first session. Here is where global history meets local history. Such close-grained histories of the conciliar era in particular dioceses hold the promise in aggregate of a fuller and richer history of the meanings and consequences of the Second Vatican Council than is currently possible given the state of historical knowledge. The trajectory of the historiography of another era of Christian history offers a revealing analogy here. Early studies of the Reformation, the Catholic Reformation, and the Counter-Reformation divided along confessional lines, as Protestant and Catholic historians and their secular heirs vied with one another to take hold of the immense transformations in religion and society within Europe and around the world in the sixteenth century. They did so by means of large countervailing historical claims – here and now were the birth of modern freedom, the origin of modernity's chaos, the root of the Enlightenment, the beginnings of the secularization of knowledge. But these macro accounts of the times were eventually succeeded by micro social historical studies of the Reformation and Catholic Reformation in *particular* towns, villages, religious houses, even in individual households, by a new generation of historians. The accumulation of local studies in turn served as the basis for more richly described and subtly nuanced histories of the period in which the former confidence of broad generalizations yielded to messier and more equivocal conclusions. The Protestant defense of religious liberty in certain places served to cloak religious violence and exclusion; the new sciences coexisted with the miraculous; the ascendancy of the seemingly democratic congregations opened up unexpected opportunities for domination. We hope that this volume may encourage a parallel trajectory leading to a similar messiness – and greater insights – in the history of the Second Vatican Council.

Taken together Parts I and II offer a basis for comparative studies of the Council meanings as they were worked out within a single region with interwoven destinies among the populations, as in Canada, the United States, and Mexico (Part I), and also more expansively across the Catholic globe (Part II). The conciliar era is generally understood as the awakening of the laity to their distinctive vocation in the church, for example; it was the age of the "new Catholic laity." Parish Councils, one of the institutional innovations that grew out of conciliar ecclesiology, were meant to introduce a spirit of shared responsibility between clergy and laity in the management of everyday church affairs. Did this happen? What sorts of resistance did such efforts encounter and who from – bishops and priests, but perhaps also from laypeople themselves? Was the laity ready to assume such responsibilities, and if not was any provision made to prepare them? Was Catholic church life truly transformed by the Council's vision of the church as "the people of God on pilgrimage in the world"? "Many laypersons and some priests ... complained," Vaidyanathan quotes a knowledgeable and active laywoman on the status of parish Councils in

Bangalore, "The priests made the point to have these Councils going. But it was perceived as gracious permission of the clergy to allow the laity to come and sit with them. But you know who's holding the reins. It was *dhikhava* [window-dressing] ... There's more show than substance." At the same time, even the most sympathetic theologians occasionally fretted about an overly assertive laity demanding too much of their own right in the church.

Taking up such questions of lived experience, the chapters ahead point toward further research to enhance comparative analyses of diocesan histories during the Vatican II era.[10]

★

Arguably the most understudied aspect of the lived history of the Council, one that impacted Catholics in every corner of the globe, is the way it shaped relations between Catholics of every background: priests, nuns, laypeople, bishops. Their responses to the Council in its times were all shaped by their relationships with one another. When Catholic activists burned draft files in protest against the Vietnam War at Catonsville, Maryland, on May 17, 1968, the appearance in the next morning's newspapers of Fathers Daniel and Philip Berrigan in their Roman collars praying over the flaming records reportedly led to fierce conversations at Catholic dinner tables around the country. What seemed like an event in the public sphere had deep personal and domestic resonance. Comparative analysis of institutional changes across dioceses – mandated liturgical reforms, engagement in political and social concerns, new structures of parochial and diocesan governance, official participation in ecumenical initiatives, and the like – is of course both essential and intricately intertwined with the interpersonal histories of Catholics. But a relational focus for the conciliar era provides the clearest example of how profoundly a comparative lived history approach can expand our knowledge of Vatican II.[11]

In his probing and influential study of the rhetorical style and language of the Council's documents, O'Malley notes the predominance in them of what he calls "horizontal words," which he contrasts with the "vertical words" of earlier church Councils. Such verticality was especially true of Vatican I (1869–1870). It was at this meeting that the dogma of papal infallibility was proclaimed despite the best efforts of churchmen in the United States and Europe anxious about what it would do to the church's moral authority in the modern world to table it. As the First Vatican Council hastily finished its work and the prelates rushed to flee Rome, Giuseppe Garibaldi's troops broke through the papal lines, leaving Pius IX "a prisoner in the Vatican." Relations between the church and "the modern world" had reached a nadir. Among the horizontal words of Vatican II, on the other hand, O'Malley writes, were "reciprocity words," the most important of which were "dialogue" and "collegiality"; "friendship words," such as those Pope John addressed to the separated brethren in his announcement of the Council; words that speak of the desire for change, such as *aggiornamento*; and "interiority-words" – the most famous of these was the opening phrase of *Gaudium et Spes*, which gives the document its title. "Joy and hope, grief and anguish."[12]

Such a hermeneutics of horizontality points to a central dimension of the lived history of the Second Vatican Council in its times – namely, the profound impact it had on the web of relationships that constitute the lived experience of the faith among priests, between priests and bishops, between clergy and laity, within religious orders, among vowed women religious, between gay and straight Catholics, between parishioners at Mass, between Catholics of different races, cultures, classes, and age groups. All of these personal ties, many of them long standing, governed by inherited protocols, hierarchies, and expectations, were implicated in the others, so that to pull on any one strand in the web was to set all of them moving. "The real issue of renewal," Chicago sister Karol Jackowski writes of this period in her convent life, "had little to do with clothes, or names, or schedules, and everything to do with how we lived in community and how well we loved one another."[13]

A focus on the interpersonal must be attentive to harmful and even abusive relations in dioceses and parishes. Revelations about the sexual abuse of children by priests, often in distinctly Catholic spaces and times – rectories, convents, sacristies, and sanctuaries – in particular have cast a harsh retrospective light on the relational history of this period. Did the new informality in social relations among priests, nuns, and laypeople; the restiveness of young men and women with seminary and convent discipline; their desire for greater intimacy; the diminishing emphasis on sin and confession; and even perhaps the era's theology of an accepting and forgiving God converge to create the circumstances that facilitated abuse, if they did not actually encourage it? Some commentators have thought so, yet most reported incidents of abuse go well back into the pre-conciliar church in the United States and elsewhere. The belief that priests are special beings, far superior to ordinary humans, which was commonplace in Catholic culture before the Council, contributed to the impunity with which clerical abusers acted and to the collusion of bishops and chancery officials that protected priests and put more children at risk.

Such an understanding of episcopal authority and responsibility cannot be attributed to the Council's ecclesiology. John Seitz's chapter on Boston, which was ground zero of the crisis in the early twenty-first century, reminds us to situate that crisis in a wider historical frame, even as it underscores the need to address it in historical studies of the conciliar era.

More broadly, relationships were one source – perhaps *the* source – of the most intense anxieties of the era. Priests worried that the emphasis on the special vocation of the laity would muddle clerical authority and status. "The role of laity and clergy is becoming vaguer day by day," Tentler quotes Catholic Family Life activists Dorothy and John Drish, writing in 1966, "Priests do not know what their role is. They all say that." Likewise, many bishops at the meetings in

Rome expressed concern that the Council's emphasis on ecclesial collegiality threatened to upend the church's chain of command. Many vowed women religious who until the mid-1960s had lived under the strictest regimes of discipline, obedience, and submission that governed every aspect of their every-day lives, in particular the quality of their intimacy with other sisters, worried that they would not know how to enter the new ways of being in relationship to others that were not only open to them now but expected of them.

But the fact that all relationships had been suddenly thrown into question enlivened the most profound hopes of the era, too, and was its greatest excite-ment. In his study of what he calls the "emotional history" of the Second Vatican Council, Seitz describes the desire among students at Saint John's Seminary in the Archdiocese of Boston for warmer and more sustaining friendships with their classmates in place of the stunted opportunities previously allowed them, as they had come to see these. Small groups of nuns were given permission to move together out of their convents into apartments closer to their workplaces, which afforded them greater opportunity for friendship and community. Laypeople and clergy reached for new understandings of themselves in their roles in the church and toward each other. How was a layman or laywoman to participate in the Eucharist now? The Council's liturgical reforms opened the way for more active participatory roles for laypeople in the liturgy; parochial committees planned the weekly worship services; parish priests celebrated Masses in the living rooms and backyards of their parishioners. What did it mean to be a priest in such circum-stances, to be in relationship with laypeople, whose rights and freedom of conscience the Council had endorsed? Or to be a communicant in them? Such questions inevitably become issues of authority within Catholicism. How was one to be a mature adult and at the same time obedient to the authority of his or her superiors in religious orders? How were laypeople to be faithful to the teaching authority of the church and at the same time honor the lives and choices to which they believed God had called them? In this new ecumenical era, how were Catholics to behave toward other Christians or toward people of other faiths?

The relationships at stake in the conciliar era were not only those among humans but also, perhaps most importantly, between humans and God, between men and women and the Virgin Mary and the saints, and between the living and the dead. In the minds of many Catholics who grew up in these times, the Council was about love, especially the love of God for men and women. The God Catholics were offered before the Council was very often a watchful and punitive judge who they might not have known loved them. This is what many Catholics report of their religious formation before the Council. The God of the conciliar years, on the other hand, was more the dispenser of the medicine of mercy than the calculator of faults. "What a fantastic summer I had," an American nun, Sister Patricia Lucas, DHM, wrote in her diary on September 6, 1966. "The best part of the whole summer," Sister Lucas continued, "occurred when some of us celebrated the death of God. That God, the Untouchable One in the heavens, the Recorder of all our misdeeds, that Great Chess Player that moves us like pawns, had to die so that the 'Ground of My Being,' as [Protestant theologian Paul] Tillich calls him, could truly live in me."[14]

Conciliar-era theologians and liturgists set about thinning the ranks of the saints, who were as familiar to Catholics and as much a part of their lives as family members, and eliminating the vast array of devotional practices associated with their cults. This led to a stripping of the altars around the Catholic world and to a season of iconoclasm within the churches but also to resistance and alienation. Purgatory disappeared from the Catholic map, white became the color of funeral vestments, and the practice of saying the rosary alongside the coffins of the dead was discouraged. How were living people to remain in relationship with their dead now, to assist them in the afterlife, as they had done by praying them out of Purgatory?

Changing relationships in the church, the dilemmas they raised, and the opportunities they opened are at stake in every chapter in the pages ahead; in most cases, they provide the underlying dynamics of the history described. The insights a comparative reading of these chapters affords for understanding relational, institutional, and other dimensions of the history of Vatican II are the primary contributions of this book. Our hope as editors is that the lived history approach employed here will spark a new generation of research that will expand knowledge and understanding of Vatican II in the way previous scholarship has for international religious events such as the Reformation.

★

In his opening address to the Council, quoted at the beginning of this Preface, Pope John sternly cautioned those in the church, which is to say, those sitting before him in the serried ranks of prelates in Saint Peter's Basilica, who were only able to imagine the world around them in dystopian terms. These "prophets of doom" incessantly lament that "our times, if compared to past centuries, have been getting worse." It was clear that Pope John took such an attitude to be the result of willful ignorance and of a refusal to look at the world as the world actually is: "They act as if they have nothing to learn from history, which is the teacher of life, and as if at the time of past Councils everything went favorably and correctly, with respect to Christian doctrine, morality, and the Church's proper freedom."[15]

"The teacher of life." Pope John is calling here not only for attention to the past but for a particular quality of attention, one that sees the past as it was, rather than "as if . . . everything went faithfully and correctly." He does not denounce such contingencies as mere errors, however. Instead, he invites the bishops in front of him and at the beginning of their meeting to learn from what was unforeseen, unpredictable, even unfortunate about the past. This will require "discretion and prudence of judgment," he adds, which sounds like the pope's way of challenging his hearers to be critical of the prejudices and presuppositions that distort their vision of history and contemporary life. The pope wanted the church's leaders to open their eyes to the way life in the past was and in the present around them is actually lived. This opening day's message was congruent with a broader shift in Catholic intellectual life that was underway before the Council; in this address, he gives it a strong endorsement. In his chapter on the Diocese of Ferrara, in northeast Italy, Massimo Faggioli refers to the shift as the "anthropological turn" in Catholicism. It entailed a reorientation in knowledge away from the Scholastic methodology that had reigned supreme in Catholicism throughout the nineteenth and twentieth centuries, according to which truth is known deductively, moving from general propositions to specific instances, toward an inductive approach, grounded in particularities. It is undoubtedly too much, too presumptuous of us, to say that Pope John was calling for the methodology of lived history. But this is what the chapters ahead offer to readers, a step toward what we hope will be a longer and more comprehensive ongoing project.

NOTES

1. Quoted in John W. O'Malley, *What Happened at Vatican II* (Cambridge, MA: Belknap Press of Harvard University Press, 2008), p. 17; on the controversies surrounding the announcement, see Giuseppe Alberigo and Joseph A. Komonchak (eds.), *History of Vatican II:* Volume One*, Announcing and Preparing Vatican Council II, Toward a New Era in Catholicism* (Maryknoll, NY: Orbis Books, 1995), pp. 1–54. Pope John's address on the Council's opening day, *Gaudet Mater Ecclesia*, may be found at jakomonchak.files.wordpress.com/2012/10/john-xxiii-opening-speech.pdf, and in Latin at w2.vatican.va/content/john-xxiii/la/speeches/1962/documents/hf_j-xxiii_spe_19621011_opening-Council.html

2. Gaudet Mater Ecclesia, 8.

3. Gaudet Mater Ecclesia, 8, 16.

4. John T. Noonan Jr., *A Church that Can and Cannot Change: The Development of Catholic Moral Teaching* (Notre Dame, IN: University of Notre Dame Press, 2005); for the contemporary controversies within Catholicism over the Council's meanings, see Massimo Faggioli, *Vatican II: The Battle for Meaning* (Mahwah, NJ: Paulist Press, 2012) and David G. Schultenover (ed.), *Vatican II: Did Anything Happen?* (New York: Continuum, 2007).

5. "Biopolitics and the Construction of Postconciliar Catholicism" in Christopher Denny, Patrick Hayes, and Nicholas Rademacher (eds.), *A Realist's Church: Essays in Honor of Joseph Komonchak* (Maryknoll, NY: Orbis Books, 2015), pp. 147–166; on "the spirit of the Council," see John W. O'Malley, "Vatican II: Did Anything Happen?" in Schultenover, *Vatican II*, p. 56. While he acknowledges the inadequacy of the term, because one person's "spirit of the Council" might not be another's, O'Malley writes, "Many of us, I believe, still cannot shake the feeling that the expression got hold of something that was both real and important. 'Spirit' suggested that the Council had an overall orientation or pointed in a certain direction." Peter Steinfels's book is *A People*

Adrift: The Crisis of the Roman Catholic Church in America (New York: Simon & Schuster, 2003). For O'Malley's judgment on the importance of understanding the Council for understanding Roman Catholicism, see *What Happened at Vatican II*, p. 2.

6. The detail about press passes is from O'Malley, "Vatican II: Did Anything Happen?" p. 61; for press coverage in real time, see the compilation of selected dispatches a reporter calling himself "Xavier Rynne" (a pseudonym for late Redemptorist priest Father Francis X. Murphy) sent from Rome to the *New Yorker* during the Council's sessions, Xavier Rynne, *Vatican Council II: An Authoritative One-Volume Version of the Four Historic Books* (New York: Farrar, Straus and Giroux, 1968). For a lively account of the goings-on among reporters gathered in Rome and of their relationships with prelates attending the meetings, see Robert Blair Kaiser, *Clerical Error: A True Story* (New York: Continuum, 2003). A helpful discussion of the challenge of reading religious documents in their many contexts is Anne M. Blackburn, "The Text and the World" in Robert A. Orsi (ed.), *The Cambridge Companion to Religious Studies* (New York: Cambridge University Press, 2012), pp. 151–167.

7. *Gaudium et Spes*, part 1, chap. 2, 26, www.vatican.va/archive/hist_Councils/ ii_vatican_Council/documents/vat-ii_const_19651207_gaudium-et-spes_en.html.

8. Joseph M. Champlin, *The New Yet Old Mass* (Notre Dame, IN: Ave Maria Press, 1977), p. 91.

9. O'Malley, "Vatican II: Did Anything Happen?" p. 58.

10. For examples of contemporary excitement about the "new laity" in the U.S. context, see Daniel Callahan, *The Mind of the Catholic Layman* (New York: Charles Scribner's Sons, 1963); Robert G. Hoyt (ed.), *Issues that Divide the Church* (New York: Macmillan, 1967); and Russell Barta (ed.), *Challenge to the Laity* (Huntington, IN: Our Sunday Visitor, 1980).

11. Of the many books about the Catonsville Nine, interested readers might begin with Daniel Berrigan, *The Trial of the Catonsville Nine* (Boston: Beacon Press, 1970); Daniel Berrigan, *To Dwell in Peace: An Autobiography* (San Francisco: Harper & Row, 1987); and Murray Polner and Jim O'Grady, *Disarmed and Dangerous: The Radical Lives and Times of Daniel and Philip Berrigan, Brothers in Religious Faith and Civil Disobedience* (New York: Basic Books, 1997).

12. O'Malley, "Vatican II: Did Anything Happen?" p. 58.

13. Sister Karol Jackowski, *Forever and Ever, Amen: Becoming a Nun in the Sixties* (New York: Riverhead Books, 2007), p. 175.

14. Sister Patricia Lucas, "Diary of Change" in Ann Patrick Ware (ed.), *Midwives of the Future: American Sisters Tell Their Story* (Kansas City, MO: Leaven Press, 1985), pp. 172–180, at 175

15. Gaudet Mater Ecclesia, 8.

PART I

North American Essays

I

SEXUALITY AFTER THE COUNCIL: GAY CATHOLICS, MARRIED CLERGY, RIGHTS, AND CHANGE IN SAN FRANCISCO, 1962–1987

JEFFREY M. BURNS

The Second Vatican Council only glancingly addressed such sexual issues as birth control, clerical celibacy, and homosexuality. Meanwhile, the city of San Francisco became a center of the ongoing sexual revolution in the 1960s and beyond. This chapter examines the church in San Francisco's response to the challenges presented by the lived experience of married clergy and gay and lesbian Catholics, who struggled to change church teaching on sexuality.

I N OCTOBER 1961, MORE THAN 500,000 CATHOLICS GATHERED at Golden Gate Park in San Francisco to pray the rosary with famed international Rosary Crusade priest Father Patrick Peyton, CSC. Devotional Catholicism appeared to be thriving in San Francisco. Moreover, Catholic San Franciscans had a strong record of support for social justice. They had long supported the labor activism encouraged by papal social encyclicals and had venerated the memory of legendary labor priest Father Peter C. Yorke, who had risen to fame in the 1901 Teamsters strike. From the early 1930s through the 1950s, the archdiocese had an active laity committed to a range of Catholic Action programs, a well-educated and socially progressive clergy, and a burgeoning religious sisterhood. From the 1960s through the mid-1970s, Catholic social liberalism remained robust in San Francisco, as indicated by the election of and the policies initiated in the years 1964 to 1978 by mayors Jack Shelley, Joseph Alioto, and George Moscone, all of them Catholic.[1]

At the same time, San Franciscan Catholicism reflected a decided theological conservatism. Catholic Action boomed with the encouragement of Archbishop John Mitty, but Mitty assigned a clerical watchdog to make sure "that the group would keep within the reservation."[2] Catholic Action's agenda included a strong "moral apostolate" focused on the need to eliminate sexual vices. Catholic laywomen launched crusades in the city against indecent literature, pornography, and immoral movies. Perhaps most telling was Archbishop Mitty's response to the Vatican Council's Ante-Preparatory Commission's letter inquiring as to what the archbishop's concerns were for the coming Council. The archbishop responded that the number one topic he wished the Council to address was "The dogmatic definition of the objective reality of the fire of hell" (*Definitio dogmatica de realitate objective ignis infernalis*).[3]

Perhaps the archbishop was giving voice to apprehensions about the future. The church and the city of San Francisco were about to embark on two of the most tumultuous decades in their entwined histories. The San Francisco Bay Area attained iconic status as a center of social, political, and cultural dissent, protest, and demands for radical social and cultural change in the 1960s and 1970s. Tumult became the norm as natives and newcomers alike challenged tradition and questioned authority, beginning with the student protests against House Un-American Activities Committee hearings in 1960 continuing through the many movements for civil rights. Violence erupted in the city in response to such deep cultural shifts, most notably the tragic assassinations of Mayor George Moscone and Harvey Milk, the first openly gay person to win a seat on the San Francisco Board of Supervisors, by former supervisor Dan White in 1978.[4] As was the case in the rest of the United States, "rights language" became a central feature of public discourse in San Francisco, buoyed by these various movements and events.[5]

At precisely this moment the conciliar era began. The Second Vatican Council intersected with these many diverse currents in American culture, which had a major impact on the manner in which the Council was received and interpreted. While the Council's reputed opening to the world meshed well with movements for social justice, San Francisco became particularly known for its promotion of the sexual revolution. The counterculture, anchored in the city's Haight-Ashbury, rejected the traditional, monogamous, and exclusive sexual ethic, preferring instead what critics came to label simply "free love." And while San Francisco supported the various rights move-ments, civil rights activist Reverend Amos Brown has noted, "San Francisco was only truly liberal when it came to sex."[6] The Council, by contrast, was not at ease with the sexual issues; discussion of birth control and clerical celibacy was removed from the Council's agenda. Nonetheless some discus-sion of sexual issues seemed unavoidable as the Council addressed the primary and secondary ends of marriage, as well as the restoration of the permanent diaconate, which appeared to call into question the discipline of clerical celibacy. The Council's final document, *Gaudium et Spes*, explicitly addressed the topic of "conjugal love," albeit not with the forthrightness some reformers desired. Many Catholic San Franciscans, poised at the "dawning of the Age of Aquarius," seized on the Council's deliberations as an invitation to imagine a more general liberalization of the church's doctrines of sexual morality and ethics. Like other Americans, San Franciscans in the 1960s, 1970s, and 1980s tended to associate Council deliberations about change with individual rights, and they questioned traditional Catholic sexual teaching.

Catholics who sought to reform such teaching drew on three particular streams from the Council. First, there was the Council's attempt to achieve an integrated view of sexuality.[7] Emphasis was placed on the Council's positive avowal of sexuality, which diverged with what was perceived as the church's traditionally negative sexual ethic. Second, reformers emphasized the Council's promotion of dialogue and consultation, especially asserting the importance of the faithful's "lived experience" as a basis for dialogue. Reflecting on lived experience would result in a new, more positive sexual ethic, attuned to the realities of the modern world and so capable of speaking to the men and women who lived in that world. Third, reformers argued the Council endorsed the primacy of conscience. Though what the Council intended has been debated, reformers used conscience as the lynchpin in developing a "counter" theology and validating a sexual ethic previously unthinkable. Individual Catholics could arrive at conclusions at variance with the traditional teachings of the church and still remain loyal Catholics.

Developments in the broader culture supported these new orientations in Catholic theology and ethics and the new aspirations they aroused for everyday life. As Americans had seen in the civil rights movement, conscience validated standing up to corrupt and oppressive authority. The primacy of conscience stressed by Catholic activists meshed well with this national awakening to social justice. The ongoing sexual revolution opened up topics and subjects previously considered taboo, and the increasing discussion of sexual topics in public throughout the nation emboldened San Francisco Catholic activists who questioned the church's sexual ethic. Undergirding all of this was a popular rhetoric of participatory democracy, calling for "all the power to all the people," that easily blended with the notion of the People of God and the shared responsibility of and for God's people.

The Archbishop Goes to Rome

Joseph T. McGucken became the fifth archbishop of San Francisco in February 1962, shortly before the opening of the Council.[8] At the Council, he served on the relatively minor Commission on Social Communication. The "Decree" developed by this commission and approved by the Council has been dismissed as "perfunctory" by John W. O'Malley,[9] who does not mention McGucken in his history of Vatican II. McGucken did not appear to be overly engaged by the Council, truth be told, remaining instead preoccupied with the day-to-day functioning of his archdiocese. Shortly after his arrival in San Francisco, the historic St. Mary's Cathedral burned to the ground. From Rome, McGucken negotiated the construction of an ultramodern cathedral, described by his engineer, Luigi Nervi, as "the first Cathedral truly of our time and in harmony with the liturgical reforms of the Council."[10] McGucken faced stiff opposition from protestors who asserted that the millions of dollars being spent on a cathedral would have been better spent on the needs of poor people.

The third year of the Council, 1964, was a crucial one for McGucken. His concerns that fateful year presaged themes that dominated the next two decades. During the Council's intersession, McGucken issued an "official letter" on contraception. He worried that discussions among Catholics concerning the newly available birth control pill in light of the Council had given rise to the false impression that church teaching was about to change. The archbishop forcefully condemned artificial contraception as "against nature," "shameful and intrinsically immoral," as an "abominable crime." Later, similar language was used in condemning homosexual acts, and as gay people were later counseled, couples were encouraged to ask God "to help them to do what is beyond their unaided strength."[11] McGucken hoped his statement would curtail future discussion and controversy; instead, it prepared the way for more conflict. Though many supported the letter, not all Catholics in the city received it with enthusiasm. One parishioner tellingly wrote McGucken that his views were not in keeping with the spirit of the Council: "What is the Church? The Council says it is US. Your message emphatically states that it is not Us, but something over and above us." The writer stressed what he understood as a central theme of the Council, the raising up of the "mature committed Christian."[12] As such, he rejected the archbishop's letter and called for a discussion on the issue rather than a decree.

Dissatisfaction with the church's teaching on contraception continued to grow, so much so that McGucken felt obliged to condemn the practice again in 1966. In what became standard operating procedure in the post-conciliar church, McGucken cited the Council to challenge/correct the erroneous viewpoints on contraception, just as those holding these viewpoints likewise cited the Council's documents. In McGucken's words, "the Council is quite clear that Catholics are forbidden to undertake methods of birth control forbidden by the official Magisterium."[13] While this was technically true, the creation of a special papal commission raised hopes, rightly or wrongly, that the teaching might change. These hopes were dashed in July 1968 with the promulgation of Pope Paul VI's *Humanae Vitae*, which reiterated the traditional teaching against artificial contraception. The editor of the archdiocesan newspaper in San Francisco reflected on the new encyclical by challenging McGucken's understanding of it. "An encyclical does not qualify as an infallible pronouncement," he reminded readers, though it was "solemn teaching." The editorial continued, "In forming our conscience as members of the Church we will study this document seriously, pray over it, and act honestly and conscientiously as a result of our study."[14] Here was the blueprint for Catholics to dissent from church teaching and yet remain within the church. These arguments would resurface in the later debate over homosexuality.

Finally, still in 1964, McGucken addressed from Rome an increasingly contentious political and social issue back home, fair housing. In 1963, the Rumford Fair Housing Act was passed, then immediately challenged by the California Real Estate Association. The initiative opponents sponsored, Proposition 14, threatened to overturn the Rumford Act. A raucous and polarizing election ensued. McGucken issued a pastoral letter on "Christian Justice and Love," clearly denouncing the proposition without explicitly telling Catholics how to vote. "Racial discrimination and Christian love cannot abide together in the Christian heart," the letter declared. "Inequality in the opportunity to enjoy decent housing based solely on race is an insult to human dignity," it read.[15] Despite the archbishop's efforts, the initiative passed statewide by a nearly two to one margin.

By the end of the third session of the Council, then, writing always from Rome, McGucken had addressed the urgent issues that would come to dominate the lives of San Franciscans and Catholic San Franciscans over the course of the next two decades, questions of change, of rights, and of sexuality. These three issues repeatedly intersected as advocates for change in the church used "rights" language to justify a rethinking and reform of Catholic sexual teaching. Advocates of racial equality, social reform, and labor justice were able to find a place within the church; those who advocated for change in the church's sexual teaching encountered the strong headwinds of "immutable law" and "unchanging natural law." John O'Malley has argued that one of the underlying questions of the Council was "how far can change go?"[16] In terms of sexuality, it appeared, not very far. Nonetheless, as historian Mark Massa has pointed out, the changes mandated by the Council had "unintended consequences."[17]

In the decades following the Council, sexuality and the church's teaching on the same became pressing issues, indeed, at times, all-consuming issues. Whether or not the Council intended it, advocates in the post-conciliar church pushed the church to take a fresh look at its sexual teaching. And though the church showed little inclination to change, the expectation that it would increased.

An Inalienable Right to Marriage

Nowhere was this more evident than in the issue of priestly celibacy. Pope Paul VI had removed the topic from the Council agenda, but immediately following the Council, a trickle of priests began to leave the priesthood, a number that grew as the decade progressed. The vast majority of priests left the priesthood to marry. At the same time, a strong belief developed among the clergy, particularly the younger clergy, that celibacy was about to be made optional. A sociological study of priests and seminarians in the Archdiocese of San Francisco conducted by Eugene Schallert, SJ, of the University of San Francisco, concluded that a new consensus for change was emerging. In the study, 49.8 percent of priests surveyed agreed that celibacy should be optional; only 37.5 percent disagreed. A stunning 78.6 percent of the seminarians believed there should be a choice. While close to half of the ordained clergy thought the celibate priesthood was still the "best model," 62.5 percent of the seminarians did not. Both groups believed that the way celibacy had been taught had contributed to a "negative attitude toward human sexuality."[18]

The issue of clerical celibacy was addressed head on in 1969, at the San Francisco Provincial Conference of Priests Councils, held in St. Helena, California. Priests Councils were consultative bodies mandated by the Council. Delegates from the Councils of San Francisco, Oakland, Santa Rosa, Stockton, and Sacramento met to consider a number of post-conciliar issues. After passing a series of controversial resolutions, the Provincial Conference further resolved that priests enjoyed "an inalienable right to marriage" and recommended that priests who had left ministry to get married should be allowed to return to active ministry. The resolution passed by a vote of 32–2.[19] Of particular note is the language – again "rights" language is employed to make their point. Once again, rights, change, and sexuality merge.

Not all clergy were enthusiastic about the resolution. Eighty Oakland priests, led by four monsignors, circulated a petition to reject the resolution. Twenty-five Stockton priests did the same, as did a small group of San Francisco priests. Archbishop McGucken developed a position paper that, in what became standard operating procedure for proponents and opponents of an issue, invoked the Council to reject the very claim of an "inalienable right." The conference had asserted that the Council regarded the issue as "too hot to handle," but McGucken claimed the issue had in fact been addressed. Pope Paul VI had sent the Council a message, the archbishop wrote, that "a lengthy series of speeches [on celibacy] would not be opportune." According to McGucken, "the announcement was greeted with the most prolonged applause of the Council."[20] Paul VI did remove celibacy from the Council agenda though he did allow submissions to be given to the Council of Presidents.[21] The position paper concluded, evidently on the basis of the resounding silence on the issue, that the Council had endorsed celibacy.

While the discussion of priestly celibacy remained largely academic, the exodus of men from the priesthood represented a practical rejection of the practice. Two cases of clerical marriage electrified the Bay Area, those of Monsignor James M. Murray and Father Robert Duryea. Monsignor Murray was one of the most distinguished clerics in the city. From a well-known Catholic family, Murray was educated at the archdiocesan seminaries and ordained in 1941. Obtaining a master's degree in social work, he ultimately served as the head of archdiocesan Catholic Charities. In 1962, Murray was named pastor of St. John the Evangelist Parish in San Francisco, which was soon being touted throughout the city as a "Vatican II Parish" with an active laity, dynamic liturgy, and decentralized authority structure. Then, in late December 1969, Murray shocked his parishioners by announcing at Sunday Mass that he was "retiring from active ministry" to wed. He would seek official dispensation from the priesthood to be married in the church. His wife-to-be was a "mature woman" whom he had known for fourteen years, a "department head of a large public utility" in the Midwest. Murray's announcement was major news, appearing on the front page of the local dailies. He was careful to emphasize that he was not a rebel. Rather, he was choosing between two "cherished values"– marriage and the priesthood: "I carry no banners and represent no causes ... [I am] not riding the new wave of the future."[22] His future wife, Kathleen Martin, saw things differently. In a front-page interview that appeared the following day, the paper reported, "Miss Martin wishes that all priests could marry." Martin asserted, "I have no hang ups about it ... the fact that he is a priest means nothing to me. He is a person ... it is a good thing." The trend, she noted, was developing across the country.[23]

Despite Murray's disclaimers, even his more cautious announcement had an edge to it. His choice was, in his words, an "affirmation of ... married love ... [and] of the holiness and wholeness of sex." Particularly telling was his use of the quintessential language of the era to justify his action. His decision to marry was "an affirmation of respect for the individual person, his rights and duties ... and his privilege to serve his God and his brothers according to his conscience in freedom."[24]

Even more compelling was the story of Father Robert Duryea, who, it was discovered in 1971, had been married since 1964, while remaining in active ministry. Duryea, ordained in 1946, served in several parishes, before becoming a U.S. Air Force chaplain during the Korean War. On his return, he was assigned chaplain to O'Connor Hospital in San Jose. There in the early 1960s, he met his future wife, Lualan, a nurse at the hospital, an unchurched Christian from Idaho (she would later be received into the Catholic Church), nineteen years his junior. "A sympathetic priest" married the couple on June 15, 1964. For the next seven years, the newlyweds kept their marriage a secret, as Duryea remained an active priest, and "Lu," as she was known, continued working at O'Connor Hospital. Lu lived in an apartment in Los Altos where she and Duryea rendezvoused once or twice a week. In 1966, Lu gave birth to a son they named Paul; rumor had it that he was named after the pope. That same year, Duryea was named pastor of St. Peter's in Pacifica, a secluded town along the Pacific coast. Over the course of time, more and more people became aware of the secret – some two dozen parishioners, several associate pastors, a parish sister, staff, and a seminarian – but no one leaked it, which may have been a sign of parochial support. As time went on, the routine became normalized. "My wife Lu and our very young son Paul came to Sunday Mass and other special events without feeling uncomfortable," Duryea recorded in a series of autobiographical articles he wrote for the *San Francisco Chronicle* entitled "I Was a Married Priest." Duryea was a popular pastor, introducing the changes mandated by the Council and creating another "Vatican II Parish." The parish sponsored ecumenical gatherings and adult education and developed an active parish council. Duryea observed, "'The people' could be trusted a lot more than they were. The Church is made up of all her members." "Shared responsibility" was the watchword at St. Peter's.

In 1971, Archbishop McGucken learned of the marriage and removed Duryea, announcing that Duryea was "automatically excommunicated" for marrying while still a priest. Unlike Murray, Duryea did not leave willingly or quietly. He boldly stated, as the church door was closing on him and his family, "The law is wrong and should be changed ... I have proved to myself and to anyone with an open mind that the traditional objection to married priesthood is nonsense ... my family life kept growing stronger and deeper while I remained an effective and popular pastor." Though Duryea acknowledged that the Vatican Council was not responsible for his decision to marry – human love was – he believed the Council validated his decision.

Pope John XXIII, Duryea insisted, had made an "honest call for renewal . . . He invited change . . . in a world of real people." He refused to see his marriage as a scandal. The real scandal, he said, was "the Church's unwillingness to listen to its members and to respond to the consistent urging of the Second Vatican Council toward openness and constructive change."[25]

News of Duryea's secret life was, like reports of Murray's marriage, front-page news. He received continued support from his parish. St. Peter's Parish Council issued a statement supporting its pastor. It read, in part, "We feel that the Church's rule on celibacy, which deprives our community of ministers such as Father Duryea, should be changed as soon possible." Later on in the document, signatories asserted in bold uppercase letters, "**THE PEOPLE OF ST. PETER'S ARE TRYING TO CONTINUOUSLY GROW IN THE SPIRIT OF VATICAN II**."[26] The assistant pastor, seminarian, and parish sister affirmed that Duryea was "living testimony that a married priest can be effective in today's Church." Several parishioners set up "Save Duryea From Extinction" clubs.[27]

Not everyone was so enthusiastic. Val King, a conservative columnist for the archdiocesan newspaper the *San Francisco Monitor*, blasted Duryea. "He has lived a lie for seven years," King thundered, "He has mocked and betrayed the confidence, trust and faith of those who mistook him for a priest validly exercising his priestly office."[28] King was a highly visible lay spokesman, the host of a weekly local Catholic television show called *Heritage*. Another San Franciscan, Jesuit Father Joseph Brusher, professor of history at the University of San Francisco, was inspired to write "An Open Letter to the American Bishops," in order "to counteract," in his words, "the presence of a gaggle of discontented priests and ex-priests who are trying to push you to abandon the traditional celibacy of the clergy of the Western Church."[29] For several weeks, letters to the editor of the archdiocesan newspaper ran both in favor and against Duryea. The celibacy issue, like so much else in the church and society in the 1960s, led to ever-increasing polarization.

Legitimate Opinions on Both Sides

As the controversy over Duryea and a married clergy waned, the issue of homosexuality moved to center stage. Following World War II, when San Francisco was a port of call for the U.S. Navy, a gay subculture had begun to expand in San Francisco. By 1964, the city was regarded by many as the "gay capital of the United States."[30] An estimated 120,000 gay men and women lived in San Francisco in 1980, just less than 20 percent of the population. As their number increased, so did their visibility. Drawing on the advances made by other movements, gay San Francisco began to assert its rights. During the 1960s, gays and lesbians refused to be relegated to the periphery of society, as they figuratively "came out of the closet." They rejected standard accounts, in church and society, of gays as sick, pathological, and sinful; they affirmed their "right to be" and their "freedom to be gay."[31] They protested and resisted police harassment and refused to accept antigay violence. The newfound confidence was evident in the first Gay Freedom Day Parade or gay pride parade in San Francisco, held June 25, 1972.

The embrace of change as positive and necessary and the language of rights inspired the Catholic Church's first public engagement with the gay community. In the summer of 1971, the archdiocesan Commission on Social Justice (SJC), under the direction of Father Eugene Boyle[32] and layman John Delury, became embroiled in controversy. At the prompting of the Religion Committee of the Society for Individual Rights, a pro–gay rights advocacy group, the SJC endorsed two controversial bills. The first added "sexual orientation" to the city's anti-discrimination legislation; the second removed all "private acts between consenting adults" from the California State Criminal Code. The SJC argued it was not approving homosexual actions but was solely concerned with the "justice" issues – discrimination against any group was unacceptable. The statement provoked outrage. Once again, the redoubtable Val King led the attack on the SJC; outraged letters to the editor and to the archbishop loudly seconded his opinion. Typical of the letters received was that of one pastor who objected to the "six jokers" who had embarrassed the church: "For the life of me, I cannot understand why sodomy and a few other unsavory and unnatural acts are no longer morally wrong."[33] Anyone supporting the position of the SJC "does not know anything (more probably, does not give a damn) about scripture or moral theology."[34] Others concurred.

The archbishop responded by stressing that he did not endorse the commission's actions and disagreed with its advocacy in this instance. McGucken had established a policy during the Proposition 14 battle that the SJC was free to make public statements, but that the archbishop did not guarantee them. The commission was allowed to work in areas in which "there might be legitimate opinions on both sides of the controversial questions."[35] (This was revoked later amid the controversies of 1982–1983.) Nonetheless, McGucken lamented to one of the letter writers, "One of the frustrating difficulties that we endure these days is the fact that errors have been spread that cause great confusion to the Catholic people, even to our priests and religious."[36] Still, McGucken believed, to rule with an iron hand was counterproductive.

   While the SJC's actions were being debated, former priest Tom Fry began
the city's first Catholic ministry to gays and lesbians. Fry, an activist priest,
had studied at St. Patrick's Seminary; ordained in 1963, he had participated in
the march on Selma. Back home, he protested the construction of the new
cathedral, opposed the war in Vietnam, and circulated a petition against
Humanae Vitae.[37] In 1969, Fry left the priesthood to get married, but before
marrying he came to the realization he was gay. Accepting his sexual
orientation freed him for further service. In 1971, he began the Catholic
Gay Ministry, with the support of sixty priests and several Franciscans,[38]
which provided support for Catholics struggling to reconcile their religion
with their sexuality. The primary aim of Fry's ministry might be described as
"consciousness raising." He spoke at venues throughout San Francisco trying
to assure gay and lesbian Catholics that they were not alone, that the issue of
being gay and Catholic could be addressed openly.
   Two years later, Fry and Franciscan Father David McBriar established
a branch of Dignity, an organization for gay Catholics. Founded in San
Diego in 1969 by Father Patrick Nidorf, OSA, Dignity was expanding across
the country. According to New York Dignity co-founder, author, and
activist John J. McNeill, Dignity was rooted in the theology of the Second
Vatican Council, particularly the teaching on "the freedom of conscience."
The Council had given the group its name. *Gaudium et Spes* had proclaimed,
"Humans have in their heart a law written by God. To obey it is the *dignity*
(emphasis mine) of the human." The document continues, "According to
[conscience] we will be judged. Conscience is the most secret core and
sanctuary of the human. There we are alone with God whose voice echoes
in our depths."[39] Gays and lesbians were to listen to their hearts. The Council
had ignited the deepest aspirations to dignity among those long denied it by
church and society.
   Dignity San Francisco was dedicated to the spiritual growth and healing of
Catholic gays and lesbians. As one participant remembered, at the first Dignity
San Francisco meeting, "most of us told of the extremely difficult experiences
that we had previously, by trying to stay within the church, continue with the
sacraments, and still stay honest with ourselves and our spiritual advisers by
admitting our sexuality."[40] The group also hoped to open a dialogue with the
church and to be a witness to the entire gay community, Catholic and non-
Catholic.[41] At the center of Dignity was an acceptance of one's sexuality. What
did that mean in practice? How could one be gay and Catholic? Catholics who
admitted of no possibility of a gay Catholicism immediately protested the new
organization, but, surprisingly, the archdiocesan newspaper wrote a relatively
positive editorial. While condemning the homosexual lifestyle, it cautioned

against demonizing gay men and women, who "were no more virtuous or exploitive than any other group of people . . . Charity and love" should guide the church's ministry to the homosexual.[42] The debate inspired by the editorial included letters from two gay men, one of whom lauded the editorial for acknowledging that "We are human beings."[43] The second condemned the "homophobic attitudes" of the church. Christians needed to realize that Jesus's love for the homosexual "is just as profound and mysterious as it is" for the heterosexual.[44]

The debate was revived three years later when *Monitor* columnist Michael P. Cavanagh, a psychologist and popular lecturer, wrote two gay-friendly columns on homosexuality.[45] Cavanagh debunked a number of myths about gay people, including the danger or depravity of gay men and women. The thrust of the articles was that gay men and women are human beings in need of and deserving pastoral care. Reactions to the column, which required several pages in the *Monitor*, went from the usual "I consider homosexuality a filthy, evil thing" to a more nuanced and reasoned critique of what some writers considered Cavanagh's simplistic approach to moral theology. Twenty priests of the archdiocese signed a letter supporting Cavanagh, provoking a number of reactions of its own. Another letter expressed a recurring theme from gay Catholics, "It often takes many painful years for a homosexual Christian to realize that God loves him too, just the way he is."[46]

Cavanagh answered his critics in another column, stating that his intent was to minimize the isolation felt by gay people and to encourage their participation in the life of the church. He emphasized the complexity of homosexuality. "No one can legitimately make definitive pronouncements with regard to homosexuality," he cautioned. He concluded citing contemporary theologian John Dedek, who wrote in classic post-conciliar rhetoric, "any Catholic has the fundamental right to dissent privately even publicly from the authoritative non-infallible teaching of the official magisterium."[47] The implication was clear – gay men and women, possibly even sexually active ones, had a place within the church.

Cavanagh's rejoinder to the responses inspired a private letter from Archbishop McGucken, who gently corrected the psychologist. McGucken believed that his experience with gay people in Los Angeles/Hollywood had given him an appreciation of the difficulties gay men and women faced in keeping chaste. He advised compassionately providing the poor souls with personal, pastoral, and perhaps psychological care. Nonetheless, he cautioned, the teaching of the church must be stated clearly, taken seriously, and at times accepted as "infallible." Again citing Council documents, he argued that the *Dogmatic Constitution on the Church*, Chap. III, no. 25, validated certain magisterial teachings as infallible even when they were not pronounced "ex cathedra." Dedek's assertion, according to McGucken, was not well grounded in conciliar thought.[48]

Archbishop John R. Quinn

John R. Quinn succeeded McGucken as archbishop of San Francisco in 1977. An alumnus of the North American College in Rome, he had previously served as bishop (1972) and archbishop (1973) of Oklahoma City. Quinn developed a thoughtful style that placed a high priority on dialogue and consultation. His statements on nuclear proliferation and military aid to Latin America gained him national attention, but the issue of homosexuality proved more problematic. Tensions between the church and the gay community intensified shortly after Quinn's arrival in San Francisco. After the assassinations of Mayor George Moscone and Supervisor Harvey Milk in November 1978, much was made in the press of Dan White's Catholic school training and of the fact that the district he represented was heavily Irish Catholic. From the perspective of many in the gay community, to be Catholic was to be homophobic; many gay San Franciscans suspected Catholics of being sympathetic to Dan White.[49]

Conscious of growing tensions, on May 5, 1980, Quinn issued a "Pastoral Letter on Homosexuality,"[50] which made a clear distinction between homosexual "orientation," which was not sinful, and homosexual "behavior," which was. Catholics were encouraged to oppose violence against gays. Nonetheless, "there is a clear difference between the acceptance of homosexual persons as worthy of respect and as having human rights, and approval of the homosexual lifestyle . . . Homosexual behavior cannot be viewed as an acceptable form of behavior morally or socially." Even so, like everyone else, gay people had to struggle to achieve moral perfection and "become rooted in the person of Jesus Christ." Many San Franciscans, Catholic and not, hailed Quinn's letter for its pastoral sensitivity, but conservatives criticized him for allegedly soft-pedaling the church's condemnation of homosexuality. In the gay community, Quinn was viewed as expressing the same old church line. The pastoral did little to resolve long-standing tensions.

Quinn set off another controversy the same year with a speech at the Synod on the Family in Rome. He acknowledged the reality, evident to church leaders in the United States, that the vast majority of American Catholics opposed the church's teachings on birth control. While he did not challenge the teaching on birth control specifically, he asked whether the manner in which the doctrine was being taught was effective and if not, as he clearly thought, how this might be improved. The popular press immediately hailed it as an attack on *Humanae Vitae*. Quinn's letter raised the prospect that if this matter were open to question, by a prelate no less, then why not other sexual matters? Gay activists repeatedly cited the blatant disregard of many Catholics for the church's teaching on birth control to justify their own dissent on homosexuality. In 1981, two archdiocesan task forces were formed to examine the issue of homosexuality, one, under the auspices of the archdiocesan Commission on Social Justice – the Task Force on Gay/Lesbian Issues – to address the problem of increasing violence against gays in San Francisco, and the second, under the archdiocesan Priests' Senate, to consider pastoral ministry to gays.

Homosexuality and Social Justice

The members of the Social Justice task force brought a vast wealth of experience, and a marked openness and sympathy to gay men and women and their struggles. There were fourteen members – two priests, two women religious, one lay brother, five laymen, and four laywomen. Among them were prominent members of the Catholic gay community, notably Dignity San Francisco Co-chair James Ehrhart. Another member of the task force was Larry Agriesti, a Peace Corps veteran. Agriesti was a minor celebrity in the San Francisco gay community for having created the famous "Bigots on Parade" demonstration during the 1977 Gay Pride celebration. Agriesti had placed a poster of Anita Bryant, who had recently engineered an antigay ordinance in Florida, alongside images of Hitler, Stalin, and the Ku Klux Klan. He followed this up the next year with posters of the crucified Christ that listed the cities that had passed antigay ordinances. Most task force members were involved in pastoral ministry, education, or counseling. It was an impressive, committed group.

Women were well represented on the task force, a significant fact considering women often had a lower profile within the LGBT Catholic community. Dignity San Francisco repeatedly pleaded for greater participation by lesbian Catholic women.[51] Dignity Co-chair Madeline Ritchie maintained that Catholic lesbians, many of whom were feminists, faced what one woman called a "double whammy,"[52] a repressive sexual theology and an oppressive male hierarchy.[53] Many saw Dignity as a "men-only organization."[54] The message was heard. The women appointed to the task force were of considerable substance and experience.

Ritchie, a public health nurse, had established a clinic for Southeast Asian refugees at San Francisco General Hospital in the 1970s. She had served several terms as co-chair of Dignity San Francisco and one term on the National Dignity board. She was affectionately called "our own Madeline R." in the Dignity newsletter.[55] Ritchie deeply felt the pain of being lesbian and Catholic. She recalled the fear that pervaded early Dignity meetings, where members used only their first names, and taking photos of members was forbidden – to be publicly LGBT remained a risk.[56] Sister Eileen DeLong, RGS, was a Good Shepherd sister who had served many years as a high school teacher and administrator. In 1977, she enrolled at the Graduate Theological Union in Berkeley to pursue a master's of divinity degree. She became active in gay and lesbian support groups as well as with Dignity; in 1978, she was instrumental in the creation of Catholics for Human Dignity to oppose the Briggs Initiative, which sought to remove gay and lesbian teachers from California's public schools. Sister Eileen lamented shortly before her death the fact that "it had taken her many decades to become free with the increasing freedoms brought by Vatican Council II."[57] Another task force member, Leslie Bunch, was the mother of four children, one of whom was gay. In 1978, she co-founded and served on the board of Parents and Friends of Gays, San Francisco. The other three women on the board all had advanced degrees and had been active in a variety of community and educational ministries.

Over time, a local activist named Kevin Gordon, chosen by the others to chair the task force, emerged as its driving force. Gordon had been a Christian Brother in New York. He held advanced degrees in religious education and systematic theology from Manhattan College and the Union Theological Seminary, respectively. Gordon left the Christian Brothers in 1972 and moved to San Francisco, where he did a "clinical internship in human sexuality" at UCSF's medical school. Subsequently, he began a private practice. Gordon saw the task force as an opportunity to address honestly the status of gay and lesbian Catholics and as he later wrote "an opportunity for dialogue and reflection in the Spirit of Vatican II."[58] Throughout the deliberations of the task force, the language Gordon and his colleagues used to explore and articulate theological and ethical positions pulsed with the rhetoric of the Vatican Council. Gordon insisted that the concept of the People of God meant looking at the real lives of real people, of people with bodies. He called for "an embodied sexual theology."

After consulting for more than a year, on July 29, 1982, the task force approved a report entitled *Homosexuality and Social Justice*. The archdiocesan Commission on Social Justice accepted it as a "working document." This meant, Commission Director Thomas Ambrogi explained in his introduction, that the report "is not an official document of the Archdiocese itself."[59]

The 150-page report called for nothing short of a Catholic sexual revolution. It directly attacked the church's teachings on sexuality as inadequate and called for a new and positive sexual ethic that would include gay sexuality. The report charged, correctly, that the church condemned gay men and women to lives of celibacy. It went further with the claim that the Catholic Church's negative assessment of gays invited violence by legitimizing discrimination. In the words of the report, "The church, by its moral teaching on the intrinsic evil of homosexuality, and despite its disclaimers about homosexuals as persons, is a conspirator in the violence perpetrated against the gay and lesbian community."[60] Quinn himself was not spared. One task force recommendation advised "that the Archdiocese representatives refrain from making empirically unsupported, and inflammatory statements about homosexuality such as contained in the *Pastoral Letter on Homosexuality*."[61]

The task force report addressed the issues of violence, homosexuality in the Latino community, language, family, gay life, gay religious and priests, the sexually disenfranchised, and education, and it made fifty-four recommendations for reform. Chap. 5 was particularly poignant: "Spiritual Lives of Lesbian Women and Gay Men," which presented the verbatim testimony of a gay man and a lesbian woman, not named in the report, who expressed their love for the church but went on to described how deeply wounded they were by the church's categorization of their way of loving as evil. They had arrived at a place now, they said, where they understood that their sexuality was healthy and pleasing to God. The gay man testified, "To be condemned by society as a criminal, denounced by family as a pervert, and finally a sinner by the Church, was enough to break my will to live." Yet his search for meaning led him "to believe that my form of love was holy and good because it came from Him . . . [Jesus] knows who I am, loves me as I am." The gay woman concurred, "I cannot be a person of Jesus and, as sectors of my Church ask me to do, deny my expression of sexuality." The gay man appealed several times to the Vatican Council's *Declaration on Religious Freedom*, with its emphasis on conscience, for validation of his beliefs.[62] The report concluded this wrenching chapter by affirming that task force members had "listened" and "learned." They had found that by and large gay and lesbian Catholics "were committed, fully active Roman Catholics" whose lives "reflect an admirable moral integrity," who consider their sexuality good. "We do not experience our active sexual lives as evil, but as good, worthy of human beings, and often beautiful."[63]

The *Bay Area Reporter*, a gay community newspaper, hailed the report as "flying out of the closet of the Roman Catholic Archdiocese with a stinging, driving force."[64] The official Catholic response was slow and measured.

Though Quinn privately fumed that the task force had exceeded its mandate, in public he made no immediate comment, permitting debate. In a press release, Quinn affirmed that though the report contained much that is contrary to church teaching, it represents a point of view "which cannot be simply ignored or dismissed out of hand."[65] To the Priests' Senate he wrote, "I ask the senate to listen to many voices, including those voices found in the recently published task force report."[66] Nonetheless, over the course of the next eight months, Quinn distanced himself from the report.

In the meantime, debate over the report raged among San Francisco Catholics. The archdiocesan newspaper published an editorial signed by editor Father John P. Penebsky entitled "Will We Listen?" that counseled readers to attend "thoughtfully and thoroughly" to the report. "We do not agree with many of the Report's findings and recommendations," Father Penebsky noted, "On the other hand, we respect the report for what it is – a working document voicing the real feelings of real people who have had the courage to speak out ... We hope the report will be read, studied, discussed, and, yes, prayed over."[67]

Dignity San Francisco passionately endorsed the report. Writing to Quinn, the chair of Dignity SF asserted, "The publication accurately portrays the minds and hearts of gay and lesbian people in the Archdiocese of San Francisco." And in a clear echo of *Gaudium et Spes*, the letter observed the report presented "their pain and joy, their fears and hopes ... poignantly offered as essential elements in a crucial dialogue."[68]

The wrangling between the archdiocese, the Commission on Social Justice, and the task force went back and forth for several months. Though Quinn kept a low public profile, behind the scenes he sought to minimize the report. He replaced the director of the Commission on Social Justice, installed a more vocal clerical presence on the commission, and enjoined two seminary professors to write a critical response to the report. Then Quinn overrode the report with the findings of the archdiocesan Senate of Priests, issued on May 19, 1983, titled "Ministry and Sexuality in the Archdiocese of San Francisco."[69] This became the official archdiocesan policy. The document would have been regarded as a major progressive innovation in ministry to gay people had it not followed the Social Justice task force's report. The forty-page "Ministry and Sexuality" called on ministers to be compassionate and nonjudgmental in dealing with gay men and women. Although it repeatedly reaffirmed traditional church sexual teaching that sexual activity was acceptable only within the married state, it made a number of important recalibrations. It debunked many of the commonly held stereotypes of gay people, especially the notion that gays were "mentally disordered" or that they could overcome their orientation through willpower. The report also strongly stated that "homosexual orientation is not held to be a sinful condition ... Rather, it entails living out the demands of chastity within that orientation." Most remarkably, the report advocated a policy of "gradualism" in counseling gay men and lesbian women:

> Chastity is always the responsibility and goal of the Christian life ... the homosexual person should not be surprised by periodic tensions and some relapses ... Homosexual people fall in love. And as long as this is so, sexual activity may occur ... Objectively, the Church teaches that homosexual activity in such unions ... is morally unacceptable. The principle of gradualism recognizes this fact and assists the person toward a progressive assimilation of the Church's ethical values. Ministry in this area demands an awareness that purification and growth in holiness come about only gradually ... We are all sinners who at times violate our best moral convictions, but we can be healed and forgiven.

"Ministry and Sexuality" also stressed that the protection of human and civil rights for homosexual persons was not merely encouraged, but "mandated."[70]

Once again, responses ranged from outrage to support. Of note, prior to the Senate of Priests' report's publication, a group of priests had filed what they called a "minority report" objecting to much of what was to come in the official document. The writers belittled the Senate of Priests' report for its trendiness, as well as its lack of doctrinal rigor. "Ministry and Sexuality" contained "little about the ordinary teaching/magisterium of the Church," lacking any "clear, objective statement that sexual intercourse outside of marriage is sinful," or any statement "about homosexuality being aberrant on the natural level." As one of the authors of the minority report observed, "'Ministry and Sexuality' seems to condone homosexuality."[71] Conservative Catholics such as Parents for Orthodoxy in Parochial Education (POPE) likewise condemned it. Even before the two contrasting reports were issued, POPE had complained, "The 'Spirit of the Council,' whatever that is, was the reference given by the sexperts who made sweeping changes contrary to tradition." Moreover, "the documents of the 2nd Vatican Council have been misapplied, misinterpreted and misconstrued."[72]

Of equal note was the response by members of the gay community to "Ministry and Sexuality." On June 28, the anniversary of the Stonewall uprising in New York, Kevin Gordon, representing the Social Justice task force, along with members of Dignity San Francisco, Catholics for Human Dignity, and the San Francisco Coalition for Human Rights held a press conference to issue a statement asserting, "Standing within the centuries old tradition of the reception and non-reception of Church teaching, we cannot receive, in conscience, a product whose process disregards Vatican II's own best theological insights into consulting the sense of the faithful and seeing the Church as the People of God in dialogue and participation by due process."[73] The report was "theologically and pastorally inadequate and therefore unacceptable ... [the report] neither comes out of, nor speaks to, the real lives and loves of lesbian women and gay men."[74] As such, the gay community "returned" the report; gay Catholic San Franciscans said it was not "received." "Thank you, but no thank you."[75] Gordon dubbed the non-reception press conference, the "Catholic Stonewall."[76] The archdiocese reacted quickly. Two days after the press conference, the Task Force on Gay/Lesbian Issues was dissolved.

The controversy did not end there, however. Several months later, Gordon resurfaced with "The Consultation on Homosexuality, Social Justice and Roman Catholic Theology." Composed of scholars, theologians, and activists, the consultation would continue to reflect on the issues addressed by the Social Justice task force, but as an independent research group "within the Roman Catholic Church, but not under the control of any diocese." In the margins of the press release announcing the creation of the consultation, the archdiocesan director of communication wrote simply, "Read and weep."[77] The consultation included a national board of scholars and activists that included famed feminist theologian Rosemary Radford Ruether, feminist theologian Mary Hunt, NYU catechist Gabriel Moran, Yale historian John Boswell, and Marquette ethicist Daniel Maguire. In 1986, the consultation reissued the task force report with more than a hundred additional pages of data and reflections. Gordon, through the consultation, continued to develop two themes: the importance of the Second Vatican Council in opening a new understanding of the church and the need to develop an embodied sexual theology.

In 1982, on the completion of the task force report, Gordon had written Archbishop Quinn, "This Task Force stands with ultimate seriousness for the integrity of the issue of homosexuality, as well as the integrity of the Vatican II church."[78] Gordon later wrote that a reformulation of the church's sexual teaching could not have taken place without Vatican II: "Vatican II is what has helped more than anything else." The Council created a new paradigm, which rejected the "classicist mentality" that understood the church as unchanging and unchangeable, above history. "In a church that has all the truth of the *one* way, we can only be perverts, deviates, faggots, lezzies, and queers." This changed with the Council. The new paradigm spoke of the church as the People of God (embodied), moving through history as pilgrims. It was a church that could learn. Vatican II opened up a "bodily, social way of being in the world." It offered the possibility of an "embodied sexual theology."[79]

The new sexual theology that Gordon envisioned was to grow out of the actual lives of real people. Gay men and lesbian women no longer regarded their sexual selves as sinful. Gordon argued that the distinction between orientation and behavior was "practically meaningless and pastorally useless."[80] As he later wrote, "Sexuality is experienced by gay men as an extremely important, indeed, central constitutive factor of bodily existence and human experience, not a subsidiary characteristic, but neither as the one lens through which to filter one's entire personhood." In a tradition of belief and practice that was incarnational and sacramental, the body took on profound implications. As such, gay men and lesbian women respectfully dissented from the church's sexual teaching. They loved the church but no longer looked to it for sexual validation. Gordon observes, "An older ecclesiological logic would expect that they would leave the Church." But gay men say to the church, "we have experienced and received such riches and light and strength from you, we don't want you to be dismissed" because of an inadequate sexual ethic. "Gay Catholic men expect to, and do, fully participate in the sacramental life of the Church (much like couples practicing birth control)."[81]

The new sexual ethic espoused by Gordon, and by the task force report, developed a way for gay Catholics to reconcile theologically and existentially being gay and Catholic. They were able now to accept the church on their own terms, if they wanted to, rather than adhering to an institution whose teachings condemned them. Nowhere was this more apparent than in the conversion of Jack Fertig, better known as "Sister Boom Boom," the spokesperson for the notorious (to some), glorious (to others) Sisters of Perpetual Indulgence. Founded in 1979, the Sisters had been enraging Catholics since the group's founding – those Catholics, that is, who saw the group's antics as an insult to actual women religious and to the church.[82] By the early 1990s, Fertig came to the conclusion that the Sisters' act had "grown stale," and he found his way to the church, with the emphasis on *his way*. "When I went to the Catholic Mass," Fertig wrote, "asking if this was really my direction, the answer was clear. I had finally come home." Fertig approached Sister Cleta Herold about entering the Rite of Catholic Initiation (RCIA) program at Most Holy Redeemer Parish in the Castro, with the proviso "I was clearly not about to compromise anything regarding my sexuality."

Fertig told Sister Cleta his history as a gay activist and his participation in the Sisters of Perpetual Indulgence, along with "my disagreements with certain points of the catechism. Sister never batted an eyelash, but asked if I could show up Sunday mornings at 8." Fertig reflected on the wonderful diversity of the church, and while he did not specifically cite the Council, his words echoed the language and teachings of Vatican II:

> The Church is not monolithic ... The Church is all of us ... Through God's creation of humanity in the divine image, through Christ's life on Earth, through the communion of Saints, we see in this special Church how our humanity is sacred ... I feel extremely blessed to have found a home in this wonderful family of God and Humanity, this fallibly human, yet gloriously divine Roman Catholic Church.[83]

The parish in which Fertig found a home was Most Holy Redeemer, operating in the heart of the Castro. Most Holy Redeemer welcomed gay parishioners, including them in positions of parish leadership and sacramental ministries. The parish was widely respected for the quality of its liturgies, which were reputed to be the best musically and aesthetically in the archdiocese, as well as for its commitment to social justice.

"On the Pastoral Care of Homosexuals"

By 1986, the mood of the gay community had darkened. The AIDS epidemic cast a pall over the city, as the number of AIDS-related deaths increased dramatically. Among those who died of AIDS was Kevin Gordon, in 1992. The plague, which disproportionately affected gay men, was seen by some as a sign of divine retribution for the sin of homosexuality. It was in the midst of this pain and suffering and dying that on October 30, 1986, Cardinal Joseph Ratzinger, prefect of the Congregation for the Doctrine of Faith, issued "On the Pastoral Care of Homosexual Persons." Popularly known as the "Ratzinger Letter," in the gay community it was derided as the "Halloween Letter." The ironically titled "On the Pastoral Care of Homosexual Persons" was reported in the San Francisco popular press as a vicious assault on gays and lesbians. The *Bay Area Reporter* captured the mood of the gay community with its front-page headline "Pope to Gays: Drop Dead."[84] While the whole letter was regarded as an insult, particularly galling was the assertion that gay men and women had a "strong tendency ordered toward an intrinsic moral evil, and thus the inclination itself must be seen as an objective disorder." More distressing was the brutal observation that when same-sex activity is "condoned" by society, or when society protects "behavior to which no one has any conceivable right," it ought to be no surprise when "irrational and violent reactions increase."

Cardinal Ratzinger came just short of blaming gay people for the violence against them. One national gay advocacy group warned, "The danger and terrorism represented by the Vatican's new statement cannot be understated: it will unleash the flames of ignorance and violence more effectively than a bomb ever could."[85]

By the time Pope John Paul II visited San Francisco in 1987, the optimistic belief that Vatican II would be the harbinger for change in the church's teachings on individual rights and sexuality was fading fast. At the beginning of the 1960s, Catholic critics of theological conservatism on matters of sexual morality and ethics were optimistic; a new sexual ethic based on the actual lives of real men and women seemed possible. But the San Francisco liberal reformers discovered they had exaggerated the potential of the Council for fundamental change and overestimated the willingness of the archdiocese to embrace dissent. Nonetheless, the gay and lesbian communities were no longer the same; neither were gay and lesbian Catholics.

There was no going back into the closet. A vibrant LGBT Catholic community had emerged at Most Holy Redeemer Parish in the Castro, providing a contemporary witness of the ongoing struggle of what it means to be gay and Catholic, of the ongoing struggle as to what the Council meant in the real lives of ordinary people.

NOTES

1. See William Issel, *Church and State in the City: Catholics and Politics in Twentieth Century San Francisco* (Philadelphia: Temple University Press, 2012).

2. John J. Mitty quoted in William Issel, *For Both Cross and Flag: Catholic Action, Anti-Catholicism, and National Security Politics in World War II San Francisco* (Philadelphia: Temple University Press, 2010), p. 60.

3. John J. Mitty to Dominico Cardinali Tardini, September 1, 1959, Vatican Council files, Archives of the Archdiocese of San Francisco (hereafter referred to as AASF).

4. See David Talbot, *Season of the Witch: Enchantment, Deliverance, and Fear in the City of Love* (New York: Free Press, 2012).

5. See James T. Patterson, *Great Expectations: The United States, 1945–1974* (New York: Oxford University Press, 1996) and James T. Patterson, *Eve of Destruction: How 1965 Transformed America* (New York: Basic Books, 2012).

6. Amos Brown quoted in Talbot, *Season of the Witch*, p. 208.

7. See *Homosexuality and Social Justice: Reissue of the Report of the Task Force on Gay/Lesbian Issues, San Francisco: New, Updated, Expanded Edition* (San Francisco: The Consultation on Homosexuality, Social Justice, and Roman Catholic Theology, 1986).

8. See Jeffrey M. Burns, "Postconciliar Church as Unfamiliar Sky: The Episcopal Style of Cardinal James Francis McIntyre and Archbishop Joseph T. McGucken," *U.S. Catholic Historian* 17 (1999), 64–82.

9. John W. O'Malley, *What Happened at Vatican II* (Cambridge, MA: Belknap Press of Harvard University Press, 2008), p. 152.

10. Luigi Nervi quoted in James Gaffey, "The Anatomy of Transition: Cathedral Building and Social Justice in San Francisco, 1962–1971," *Catholic Historical Review* 70 (1984), 60.

11. Joseph T. McGucken, "Archbishop's Message," *San Francisco Monitor* (hereafter referred to as *SFM*), May 1, 1964, p. 1.

12. Charles Baireuther to Joseph T. McGucken, May 4, 1964, Birth Control files, AASF.

13. Joseph T. McGucken to Rev. Bernard A. Cummins, January 27, 1966, Birth Control files, AASF.

14. "Editorial: Encyclical," *SFM*, August 1, 1968, p. 16.

15. "Archbishop's Letter on Christian Justice and Love," *SFM*, p. 1.

16. John W. O'Malley, "Vatican II: Twelve 25-minute talks on four audio CDs" (Rockville, MD: Now You Know Media, 2011), Disc One.

17. Mark Massa, *The American Catholic Revolution: How the Sixties Changed the Church Forever* (New York: Oxford University Press, 2010), p. xvi.

18. Eugene Schallert, SJ, "A Study of the Archdiocesan Priesthood, 1969," Priests' Senate files, AASF.

19. "Proceedings of the San Francisco Provincial Conference of Priests' Councils," January 1969, Association of Priests files, AASF.

20. "The 'Inalienable Right to Marriage,' February 26, 1969," position paper, Association of Priests files, AASF.

21. See O'Malley, *What Happened at Vatican II*, p. 271.

22. James Murray, quoted in "Monsignor Murray Retires from Active Ministry," *SFM*, January 1, 1970, p. 3; and Murray, quoted in "Monsignor Murray to Wed, Quit Priesthood," *San Francisco Chronicle*, December 29, 1969, p. 1.

23. Kathleen Martin, quoted in "Monsignor's Bride-to-Be Talks," *San Francisco Chronicle*, December 30, 1969, p. 1.

24. James Murray, quoted in "Monsignor Murray Retires," and "Monsignor Murray To Wed."

25. Robert Duryea quoted in "I Was a Married Priest," series of articles in *San Francisco Chronicle*, January 24, 1972 to February 5, 1972.

26. Position Paper of the St. Peter's Parish Council, April 12, 1971, St. Peter's, Pacifica parish file, AASF.

27. "Married Priest Is Removed as Pastor." *SFM*, April 15, 1971, p. 3.

28. Val King, "Duryea," *SFM*, April 22, 1971, p. 4.

29. Joseph Brusher, "Open Letter to American Bishops," *SFM*, May 6, 1971, p. 4.

30. For the development of San Francisco as a gay and lesbian center, see Josh Sides, *Erotic City: Sexual Revolutions and the Making of Modern San Francisco* (New York: Oxford University Press, 2009) and Nan Alamilla Boyd, *Wide-Open Town: A History of Queer San Francisco to 1965* (Berkeley: University of California Press, 2003).

31. See J. Todd Ormsbee, *The Meaning of Gay: Interaction, Publicity, and Community among Homosexual Men in 1960s San Francisco* (Lanham, MD: Lexington Books, 2010) and Elizabeth A. Armstrong, *Forging Gay Identities: Organizing Sexuality in San Francisco, 1950–1994* (Chicago: University of Chicago Press, 2002).

32. Boyle was the leading Catholic social justice figure in San Francisco. See Jeffrey M. Burns, "Eugene Boyle, the Black Panther Party and the New Clerical Activism," *U.S. Catholic Historian* 13 (1995), 137–158.
33. Thomas Regan to Joseph McGucken, June 24, 1971, Social Justice files, AASF.
34. Thomas Regan to Commission on Social Justice, June 24, 1971, Social Justice files, AASF.
35. Joseph McGucken to James Flynn, June 6, 1973, Social Justice files, AASF.
36. Joseph McGucken to Stephen Firenze, September 1, 1971, Social Justice files, AASF.
37. Interview with Tom Fry, December 28, 1996. GLHS OHP #96–120, Voices of Oral History Project, GLBT Historical Society, San Francisco.
38. Ibid.
39. John J. McNeill, "Contributions of Gay and Lesbian Catholics" in *Radical Suspicion and Fundamental Trust: Reshaping Catholic Sexual Ethics*, manuscript of a proposed book, 1992 collection, Graduate Theological Union Archives, Berkeley.
40. Quoted in William Eugene McMullan, "Queer Witness: Religion and the History of the LGBT Movement in San Francisco, 1948–1981," PhD diss., Graduate Theological Union, Berkeley, 2011, p. 178.
41. Kevin J. Calegari to Rick Weatherly, January 28, 1981, Dignity SF records 1972–2005, BANC/MSS 2002/73, Bancroft Library, University of California, Berkeley (hereafter referred to as BL).
42. "Editorial: Homosexuality," *SFM*, January 25, 1973, p. 4.
43. "Letter to the Editor," Thomas M. Edwards, *SFM*, February 8, 1973, p. 4.
44. "Letter to the Editor," Ronald D. Lee, *SFM*, February 15, 1973, p. 4.
45. Michael P. Cavanagh, "Homosexuality and Mental Health," *SFM*, October 16, 1975, p. 12, and "Morality and Homosexuality," SFM, October 30, 1975, p. 8.
46. "Responses to Dr. Cavanagh," *SFM*, November 13, 1975, p. 5, and "More Responses to Dr. Cavanagh," *SFM*, December 4, 1975, p. 5.
47. Cavanagh, "Response on Homosexuality," *SFM*, December 25, 1975, p. 7.
48. Joseph T. McGucken to Dr. Michael P. Cavanagh, January 20, 1976, Homosexuality files, AASF.
49. Randy Shilts, *The Mayor of Castro Street: The Life and Times of Harvey Milk* (New York: St. Martin's Press, 1982), p. 185.
50. John R. Quinn, *Pastoral Letter on Homosexuality* (Boston: Daughters of St. Paul, 1980).
51. See Women's Concerns files, Dignity SF records, BL. Also see Tom Carroll, "Co-Chair's Column: What About the Women?" *Bridges: Newsletter of Dignity San Francisco* 9 (May 1982), 2 and Sophie Miranda, "Lesbians and Dignity," *Bridges* 10 (September 1983), 1.
52. Miranda, "Lesbians and Dignity."
53. Author interview with Madeline Ritchie, August 11, 2013, San Rafael, CA. Tape in AASF.
54. Miranda, "Lesbians and Dignity."
55. "Here's Hedda," *Bridges* 9 (January 1982), 3.
56. Ritchie interview.
57. "Eileen DeLong, RGS," Sisters of the Good Shepherd Necrology, Good Shepherd Sisters Archives. See also "Eileen DeLong, RGS: A Tribute," *Bridges* 11 (September 1984), 3.

58. Kevin Gordon to John Quinn, August 4, 1982, Homosexuality files, AASF.

59. Thomas Ambrogi in *Homosexuality and Social Justice: Report of the Task Force on Gay/Lesbian Issues* (San Francisco: Commission on Social Justice, 1982), p. iii.

60. *Homosexuality and Social Justice*, p. 7.

61. *Homosexuality and Social Justice*, p. 71.

62. *Homosexuality and Social Justice*, pp. 75–81.

63. *Homosexuality and Social Justice*, p. 71.

64. Allen White, "Local Catholics Issue Revolutionary Report," *Bay Area Reporter*, September 23, 1982, p. 4.

65. "Archbishop Says Report on Homosexuality Is Contrary to Church Teaching," press release, October 27, 1982, Homosexuality files, AASF.

66. Quinn quoted in "Senate of Priests, Minutes of Session XVII, September 28, 1982," Priests' Senate files, AASF.

67. John P. Penebsky, "Editorial: Will We Listen?" *SFM*, September 16, 1982, p. 4.

68. Tom Murray to John R. Quinn, January 19, 1983, Dignity SF records, BL.

69. For a fuller description of the controversy, see Jeffrey M. Burns, "Beyond the Immigrant Church: Gays and Lesbians in the Archdiocese of San Francisco, 1977–1987, *U.S. Catholic Historian* 19 (2001), 79–92.

70. Roberta Ward, "S.F. Senate of Priests Creates New Policy for Archdiocese," *SFM*, June 2, 1983, pp. 1, 12.

71. "Senate of Priests, Minutes of Session XVI, June 10, 1982," Priests' Senate files, AASF.

72. Francis Bodeen to *National Catholic Register*, September 24, 1982, POPE files, AASF.

73. "The Members of the San Francisco Lesbian and Gay Community Return to the San Francisco Archdiocese, The Senate of Priests Pastoral Plan on 'Ministry and Homosexuality,'" June 27, 1983, Dignity SF records, BL.

74. Don Lattin, "Gays Reply to Catholics: 'Unacceptable,'" *SF Examiner*, June 28, 1983, p. B4.

75. "Joint Meeting with Archdiocesan Task Force," May 24, 1983, Dignity SF records, BL.

76. "Notes," Dignity SF records, BL.

77. "The Consultation on Homosexuality, Social Justice, and Roman Catholic Theology," press release, March 1984, Homosexuality files, AASF.

78. Kevin Gordon to John Quinn, August 4, 1982, Homosexuality files, AASF.

79. Kevin Gordon in *Homosexuality and Social Justice Reissue*, pp. 33–34.

80. Ibid, p. 47.

81. Kevin Gordon, "Gay Men's Experience and Christian Sexual Ethics" from GTU Archives, *Radical Suspicion and Fundamental Trust: Reshaping Catholic Sexual Ethics*, manuscript of a proposed book, 1992.

82. For an interesting perspective on the sisters, see Cathy B. Glenn, "Queering the (Sacred) Body Politic: Considering the Performative Cultural Politics of the Sisters of Perpetual Indulgence," *Theory and Event* (2003), 7.

83. Jack Fertig quoted in Donal Godfrey, *Gays and Grays*, pp. 42–33. Shortly before his death, Fertig converted to Islam.

84. "Pope to Gays: Drop Dead," *BAR*, November 6, 1986, p. 1.

85. "Editorial Opinion: Unleashing the Flames of Ignorance," *BAR*, November 6, 1986, p. 6.

2

PRIESTS AS PERSONS: AN EMOTIONAL HISTORY OF ST. JOHN'S SEMINARY, BOSTON, IN THE ERA OF THE COUNCIL

John C. Seitz

This chapter explores the impact of the Second Vatican Council – its texts, style, and tone – as it shaped Boston seminarians' understanding of their calling. The Council and the wider 1960s invited seminarians not just toward new freedoms but also, and more importantly, toward new kinds of affective relationships within the church.

THE HISTORY OF VATICAN II (AND OF THE 1960S IN THE UNITED States as well) has for too long been caught up in ideological debate hinging on questions of freedom versus authority. It is impossible wholly to deny the relevance of this modern problematic, and the historical subjects of this study, the seminarians at the major seminary in the Roman Catholic Archdiocese of Boston, sometimes situated themselves within this very frame. But Boston's seminary forces historians to begin asking new questions of this period. We cannot understand the experience of Vatican II in Boston if we rely on this familiar plot. Instead, we must consider what people mean when they shout "freedom!" or "authority!" and explore the range of ways these cries radiate out into lives. This advice is especially pertinent in treating people who have, or have at least taken seriously the possibility – as all priests and seminarians did – of promising obedience to a recognized religious authority such as the Roman Catholic archbishop of Boston.

"We are Men"

For Fr. William Clarke (1968), a retired priest in Boston, one date, March 22, 1966, captures all the promise and tragedy of the past half century of his life as Catholic.[1] Clarke was enrolled at St. John's Seminary, the major training ground for priests located in the Brighton neighborhood. He had already been training for the priesthood for six years by the spring of 1966. Beginning at age eighteen, he had spent two years at the minor seminary in the Jamaica Plain neighborhood. This initial post–high school training was to be followed by six years at the major seminary at the center of Catholic Boston. In 1966, Clarke had passed through two years of philosophy at St. John's, and he was halfway through the advanced training in theology required of all priests in Boston. Reports about precisely what happened at St. John's on March 22, 1966, vary. Clarke remembers it this way:

> On March 22nd Daniel Hoo . . . went up the hill to where the cardinal was meeting with the priests of the archdiocese. And Daniel had a sign of protest. Guys . . . broke into classrooms and told us that Daniel went up the hill. Guys left their classrooms and left the professor behind. It was unbelievable.[2]

The sign Hoo carried read, simply, "We are Men, Not Boys." As Clarke recalls, no one else had a sign. Inside, Richard Cardinal Cushing, the long-serving archbishop of Boston, was holding one of a series of meetings planned with priests of the archdiocese in pursuit of "adequate communication" and "the spirit of collegiality" in the implementation of Vatican II reforms.[3] Cushing was immediately informed of the protest outside. He quickly forbade *The Pilot*, the archdiocesan newspaper, from reporting on it. In the meantime, someone began writing down names of the seminarians in view.[4]

Clarke elaborated on the intensity of the moment for everyone at St. John's. He called it a "gut-wrenching experience" and recalled a few peers "so emotionally in turmoil, they were distraught" and even "throwing up" as they faced the decision to join or stay behind. News stories of the event indicated that about 125, or about one-third of the seminary's students, had at one point been alongside a smaller contingent of those who seemed to have arrived in front of the library first. After about a half hour, the gathering of seminarians broke up, but the school did not return to business as usual.

Seven of those who had joined Hoo were soon identified, with him, by seminary officials as ringleaders of a "revolt." Some of the students involved spoke out to news media and described their mission as a desperate effort to secure a meeting with the cardinal (after he had ignored their letters) about issues related to academic and personal policies at the seminary. They framed their complaints with reference to *aggiornamento*, but they were also seeking a return of opportunities for ecumenical academic encounters and political expression that had been implemented a few years before by a recently retired rector, Matthew Stapleton. The new rector, Lawrence J. Riley, had been promoted from his faculty position with a mandate to curtail or slow the changes that were underway. His selection, and the subsequent changes he implemented, offered a striking reversal of Stapleton's interpretation of the conciliar documents. Cushing and Riley were clearly worried that the windows of St. John's had been opened too widely; their efforts to close them again would not go well.

On the day of the demonstration, seminarians distributed a letter to the local press that drew on the Second Vatican Council's *Decree on Priestly Training* to make the case for more practical and world-oriented ministries.[5] Language was an issue, too. The day before the protest, Riley had received approval from the cardinal for his proposal to implement liturgical changes at the seminary. Cushing called the proposals – which increased the amount of Latin to be used at the seminary – "very liberal." But aggrieved seminarians considered them a triumph of "medieval" and "old" over "new" and "meaningful." Riley's move to reduce the vernacular at St. John's provided the immediate trigger for the demonstration.

As astonishing as it was, Clarke said the eruption could have been antici-pated. In the months leading up to March, a group had been secretly producing pamphlets related to Riley's administration and Vatican II on a machine they had smuggled into a dormitory room. They nicknamed it the "Immaculate Press." Unprecedented displays of "rudeness you wouldn't believe" (seminarians once banged auditorium chairs up and down while Riley spoke) had already signaled the beginning of the end of Riley's short tenure as rector at St. John's. But before Riley would be allowed to step down (later to be promoted to auxiliary bishop), eight seminarians identified as leaders were expelled from the seminary. During that Easter season, a group of lay supporters marched in front of Cushing's residence and joined seminarians in a Lenten fast. They called for reinstatement of the expelled students and consideration of their pleas.[6] No one would be reinstated, but the event had a profound influence on the seminary and its residents' encounters with Vatican II.

Contexts of Change in Boston

This chapter moves back and forward in time from March 22, 1966, to consider life at St. John's Seminary as it contributes to the lived history of Vatican II. It does not attempt to provide an exhaustive account of every-thing that happened at St. John's in this period. The story crisscrosses in and out of daily routines, institutional structures, and remarkable events in search of illustrative moments. And the chapter does not treat the con-tributions of Boston's archbishop to the Vatican II proceedings in Rome. Cardinal Cushing profoundly influenced the third and fourth sessions of the

Council when he spoke out in favor of stronger language in support of religious liberty and a more robust posture of brotherhood toward the world's Jewish population.[7]

Despite these important interventions by Boston's ordinary, the Council itself sits in the background of this work, just as it did for seminarians at the time. Instead, I focus attention on the aspects of the Council text, "style," and "tone" that appear in historical sources emerging from the seminary.[8] Seminarians first came in contact with "the Council" through news reports; occasional lectures; and, eventually, new instructions related especially to liturgy and the priesthood. In the latter years of the 1960s, Council documents began to be studied in classrooms and were quoted in the newly formed student newspaper *Impact*. This latter source, which began publication as a student mouthpiece several months after the 1966 controversies, is a remarkably rich access point to student life in the late 1960s and early 1970s. It teems with citations from Council documents.

But while it sat behind the seminarians' actions, Vatican II was not the only force transforming their lives. Although isolated behind seminary walls, seminarians and their faculty were not wholly set apart from the broader social environment of Boston. Many seminarians in these years entered directly out of high school, but some had one or more years of experience in college. Newspapers, or sections of them, were available at the seminary lounge. Holidays and summer breaks also provided opportunities for brief immersion in the world beyond the seminary walls.

What they read in the news and saw on their trips home was a city and region undergoing significant change. Like many cities of the urban Northeast and Midwest, Boston had seen a massive building up of surrounding communities. Especially after the Second World War, Catholics and others increasingly left urban centers for single-family homes in suburbs such as Revere, Watertown, Medford, and Quincy. Those who remained in Boston had to contend with a deteriorating infrastructure and good-intentioned but often disastrous official attempts to improve it through "modernization" and "redevelopment."

Post-WWII migration of African Americans into Boston, especially into Dorchester and Roxbury, added to Boston's racial diversity. But de facto segregation, racist housing practices, and other forms of hostility and unequal opportunity challenged African American and other families of color and limited the possibilities for a meaningful racial pluralism. Middle-class whites left the city in record numbers between 1950 and 1970. Ethnic identities, which had once been primary in this region, gradually faded in significance as the divisions between "white" and "black" and "urban" and "suburban" came to the fore.[9]

Amid these changes and challenges, which were often defined by the potential fracture of community and family bonds, Boston's Catholics had reason to trust in their capacities to adapt or to restore good order. The institutional structure of the Catholic Church seemed to promise a continuing Catholic presence in the cities. While dozens of new parishes were being established in the suburbs, older urban parishes were not being dismantled. Unlike most of their Jewish and Protestant counterparts, Catholic churches were understood to be permanent fixtures, established to serve in perpetuity all the Catholics in a particular part of the city. Even as many Catholics left urban areas, Catholic parishes remained.[10] As the church's future priests, young Catholics joining the seminary in the late 1950s and early 1960s did so with great confidence that they would be crucial players in guiding the heavily Catholic area of greater Boston through a tumultuous period. When John F. Kennedy, a youthful Catholic senator from Massachusetts, won the nation's highest office, Boston's future priests could hardly be blamed for their intensity and exuberance in facing the challenges of the day.

The variety of speakers invited to visit the seminary signals the range of concerns circulating in Boston and the seminary during the 1960s. Visits from Bernard Häring and Henri de Lubac offered spiritual advice from the vantage point of insiders at the Council. Even before the Council concluded, seminarians were visited by speakers with acute social concerns. Martin Luther King Jr. spoke to seminarians' worries about poverty, segregation, and intensifying racial politics in Boston. Dorothy Day's visit provided an opportunity for seminarians to continue reflection on the possibilities for priestly unity with the poor. Later, a visit by Fr. Bryan Hehir (1966), who played a mediating role during the standoff of 1966, offered a chance for reflection on the church in relation to urgent matters of war and peace. Like many other Americans, seminarians were increasingly worried about U.S. involvement in Vietnam.

These visits are perhaps the clearest markers of a widening field of interest incorporated into seminary training across the 1960s. Seminary coursework also began to change in the years leading up to the Council. In particular, the introduction of a historical-critical approach to scripture had helped open the seminary to wider academic conversations.[11] Social problems and friction at the seminary before the Council were put in a whole new register once seminarians began to absorb conciliar language. The Council seemed to offer a path toward reconciliation, unity, and holism for a church, city, and world plagued by division and even fracture.

Given the recognizable litany of social and church concerns at work at St. John's, it is perhaps tempting to consider the demonstration of March 22 in light of familiar tropes related to the history of Vatican II and the 1960s in the United States. These tropes, perhaps most clearly articulated by former *First Things* editor Richard John Neuhaus in a 2002 retrospective essay, make the case that the era's spirit of liberation and experimentation combined with the haphazard introduction of the modernizing impulses of Vatican II to devastate U.S. seminaries. Untested liturgies, distracting obsessions with social justice at the expense of care of souls, and slackening of priestly discipline supposedly destroyed ancient traditions of priestly formation. Social and church leveling limited priests' special responsibilities and diminished their exalted status, killing off the remaining attraction young Catholic men might have felt toward the priesthood.

Declining seminary enrollments, a contemporary shortage of priests, and the shuttering of hundreds of U.S. Catholic churches have been the result. Moreover, seminaries' openness in the 1960s to "culture" diluted the purity and discipline of priestly training, emboldening those with homosexual, pedophilic, or ephebophilic tendencies.[12]

These arguments locate the origins of the Catholic crisis of sexual abuse and cover-up in the "liberal" 1960s and in the supposedly porous seminaries that over-zealous interpretations of Vatican II enabled. While this chapter is not primarily an exploration of the sexual abuse crisis, the evidence about seminary life it discloses militates against any such simplistic reading of the Catholic 1960s. I return to the abuse crisis later. But for now I simply want to posit that it was the fear of a life of relational aridity, not rules per se, that troubled and motivated the seminarians of the late 1960s and early 1970s. The language and documents of Vatican II resonated with seminarians' emotional state and authorized an airing of these feelings.

The conflict and upheaval at St. John's during the era of Vatican II is a history not only of ideologies or theologies but also of emotions. Drawing on interviews with St. John's alumni, archived memos, and the seminary student newspaper, it becomes clear that Vatican II was felt at St. John's primarily as an invitation to new kinds of affective relationships in the church.[13] These documents and conversations suggest that these young men saw in the tumult of the 1960s and early 1970s an opportunity to gain not just unexpected freedom to shape their own training and ministry but also – and even more importantly – respect, friendship, and authentic bonds. As Council-inspired schema and social changes began to influence the seminary in the late 1960s, it was the fulfillment and failures of these relational promises that most profoundly animated and vexed Boston's future priests.

The evidence of these passions offers one means, in one locale, for uncovering the emotional history of Vatican II in Boston.

'All-Americans' and 'The New Breed'

Older priests, therefore, should receive younger priests as true brothers and help them in their first undertakings and priestly duties. The older ones should likewise endeavor to understand the mentality of younger priests, even though it be different from their own, and follow their projects with good will. By the same token, young priests should respect the age and experience of their seniors.[14]

The harmonious interchange of wisdom and energy envisioned in this passage from the Second Vatican Council's December 1965 *Decree on the Ministry and Life of Priests* almost certainly struck priests and seminarians in Boston with a peculiar force. For seminarians, this description would likely have read more as fantasy than realistic expectation. Some of the older priests also may have been prone to skepticism about the possibilities for brotherly bonds with their up-and-coming new colleagues. Relations between junior and senior priests had come to be shadowed by mutual fear and suspicion.

One episode communicates the pains attending these divisions with poignant clarity. In a correspondence with the cardinal related to parish fundraising to defray the costs of the Council, Fr. Francis A. Barry of Weymouth took the opportunity to report the challenges of his personal life: 1965, he wrote, "had been one of the loneliest, most unhappy years of my life." Family health challenges and a church construction project had drained the senior priest's energy. But there was another factor: "My lot has not been easier," he confided, "with the 'New Breedism' I have to contend with – but I hope to do a better job in the year just ahead."

Ordained in 1928 after training at Boston's St. John's Seminary, Barry had served as the archdiocesan director of vocations and as the spiritual director for Boston's minor seminary. Barry's experience in these positions of responsibility for priests' recruitment and training surely emboldened him to offer his candid and critical assessment of the new priests of the era, some of whom would have served as curates in his parish. The phrase "New Breedism" – a term common in the early 1960s to refer to up-and-coming priests' new understandings of the meanings and responsibilities of the priesthood and the church – was not lost on Cardinal Cushing, who had himself finished his preparations for the priesthood at St. John's Seminary only seven years before Barry.[15] Sharing a generational outlook, the cardinal assured Barry of his understanding of the pastor's troubles: "The new breed either in the seminary or in the priesthood has all of us bewildered," the cardinal wrote Barry. "I can appreciate, therefore, your present frame of mind." "God help us all," Cushing ominously concluded. Only two months later, Cushing's seminarians befuddled him further by staging their demonstration. Rather than a "better job" in 1966, the year saw Fr. Barry's retirement at the age of sixty-six due to failing health. Instead of providing support through a difficult time, the rising curates had only deepened Barry's woes.[16]

When I spoke with him in 2013, Fr. Joseph Tyron provided a seminarian's view of this same generational gap. Tyron, who was ordained from St. John's Seminary in 1963 and had recently retired when we met, recalled widespread concern among his seminary peers about a small class of priests they called the "All-Americans." These were pastors who were widely respected by officials in the seminary but who struck fear in the hearts of soon-to-be priests. They were the stars of the archdiocese, in part, it seemed to the seminarians, because of the tight control they exerted over the junior priests who were sent to serve at their parishes. They were essential to the cardinal's ability to run the archdiocese because of their access to laity who could be of help in the cardinal's relentless fundraising duties. He reported having to raise $30,000 a day to keep the archdiocese running.[17] This position of value shielded the All-Americans, seminarians believed, from critique or reprimand. Tyron described the situation with a double-edged military analogy. He was willing to be a "marine" and suffer under harsh discipline, but he was not ready to be "cannon fodder" for the All-Americans to "mow down."[18] Education at St. John's Seminary in the era of Vatican II took place against a backdrop of intimidation and foreboding.

Boundaries, Minute Management

In this understanding, the priesthood – or at least the first twenty or thirty years until promotion to pastor – was troubled by the continuing presence of the minute management of time, body, and space facing the men during their training at St. John's. Worse, it threatened to perpetuate or even exacerbate the relational aridity many seminarians understood to be systematically cultivated at St. John's. By contrast, the relational promises of Vatican II, especially its promotion of ideals of brotherhood, communion, and unity, offered an exhilarating alternative. Pursuit of these ideals, not a rejection of obedience or even longing for freedom, drove seminarians zealously to embrace change at St. John's in the late 1960s and early 1970s.

A brief survey of the seminary's *Common Rule* sheds light on the emotional environment into which Vatican II's calls for "friendship," "human dignity,"

and "brotherhood" took shape.[19] The *Common Rule*, which had changed
only slightly since the early twentieth century, provided the comprehensive
set of observances – in its words "an instrument of self-discipline" – by which
individuals could seek "personal sanctification" for the good of all.[20] The most
distinctive elements of the *Common Rule* concerned the regimes of time, space,
and comportment. Each moment of a seminarian's time was carefully
accounted for. A "rising signal" woke seminarians early for prayers followed
by daily Mass. A tight schedule of prayer, meals (in silence), recreation, study,
and the nighttime "great silence," were directed by a bell, which came "half-
jokingly" to be called the "*Vox Dei.*"[21] Until the late 1960s, seminarians would
spend much of the summer at a New Hampshire "Villa," where they would
continue the routines, but with slightly less rigidity and in the surroundings of
Lake Winnipesaukee.

Time discipline worked in tandem with specific spatial arrangements.
The ringing of the bell marked the proper moment to move directly into
a different, predetermined space with its own particular rules. The upper
floors of the dormitories – where seminarians' single rooms could be found –
were designated as areas of silence. Individual rooms were to be entered only
by the seminarian occupying them. Visiting another seminarian's room was
grounds for "the severest sanctions." "Each student," the *Common Rule*
indicated in 1946, "must learn to content himself with the solitude of his
own room and to resist temptations to leave it" during designated study
periods. A similar principle applied in 1954, when seminarians were
reminded not even to "speak at the door" of another seminarian. Beyond
the dorms, an imaginary line ran through campus, dividing advanced and
beginning students.

Famously, seminarians were also to avoid "particular friendships."
Recreational activities, either inside or occasionally outside the seminary
walls, were to be performed in groups and in a spirit of "free association" so as
to avoid the temptation of "narrow or exclusive companionships." Holidays,
including a "weekly holiday" on either Wednesday or Thursday afternoons,
included the obligation for "holiday walks" through the city in preassigned
groups of four. Preceded by and culminated with a group prayer, these walks
offered two hours, under the leadership of an upper classman, to explore the
city.[22] Entry into buildings was not permitted. In retrospect, the alumni
I spoke with saw a clear but unspoken fear of homosexuality embedded in
many of these rules.[23] The integrity of boundaries, whether personal or
institutional, was paramount.

Along with consumption of alcohol or drugs and the possession of
immoral publications, seminary rules identified leaving the seminary without

permission as the most dangerous and severely penalized offense. Newspapers and radios were contraband unless received in the controlled environment of the library or, later, a radio in the lounge. Telephones were likewise supervised. Mail was permitted at any time but was subject to opening and reading at the rector's discretion. Faculty lived on campus and were responsible for supporting seminarians in their formation and monitoring their behavior.[24]

Some degree of play inevitably adheres in day-to-day practice of precise rules like these. It is not surprising that all of these rules were contravened in various ways across the years. Mass, meals, prayers, and classes were rarely skipped. More commonly, students talked in the dorms and read newspapers or listened to radios they had smuggled in. They smoked and conversed in the bathrooms, which seem to have been less closely supervised than other parts of the campus. They sometimes left campus, drank beer, or visited others' rooms. They sometimes ended up creating close, particular friendships with one another. Aggressive sporting events, often called "violent rec," were often cited as the prime opportunity for the development of friendships. Sexual relationships were less common; no one expressed knowledge of sexual activity, but they acknowledged that sex between seminarians may well have been happening without their awareness. The clarity and specificity of the disciplines of academics, time, and space made it possible for seminarians – however much they may have liked or disliked the rules – to work with and sometimes around them. "The Rule" was not the same thing as life under the Rule.

But it is crucial as well to note that order, discipline, silence, and even obedience were not altogether anathema to the seminarians of the 1960s. Many of the men I spoke with spent considerable time explaining the radical severity of the Rule only to follow those descriptions with an affirmation of their success and even joy living within it. Would-be priests knew that they were entering into a life that was "nonnatural" and "strange." "Some guys," Fr. Tyron recalled, "complained about the strangeness of some of the rules. I used to say, 'well, you know, the life we are getting into is pretty irrational so it's appropriate that, you know, we get used to the irrationality.'" From this point of view, the tight rules and discipline at the seminary were simply preparation for an entire life in a vocation that would require a level of self-sacrifice perhaps not called for in other professions. Even Fr. Clarke, who was so disillusioned with his training at St. John's, explained his staying on by noting that he got used to the pattern of life, became comfortable within it, and remained even more uncertain about what life would be like outside. When asked about daily disciplines, Daniel Hoo recalled his entry into seminary life as "a seamless transition" into familiar patterns of chapel, prayer, and classes. Seminarians understood and appreciated, even in the Vatican II era, the virtues of a starkly disciplined life. As Cardinal Cushing put it in a vocations recruitment letter to be read in all parishes in November 1959, St. John's was primed to help students fulfill "the grave requirements which Holy Mother Church lays down for the formation of the priesthood."[25] Seminarians entered formation aware of the gravity of their decision.[26]

But more than in previous decades, the priesthood faced strong competition in the mid-1960s from other professions. With a variety of professional arenas increasingly open to Catholics, the number of men enrolled in the seminary began to decline from an all-time high of 490 in 1956.[27] Significant numbers of men were leaving the seminary as well, most of them willingly, others after being removed by a process of administrative review.[28] For some, the dashed hope that Vatican II would usher in a married priesthood sent them packing. If seminarians were still willing in the mid-1960s to enter the disciplined life of priestly formation, they were less willing (or able) to do so while hiding or suppressing their need for meaningful relational networks. The seminarians' pursuit of social justice and personal freedom must be read in light of this desire: both goals would allow seminarians to be known as subjects. Different from respect or power, this recognition meant feeling satisfactorily constituted through and with particular others. It signaled the availability of an inner life where emotions were relational constituents of selfhood, not merely instinctual liabilities.[29] Training oriented toward the ideal of the "Lone Ranger" priest came into conflict with what some seminarians saw as the interconnected ideal of both Vatican II and the social movements of the 1960s.[30]

"Needs and Feelings"

The seminary made changes in the wake of the demonstration. In addition to the eight expelled, twenty-one seminarians were denied advancement, nearly triple the previous year and ten times higher than in many previous years.[31] Riley, the rector whose policies had helped provoke the event, left in April. A post-demonstration memo written by the seminary's "prefects" (advanced students in positions of leadership in the dormitories) may have facilitated this last change. While distancing themselves from the demonstrators, whose action they deemed "impulsive" and showy, the group drew on Karl Rahner and other Vatican II theologians to defend the "spirit" of the Council through an "incarnational" view of the formation of "secular priests." This meant diminishing separation between seminarians and "the world." But it was not a rejection of authority. "Freedom in the Church," they wrote, means recognition that "the Spirit" resides in subordinates as much as in superiors. Respect for "the needs and feelings of the students," they believed, would foster the "closely knit" "community of love" they sought.[32] By November, the new rector could report that students had warmly received his initial steps in the formation of a student Council.[33]

Undercurrents of resentment and distrust were still strong. Cushing warned Fr. John A. Broderick, the new rector, to "make haste slowly" in implementing changes at the seminary. Cushing's confusion about the "new breed" had begun to boil over into incredulity and anger: "All I have are problems, problems, problems with young priests who have been ordained during the past five years," he lamented. In a rare indication of potential faculty collaboration in the demonstration, Cushing instructed Broderick not to tolerate any lack of cooperation from the faculty.

Cushing may well have taken the demonstration – which he termed a "revolt" – personally. He was seriously ill off and on for much of the late 1960s and had come, as he noted in a speech after the demonstration, with "weary steps and a heavy heart" to the "evening of my life." His grief and fatigue were laced with firm resolve. He personally instructed Broderick to provide evidence "to prove" that one of the expelled students had been a ringleader and should not be awarded reinstatement on appeal to the apostolic delegate.[34] The angst spread beyond the chancery. Fr. Robert Hale (1963), a former director of education for the archdiocese, recalled being a young curate at the time and watching his pastor storm into the room cursing "those bastards" who had gone "on strike" at the seminary. Cushing, Hale remembered hearing, was "very downhearted and disappointed."

Daniel Hoo (1968), the expelled seminarian holding the sign and leading the way on March 22, seems to have particularly aggravated the cardinal. Hale reported that Cushing believed he had been especially betrayed by this young man. According to this story – again relayed from Hale's pastor around the time of the strike – Cushing believed he had been particularly generous with the Jamaican seminarian. Race and class biases intermingled here in the singling out of Hoo. When James Murray, a former Boston priest who had been a seminary friend of Hoo's, visited the cardinal to discuss Hoo's expulsion, Cushing's response was so "inappropriate" that Murray refused to repeat it when we spoke. He did report that Cushing had "dismissed" Hoo as a "Chinese communist."

These pained and scurrilous comments obscured a more complicated reality indicative of the emotional quality of the reception of Vatican II at St. John's. Hoo had indeed been sponsored by the archdiocese as a promising

candidate for the priesthood from Jamaica. Son of a Chinese father and
a Chinese Jamaican mother, Hoo arrived at St. John's in 1962. As one of
a small number of nonwhite members of the seminary, Hoo's experience
there was different from that of others. He recalls that he did not "quite fit in"
and experienced many instances of prejudice and exclusion from the majority
Irish American students. He and other racial outsiders had even taken the risk
of organizing "almost clandestine" support meetings with one another in
the basement of a seminary building. But Hoo was not wholly alienated from
the community and in fact had developed friendships within his cohort and
had found inspiration in the combined rigor and adaptability of his first
rector, Matthew Stapleton.

Under Riley's leadership, Hoo's experience changed. Only a few months
before the demonstration, Hoo's father had died. Typical seminary practice
had been to honor the deceased family members of seminarians with a community Mass. Riley and Cushing above him refused to grant Hoo's request for
a memorial Mass, since his father was not *Roman* Catholic, but a member of
the Chinese Patriotic Catholic Association (the state-run Catholic Church,
which did not acknowledge the authority of the Vatican). This wound –
which had the added effect of highlighting Hoo's difference from his
fellow seminarians – helped inspire him to become a reluctant spearhead.
Although in retrospect he thought of himself as a "social justice . . . activist,"
Hoo did not consider himself an organizer of the planned demonstration.
But when the appointed day arrived, a group of seminarians had gathered
uncertainly; in conversation with one of their faculty members, they soon
resolved to call off the protest. Hoo ignored this change of plans, proceeded
to his room to gather his sign, and walked with another seminarian past the
cautious crowd and up the hill. Soon he would be expelled and given only
one day to leave the seminary.

The angst and confusions of this event still radiate today. Despite a successful
social work career, a marriage, and a rich life lived between New York and
Kingston, Hoo called the expulsion a "very fresh experience." Even some
of those who were not expelled have lingering doubts about what happened. Clarke recalled that "not one of us had the damn courage to stand
up" for reinstatement of the expelled. Others revealed they had tried to
work back channels in defense of their friends, but to no avail. The personal
and pained reasoning of these assessments augments the sense that this
history must be told not only with an eye on ideological or theological
orientations to authority and freedom but also with attention to interpersonal relationships and the kinds of powerful feelings that go along with
them. Being a "man" and not a "boy" did not mean being free from

discipline; it meant being able to be recognized by others in one's wholeness.[35]

'All Present Facades'

Each man has a great deal to offer to every other man, but how many of these men are willing to give themselves completely to others?

Thomas Garrett, St. John's class of 1973, in *Impact*, February 14, 1968

Impact, the seminary's student newspaper, which began circulating in December 1967, is nothing if not a record of strained feelings. Originally intended to provide a voice for the student Council to communicate with students, the paper evolved into a wider forum for reporting on seminary affairs, conducting surveys, and publishing editorials, along with regular sports and culture reviews. The paper offers a fascinating record of seminarians trying to make sense of priestly formation in Boston in light of the expulsions of 1966, the Vietnam War and the draft, the civil rights movement along with class and racial inequality in Boston, and the unfolding significance of the Second Vatican Council.[36]

In all these cases, the newspaper demonstrates the radically transformed, and fitfully transforming, quality of the seminary in the late 1960s. By the time *Impact* began printing, many of the rules under which seminarians were supposed to live their lives had either been eliminated or radically altered.[37] Just to take one example, one of the three actions considered most grave in the 1954 manual – leaving campus – was not only widely in practice but officially sanctioned in a variety of ways. By the 1967–1968 academic year, the Boston Theological Institute began opening classes at its member institutions to students in all the consortium's schools. St. John's was a member and many of its students immediately took advantage of the chance to augment their St. John's curriculum with courses at Weston, Harvard Divinity School, Boston University, Episcopal Divinity School, and elsewhere.

Even greater mobility was less than a year away. By 1968, the seminary's board had approved a new policy allowing seminarians to leave campus at night without securing special permission, so long as they returned by eleven o'clock. Cushing immediately regretted the decision, fearing it would hinder development of "an aptitude for being alone in one room" and would stunt the growth of a "love for and interest in study and research." He suggested allowing the open policy perhaps only two days a week instead.[38] But this would have involved more of the kinds of intricate rules that were nationally being phased out of the diocesan seminaries.

Along with liturgy and strong academics, genuine and powerful bonds of affection and respect were supposed to replace "detailed regulations" in the formational program of the seminaries.[39] This is precisely what Cushing's worry about "being alone in one room" failed to grasp. But seminarians in this era were driven by the possibility of these kinds of relationships and their own sense of their enlivening capacities. *Impact* is a record of their mighty struggles in the late 1960s to forge communion among themselves and with their faculty. Freedom – to be political, to leave campus, to experiment with liturgy – meant nothing without the emotionally satisfying support of peers and superiors who respected and tried to understand you. Seminarian Thomas Garrett expressed this in a lament about what he saw as seminarians' fixation on trivial and superficial aspects of seminary life. Instead of obsession with rules such as "'to watch or not to watch' television," Garrett sought focus on "internal qualities of priestly training," especially self-scrutiny and honest communion inspired by the Eucharist. While not always as stark as Garrett's "disgust," virtually every issue discussed in the pages of *Impact* radiates with the hope or dismay of intra-church bonds made or broken.

Divisions within the community rankled many who wrote to the newspaper. Relationships between the upperclassmen (the Theologians) and the lowerclassmen (the Philosophers) were particularly strained. "Why do we even bother seeking a strong unity between faculty and students," Roger Le Blanc (1972) asked, "if we make no attempt to establish a unity between the two houses? Unity involves much more than participation in common exercises." Another student posed the problem even more broadly: "If we can't form this community here," he wrote, "how can we expect the community in the world, or the Community of the World to be at peace and one?"[40] Fr. Randall Stiles (1970), an active college chaplain, considered the possibility of brotherly unity to be the prime legacy, two years later, of the expulsions of 1966. For Stiles and others, strained relationships between faculty and students remained the key hurdle: "All present facades existing between faculty and students should be dropped," he declared, so that a "maximum degree of sincerity, openness and cooperation" could be sought.[41]

The "Council System," which was the name for the annual review of seminarians by the faculty for promotion through the ranks of the seminary, gave this issue a focal point and exposed seminarians' ongoing desire "to be accepted on our own terms and understood likewise." After an anonymous seminarian openly fretted about the secrecy of the review process, others wrote to defend him against the accusation that he simply did not want to be judged. Instead, seminarian Lawrence J. McGuire wrote, the concern with the Council System stems from the risk that judgments will be made based on surface impressions: "Judged only on externals and according to varying standards, students are not rarely denied promotion to orders and even expelled due to some minor personality trait," he wrote in 1968. As tragic as this can be for those involved, another risk radiated out from the process, potentially to infect the whole community: "In an attempt to garner 'yes' votes, the student is often led to play different roles for different faculty members." Should it spread, such disingenuousness would circumvent the kinds of mutually enriching intra-church relationships so profoundly celebrated by the Second Vatican Council and so devoutly sought at St. John's in its wake.[42]

By 1970, *Impact* had lost some of the relentless introspection and concern with the seminary's identity and community life. The new national "Program of Priestly Formation" began to appear in 1971, offering a level of stability in seminary approaches to spirituality, academics, and discipline.[43] Political items took a more prominent place on its pages. Theological discussion became richer as well. The paper began to feature faculty essays. The gaps between faculty and students were narrowing.

The urgency of those early few years may have faded, but the emotionally fraught struggle to realize a brotherhood founded on honesty and integrity continued. Stiles, the *Impact* author seeking a "maximum degree of sincerity, openness and cooperation" at the seminary in 1968, continued that pursuit as a priest. When Fr. Stiles was assigned to his first parish, a promising mentorship with the pastor came to an abrupt end when the elder priest died. Under new leadership, Stiles again felt relationally stifled. The new pastor changed the locks to the church buildings, effectively halting Stiles's efforts to minister to the parish's high school students. Stiles saw in his pastor's "cynical and bitter" style a horrifying snapshot of his own future. Against the prudent advice of the archbishop, he requested a transfer away from his first parish. Under a plan proposed by the short-lived "Priests Senate," Stiles would go on to develop Boston's first "team ministry" with two senior priests. By his reckoning, these unorthodox decisions put him "on the edge" of the official church in Boston. But they offered him a way forward to minister in a nurturing environment of mutual respect and support. It is not freedom from judgment that the seminarians sought, but sincerity and deep personal communion open to a holistic sense of selves as made in God's image.

"Their Reality as Persons"

These ambitions risk becoming juvenile and maudlin or, worse, subject to fantasies of purity and authenticity that may underestimate the capacity for self-delusion. This world remained male-dominated, and so "brotherhood" could only theoretically be translated into universal solidarity. Just as urgently, the value of clerical unity can potentially put broader human commitments at risk. Here we must turn attention again to the clerical sexual abuse crisis, which exploded publicly in Boston in 2002 with damning news reports about systemic problems in the church's response to reports of clerical abuse dating from the 1950s through the 1990s.[44]

No evidence indicates that the slackening of rules at the seminary emboldened or attracted abusers. The most heinous clerical abusers, Eugene M. O'Sullivan (1959), Paul R. Shanley (1960), Joseph E. Birmingham (1960), and John J. Geoghan (1962) all finished at the seminary well before any rule changes had been implemented and before the national wave of student protests and cultural unrest later in the decade. Those St. John's alumni who became most responsible for passing known or suspected abusers from parish to parish – Robert J. Banks (1952), Thomas V. Daily (1952), and John B. McCormack (1960) – were likewise ordained before Vatican II and "the 1960s" of popular imagination. The classes of 1968 and 1969 have received a lot of attention as particularly problematic (seven and six accused abusers, respectively). But the classes of 1955 (six accused), 1957 (seven accused), 1960 (eight accused), 1962 (six accused), and 1963 (ten accused) were only modestly different, even when accounting for decreasing ordination classes. For example, as a proportion of ordination classes, the rate of accused abusers in Boston is higher for the class of 1968 (approx. 14 percent) than it was for the class of 1960 (approx. 10 percent). But comparing 1960 to 1970 (approx. 7 percent), the numbers are reversed. Priestly formation under the more severe rule did not translate into lower incidence of abuse.

Just as the 1960s cannot be blamed for St. John's production of abuser priests and enabling bishops, neither can Vatican II's impact on seminary life. Of the St. John's alumni credibly accused of sexual abuse in Boston, sixty-eight were ordained – again, typically after six years at the seminary and two at the minor seminary – between 1950 and 1965, when the Council ended. In the fifteen years following the Council, thirty-six St. John's alumni were credibly accused of sexual abuse. While nationally more known abusers were ordained in the 1970s than in any other decade, in Boston most accused abusers were ordained in the 1950s (thirty-four) or the 1960s (fifty-two). Nineteen St. John's alumni from the 1970s were later accused. Of those ordained in the 1960s, thirty-four of the accused finished between 1960 and 1965. Of those who finished in the latter half of the decade (1966–1970), twenty-one were later accused of abuse.[45]

These numbers must be read with caution: most abuse goes unreported, so incidences were likely higher in all years. Obviously lost to history are memories of abuse that were taken to the grave before the stigma on reporting was slightly eased after 2002. But when it comes to the 1960s, Vatican II, and abusive St. John's alumni, some observations can be made. St. John's did educate some of the most notorious clerical abusers and some of the country's worst episcopal enablers of abuse. But it cannot be concluded that the relative openness of seminary training in the late 1960s offered a slippery slope toward sexually abusive behavior among clergy. Only those ordained after 1973 (most of whom would have begun at St. John's in 1967) would have spent their entire time at St. John's under the freer "emotional community" that prevailed after the uprising of 1966.[46] Lower incidence of abuse among priests ordained after 1973 may speak to the healthfulness of changes made in the late 1960s. While especially vicious cases such as that of Ronald H. Paquin (1973) offer counter examples, by these measures the easing of certain daily constraints at St. John's and seminary openness to the cultural movements of the 1960s may have actually led to a decrease in the incidences of abuse among the ordained.

But it would be a mistake to end the discussion without addressing the relational components of the abusive and insular behaviors that together produced the sexual abuse crisis in the Catholic Church. The people I encountered – alumni who volunteered to speak with me, seminarians who wrote for *Impact*, officials whose voices appear in archival records – were unlikely to provide much information about the dark side of the relational desires circulating at St. John's.[47] We must acknowledge, however, the connections between what we know about the rationale of clerical abusers and their episcopal protectors and the relational longing expressed among seminarians at St. John's.

The desire to have a relationally rich and emotionally satisfying life as a priest is not necessarily narcissistic; St. John's seminarians saw these goals as unambiguously tied to the calling they felt to serve others and build the beloved community. But it is striking to note that abusers often described their goal in their pursuit of their victims as one of connection and relational depth. As Marie Keenan has noted in her study of abuser priests, clerical perpetrators sometimes aligned themselves with younger men and boys as part of their search for special friendships and intimacy, experiences that they were otherwise often denied. Stunted in their human development by their embrace of the church's rigid and asexual definition of clerical masculinity, some abusers manifested their frustrations in abusive relationships with young men and boys, with whom they perceived an "emotional congruence."[48] Closer to St. John's, Paul Shanley (1960) was widely respected in Boston and beyond for his ability to lower the barriers between the priesthood and Boston's troubled youth. As fawning letters from Church officials to Shanley and other Boston abusers suggest, this ability to connect was powerful enough to encourage churchmen to overlook or soft-pedal the predatory realities.[49] And here another troubling consonance emerges, as the profoundly valorized brotherhood of priests – even sometimes across generations – again and again trumped the pursuit of justice and safety for abusers' victims.

This is uncomfortable terrain. It suggests, following Keenan, that abusers and enablers must be understood not apart from us. They must not be cast simply as "monsters" nor merely sick or "flawed individuals," but as people whose characters and behaviors emerged at the intersection of biography, body, and culture.[50] The desire to know and be known, to have deep friendships, to collapse boundaries that divide people from one another, to reconcile with offensive others in the name of holism, these are values that emerged with particular force as seminarians at St. John's swam in the confluence of Vatican II and Boston's 1960s. These desires are not to be blamed for clerical sexual abuse or its cover-up. The key factor is the varying ground – individual, social, ecclesial – on which these desires played out across the latter half of the twentieth century. But as *Impact* and the ongoing difficulties in the Catholic priesthood in the United States suggest, Vatican II did not resolve the emotional challenges of priestly formation and life. It did not erase secrecy, authoritarianism, or self-protection in the church. It did not end emotional isolation among clergy. In some cases, it gave these tendencies cover. Priesthood – because it hinges on a certain set-apartness and "mystery" – may always pose such dilemmas.[51]

But seminarians at St. John's saw in the language and tone of Vatican II an invitation to new and more open connections that could make their isolation less complete, the need for secrecy less total. As one seminarian put it in 1970, "community is a process where people are united, not in terms of their ordered preparation for a goal, but in terms of their reality as persons."[52] They wanted to be the kind of subjects and community, in other words, that previous generations at St. John's had been instructed to avoid for fear of distracting from the pursuit of defiant, heroic, "perfect, celibate, clerical masculinity."[53] Vatican II inspired St. John's seminarians to seek out a version of communion that would be both more honest and more dynamic. Part of the lived history of this era, then, is the poignant and painful documentation of the difficult pursuit of that dream.

NOTES

1. I have changed the names of St. John's alumni with whom I spoke in my research for this project. I have kept intact other details of their identity, such as their year of graduation (if any) from the seminary. After I sent a description of my research and an invitation to contribute to all of St. John's alumni currently receiving mail from the seminary, I received twelve responses and recorded conversations with nine. Additional outreach resulted in a second season of interviews, which included nine new St. John's alumni and a second session with two more. Two of those I got to know were among those expelled in 1966. The life story of a third, Fr. Ronald Lawson, appears in a recent biography, Richard Rotelli, *"Let Me Be a Light": The Faith Journey of Father Ron Lawson* (West Conshohocken, PA: Infinity Publishing, 2010). I have created no composites and have always quoted verbatim from my transcripts of the conversations. At their first mention, I indicate the alumnus's class at St. John's, even if the speaker did not go on to finish priestly training at St. John's. Unless the speaker is not clear from the context, I do not cite the interview transcripts. All the interviews took place between 2012 and 2015. I also corresponded via email with other St. John's alumni whose names I found through archival research at the headquarters of the Archdiocese of Boston. Thanks are due especially to those who volunteered their stories and to Robert Johnson-Lally, the archivist.

2. I've changed this quote to use the pseudonym "Daniel Hoo," whose voice appears later in the essay.

3. "Cardinal Begins Series of Meetings with Priests," *Boston Globe*, February 25, 1966.

4. Thomas H. O'Connor, *Boston Catholics: A History of the Church and Its People* (Boston, MA: Northeastern University Press, 1998), p. 270. A series of informal written recollections from several alumni, as well as a longer unpublished narrative by Lawrence F. Murphy, a faculty member, entitled "The Storm: A Story of Collision in the Catholic Church" offer a rich set of narratives centered on the demonstration. These were copied and given to me by one of the alumni.

5. *Decree on Priestly Training, Optatam Totius*, October 28, 1965.

6. "Academic Freedom Balked, Seminarians Claim," *Quincy Patriot Ledger*, March 23, 1966; "125 Seminarians Stage Protest While Cardinal Speaks," *Woburn Daily Times*, March 23, 1966; "Laymen Continue Vigil at St. John's Seminary," *Boston Globe*, April 8, 1966; "Student Fast at St. John's Scheduled to End Today," *Boston Sunday Herald*, April 10, 1966; "Please Reconsider, Cardinal Cushing," *Christian Century*, April 13, 1966, pp. 453–454. Archbishop Richard Cardinal Cushing to Fr. Lawrence J. Riley, March 21, 1966. Archives of the Archdiocese of Boston, St. John's Seminary Correspondence (SJSC hereafter).

7. Archbishop Richard Cardinal Cushing, "Venerable Fathers, Esteemed Observers," and Address to the Fathers of the Second Vatican Council in the Third Session at the 89th General Congregation," September 28, 1964, SJSC. Paul VI, "Declaration on the Relation of the Church to Non-Christian Religions," October 28, 1965.

8. On "style" and "tone" see John W. O'Malley, *What Happened at Vatican II?* (Cambridge, MA: Harvard University Press, 2008), p. 11 and John W. O'Malley, "Vatican II: Did Anything Happen," in *Vatican II: Did Anything Happen*, ed. David G. Schultenover (New York: Continuum, 2007) pp. 52–91.

9. Ronald P. Formisano, *Boston Against Busing: Race, Class, and Ethnicity in the 1960s and 1970s* (Chapel Hill and London: University of North Carolina Press, 1991), pp. 1–21; Michael Patrick MacDonald, *All Souls: A Family Story from Southie* (Boston: Beacon Press, 1999) pp. 74–106.

10. Gerald Gamm, *Urban Exodus: Why the Jews Left Boston and the Catholics Stayed* (Cambridge, MA: Harvard University Press, 2001); John C. Seitz, *No Closure: Catholic Practice and Boston's Parish Shutdowns* (Cambridge, MA: Harvard University Press, 2011), p. 87.

11. On curricular debate, see especially Joseph M. White, *The Diocesan Seminary in the United States* (Notre Dame, IN: University of Notre Dame Press, 1990).

12. Richard John Neuhaus, "Scandal Time (Continued)," *First Things* (June/July 2002), www.firstthings.com/ftissues/ft0206/public.html; see also Karen J. Terry (principal investigator), "The Causes and Contexts of Sexual Abuse of Minors by Catholic Priests in the United States, 1950–2010," pp. 26–47. Accessed April 4, 2017.

13. On the interplay of the study of emotions and the study of relationships, see Michael Roper, "Slipping Out of View: Subjectivity and Emotion in Gender History," *History Workshop Journal* 59 (2005), pp. 57–72.

14. Paul VI, December 1965 *Decree on the Ministry and Life of Priests* (*Presbyterorum Ordinis*), #8.

15. Andrew Greeley, "The New Breed," *America*, May 23, 1964; Joseph M. White, *The Diocesan Seminary in the United States: A History from the 1780s to the Present* (Notre Dame, IN: University of Notre Dame Press) 1989, p. 412.

16. Barry to Cushing, February 2, 1966; Cushing to Barry, February 3, 1966 (Roman Catholic Archdiocese of Boston Archives, SVC Files, M-2750, "SVC" hereafter), "Rev. Francis Barry, Vocations Leader" (Obit.), *Boston Globe*, October 5, 1977, p. 21.

17. Thomas H. O'Connor, *Boston Catholics: A History of the Church and Its People* (Boston: Northeastern University Press, 1998), p. 272.

18. Clarke (1968), Fr. Stiles (1970), an active Catholic college chaplain, Tyron, and Fr. James Wright (1963, retired from suburban pastorate in 2007).

19. See especially Paul VI, *Gaudium et Spes*, December 7, 1965, and Paul VI, *Lumen Gentium*, November 21, 1964.

20. *The Common Rule of St. John's Seminary* (CR hereafter) (Brighton, MA: Roman Catholic Archdiocese of Boston), 1954, pp. 2, 9.

21. Fr. Wright (1963).

22. CR (1954), pp. 10, 32–33, 35–37, 39–42.

23. Fr. Wright, Fr. Clarke, Ryan Cratty, an ex-priest (1969).

24. CR (1954), pp. 3, 30, 35–36.

25. Cushing, letter to be read in parishes, October 27, 1959, SJSC.

26. See for example Raymond Hedin, *Married to the Church* (Bloomington: Indiana University Press, 1995), pp. 43, 58, 79.

27. *Boston Catholic Directory* (Roman Catholic Archdiocese of Boston, 1945–1973).

28. Broderick to Cushing, June 13, 1967, SJSC.

29. Michael Roper, "Slipping Out of View: Subjectivity and Emotion in Gender History," *History Workshop Journal*, 65.

30. Fr. Robert Hale (1963), a former director of education for the archdiocese, Fr. Clarke, and Fr. Stiles (1970).

31. The personal evaluations cease to appear in the SJSC archives in the early 1970s.

32. St. John's Seminary Prefects, spring 1966, untitled, undated memo.

33. Broderick to Cushing, Nov. 17, 1966, SJSC.

34. Cushing to Broderick, September 16, 1966, SJSC; "Cardinal's Statement," *Boston Globe*, April 21, 1966.

35. For more on this theme and other issues related to this period at St. John's, see John C. Seitz, "What Better Place?: Refiguring Priesthood at St. John's Seminary, 1965–1970," *U.S. Catholic Historian* 33:2 (Spring 2015), 49–82.

36. The Archives of the Roman Catholic Archdiocese of Boston holds copies of the newspaper from its 1967 beginning through 1970.

37. On various reform efforts and interim reports, see Stafford Poole, CM, *Seminary in Crisis* (New York: Herder and Herder, 1965); James Michael Lee and Louis J. Putz, CSC (eds.), *Seminary Education in a Time of Change* (Notre Dame, IN: Fides Publishers, 1965); Richard Armstrong and James Keller (eds.), *Apostolic Renewal in the Seminary in the Light of Vatican Council II, The Papers of the 2nd Christopher Study Week* (New York: The Christophers, 1964).

38. Cushing to Broderick, August 1, 1968, SJSC.

39. Bishops' Committee on Priestly Formation, "Report of November 1967," *Interim Guide for Seminary Renewal*, May 1968, pp. 19–20, SJSC.

40. *Impact*, February 14, 1968; February 7, 1968; D. Richard Doherty, Class of 1973, "Our Schism," *Impact*, April 10, 1968.

41. *Impact*, March 20, 1968; "Stiles" is a pseudonym since he was also among those I interviewed in 2012–2014.

42. Lawrence J. McGuire, Jack Craib, *Impact*, January 11, 1968.

43. White, *The Diocesan Seminary in the United States*, p. 417.

44. Earlier reporting related to abuse and cover-up in the 1980s raised a flag that the 2002 reporters would wave again. See Jason Berry, *Lead Us Not Into Temptation: Catholic Priests and the Sexual Abuse of Children* (New York: Doubleday, 1992).

45. *Boston Catholic Directory* (Roman Catholic Archdiocese of Boston, 1958–1973); Massachusetts Attorney General Thomas F. Reilly, "Accused Priests Who Graduated from the Archdiocese of Boston's St. John's Seminary," Appendix 2 of "The Sexual Abuse of Children in the Roman Catholic Archdiocese of Boston: A Report by the Attorney General," June 23, 2003, www.bishop-accountability.org /reports/2003_07_23_Reilly_AGReport/boston_appendix_2.pdf; Laurie Goodstein, "Trail of Pain in Church Leads to Nearly Every Diocese," *New York Times*, January 12, 2003; Eric Convey, "Hub Seminary Linked to Problem Priests," *Boston Herald*, March 3, 2002; Sean O'Malley, "Statement of Archbishop Sean P. O'Malley, Regarding Clergy Sexual Abuse in the Archdiocese of Boston from 1950– 2003," February 26, 2004, www.bishop-accountability.org/usccb/nature andscope/dioceses/bostonma.htm; Denise Lavoie, "Boston Archdiocese Releases Abuse Report," *Boston Globe*, February 26, 2004.

46. Barbara H. Rosenwein, *Emotional Communities in the Early Middle Ages* (Ithaca, NY: Cornell University Press, 2006).

47. On blind spots in empathic research, see Marci Shore, "Can We *See* Ideas? On Evocation, Experience, and Empathy" in Darrin M. McMahon and Samuel Moyn (eds.), *Rethinking Modern European Intellectual History* (New York: Oxford University Press, 2014), pp. 205–206.

48. Marie Keenan, *Child Sexual Abuse and the Catholic Church: Gender, Power, and Organizational Culture*, pp. xiii, 15, 110, 225, 237, 251. On page 15, Keenan flags the concept of "flawed individuals" as a convenient and oft-used rationale for ignoring the systemic or cultural components of abusive situations.

49. Cardinal Bernard Law to Fr. Paul R. Shanley, Letter Accepting Shanley's Resignation from St. Jean's, December 7, 1989; Bishop Robert Banks to Fr. Philip Behan, San Bernadino Told Shanley is in Good Standing, January 16, 1990; Fr. John B. McCormack, Report on Meeting With Shanley and Rochester Talk (with handwritten note at bottom of page), May 15, 1985. Bishop Accountability, Boston Documents: A Selection, at www.bishop-accountability.org/ma-boston/archives/PatternAndPractice/doc-list-1.html?

50. Keenan, *Child Sexual Abuse and the Catholic Church*, pp. xiii, 110, 225, 237, 251.

51. Cardinal Emmanuel Suhard, cf. John Tracy Ellis, "The Formation of the American Priest: An Historical Perspective," in John Tracy Ellis (ed.), *The Catholic Priest in the United States: Historical Investigations* (New York: St. John's University Press, 1971) p. 90.

52. *Impact*, May 6, 1970.

53. Keenan, *Child Sex Abuse and the Catholic Church*, pp. 245–246.

3

VATICAN II AND THE QUIET REVOLUTION IN THE ARCHDIOCESE OF QUEBEC

Gilles Routhier

Like the sown seed of the Gospels, the teaching of Vatican II bore different fruit depending on the soil that received it. In Quebec, Vatican II met a society in full effervescence, agitated by the strong currents produced by the Quiet Revolution, an encounter that reconfigured post-conciliar Quebec Catholicism as bishops negotiated their new role as citizens of the province rather than as superior to it.

A COMPARISON OF THE 1947 AND 1981 EDITIONS OF *Le Canada ecclésiastique* (an annual directory of the church in Canada) yields some striking contrasts. When Maurice Roy was named archbishop of Quebec in 1947, he became the head of a local church endowed with Catholic institutions. The archdiocese had a university, a major seminary, 9 minor seminaries, 6 classical colleges, 332 convents and academies, a teachers training college for instructors of boys and 8 for girls, 31 hospitals, and 18 orphanages or charitable homes. This church was therefore well established and, by virtue of its institutions, assumed a visible presence in society. It also required the services of an enormous management personnel. The Archdiocese of Quebec hosted in its territory 41 female and 29 male congregations or religious institutes (18 clerical and 11 nonclerical). It also had a central apostolates council, a family service, a department of rehabilitation and preservation of childhood, as well as several professional, employer, and worker associations. When Cardinal Roy left office in 1981, this vast network of institutional presence was severely diminished.

Some analysts attribute this institutional shift solely to Vatican II, failing to distinguish between the *post concilium* (what happened after the Council) and the *propter concilium* (what was caused by the Council). They neglect to conduct sufficient investigation into the actual condition of the local church; warning signs were on the horizon since the end of World War II. Even before the Council was called, the Catholic Church in Quebec was beginning to show signs of weakness; its majestic appearance could not hide the changes that were already underway. The most attentive were not fooled, since the figures spoke for themselves: in relative terms (absolute number in proportion to the population), the recruitment of priests and women and men religious declined. For the first time since the 1920s, their numbers no longer grew faster than the population. At the same time, the number of children to educate increased rapidly and the demand for health care increased significantly. Meanwhile, the number of religious in the education and health care sectors declined. Financial pressure grew stronger; the church of Quebec could no longer financially support the networks that it had helped to establish.

The Catholic Action movements also declined and religious practice recorded a worrying decrease. Both the laity and priests expressed a strong desire for renewal. Eventually, important debates took place within church circles such as those concerning the ecclesial ties of organizations such as trade unions, cooperatives, and the education system, as well as religious pluralism, the neutrality of the state and its secularism. It could no longer be "business as usual" amid major shifts in the surrounding society. Henceforth, things had to be imagined differently. A new page in the history of the church was opening itself. It was necessary to imagine the face of Catholicism in the new culture and society as they unfolded.

A Church in the Making

In the space of forty years, the Catholic Church in Quebec experienced an enormous transformation, a mutation that began before the opening of Vatican II. One cannot attribute solely to Vatican II the profound remodeling of the church of Quebec. In fact, at that time, the province of Quebec, governed since 1944 by Premier Maurice Duplessis, was going through what has been termed the Quiet Revolution at the very moment that the West more broadly was experiencing a large-scale cultural change. In Rome, people were talking about the *aggiornamento* of the church, about its renewal. Thus the church of Quebec was under the influence of three currents: the Quiet Revolution, which accelerated the already obvious social and cultural changes since the end of World War II; a more general cultural revolution that engulfed the West; and the Second Vatican Council. The conciliar event and its teaching interacted with the social, political, and cultural context in a manner that drew a new image of the church of Quebec. It is this phenomenon of encounter that one has to understand and observe to comprehend the transformations of the Vatican II era in Quebec.

The first response of Quebec bishops to the announcement of the *aggiorna-mento* of the Catholic Church was silence. But the faithful and especially the media quickly perceived the Council as an opportunity to engage the arch-diocesan church and its future. Even before the opening of the Council, the expectations of the clergy and the laity were resonant with its reform program. Archbishop Roy was well aware of the renewal movements in his archdiocese and also of ongoing debates about the confessional ties of institutions and religious freedom. He was aware that the Council had arrived at a moment when the church of Quebec was at a crossroads. The Quiet Revolution required that throughout the province, the church, whose presence in society rested on its institutions, advance its own *aggiornamento* and reexamine what *Gaudium et Spes* was soon to call its place in the world of today.

The major reforms of the Quiet Revolution, the period of intense change in 1960s Quebec, encompassed the creation of a welfare state with major overhauls in the educational, health care, and social systems.[1] All of this took place in concert with the Council and its aftermath and placed in govern-mental hands social functions that the church had previously overseen. The provincial government created the Ministries of Health and of Education, expanded public services, and made massive investments in the public education system and provincial infrastructure.

This was also a period of noteworthy ideological update. Although Quebec was a highly industrialized, urban society in 1960, the Union Nationale party, in power since 1944, held tenaciously to a conservative ideology and relent-lessly defended what many citizens saw as outdated traditional values. Societal changes and debates about them did not simply question the place of the church in society but fundamentally changed the relationship between the church and the state. Even to a greater extent than the Vatican II document on religious life, *Perfectae Caritatis*,[2] the reforms compelled religious institutes of men and women to rethink their mission, putting into question the overall mode of religious socialization of the faithful who increasingly had less contact with the church. Archbishop Roy, a diplomat and skilled negotiator, was able to protect the interests of the church during this period as the educational, health care, and social well-being institutions were completely restructured. His interventions with government officials helped protect the right of parental choice over the religious education of their children and ensure pastoral ministry in the public schools and hospitals.

The result was a compromise between the church and the government of Quebec. In exchange for the bishops' consent to the government reform of the educational system, the preamble to the Public Education Act guaranteed the rights of Catholics to a Catholic education in public schools, the provision of Catholic religious instruction, and Catholic chaplaincies in both schools and hospitals. These concessions led the epithet "quiet" to be attached to this "revolution," which nonetheless fundamentally called into question the role and place of the church in the society of Quebec.

Vatican II and the ways it envisioned the relationship between the church and the state as well as between the church, culture, and society helped shape the contours of this compromise. An illuminating example of how the Council teaching and local events coalesced occurred in 1965 when Pope Paul VI named Archbishop Roy a cardinal. At the reception the parliamentarians of Quebec gave in his honor, Roy applied the words of the apostle Paul to himself, "I am a Roman citizen . . . the warmth of your welcome," he pointed out, "allows me to say, with more gratitude and more pride than ever: I am a citizen of Quebec."[3] This statement contrasted sharply with an 1875 joint letter of the bishops of Quebec in which they wrote: "The Church is not only independent of the civil society, but is superior to it . . . the State is in the Church and not the Church in the State." Subsequent Quebec bishops have similarly tended to present themselves as citizens within the framework of the state of Quebec.

The *Grande Mission*

The repositioning of the church in society necessitated that the entire life of the church be reviewed: liturgy, clergy formation, catechesis, archdiocesan governance, parish ministry, religious life, and much more. Liturgical reform was the first to be implemented, even before the close of the Council. The expectations of the faithful and the information they received during and after the Council facilitated a relatively smooth transition to new forms of liturgical celebration, beginning in 1964.[4] Liturgical education included the formation of liturgical committees and in March 1968 the creation of the archdiocesan journal *Vie liturgique* (Liturgical Life), which served as a link between the archdiocesan commission on liturgy and the regional and parish liturgy committees. Education of both priests and the faithful concerning the conciliar liturgy facilitated a positive reception and even genuine enthusiasm for the active role of the faithful in the new, vernacular Mass rite.

Judging from the number of letters to newspaper editors, the reform of catechesis – which the Council only indirectly programmed – met more opposition. This reform depended largely on the restructuring of education and the pedagogy that accompanied it, but it was also shaped by the Council. Not only had the Council deeply renewed the discourse on the church, the Virgin Mary, ecumenism, the other world religions, religious freedom, and so forth, but it also had especially influenced the Catholic Church's manner of speaking and its manner of speech and of teaching the Christian faith. A more discursive style of teaching was supposed to lead to a renewal of catechetical discourse. While the opposition to this revival was ardent, it was nonetheless limited to a small group of protesters who failed to win large numbers of supporters. The abundant letters to the editor on this topic published in the daily newspapers of Quebec City, *L'Action catholique* and *Le Soleil*, show that only a small circle of writers openly contested the new catechetical approach. They tended to focus on concerns such as the rise of "naturalistic" teaching and the mix of religious backgrounds and the lack of discipline in the new public high schools.

Even more consequential for the lives of Quebec Catholics was the reform of the archdiocesan structure. The task of rethinking the entire pastoral action and administrative government bodies of the archdiocese was the responsibility of the *Grande Mission*, established in 1964. Employing new social science tools, particularly the survey methods of the sociologist Fernand Dumont, the *Grande Mission* was an effort to revitalize pastoral action in all parts of the diocese. Sociologists conducted a thorough investigation of the human, social, economic, and pastoral reality in each region of the archdiocese.[5] Then a mission leadership team moved into the respective regions for a year. The team promoted cooperation among priests, religious, and laity to renew pastoral life. An overarching goal was to foster a new image of the church and its activity in the world. The diocesan mission coincided with the first stage of the reception of Vatican II. It was also the most substantive way archdiocesan leaders promoted the Council's ecclesiology and teachings among local Catholics.

The *Grande Mission* imported into the church the methods the state used to develop regional planning and activity. A distinctive feature of the *Grande Mission* vis-à-vis the archdiocese was its geographical base, which was no longer the parish, the undisputed basis of pastoral action since the Council of Trent, but a sociologically homogeneous region. It was also unique because of the importance and novelty of the tools of sociological analysis employed to achieve a more unified pastoral plan. Leaders of the *Grande Mission* were convinced that

> before operating on the ground and establishing a plan of evangelization, it is necessary to take a synthetic and explanatory vision, as far as possible, of the socio-religious universe in question. There is no need to repeat again that the quality and dynamism of faith are conditioned, for better or worse, by the human environment in which it is rooted: people's mentality is

shaped by the geography, and history and relationships of all kinds between man and his fellows or the physical environment, for example the types of occupations, social institutions, etc.[6]

For the data collection, team members employed different techniques, such as gathering the priests and the laity of a region to record their thoughts. Then the leadership team presented the results of these investigations during sociological forums involving the leaders of the socio-parochial life of a region. Investigation, participation, and community engagement became the hallmarks of this experience. On the ecclesiological level, the emphasis was on the people of God and on encouraging collaboration between priests and the laity.

This initiative was concurrent with the first experiments of economic planning and regionalization of state action that the government led by Jean Lesage proposed in 1961, following the adoption of legislation establishing economic advisory Councils in Quebec and the consequent efforts to prepare a plan for the economic development of the province. The investigations that led to the establishment of comprehensive pastoral ministry had the same characteristics as those found at the time in the regional development committees of the government of Quebec. Once again, these developments are also consistent with the influence of the Second Vatican Council, which in various texts promoted the use of social sciences in pastoral work (see *Christus Dominus* 16 and 17, *Optatam Totius* 20 and *Apostolicam Actuositatem* 32). Moreover, the same team of sociologists from Laval University, which active Catholic Fernand Dumont led, played a pivotal role in both operations.[7] Even the terms used in these respective efforts reveal their close correlation, such as the archdiocese's "pastoral plan" and "holistic pastoral ministry" with the government's "regional development plan" and "comprehensive plan."

Furthermore, as with new regional state structures, new central institutions for the coordination of "all the forces of the Church" were implemented.[8] The *Grande Mission* claimed to use "*all* apostolic forces to work on a socially homogeneous geographical *whole* in order to get in it the totality of the conditions of life ... and thus to join the whole man in his entirety ... his religious, professional, family and leisure life."[9] As in the case of the governmental regional planning operations, the *Grande Mission* established new institutions at the regional level: a regional pastoral Council, a regional priests Council, a regional liturgy Council, a regional commission of the religious, regional boards, a regional secretariat, and so on. The *Grande Mission* thus resulted in an institutional framework that reconfigured the governance of the archdiocese in tandem with a similar regional restructuring of the civil government of Quebec.

While this shift did not negate the importance of the parish, it placed the parish under the auspices of new regional bodies and enhanced the tendency for Catholics to perceive the parish as a community rather than a geographical unit. The *Grande Mission* also laid the foundation for a new body that would lead parish governance: the parish pastoral council. To get in touch with parishioners, the Council of Trent proposed pastors visiting their parishioners and keeping sacramental records. The focus in the Quebec archdiocese during the Vatican II era was more on sociological surveys and group meetings. This led to a fundamental revision of pastoral ministry. Whereas Trent acclaimed the mapure of the priest, the emphasis of the *Grande Mission* on the involvement of all the faithful encouraged shared responsibility between priests and the laity. As one leader noted, a "living liturgy in which all the faithful participate consciously and freely" must correspond to an apostolate nourished and rooted in "a revision of Christian life throughout the region and the taking of responsibility of the Church . . . by all, the priests, the religious and the laity."[10] At the end of the *Grande Mission*, leaders opined that in the parish pastoral council "one must find around the Parish Priest the principal representatives of apostolic forces: representatives of the laity, Brothers, Sisters, representatives of apostolic movements, some good lay leaders . . . In a word, the Parish Council must be some kind of an office for the coordination of the religious life of the parish."[11]

In sum, the main idea of the *Grande Mission* was shared responsibility: it was intended to advance, in a concrete and experiential way, the ecclesiology of Vatican II. Pastoral leaders concluded that they needed to rethink the structures that undergirded pastoral action, not only by focusing on the parish movements and works but also by addressing pastoral problems on the basis of a homogeneous human region. They also concluded that pastoral ministry depended not only on the clergy but also on all the baptized.

Central Government of the Archdiocese

The new regional focus of pastoral action quite naturally led to changes in the central government of the archdiocese. In 1947, the diocesan curia consisted of just a few permanent staff. Installed in the episcopal palace, it had scarcely a dozen people attached to it. Laval University, the minor and the major seminaries, as well as the rectory of the cathedral constituted a reservoir of priests who, in addition to their primary responsibilities, oversaw various archdiocesan agencies. On this first level of archdiocesan organization was superimposed another level that included many chaplains attached to the Department of Catholic Action and apostolates created mostly during the first third of the twentieth century. This department oversaw groups such as the specialized and general Catholic Action movements, pious associations, the Catholic press, works of charity and social service, the economic and social apostolates, the national associations, and the management of missionary apostolates and vocation promotion.

By 1964, while the decree *Christus Dominus* on the pastoral office of bishops was being discussed in Rome, significant changes began to appear in this chart. Some cracks were opened in 1960 with the creation of a catechetical office and then, in 1964, with the establishment of a commission for ecumenism and, in the same year, the reform of the Liturgy Commission. The *Grande Mission* and the impetus for comprehensive pastoral ministry helped break old administrative patterns. Discussions begun in 1962 introduced the establishment of a general commission for pastoral ministry for the archdiocese, a diocesan pastoral council. Over the following two years, numerous proposals to reorganize the archdiocesan government emerged.

Two broad approaches were evident in these varied proposals. One suggested the creation of a vast body representing the archdiocesan church encompassing people who "represent the totality of pastoral issues, institutions, associations, etc."[12] The other was the approach that gained greater traction in the transformation of the archdiocesan structures. It proposed the "grouping of a small number of people capable of thinking the diocesan pastoral ministry and capable of helping to put it in place. So, we are less concerned about uniting all the major diocesan representatives of the regions, apostolates, *et cetera*. It is less about having representatives than having officials."[13] In this perspective, the diocesan pastoral council was to be the leading organ for the entire archdiocesan pastoral organization. It would be a relatively small group charged as the "first committee of the diocese ... it coordinates the work of all other committees."[14] The council would be the engine of the overall pastoral ministry, an agency of the archdiocesan curia that monitored the implementation of the archdiocesan pastoral plan. Its oversight role would not merely extend to other agencies of the archdiocesan curia, but to all pastoral areas. Its purpose was to animate comprehensive pastoral ministry, for which it had the authority to create and coordinate diocesan commissions and regional institutions.

The new centralized administrative body enacted conciliar discussions on the establishment of diocesan pastoral councils;[15] it also mirrored the establishment of oversight agencies within the Quebec government. Significantly, the second draft of the archdiocesan circular aimed at the establishment of this body makes it almost a *consilium coordinans* (coordinating council) as envisioned in ecclesial discussions of the council at the same time. The term "coordination" or its derivatives comes up nine times in the last two pages, making explicit reference to the Coordinating Commission of Vatican II, which was above the other commissions of the council. The archdiocesan circular notes that

> as the problems become more numerous, as the action diversifies itself, as the agencies proliferate, it is even more important to monitor the coordination of efforts ... In fact, the more the action diversifies itself, the greater the need for order and coordination. We believe that such a body will be fully present in diocesan structures, helping us and our closest collaborators to plan and coordinate the efforts geared at building in our diocese a growing Christian community.[16]

Here we have a clear example of how a particular social context shaped the reception of the Second Vatican Council, in this case on the matter of overseeing archdiocesan pastoral life. While the council called for diocesan pastoral Councils, the first justification for establishing such a council in Quebec is the efficiency and rationality of administration. The more the action diversifies itself and the more the bodies multiply, the more the need for a central coordinating body, especially when we accept in principle that only a comprehensive pastoral ministry can contribute effectively to the proclamation of the Gospel. But both drafts of the decree offer the rationale of imitating governmental restructuring. The first states, "A more intense life calls for an increasingly diverse organization. We see in the secular world how they organize all dimensions, how they organize without ceasing."[17] The second draft is even more explicit: "We also see today that the civilian and secular world gives itself the institutions it needs. The governmental structures become diverse. The administrative structures of commerce and industry perfect themselves. People build and coordinate everywhere. For its part, the church does not want to stay behind."[18] Thus the diocesan pastoral council (DPC), following the example of the central councils of the state, was defined as an agency of management and action: the council was

> an executive agency of the entire diocesan pastoral ministry, consisting of people capable of rethinking, in an overall perspective, the diocesan pastoral ministry, capable of helping to establish and provide for its start and its proper functioning. It is not the representative role of the members that is highlighted here ... The DPC helps the bishop in terms of action. Under the leadership of the latter, it creates, renovates and stimulates the necessary bodies to execute the episcopal decisions.[19]

The pastoral council that archdiocesan officials established in 1963 structured all the institutions that influenced the post-conciliar years. Eight years
later, taking stock of their work to date, members of the council noted:

> This DPC provides for the establishment and the running of the compre-
> hensive pastoral ministry, for the life and the coordination of committees
> and regions: It is clear that its role is largely executive. In fact, in close liaison
> with the Office for Pastoral Ministry, the DPC creates many diocesan
> bodies grouped by categories. With the support of the *Grande Mission*, it
> created 10 pastoral zones with their regional pastoral council. Directly or
> indirectly, it contributes to the creation of the Diocesan Commission for
> the Religious (September 1966), the Council of Priests (February 1967) and
> the Council of the Laity (1968).[20]

These new entities were put at the forefront of the operation of the archdiocese, replacing the central role of the institutions cited in the ecclesiastical
yearbook of 1947. A marked shift in emphasis was clear. Some previously
leading institutions, such as Catholic hospitals, no longer existed as Catholic
entities. Others gradually followed along the same path, such as Laval
University, which was willingly secularized in 1971.

A first assessment of the diocesan pastoral council in 1969 was even more
revealing of the major transformation in the administration and pastoral oversight of the archdiocese. The enumerated achievements of the council
included the following: the general organization of the comprehensive pastoral
ministry of the archdiocese; the regionalization of the diocesan pastoral ministry with the establishment of ten pastoral regions and regional pastoral
councils; the establishment of a parish pastoral Council in almost all parishes;
and the creation of an archdiocesan secretariat, office for pastoral ministry,
liturgy commission, catechetical office, pastoral education office, social communications office, council of priests, commission of the religious, office of the
clergy, council of diocesan offices, and council of regions.[21] The formation of
such bodies comprised a major institutional overhaul of both the archdiocesan
organizational chart and the kinds of leaders that were needed to occupy it.
The executive bodies established tended to reserve leadership roles for ministry
professionals with expertise in areas such as pastoral research, collaborative
ministerial efforts, and bureaucratic processes.

Once again, it is noteworthy that developments in the archdiocese
parallel those in Quebec's civil government, which in 1966 was divided
into ten administrative regions with eighteen subregional centers. These
phenomena were not only concurrent but also followed the same logic.
Indeed, the experts who drove the changes in both sectors trained in the

same schools, belonged to the same administrative culture, used the same methods, and induced the same effects. Catholics themselves contributed significantly to their training as the faculty of social sciences at two Catholic institutions, Laval University and Maison Montmorency, helped elaborate the major features of the Quiet Revolution and taught them to their students. These two institutions of higher learning were places of meeting and formation for intellectuals who in time held leadership positions in the Quebec government, as well as in the archdiocesan offices and commissions. A close link between Quebec's Quiet Revolution and the history of the archdiocese during the Vatican II era is abundantly clear.

The transformation of the church of Quebec during the post-conciliar years illustrates the many interactions between the Second Vatican Council and a local society and culture. In Quebec City, this interaction was particularly obvious because of the intimate and narrow links between church and society, so much that we cannot easily distinguish what relates to one or the other. In fact, the same social actors, especially those found at Laval University, were Catholics who functioned as experts within the structures of both the state and the church. This Catholic elite contributed to the construction of the Quebec state, defining its areas of competence and transforming its institutions and administrative procedures. At the same time, they advised Cardinal Roy, who was trying to imagine the place of the church in a changing society and who desired to enact a Vatican II renewal of his archdiocese's pastoral care in the life of the faithful. The waters of the council and the Quiet Revolution combined to produce a unique ecosystem in which we can no longer recognize either the river water or the marine water in its pure state.

NOTES

1. The paradoxical expression "Quiet Revolution" was first used by an anonymous writer in *The Globe and Mail* in 1960.

2. See the doctoral thesis by Dominique Laperle, *"Enflammer le monde et libérer la vie": L'évolution et l'adaptation de la Congrégation des sœurs des Saints Noms de Jésus et de Marie en contexte conciliaire (1954–1985)*, L'Université du Québec à Montréal (2013).

3. See Gilles Routhier, "Le pari d'un catholicisme citoyen," *Studies in Religion/Sciences Religieuses* XXXVIII:1 (2009), 113–134.

4. On the implementation of the liturgical reform in the parishes of the Quebec diocese, see Michel Mondou, *La réception de la constitution "De Sacra Liturgia" de Vatican II, au niveau paroissial dans le diocèse de Québec, entre 1964 et 1967* (Quebec: Université Laval, 2011).

5. For a good example, see V. Delalande, *Québec Métropolitain: Étude de trois zones pastorales selon la méthode de "contact global"* (Quebec: Université Laval, Centre de sociologie religieuse, 1968).

6. Roland Doyon, "La Grande Mission de Charlevoix," *Semaine Religieuse de Québec*, June 11, 1964, pp. 654–658.

7. Father Gérard Dion, also a professor at Université Laval, was regularly consulted by Cardinal Roy as well and had a great influence on these developments. See Routhier, "Dans la mouvance de Vatican II," in S. Clavette (ed.), *Gérard Dion: Artisan de la Révolution tranquille* (Quebec, Canada: Presses de l'Université Laval, 2008), pp. 599–613.

8. In 1962, the constitution of the General Commission of Pastoral Ministry on which the Secretariat of the *Grande Mission* and the Diocesan Catholic Action Committee were based; in 1963, the creation of the diocesan pastoral Council; in 1968, the establishment of a secretariat for the comprehensive pastoral ministry; in 1969, the creation of the Pastoral Ministry Office; and, in 1970, the Council of Diocesan Offices and the Committee of the Regions.

9. Doyon, "La Grande Mission."

10. Doyon, "La Grande Mission."

11. Doyon to Archbishop Roy, April 17, 1963, p. 6. Archives Archidiocèse de Québec, dossier Grande mission, 1 S, vol. 8.

12. Doyon, "Mémoire," memo, January 12, 1963, p. 7. Among the categories that he wanted to see represented were men, women, old, adult, young, progressive, conservative, clergy, religious, laity, the rural and urban inhabitants, the various occupations, and so on. Doyon, a priest in the Quebec diocese, had pursued religious sociology training in Paris under the direction of Fernand Boulard, who himself was an influential member of the *De Episcopis* Commission at the Council. It is notably through him that the idea of "overall pastoral care" and the recommendation to use sociology to reflect on pastoral action made their way to the Council. In Quebec City, Doyon was a founding member of the Centre de recherches en sociologie religieuse (Religious Sociology Research Center), established at Laval University at the request of the archbishop in 1959. It played a key role in the *Grande Mission*. Subsequently, he had been given the responsibility of reviewing the entire pastoral organization of the diocese, in the light of the conclusions afforded by religious sociology.

13. "Mémoire provisoire," January 23, 1963, p. 3, Archives of the Archdiocese of Quebec (AAQ), 1 J.

14. "Mémoire provisoire," January 23, 1963, p. 3.

15. In the schema *De animarum cura in genere* (February 1962), the formation of a diocesan pastoral council was in fact proposed, whose function would be to inform the bishop of the spiritual needs of his diocese, to advise him and to promote the apostolate through the creation of specialized committees. Its role ultimately became to coordinate the apostolate throughout the diocese. The same ideas are substantially found in *De cura animarum* (April 1963), a schema on the pastoral office of bishops. In the second appendix, we find the following text: "It is quite important that the bishop creates a *Consilium Pastorale Diocesanum*, and that he frequently convokes them ... It is the duty of the diocesan pastoral council: (1) to inform the bishop of the state of the faithful and their spiritual needs and to advise him (2) to assign issues to be addressed and determine their activity proper to the various Commissions that

have been established in the diocese so that the apostolic works should be encouraged and coordinated." *Schema decreti de cura animarum, appendix secunda*, 37 (Vatican City: Typis Polyglottis Vaticanis, 1963). See also a similar text in *Appendix secunda*, 32. The work of the Joint Preparatory Commission De Episcopis religiosis also contained a similar suggestion. The result of this work would be included in Chapter III of *De cura animarum* and in the fifth appendix of the same document. It then promotes the formation of a *consilium coordinans*, which not only advises the bishop about the works of the apostolate but also ensures the coordination of these works in the diocese. We know that, eventually, was not the way that *Christus Dominus* would take, since it did not give the pastoral council the mandate to coordinate the pastoral activity of the diocese. The board would be, above all, an advisory board whose mission is to study, research, and submit practical conclusions.

16. "Le Conseil diocésain de pastorale," draft circular, around April 1964. This version of the circular was written by Roland Doyon.
17. Doyon, "Le Conseil diocésain de pastorale," draft circular.
18. "Le Conseil diocésain de pastorale," draft circular, April 1964.
19. C. Bélanger, "Le Conseil diocésain de pastorale," L'Église de Québec 15, April 14, 1966.
20. "Le Conseil diocésain de pastorale," May 26, 1971, AAQ, 1J, vol. 9–6.
21. "Le Conseil diocésain de pastorale. Rapport global de ses activités depuis ses débuts," July 15, 1969, AAQ, 1J.

4

TRADITIONALIST CATHOLICISM AND LITURGICAL RENEWAL IN THE DIOCESE OF CUERNAVACA, MEXICO

Jennifer Scheper Hughes

In the Mexican Diocese of Cuernavaca, conciliar reforms that sought to curtail devotion to saints and make other corrections to structures of popular piety met with significant resistance. Especially in indigenous communities identifying as "traditionalist," efforts to remove saints were sometimes met with organized resistance, outright rebellion, and even violence.

THE MOVEMENT OF LITURGICAL RENEWAL IN THE MEXICAN Diocese of Cuernavaca anticipated and even shaped the sweeping transformations of the Second Vatican Council. By the late 1950s, the Mexican Bishop don Sergio Méndez Arceo had already embarked on an ambitious set of renovations in which he sought to modernize the Cuernavaca cathedral. The pioneering bishop "swept clean" his cathedral (he called the project a *limpieza*) – removing from the sanctuary more than a dozen saints' images and the imposing side altars on which they had rested for centuries. The altars and the massive, gilded altarpiece "crowded with flowers and candles and images" overwhelmed the liturgical space,[1] the bishop explained, and the devotional activity that occurred at these altars during Mass distracted from the Eucharistic celebration.[2] One of the most ambitious articulations of the Catholic liturgical renewal movement in the world at that time, the renovations to the colonial-era Cuernavaca cathedral were not only aesthetic but also pastoral in nature: intended to curb the excesses and exaggerations of the cult of the saints and thereby reorient and purify popular piety.[3]

Concerned that the saints and their altars distracted the faithful, Don Sergio (as he was popularly known) banished the now superfluous images to the cathedral basement. The basement was thus transformed into a sort of mausoleum for saints who had been *retirados del culto*, removed from their devotional context. In their place, the bishop had the cathedral walls painted with passages of biblical text: gilded verses from the Gospels now appeared where candlelight once illuminated the hallowed forms of revered saints. Of the images, all that remained was one of the Virgin Mary (an early colonial image of Our Lady of the Assumption) and the crucified Christ. Gone, however, was the pained and suffering Christ so familiar to Mexican Catholicism.[4] The new, Vatican II crucifix was stylistically modern, with head raised, eyes open, arms thrown out in a gesture of welcome and blessing. This was an image of Christ triumphant; the *Cristo triunfal*, Don Sergio called it. Suspended from the ceiling of the sanctuary the modern crucifix floated on high, remote above the congregation: not a devotional object, but rather a work of art.

Ordinary believers throughout the Diocese of Cuernavaca in the Mexican state of Morelos greatly grieved the removal of their beloved saints, or *santos*. One elderly *campesino* who came to identify with a faction of schismatic traditionalists recalled his painful encounter of the renovated cathedral for the first time:

> There were no longer any images there in the cathedral, there was nothing left. It brought us a great sadness, *una tristeza*, because the images represent our Catholicism. Maybe we do not do all the things that a good Catholic should. But this is who we are, this is our faith: We believe in God and we believe in our images.[5]

According to the *campesino*'s creed, devotion to saints is not simply one dimension of local Catholic practice – rather, it is fundamentally constitutive of faith itself. The removal of the saints from the cathedral was so distressing, the sense of loss and disorientation so profound, that the devout of the diocese felt compelled to intervene. According to popular memory, in the wake of the renovations a group of lay Catholics forcefully occupied the cathedral, blockading the bishop's access to his own seat for eight days in protest.[6]

The Second Vatican Council's *Constitution on the Sacred Liturgy, Sacrosanctum Concilium* (1963), affirmed Don Sergio's liturgical innovation at the Cuernavaca cathedral, directing that the number of images in a church be "moderate in number" so as not to "create confusion among the Christian people."[7] After the close of the Council in 1965, Don Sergio exercised a mandate to extend his labors beyond the cathedral into the rest of his diocese.[8] Over the next decade, the bishop worked the aesthetic reorientation of his parishes more generally, directing diocesan priests to purify the faith of the people by emptying the churches of Morelos of their many images.

Across the globe, bishops and priests did likewise, removing from churches the images deemed surplus, and then worried about how to dispose of the formerly revered icons. In the Australian diocese of Adelaide, one priest moved the saints' images into the garage of the parish house. He still recalls the unease he felt parking his car each evening when, illuminated by the headlights, he was greeted by rows of small, pale faces gleaming back at him from the darkness.[9] Finally, the discomforted priest made several trips in a rowboat out into the bay, bringing one or two of the statues with him each time. When he rowed his small craft back to shore, it always returned empty. In the Diocese of Cuernavaca, for the most part the retired saints were banished to church storage closets or, if of colonial-era provenance (or otherwise of particular art historical interest), occasionally exiled to museums. Humble believers worried over their *santos desaparecidos*, their patron saints who had been disappeared. Here they employed the chilling language used to describe the kidnap and murder of political activists under repressive military regimes as in Argentina's dirty war and under El Salvador's military regime.

While many of the changes that followed the Second Vatican Council were readily received in the Diocese of Cuernavaca, those conciliar reforms that sought to curtail devotion to saints and make other corrections to structures of popular piety met with significant resistance from local Catholic communities throughout the state of Morelos. Some traditional barrios and pueblos found themselves immersed in prolonged conflicts with their priests and even with the bishop himself. These conflicts centered almost entirely on the place of the *santos* within revised Catholic practice. Efforts to remove saints, or even to change their physical position within parish churches, were sometimes met with organized resistance, outright rebellion, and even violence.

The most vigorous opposition to the labor of liturgical renewal came from indigenous-descended and indigenous-identified communities, especially in the northeastern part of the state in the Morelos highlands. In these remote, rural, and economically marginalized pueblos, the unwelcome imposition of conciliar reforms was sometimes experienced as a second conquest: cast in the shadowy and menacing memory of military invasion and forced conversion to Christianity under Spanish colonial rule. The removal of saints' images was perhaps too painfully reminiscent of colonial-era extirpation campaigns in which foreign Catholic missionaries sought to eradicate indigenous religion by consigning their deities ("idols") to flames. Some communities in Morelos responded to this perceived second conquest with an aggressive defense of traditional local Catholic custom and of their own religious autonomy. In some cases, they permanently expelled priests from the parish in favor of a wholly lay-led Catholic ritual practice.

The most staunchly resistant communities were drawn to orthodox, traditionalist, and even schismatic Catholic organizations, including international organizations that appeared in protest after the Council. In their efforts to protect the local rites and practices that had defined community identity since the Spanish conquest, several parishes in the diocese of Cuernavaca declared themselves *tradicionalista*. They severed their ties to the diocese and affiliated with Cardinal Marcel Lefebvre, the French cardinal who dissented from Vatican II and established a neo-orthodox schismatic movement. Or they joined other conservative organizations espousing a Tridentine ethos. In the Diocese of Cuernavaca, traditionalist schism and factionalism were most strongly present in those communities that were closely identified with and protective of carefully guarded indigenous customary practices (known as *costumbre*).

Although the trajectory of Catholic traditionalism in Mexico after 1965 may seem to fit neatly within a pattern of resistance to Vatican II reforms worldwide, my intention here is to clarify the culturally specific local meanings of traditionalism, a category that, in fact, has a wide semantic range globally. Drawing on oral historical interviews with religious leaders (including laity, women religious, and priests), local newspapers, parish archives, and diocesan archival records, this chapter explores the internal cultural logics of local rebellion against Vatican II liturgical reforms. I deconstruct the heavily freighted cultural category *tradicionalista* to discover its local meanings and to outline its significance for the history of the Diocese of Cuernavaca and for understanding the dynamics of Mexican Catholicism more generally.

Zapatista Bishop, *Gente Rebelde* of Morelos

Under Don Sergio's direction, Cuernavaca was a dynamic center for liturgical innovation and radical Catholic thought from at least the middle of the twentieth century. The most famous liturgical development was initiation of the first Mariachi Mass. From the mid-1950s, Bishop Méndez Arceo was already envisioning a new and revitalized expression of Roman Catholicism in Latin America. The Belgian priest Grégoire Lemercier and his community of Benedictine monks began to sing the Mass in Spanish in 1951, the very year they founded their monastery in the verdant hills of Cuernavaca. They may have been the first Catholic community in the Americas to put aside the Latin liturgy in favor of the vernacular.[10] A decade later, Lemercier garnered international attention and Vatican censure for making Freudian psychoanalysis central to the spiritual formation of his monks.[11]

Diocesan leaders in Cuernavaca were also at the helm fomenting a new kind of critical, Latin American way of doing theology that anticipated the *teología de la liberación*. Liberation theology, arguably the single most important Christian theological development of the twentieth century, was a system of theological thought and praxis that was radically responsive to the economic, political, and spiritual realities of the Latin American people. It effectively shifted the center of theological production from Europe to the Global South. In 1961, at the invitation of Don Sergio, the Austrian priest and cultural theorist Ivan Illich selected the Diocese of Cuernavaca to be the home for his groundbreaking center for cultural training and critical inquiry. Illich's Centro Intercultural de Formación (later, El Centro Intercultural de Documentación, CIDOC) trained North American and European missionaries preparing to work in Latin America. Illich's students were educated to be critical of more traditional "imperialist" evangelization methods and guided instead toward liberative expressions of pastoral solidarity.

In 1962, Méndez Arceo brought many lessons from his *acción litúrgica* (his diocesan project of liturgical action and activism) to the Second Vatican Council. One of the most active and outspoken Latin American bishops present, he made eighteen formal interventions on a variety of subjects over the course of the Council.[12] Some of these interventions reflected Don Sergio's persistent concerns about the devotional practices of the Latin American people, especially popular celebration of the saints as mediators.[13] Don Sergio also spoke strongly in support of ecumenism and affiliated himself with the most progressive agenda with respect to fostering a global Catholic vision for justice and solidarity. The Conference of Latin American Bishops (CELAM) gathered at Medellín, Colombia, in 1968 to imagine how the Second Vatican Council might become fully realized, fully articulated, in Latin America. At Medellín, the bishops formally codified the key tenets of liberation theology, including, most importantly, the preferential option for the poor.

Don Sergio was both admired and disparaged as the "red bishop" of Cuernavaca when his ministry took an even more explicitly political direction after Medellín. The period of his episcopacy coincided with a time of political upheaval in Central America in the 1970s and 1980s, when oppressive military regimes and violent civil wars rocked the region. He raised funds for the Marxist-inspired Nicaraguan Sandinistas and sheltered leftist refugees from Guatemala and El Salvador, including guerrillas.[14] He also expressed strong support for local workers' unions and dedicated himself and his priests to ministering in the poorest communities. Don Sergio's commitments not only reflected the post-Medellín ethos of the Latin American church but were very much in keeping with the cultural character of the state of Morelos. The people of Morelos frequently speak of themselves as a rebellious people, *somos una gente rebelde*, they say. Outside observers agree: *Son un pueblo de lucha*," that is, they are a people who fight – a struggling, even combative, people. Known for its revolutionary spirit, a spirit frequently manifest in its rebellious and activist priests, the state takes its name from the rebel priest José María Morelos, who led the Mexican War for Independence.[15] Morelos was also the birthplace of the revolutionary hero Emiliano Zapata, who led a movement of *campesinos* as part of the effort to overthrow President Porfirio Díaz during the Mexican Revolution of the 1910s.[16] Don Sergio's predecessor, the former bishop of Cuernavaca, served as personal confessor to Zapata and many diocesan clergy ministered as chaplains in the Zapatista army.[17] Don Sergio sometimes referred to himself as a *zapatista*, precisely allying himself with the radical history and rebellious spirit of the state.[18] Affluent Catholics and conservative journalists in the diocese publically criticized the bishop. Cuernavaca's right-wing newspaper *El Informador* frequently referred to the bishop in print not as Méndez Arceo, but as "Méndez *Ateo*," Méndez the atheist, for his Marxist sympathies. Don Sergio was investigated for his political commitments by both the Vatican and the FBI.[19]

The bishop's most significant legacy in the diocese may have been the creation and proliferation of the Ecclesial Base Communities or Basic Ecclesial Communities (CEBs is the Spanish acronym). The most important institutional expression of the option for the poor, these small neighborhood groups of lay believers were dedicated to biblical reflection, social analysis, and community action. They reflected a new way of organizing the religious life of the diocese, embodying a newly conceived, post-Medellín ecclesiology premised on the role of lay believers in building up the "people's Church," a church of and for the poor. Base communities flourished in many regions in Latin America in the 1970s and 1980s and with Don Sergio's support were particularly vital in the poor barrios and pueblos of the Diocese of Cuernavaca.[20] Don Sergio invested in the work of the CEBs and integrated their members into the liturgical life of the cathedral. On Sunday mornings, lay leaders from the CEBs, humble of means and without formal education (but now empowered by the church as privileged interpreters of the Gospels), stood before the congregation and gave the homily. The CEBs began to lose momentum after 1984, when, reflecting a conservative turn in Rome, Vatican officials noted deficiencies they perceived in them as part of a systematic critique of liberation theology. The Vatican also criticized the notion of a "people's Church," which it perceived as a direct challenge to the magisterium and to the hierarchical structure of the church generally.[21]

Don Sergio's political commitments and profound solidarity with the plight of the poor of his diocese resonated deeply with many *morelenses* (natives of the state of Morelos). The bishop was deeply admired: "He was a very humane person. Everyone always said he was very humane. He did not discriminate against anyone." Another observed, "He was humble, modest, and very noble with all people." "The pope of Morelos," a scholar from Cuernavaca dubbed him. Yet, his liturgical interventions related to the saints and popular religion often brought the bishop into conflict with those parishes at the economic margins of the diocese, in the very communities that he was most committed to championing.

Resistance to Reforms in Rural Pueblos

Even as the church's global vision for liturgical renewal was in some sense germinated in Cuernavaca (as in other dioceses worldwide), communities of lay believers on the ground were sometimes hard pressed to accept those changes that they perceived to be a threat to their local Catholic customs. Don Sergio observed that even as the final session of the Council was concluding in 1965, organizations in his diocese were already mobilized in opposition to changes, even to the point of perpetrating physical attacks.[22] The rural pueblo of Atlatlahucan in the northeast corner of the state was home to some of the most dramatic and protracted conflicts of the post-conciliar period. In Atlatlahucan, local Catholics interpreted the diocesan project of *acción litúrgica* and in particular the *limpieza* as an act of violence against their beloved saints' images. They also perceived these expressions of conciliar reform as a threat to local religious autonomy: a direct assault on the authority of the *mayordomías*, the lay religious brotherhoods that had anchored local Catholic religious life and custom from the colonial period. The pueblo rebelled openly against the reforms, ousting the parish priest and, in a particularly charged moment, physically threatening the bishop himself. Don Sergio's efforts to implement liturgical renewal at the local, parish level also caused an irreconcilable and seemingly permanent rift in the town: a schism between so-called traditionalists and moderns, between those who opposed conciliar reforms to liturgy and those who accepted them, remaining loyal to the bishop. Important dimensions of the lived history of Vatican II in the Diocese of Cuernavaca are articulated in the conflict in Atlatlahucan. The conflict is best comprehended in its historical cultural context, in relation to the structures of indigenous and indigenous-descended (i.e., mestizo) Catholicism in Mexico and in relation to the colonial history of the church in Latin America.

A pueblo proud of its indigenous, pre-Hispanic origins, at one time Atlatlahucan was a tributary to the Aztec empire. After the conquest, in the second half of the sixteenth century, the Augustinian order took on the responsibility of Christian evangelization in the community. The order was active in the region, establishing their influence through a chain of mission monasteries (known as *conventos* or *ex-conventos*) in pueblos throughout Morelos. With its stone edifice and imposing walled atrial courtyard, the Atlatlahucan *convento* is an impressive monument to almost five centuries of Roman Catholicism and today a UNESCO World Heritage site. As elsewhere in Mexico, the local indigenous Nahua population of Atlatlahucan did not so much resist Christian evangelization as it did labor to gain some degree of authority and control over the ritual practices that defined the new religion. They structured their Catholic practice around a local system of lay leadership, of *mayordomías* (or *cofradías*). Under the mayordomal system, extended families take up a charge (a "*cargo*") and are designated to care for and maintain specific local *santos*, often at considerable personal expense. The *santos* are celebrated in a complex calendar of festival celebrations that has structured collective religious practice for many generations, indeed for centuries.

During the time of the Second Vatican Council, Atlatlahucan counted fewer than 4,000 residents: the mestizo (mixed indigenous and European) *poblanos* were mostly poor, agricultural laborers, and only a modest minority were literate.[23] After the close of the Council, at the height of Don Sergio's project of *limpieza*, the bishop and his priests were impassioned and assiduous in their systematic criticism of the historic *mayordomías*, which they claimed fostered excessive devotion to the saints. In the eyes of some local believers in Atlatlahucan, the bishop had declared a sort of pastoral war on the purportedly outdated saints as on the local community organizations dedicated to their maintenance. The pueblo responded accordingly.

Tensions arising over the project of liturgical renewal peaked around 1968 when open rebellion engulfed the town. An innovating diocesan priest had removed the local crucifix from its customary place in the *nicho* behind the altar and replaced it with one that hung, suspended, in the center of the sanctuary, just as Don Sergio had hung his modern crucifix in the cathedral. The suspension of the Christ image from the ceiling was accompanied by several other innovations, including alterations to the traditional liturgy, but the hanging of the crucifix was in the minds of most local believers the final straw. The tradition-defending *mayordomos* ran the offending priest out of town and took possession of the *ex-convento*, a control they maintain to this day. Their first act was to remove the *Cristo colgado*, the hanging Christ, and reinstall the original crucifix behind the altar. They disparaged those local Catholics who were supportive of the reforms as *los colgadores*, those who "hung" Jesus. The angry epithet derived its potency from the analogy it draws between the original persecutors of Christ, the Roman soldiers who hung Jesus from the cross, and those who strung him up anew in Atlatlahucan.

In an effort to maintain a strong diocesan presence in the contentious and fractured community, Don Sergio made two to three visits a year to Atlatlahucan. One particular episcopal visit looms large in local memory, forever altering the pueblo's history: it was to be the last time a diocesan bishop was allowed to enter the pueblo.[24] Don Sergio had come to celebrate the *Misa Panamericana* (a mariachi Mass) and to make a pastoral intervention by explaining the need to reduce the number of images in the churches. A large crowd gathered in the colonial *convento* for the occasion. There were too many assembled to be accommodated inside the church, and so Mass was celebrated outdoors, in the large, walled atrium courtyard (the *atrio*) that surrounds the colonial-era church.[25]

Standing in the open-air chapel, surrounded by his apprehensive flock, the bishop began his homily. He criticized the proliferation and repetition of the saints in the local churches. In one local barrio chapel, Don Sergio observed, there was not one, but two statues of Saint Mark: one of the saint sitting and another of him standing. "This repetition of the saints such as you have in the traditional church just can't be," the bishop inveighed. Local *tradicionalistas* recall, "This bishop, this Méndez Arceo, he did not believe at all in our images. He wanted to erase our Christian religion. He came and preached that the images in our church were *monos*. He said we had *monos* in our church!" Locals took great offense at the bishop's language, understanding that he was insulting their saints' images as "monkeys." Yet, the Spanish word "*mono*" can also mean replica, imitator, mimic, or caricature. It is likely this sense of the word that the bishop intended: the statues were only representations or symbols of historic saints and should not be worshiped as the saints themselves.

Regardless of the bishop's intended meaning, the ill-advised sermon caused alarm in its audience. Angered and pained at the bishop's almost unspeakable offense, the faithful leapt into action, threatening the bishop: "You say you no longer want to see these *monos* here in our church? Well luckily we have two kilos of rope here to hang you from this little tree. He comes to take away our images? To remove them from the church? Well we will hang this bishop here and now!" Don Sergio did not wait to see if the threat was real: he made a hasty retreat, departing swiftly from the pueblo never to return.

In the period that followed, the bishop struggled to regain control over the community and took dramatic steps, even prohibiting all liturgical celebrations within the pueblo. This ban was to continue "as long as there was not peace and submission in the town."[26] By 1972, Don Sergio had forbidden his parish priests from collaborating with *mayordomías* altogether, and from officiating at their celebrations.[27] He correctly perceived that the *mayordomos* were behind the rebellion.

The rebellion in Atlatlahucan against conciliar liturgical reform oriented around two axes: the place of the saints and the authority of the *mayordomías*. In an interview, a young man from Atlatlahucan who identifies as a *tradicionalista* offered an explanation for the pueblo's revolt:

> Let's talk about this idea of taking out all the images of the church. This is a very radical idea. Because our people have a tradition, each family has under their responsibility a *cargo* of an image. So the idea was that we should break with family traditions. If you took away these images, we would no longer have a reason to be, *una razón de ser*, a reason to live.

Much more than a "statue" within the Mexican analogical imagination, the *santo* is a deity, an object, and an ordering principle around which collective life is structured and community coherence is maintained.

In Atlatlahucan, as elsewhere in Latin America, the reforms of Vatican II and Medellín came into direct conflict with the jurisdiction of the *mayordomías* as protectors of the saints and guardians of local custom (*costumbre*). In Mexico, the *mayordomía* was the primary institution through which indigenous communities brokered their appropriation of Christianity: the principal mechanism for the production of the syncretic, hybrid expression of indigenous religion and local Catholicism that we understand today as Mexican Catholicism. The *cargo*, the shared burden of upholding and caring for the sacred, is one of the enduring structures of indigenous religion from before the conquest.[28] The *mayordomía* preserved the *cargo* and gave indigenous and mestizo communities some degree of local control over religious and cultural expression in the face of the full weight of colonial power and imposition. Most important, even as cultural practice necessarily shifted, the *mayordomía* and the collective celebration of the saints ensured the survival of the *ethnos*, the identity of the local community as a people. Indigenous Catholic communities fully appropriated the institution: The *mayordomía* became a flexible institution, readily adaptable to local circumstances and functioning in relationship to but also with relative autonomy from official church structures and authority.[29] In Mexico, *mayordomías* have been a site of contest and conflict between lay Catholics and their clergy from the colonial period: any challenge to the *mayordomía* was perceived as a threat to community autonomy and self-governance, so much so that during the late eighteenth century one archbishop worried that any effort to curtail them would lead to violence.[30] This historical, cultural context explains why the local laity in Atlatlahucan expected parish priests and even bishops to defer to the power of the *mayordomías*, and not, as we might expect, the other way around.

In the course of the resulting local conflicts that rocked his diocese, Don Sergio had come to regard the *santos* and the local, customary faith that surrounded them as vestiges of a colonial past, symbols of a kind of backward traditionalism that was the product of Spanish colonial rule. This was an early liberation theology critique that applied to expressions of popular Catholicism generally. Morelos anthropologist Miguel Morayta recalls a painful conversation with Méndez Arceo in which the young anthropologist boldly defended the cultural value of the veneration of images. Morayta recalls, "The bishop's answer thundered like lightening: 'Images and *mayordomías* . . . were and remain instruments of colonization. Beliefs and principles are what matter, not images!'"[31] After Medellín, some Latin American bishops utilized ecclesial base communities (CEBs) as part of a deliberate strategy to disrupt the power of *mayordomías*. As a mode of organized parish life, the CEBs were generally more easily subject to clerical and episcopal oversight. In this way, the implementation of conciliar reforms threatened local religious autonomy in indigenous-identified communities, challenging the structures of religious authority that had been engineered to facilitate cultural survival in the period of colonial rule.

For their part, the faithful believers of Atlatlahucan were protective of their culturally specific model of Catholic self-governance, an indigenous Catholic ecclesiology grounded in the authority of their community elders. In Atlatlahucan after the Second Vatican Council, the *mayordomías* protested the lack of consultation regarding modifications to liturgical practice, church buildings, and devotion to saints. A young man from Atlatlahucan identifying himself as a *tradicionalista* explains that the community is accustomed to participating with the priest in making important decisions affecting community life:

> When the priest and the community board [*junta vecinal*] reach a consensus on a topic, that decision is then submitted to the rest of the local religious organizations [i.e., *mayordomías*] for approval. These religious bodies also

have a fundamental role to play ... Each organization dedicated to the celebration of a different saint has a right to vote, shall we say, in the decisions made by the Church.

Quite striking that according to local custom, priests' (and even bishops') decisions on matters of local significance were to be submitted to the *mayordomías* for approval before implementation. In an interview with anthropologist Cecilia Salgado Viveros, one community elder from Atlatlahucan expressed the tension between clerics, bishops, and the pueblo even more boldly: "With respect to the bishop and the Pope, we have no need to obey them: we have our own leaders, after all."[32]

Another diocesan challenge to local lay authority in Atlatlahucan in this period came in the form of the introduction of a program of Bible study and biblical literacy. In 1961, Don Sergio received permission from Rome to distribute readily accessible Protestant study Bibles throughout his diocese. After the Council, these appeared in the streets of Atlatlahucan, as priests and lay catechists distributed the Bibles house by house. The Protestant Bibles were easily recognizable to locals by their distinctive bold, yellow covers and were a significant point of contention between the traditionalists and the bishop. Illiteracy was prevalent in the pueblo at the time, and even those who could read were accustomed to a more mediated and more accessible encounter with scripture brokered through a monthly religious magazine, *La semilla eucarística*, the official organ of the Archdiocese of Mexico that circulated widely in the pueblo.[33] The new appeal to biblical literacy created discomfort among some sectors of the community. Bible study and the yellow Bibles in particular became markers of Catholic "modernism" for opponents of reform. The derisive epithet *los colgadores bíblicos* created a new, double-barreled insult that conjoined the "modernists'" predilection for scriptural study with their prior offense of hanging the image of Christ from the ceiling of the church sanctuary.

Opponents surely understood that the new sort of religious authority yielded by biblical literacy represented another potential threat to the authority of the *mayordomías* and the *cargo* system. Historian of religion Ruth Chojnacki offers a brilliant study of the effects of post-conciliar, liberationist reforms in indigenous communities in Chiapas, in the Diocese of San Cristobal. Chiapas shares some common cultural context with Morelos. There, Maya catechists from traditional communities were armed with Spanish Bibles in a power struggle against the guardians of *costumbre*: "The synergistic effect [of biblical literacy] revealed the oppressive underside of *costumbre* ... Put another way, literacy bestowed the power of a textual alternative to tradition."[34] That is to say, the *mayordomías'* perception that the project of liturgical renewal was a threat to their vigilantly guarded religious authority and autonomy was in fact correct. For both the bishop and the lay believers of Morelos, the contest over implementation of liturgical reform after the Second Vatican Council was cast as a power struggle in relation to the lingering legacy of the colonial history of Mexico. Understanding the inherited structures of church self-governance enacted in indigenous Catholic communities in Mexico helps explain the vociferous rejection of Vatican II liturgical reforms in Atlatlahucan and other traditional pueblos in the diocese.

Mexico's *"Lefebvristas"*: Diversity of Catholicisms

The Atlatlahucan conflict was not only between the *mayordomías* and diocesan authorities. In fact, the implementation of liturgical reform brought about a permanent internal fracture. This fissure came to a crisis point in the mid-1970s when local upheaval again overwhelmed the town. After the ejection of the bishop from the pueblo, the traditionalist majority in Atlatlahucan had come to identify itself as a distinct faction within the pueblo. The schismatic group of lay *tradicionalistas* maintained control of the pueblo and severed ties to the diocese and to the church universal, which, in their perception, had betrayed them, their faith, and their *santos*. They maintained control over the historic *convento* and held the keys to all but two of the pueblos' more than a dozen neighborhood chapels. These remained barred and padlocked, available only for their exclusive use.

Those who tolerated the newer liturgical forms (in truth few, if any, actually preferred them) or who simply desired to remain part of the Roman Catholic Diocese of Cuernavaca and in relationship with Rome were exiled, in essence excommunicated, from the *convento* and the collective liturgical life that was anchored there. They made their exiled home in one of the town's neighborhood chapels, a *barrio capilla* dedicated to San Miguel. Today, they describe their separation from the original parish church not as a forced exile but rather in more positive terms as a *peregrinaje*, a pilgrimage. The colonial-era Iglesia de San Miguel was eventually designated the *sede parroquial*, the diocesan parish seat of Atlatlahucan.[35]

Despite the charge of modernism levied by their local opponents, Atlatlahucan residents who remained loyal to the diocese were also thoroughly traditionalist in their religious sensibilities and practice. Although they accepted the reduction of images inside the physical church structure, they did not abandon their *santos*. Those of the *sede parroquial* continued to organize their religious life outside around a calendric cycle of feast days and celebrations of local saints' images, much as they had before. The pantheon of local Catholic saints eventually came to be celebrated in parallel, with the *tradicionalistas* celebrating the saint one day, and then *modernistas* celebrating the same saint the next, in almost identical style and fashion. The loyal members of the diocese managed the preservation of their traditions entirely on their own, without a pastor: the *tradicionalistas* did not permit a diocesan priest to take up a post in the pueblo for more than two decades.

In March 1975, the *tradicionalistas* themselves finally welcomed a new cleric – not one of Don Sergio's diocesan priests but rather the Mexican-born Italian Esteban Lavagnini. Lavagnini had been trained at the diocesan seminary of Cuernavaca in the late 1940s, but now he was mobilizing dissident Catholics throughout the region in support of the apostate bishop Marcel Lefebvre. Quite taken by the ardent faith of Mexican believers, Lefebvre was active in Mexico, which he recognized as fertile territory.[36] The Mexican church felt compelled to respond to the increasingly organized resistance to Vatican II reforms taking place throughout the country. In 1976, the Conference of Mexican Bishops published a pastoral exhortation, *Fidelidad a la Iglesia* (Fidelity to the Church), which condemned extremist traditionalists (and also progressives) but nonetheless insisted that the spirit of the Second Vatican Council had been "generously accepted" by Mexican Catholics.[37] As if in direct contradiction, in January 1977 a national gathering of traditionalists gathered in Acapulco and by the end of the month the Unión Católica Trento, one of the most important orthodox Catholic secessionist organizations in Mexico, had been established.

The dissidents in Atlatlahucan had by now come to identify themselves as *lefebvristas*[38] and, in 1977, were eagerly anticipating a rumored visit from Lefebvre himself.[39] This visit was not to materialize: yielding to pressure from church leadership, the Mexican government denied entry to the schismatic bishop.[40] Catholics loyal to the diocese did not passively accept the presence of a *lefebvrista* priest in their pueblo. In the summer of 1977, one of the lay leaders of the *sede parroquial*, Severiano Prado, repeatedly called on Don Sergio and state authorities to intervene and assist him in the expulsion of the apostate Italian priest, whom he accused of creating ferment in the community. Tensions grew and came to a violent crisis when a uniformed member of the Atlatlahucan police force, Juan Bastian Guzmán, allegedly shot and killed one of the prominent *lefebvristas*, Celso Arenales Villafaña. On hearing the news of the murder, Father Lavagnini rang the church bells, sounding the age-old alarm. An angry and armed crowd of *tradicionalistas* gathered in the atrium courtyard of the *ex-convento*. The crowd pursued the fleeing officer through the streets until he fell to the ground. Then they beat

him to death. The army and state police were brought in to restore order and
five prominent *lefebvristas* of Atlatlahucan, three men and two women, were
arrested and tried for the crime.[41]

Bishop Lefebvre finally visited his Mexican flock in January 1981. His
itinerary included several cities and pueblos, most notably a small, indigenous
pueblo in Oaxaca where he confirmed an astounding 2,000 indigenous
children and adults.[42] In these communities, the dissident bishop was warmly
received on behalf of the saints' images that he claimed to protect and defend.
In his written reflections on his 1981 visit, Lefebvre recalls one local resident
who declared to him, "What we want are priests like you, priests like before,
who don't destroy our statues."[43] He admired in particular the fierce rebel-
liousness of the people of Morelos as well as their fervent devotion to images.
Lefebvre was partial to the Diocese of Cuernavaca and reported about
conflicts there, including retelling a version of the story of Atlatlahucan:

> Mexicans are naturally easy-going, but they are getting more and more
> disillusioned with the nonsense of the Modernists. Some time ago, Bishop
> Arceo, who is Archbishop [*sic*] of Cuernavaca, visited a parish in his diocese.
> He went into the church, the main feature of which is a huge Spanish-style
> crucifix in vivid colors, and surmounted by an arc of rays. The bishop
> expressed a wish to replace this with a wooden crucifix, which was
> admittedly in good taste. But he did not get his way. The people lost no
> time in telling him in all possible bluntness, "Not so fast, my Lord Bishop!
> You touch that crucifix and we hang you!"[44]

Local affiliation with Lefebvre's movement in Atlatlahucan was not long
lived. Shortly after the violent eruption, Lavagnini was ejected from the
pueblo, much as his hapless diocesan predecessor, most likely for refusing to
submit to the will of the people on some matter, or because they had come to
agree that his presence in the pueblo was causing unnecessary strife.
The traditionalists in Atlatlahucan made a series of subsequent allegiances
with a variety of dissident orthodox organization but frequently conducted
their religious life without any institutional affiliation or clerical oversight.
Some of the traditionalist Catholic organizations with which Atlatlahucan
leaders affiliated espoused conservative or right-wing politics.[45] There were
also fascist dissident Catholic groups, even some with neo-Nazi sympathies,
in Mexico during this period.[46] In Atlatlahucan, however, as in a number of
other parishes in Cuernavaca, affiliation with dissident, conservative Catholic
organizations was not fundamentally about a shared politics. Instead, these
affiliations were strategic: above all they were a mechanism for preserving
local control over religious practice.

At the height of the conflict in Atlatlahucan, the *Informador*, a typically conservative regional newspaper, described the situation of division and violence in the pueblo of Atlatlahucan as *una pequeña revolución cristera*, comparing events in Atlatlahucan to the violent Cristero war that raged from 1926 to 1929.[47] In the historic uprising, lay Catholics in rural communities throughout Mexico took up arms and engaged in violent defense of traditional Catholic religious practice against revolutionary, anti-ecclesial reforms designed to restrict and limit the church's influence in the public sphere.[48] *La Cristiada*, as the war was called, was also rooted in communities of indigenous Catholics. The movement had a strong indigenous base in the states of Michoacán and Jalisco, and virtually all the indigenous communities in Michoacán supported the uprising.[49] The internal, religious logics of the Cristero rebellion as a movement of indigenous Catholics have yet to be fully explained or understood.

The experience of the people of Atlatlahucan was not unique in the diocese. Other traditional pueblos in the region also resisted Don Sergio's *acción litúrgica*. Faced with Vatican II liturgical reforms imposed from outside and to which they had never consented, believers in the pueblos of Hueyapan, Tlayacapan, and in the Cuernavaca barrio of Acapantzingo took physical possession of parish churches and blockaded church doors, preventing entry to their parish priests and even to the bishop himself. Some of these communities then functioned for decades without a parish priest, with laypeople administering the liturgical life of the community. Conflict persisted through the 1970s. In August 1977, following a series of clashes with progressive priests, the parish church of Tlayacapan came fully under local lay control. In a letter addressed to local lay authorities, the bishop humbly, even deferentially, requested that "those currently in possession of the church ... please unlock the building" so that the newly appointed priest could occupy his post.[50] In the traditional pueblo of Acapantzingo, in 1980 the parish priest prohibited the celebration of an important local fiesta to San Isidro Labrador. The people of the parish were so outraged that they forcibly removed the priest from the church and kept twenty-four-hour watch to prevent his return and thereby protected the dignity of their saints. The stalemate lasted more than a year. Eventually, the community permitted a priest affiliated with Lefebvre to enter the church and celebrate Mass in Latin, in the pre-conciliar style.[51] This pattern was also repeated in some other Mexican dioceses. The indigenous municipality of Chamula, in the state of Chiapas, went through a similar process of ejecting ecclesial authorities in favor of their own local Catholic structures of authority. Much like Atlatlahucan, Chamula remains under autonomous self-rule with respect to Catholic practice.[52]

Atlatlahucan continues to be fractured today along the lines drawn in the early post-conciliar period: Heated arguments result in schoolyard fights, and intermarriage between the two factions is strongly discouraged. At the same time, the community remains united in the customary celebration of their saints. One resident observed to anthropologist Salgado Viveros, "In Atlatlahucan really we no longer have religious conflict, nor do we raise war banners. There is religious difference, yes: Each group has its own form of petition, of offering, and of giving thanks to God."[53] The *tradicionalista* rhetoric is more conciliatory. One young man from Atlatlahucan explains, "In my point of view, as a student of history, to be traditionalist is cultural, not ideological. Even less so is it an expression of religious fervor. Above all it is cultural. There are distinct versions of traditionalism as each person lives it."

Affective Dimension of Liturgical Renewal

Even as *tradicionalista* communities in the Diocese of Cuernavaca sometimes affiliated with international conservative, anti-conciliar groups, these affiliations were as much strategic as they were affective: they often had more to do with the assertion of local religious and cultural autonomy in a postcolonial context than they did with conservative or orthodox piety or politics.

In the Mexican diocese of Cuernavaca, to be Catholic continues to mean, above all, to be in a personal and vital relationship to an extensive pantheon of saints and saints' images.* These saints' images, including images representing particular manifestations of the Virgin Mary and Jesus Christ, are engaged and celebrated in a devotional matrix of festivals and feast days that binds human beings to the sacred and to one another in relationships that are at once affective and effectual. To be Catholic in the Diocese of Cuernavaca also means to have a particular cultural comprehension of the materiality of these saints' images (their potency as matter) and to the analogical significance of the holy objects themselves as simultaneously persons, symbols, and spirits. The nuanced complexity of these understandings is not easily accessible to clerics and other outsiders who have too often disregarded and disparaged these devotions as "folk Catholicism," "syncretism," or "superstition" – unwanted remainders of the region's indigenous cultural origins. It was precisely to these local devotions that diocesan reformers addressed themselves as they labored in the light of the Second Vatican Council.

In the last decade of Don Sergio's life, he came to abandon his antagonism toward popular Catholicism. From 1983 until his death in 1993, he even took up residence in a traditional indigenous pueblo deeply tied to its customary practices: Ocotepec. The bishop's rather surprising decision to move to this renowned pueblo expressed his more conciliatory attitude toward local Catholicism. *"Nosotros tenemos que andar con el pueblo,"* we have to walk with our people, don Sergio often repeated.[54] In Ocotepec, this meant that he participated in the many traditional local customs, including the celebration of the dead (Día de Muertos), a tradition he had long criticized and rejected. Through this process of accompaniment, the people of Ocotepec imparted to the bishop the logic of their traditions, "they gave him *la razón de su costumbre,*" his respected colleague and biographer Fr. Baltasar López explains: "Through this process he was able to understand popular religion as a subject not object. He was still critical, but from below. He lived it from inside, from below, and through a horizontal relationship. This was both a pastoral and sociological exercise." On his deathbed, the humble believers of Ocotepec surrounded the bishop, holding vigil night and day. When he died, against the ineffectual protests of his successor (Bishop Luis Reynoso), they brought his body back to their pueblo to mourn him in the traditional fashion.[55] Each November, a traditional Day of the Dead altar is constructed to honor his spirit.

My purpose here has not been to dwell on an extreme or exceptional consequence of Vatican II as it plays out on a local context in a remote and rural corner of a Mexican diocese. Rather, the specific circumstances of Atlatlahucan compel a careful and nuanced discussion of the cultural logics and potent social forces determinative of local historical outcomes in the conciliar and post-conciliar moment.

NOTES

1. Sergio Méndez Arceo, "Instrucción sobre la devoción a los santos y sus imágenes" in Baltasar López Bucio (ed.), *Cuernavaca: Fuentes para el estudio de una diócesis. CIDOC Dossier No. 31*, vol. I (Cuernavaca: CIDOC, 1960) pp. 37–38.

2. "This multiplication of altars and *retablos* is not a good thing, my beloved children. In the first place, for reasons of space, because it greatly reduces the capacity and the ability to circulate in the church, including for processions. But principally because it divides attention and creates a lack of reverence for the main altar, because on these side altars people place candles, flowers, vases, and even objects of personal use, and people even lean on them to rest." Sergio Méndez Arceo, *Exhortación pastoral acerca del reacondicionamiento de la santa iglesia catedral de Cuernavaca,* Cuernavaca, Diocese of Cuernavaca, 1959, pp. 6–7.

3. Méndez Arceo, "Instrucción sobre la devoción," pp. 37–38.

4. Jennifer Scheper Hughes, *Biography of a Mexican Crucifix: Lived Religion and Local Faith from the Conquest to the Present* (New York: Oxford University Press, 2010).

5. Oral historical interviews for this project were conducted in various pueblos in the Diocese of Cuernavaca. The quotes that appear in this essay are taken from these original interviews unless otherwise specified.

6. Diocesan priest and editor of Méndez Arceo's written works Father Ángel Sánchez recalls however that this occupation happened quite a bit later, in 1981, and was unrelated to the renovation (personal communication, email dated June 22, 2015).

7. Vatican II, *Sacrosanctum Concilium*, 125. The section on sacred art and sacred furnishings specifies: "The practice of placing sacred images in churches so that they may be venerated by the faithful is to be maintained. Nevertheless their number should be moderate and their relative positions should reflect right order. For otherwise they may create confusion among the Christian people and foster devotion of doubtful orthodoxy."

8. This included an ambitious project of restoring many of the dozens of colonial *conventos* of the diocese, a process that was well documented in the regional publication *El Correo del Sur*. See the series *"Restauración de templos y conventos de Morelos."*

9. Personal communication, Josephine Laffin, March 19, 2012.

10. Francine du Plessix Gray, *Divine Disobedience: Profiles in Catholic Radicalism* (New York: Vintage 1971), p. 261.

11. Ruben Salazar, "Priest Stands with Freud," *St. Petersburg Times*, August 12, 1967.

12. Carlos Salcedo Palacios, "Participación de don Sergio Méndez Arceo en el Concilio Vaticano II" in Giulio Girardi and Leticia Rentería Chávez (eds.), *Don Sergio Méndez Arceo, Patriarca de la Solidaridad Liberadora* (Mexico City: Ediciones Dabar, 2000).

13. Palacios, "Participación de don Sergio Méndez Arceo," pp. 145–56, at p. 150.

14. Personal communication with anonymous source (identifying as one of these guerrillas).

15. For a discussion of the rebellious spirit of Morelos as manifest in the diocesan leaders of Mendez Arceo's generation, see Lya Gutiérrez Quintanilla, *Los Volcanes de Cuernavaca: Sergio Méndez Arceo, Gregorio Lemercier, Iván Illich.* (Cuernavaca: La Joranda de Morelos, La Jornada Ediciones, 2007).

16. For a history of Zapata including his Morelos roots, see the classic work by Jesús Sotelo Inclán, *Raíz y razón de Zapata, Anenecuilco* (Mexico City: Editorial Etnos, 1943).

17. Jean A. Meyer, *The Cristero Rebellion: The Mexican People Between Church and State* (New York: Cambridge University Press, 2008), p. 12.

18. Gray, *Divine Disobedience*, p. 257.

19. In an interview, Lemercier describes being questioned about Méndez Arceo at the Vatican. Gray, *Divine Disobedience*.

20. The prevalence and impact of the CEBs are still debated. Cf. Marcel Azevedo, *Base Ecclesial Communities in Brazil: The Challenge of a New Way of Doing Church* (Washington, DC: Georgetown University Press, 1987).

21. "What are called 'base groups'... lack the necessary catechetical and theological preparation as well as the capacity for discernment." Congregation for the Doctrine of the Faith, *Instruction on Certain Aspects of the "Theology of Liberation,"* www.vatican .va/roman_curia/congregations/cfaith/documents/rc_con_cfaith_doc_ 19198 40806_theology-liberation_en.html

22. *"que hasta han comenzado a aparecer organizaciones, que se oponen a los cambios, y quieren influir en la opinión pública esparciendo ideas y sugiriendo actitudes, más aun atacando a personas."* August 31, 1965, mimeographed letter from Bishop Sergio Méndez Arceo distributed to the churches of the diocese.

23. The population of Atlatlahucan in 1970 was 3,590, with a total of 5,107 in the *municipio*. Guillermo de la Peña, *A Legacy of Promises: Agriculture, Politics, and Ritual in the Morelos Highlands of Mexico* (Austin: University of Texas Press, 1981), p. 21. Today the population has grown significantly, nearing 13,000 residents, and its class base has diversified somewhat.

24. I have reconstructed this narrative from oral histories. It may be that several different episcopal visits to the town are remembered as one, or that the chronology is inconsistent with other historical accounts.

25. The Mexican mission *atrio* was an invention of the colonial period, an open-air chapel (*capilla abierta*) that was a Spanish concession to the preference of indigenous communities for outdoor public ritual. It is also a place that has historically contained community conflict.

26. *"Por la situación de confusión y rebeldía que en considerable número de fieles prevalencia en el pueblo de Atlatlahucan, me encarga el Sr. Obispo comunicarles que se prohíbe ahí toda celebración litúrgica mientras no haya paz y sumisión."* José Espín Velasco, secretary, Bishopric of Cuernavaca, circular no. 315, June 23, 1968.

27. Scott Robinson, personal communication, May 2014. This became a diocesan policy and practice around this time.

28. For an excellent discussion of the history of this institution, see John Chance and William B. Taylor, "Cofradías and Cargos: An Historical Perspective on the Mesoamerican Civil-Religious Hierarchy," *American Ethnologist* 12:1 (1985), 1–26. In the case of Atlatlahucan, the cargo is not a shifting burden, but it is a shared one.

29. John Watanabe identified the relationship between the assertion of local identity and autonomy through colonial-era religious structures. *Maya Saints and Souls in a Changing World* (Austin: University of Texas Press, 1992), p. 3.

30. In 1794, the archbishop of Mexico reported 951 such entities in his diocese, 500 of which never requested a license and were therefore, in his estimation, illegitimate. D.A. Brading, "Tridentine Catholicism and Enlightened Despotism in Bourbon Mexico," *Journal of Latin American Studies* 15: 1 (1983), 1–22, at 12.

31. Catherine Good, Miguel Morayta Mendoza, Alfredo Paulo, and Cristina Saldaña, *"Resolviendo conflictos entre pueblos de tradición nahua de Morelos: Una ruta por la costumbre, [A1] ley y la diversidad religiosa."* Unpublished manuscript, n.d., p. 40.

32. *"Del obispo y el Papa dicen: a ellos no hay porque obedecerlos, nosotros tenemos nuestros líderes."* As cited in Cecilia Salgado Viveros, *"Identidades religiosas católicas en el oriente de Morelos,"* anthropology thesis, Universidad Autónoma Metropolitana, Unidad Iztapalapa (2000), p. 40, 148.206.53.84/tesiuami/UAM3106.pdf. See also Salgado's subsequent book, *Modernismo y tradicionalismo católico* (Cuernavaca: Universidad Autonoma del Estado Morelos, 2003).

33. A reference to local preference for reading *La semilla eucarística* over the Bible appears in an interview with don Joaquín Amaro in Cecilia Salgada Viveros, *"Identidades religiosas católicas,"* p. 36.

34. Ruth J. Chojnacki, "Religion, Autonomy, and the Priority of Place in Mexico's Maya Highlands," *Latin American Perspectives*, 43:3 (2016), pp. 31–50.

35. The church was finally renovated for this purpose sometime after 2000.

36. For a helpful survey of the various traditionalist groups in Mexico, see Artemia Fabre Zarandona, "Son lefebvristas los católicos tradicionalistas mexicanos?" in Elio Masferrer Kan (ed.), *Sectas o Iglesias: viejos o nuevos movimientos religiosos* (Mexico City: Plaza y Valdés, 2000), pp. 233–245.

37. Jean-Pierre Bastian, Miguel Concha Malo, Óscar González Gari, and Lino F. Salas, *La participación de los cristianos en el proceso popular de liberación en México (1968–1983)* (Mexico City: Siglo XXI Editores Mexico, 1986) pp. 144–145.

38. Fabre Zarandona, "*Son lefebvristas?*"

39. *El Informador*, "*En Atlatlahucan se Preparan*," p. 4.

40. Michael Wilson, "Mexico ban on Lefebvre" and "The choices facing Pope Paul on Archbishop Lefebvre's defiance," *The Catholic Herald*, July 15, 1977, pp. 1, 3. Primary historical documents accessed at archive.catholicherald.co.uk.

41. "*Fanáticos Disidentes Mantienen la División en Atlatlahucan*," *El Informador*, September 11, 1977, p. 3.

42. "Archbishop Lefebvre in Mexico" in *Apologia pro Marcel Lefebvre* vol. III, chap. 47, 1981, n.p., sspxasia.com/Documents/Archbishop-Lefebvre/Apologia/Vol_three/ Chapter_47.htm. Lefebvre's reflections are also available in print, Michael Davies, *Apologia pro Marcel Lefebvre* (Dickinson, TX: Angelus Press, 1979).

43. "Archbishop Lefebvre in Mexico" in *Apologia pro Marcel Lefebvre*, vol. III, chap. 47, 1981, n.p.

44. "Archbishop Lefebvre in Mexico" in *Apologia pro Marcel Lefebvre*, vol. III, chap. 47, 1981, n.p.

45. Todd Eisenstadt, "Usos y Costumbres and Postelectoral Conflicts in Oaxaca, Mexico, 1995–2004: An Empirical and Normative Assessment," *Latin American Research Review* 42: 1 (2007), 52–77.

46. Gray, *Divine Disobedience*, pp. 298–299.

47. "*Fanáticos Disidentes*," *El Informador*.

48. In the final analysis, it was not the government's repressive action but rather the church's decision to cease public worship in protest that ultimately sparked the rebellion, Meyer, *Cristero Rebellion*, p. 67.

49. Meyer, *Cristero Rebellion*, p. 100.

50. Don Sergio's letter to Tlayacapan, August 6, 1977, reads: "*Les pido a los actuales posesores del templo por tanto que para el lunes próximo tengan abierto el templo, de tal manera que al llegar él [Fr. Humberto Limón, the new parish priest] acompanado por el Pbro José Espín, encuentre al pueblo reunido sin discriminación y puedan escuchar su nombramiento y el pueda tomar posesión de la Parroquia.*"

51. Good et al., "*Resolviendo conflictos*," pp. 41–2.

52. Andrés Fábregas Puig, "*Entre la religión y la costumbre*," *México indígena*, 23 (1991), pp. 7–11.

53. "*Así que en Atlatlahucan ya no hay conflicto religioso, ni banderas de lucha, hay diferencia y cada grupo tiene su forma particular de pedir, de ofrendar, y dar gracias a Dios.*" As cited in Cecilia Salgado Viveros, *Identidades religiosas*, p. 40.

54. Woman religious Hermana Nieves, who cared for Don Sergio in Ocotepec until his death, recalls Don Sergio's ultimate rapprochement with popular religion.

55. At his death in 1993, a vigil over the bishop's body was held at the cathedral. Around midnight, the staff there advised the mourners from Ocotepec that the cathedral was

closing and that they would have to return the next day to continue their watch. At this, the people of Ocotepec gathered around the body of the man who had chosen their pueblo for retirement. They could not bring themselves to leave their beloved bishop alone through the night, so they requested permission from acting bishop Luis Reynoso to bring the body back to their parish church where they could continue the wake without interruption. The conservative bishop granted their request, saying to his assistant, "Let the people take his body. If not, these Indians are capable of taking him by force."

* This project could not have been completed without the generous support and participation of Fr. Baltasar López and Fr. Angel Sanchez of the Diocese of Cuernavaca. Márily Lino Dávila, coordinator of the Conacyt project on patrimony, memory, and identity for the state of Morelos (Rescate de Fuentes para la Historia Social y Religiosa de Morelos) extended generous support in providing contacts and information in Ocotepec and Atlatlahucan. Magdalena Hernandez served as research assistant and interviewer on the ground in Morelos with the utmost skill and professionalism. At the University of California, Jasmin Salais and Zulma Michaca worked as research assistants, translating, transcribing, and organizing interviews and archival materials. Scott Robinson offered important support and information in the final phase of research. I am grateful here to build on the work of respected Mexican colleagues in the field.

5

THROUGH THE PRISM OF RACE:
THE ARCHDIOCESE OF DETROIT

LESLIE WOODCOCK TENTLER

The Archdiocese of Detroit emerged as a center of ecclesial reform in the wake of the Second Vatican Council. Local reception of conciliar reform, however, was vastly complicated by the politics of race, which came to a sometimes violent head locally at just the same time. This chapter explores the consequences of the overlapping conciliar reform and civil rights movements.

W HEN PITTSBURGH'S BISHOP JOHN FRANCIS DEARDEN WAS appointed to head the Archdiocese of Detroit late in 1958, he had clearly received a promotion. With roughly 1.4 million Catholics and encompassing eight counties in southeastern Michigan, the Archdiocese of Detroit was one of the nation's most sizeable. Its previous ordinary, Edward A. Mooney, had been named a cardinal after playing a major leadership role in the predecessor body to the National Conference of Catholic Bishops. The city of Detroit in 1958 still ranked as the nation's fifth largest, though it was losing population and in the early stages of what would be a swift and traumatic transition from a mostly white city to one that was majority black. Southeastern Michigan still served as the nation's principal center of automotive manufacturing, despite the city's having seen auto-related employment shrink in recent years – a problem that would worsen significantly in subsequent decades. At the time of Dearden's arrival, however, optimism was the reigning sentiment locally. No one then could imagine the depopulation, poverty, and violence that would afflict Detroit by the time of Dearden's retirement in 1980.

The Catholic population that Dearden came to shepherd was mostly assimilated but with varied ethnic roots. Polish Americans constituted the largest and most ethnically assertive group, with numerous national parishes and schools, most of them in Detroit. Once overwhelmingly working class, the Catholic population locally experienced dramatic upward mobility in the wake of the Second World War. By the early 1960s, social class was a more potent source of division than ethnicity among local Catholics, with the newly prosperous increasingly opting for Detroit's burgeoning and virtually all-white suburbs. Rates of religious observance were high: A 1958 study found 74 percent of white working-class Catholics in metro Detroit claiming to attend Mass weekly, while 82 percent of occupationally middle-class respondents said the same.[1] Most of the city's parishes supported schools, as did many in the suburbs; more than half the school-age Catholic children in the archdiocese were attending a Catholic school in the late 1950s.[2] Catholics dominated local politics, while Catholicism continued to shape the ethos of a city that was rapidly becoming less Catholic. Many stores and movie theaters, for example, closed for "Tre Ore" observances on Good Friday afternoon.

As for Dearden himself, he came to Detroit with the reputation of an iron-willed disciplinarian – a reputation perhaps enhanced by his somewhat remote persona. Like many in the episcopate, he had spent little time as a parish priest, serving for nearly the whole of his career as a seminary professor and rector and then a bishop. Despite his reserved nature, however, Dearden was a gracious and immensely patient man, qualities that quickly won the loyalty of his clergy. He was also far more open to ideas than his reputation would have suggested. Hence his veritable transformation – for so contemporaries speak of it – as a result of his participation in the Second Vatican Council, where he served as a member of the Theological Commission and chaired the subcommittee that produced the diplomatically worded chapter on marriage and the family in *Gaudium et Spes*. His Council experience appears to have broadened his sense of church and generated a commitment to collaborative decision making. Under his post-conciliar leadership, Detroit won a deserved reputation as among the nation's most progressive dioceses. Dearden also played an important post-conciliar role on the national stage, serving as chair of the National Council of Catholic Bishops from 1966 until 1971 and presiding over the 1976 Call to Action Conference in Detroit. He was named a cardinal in 1969.

Dearden's role as an ecclesial reformer in Detroit cannot be separated from his efforts to mediate racial conflict in his archdiocese. Dearden himself often justified his chancery's racial initiatives by invoking Council documents, especially *Gaudium et Spes*. His racial activism, which will be discussed in the latter half of this chapter, proved at the time to be far more divisive than such purely ecclesial initiatives as reform of the liturgy, though for many Detroiters it was almost impossible to wholly separate the two reform modes. Attitudes toward racial change tended to inflect attitudes toward change more generally. The archdiocese would have been far less polarized by the later 1960s had ecclesial reform not been implemented in the context of an escalating racial crisis, although one could presumably say the same with regard to many locales where racial tensions were less acute than in Detroit. Nonetheless, Detroit was unusual both for the severity of its racial troubles and the extent to which its Catholic leadership, however controversially, attempted to address them.

Let us look first at the implementation of liturgical reform in Detroit, since that was the most immediate way that the laity experienced the changes wrought by Vatican II. Despite his reputed penchant for discipline, Dearden advocated greater lay participation in the Mass even prior to the Council, encouraging his clergy to offer Sunday dialogue liturgies with the pedagogical aid of a commentator. Chairman of the U.S. Bishops' Committee on the Liturgical Apostolate, he prepared his priests conscientiously for the introduction of a partly vernacular liturgy at the end of 1964. The chancery sponsored clergy study sessions on the theology of *Sacrosanctum Concilium*, the conciliar decree on liturgical reform, and Dearden required his priests' attendance at liturgical practice sessions. Clergy were also provided with sermon texts to prepare the laity for reform; these texts emphasized the communal nature of the Mass and the human solidarity it ought to generate – "We should leave Mass with more abundant love for one another and our neighbor, because we have been nourished by the Bread of Life in an atmosphere of love and unity," according to the second of four prescribed sermons.[3] Dearden remained committed to educating for change; the Archdiocese of Detroit by the mid-1960s had one of the nation's largest programs of Catholic adult education, with numerous classes in liturgy and many other subjects offered for laity as well as clergy. By the mid-1960s, however, it was clear that Dearden's hopes for a uniform and carefully monitored process of liturgical reform had run aground.

Although initial responses to liturgical reform in the archdiocese were broadly positive, discontent was also evident. A not insignificant minority of priests had reservations about some or all of the reforms – saying Mass facing the congregation seemed to be a particular bugbear – and some responded by resisting reform in more or less passive fashion.[4] There were those who refused to preach the chancery-provided sermons on upcoming liturgical changes, increasing the odds that change, when it came, would seem both bewildering and arbitrary. A few – like the Polish pastor who in 1967 had his organist bellow Latin responses to drown out the sisters who were singing in English at a weekday Mass – flouted chancery directives in more radical fashion.[5] The most potent source of liturgical polarization, however, was the growing population of priests and laity who regarded the pace of liturgical reform as intolerably slow. Young priests, especially, were prone to jump the liturgical gun, although many of the reforms thus pioneered – communion under both kinds for the laity, lay ministers of the Eucharist, communion in the hand – were eventually endorsed by the bishops' conference. Others were not. Dearden had occasion to speak in 1968 of "literally bizarre departures from established [liturgical] procedures" that had recently come to his attention. "The Mass does not belong to you and me," he reminded his clergy, "It is not our private prayer."[6]

The uneven pace of reform resulted in a liturgy that was far less uniform across the archdiocese than had earlier been the case. Growing numbers of Catholics responded by "shopping around" for liturgies that were to their liking, a long step toward redefining ecclesial community from a neighborhood or ethnic concept to one based on politics and taste. The Dearden chancery chose to put a positive spin on these developments. A 1967 chancery-issued sermon text spoke of liturgical diversity as evidence of a new freedom that Catholics ought to cherish, while Dearden's chief liturgist in 1970 endorsed the notion of "floating parishes" to serve the liturgical avant-garde and "perhaps relieve some of the tension that is being felt" in many local congregations.[7] Liturgical opinion in the archdiocese was more divided by then than in the mid-1960s. Almost half of the lay respondents to a 1970 survey expressed discontent with the liturgical status quo. Some thought change had proceeded too quickly or confusingly, while others complained that the pace of change had been too slow.[8] The survey made clear what sensitive observers had already grasped: the liturgy had ceased to be a source of unity for many Catholics.

Discontent with the liturgy was frequently part of a broader process of alienation. The culture of reform in Detroit, mediated as it was by workshops, study groups, and courses in the new theology, put a premium on participants being articulate, at home with abstractions, and confident with regard to self-presentation. Less-educated Catholics might easily come to believe that the post-conciliar church was one that privileged qualities they lacked. Detroit's path-breaking diocesan synod of 1969 provides an ironic case in point. Dearden wanted the synod to be an ambitious experiment in collaborative decision making, analogous to his own experience of the Council, and the several years of pre-synod preparation in the archdiocese unfolded accordingly. Most parishes held synod "speak up" sessions, where participants offered proposals for consideration by various preparatory commissions, which included lay members. Each commission was committed to reviewing every proposal it received. The process was time consuming, as

Dearden acknowledged: "But it is only through doing it in this fashion that we can really open up to the entire Church of the Archdiocese the prospect of giving expression to its feelings and judgments."[9]

Participation in pre-synod activities was widespread and the synod itself, with its generally progressive agenda, shaped diocesan policy for the rest of Dearden's tenure.[10] At the same time, synod participation was significantly skewed by class, race, and gender. Participation was strongest in the Detroit suburbs and weakest in the center-city parishes, particularly those for Polish Americans.[11] Individual pastors could veto synod participation in their parishes, and Polish American pastors were said to be the most likely to do so. Parish ballots were weighted in the tallies sent to the various preparatory commissions, with greater value given to those from persons who had faithfully attended the ten-week program of study that preceded the speak-up sessions.[12] The wholly unintended result was to mute the voices of working-class Catholics, less likely than their highly educated coreligionists to find study groups congenial and frequently less in control of their schedules. Those on the night shift could not participate at all, since pre-synod activities were invariably held in the evening, which also deterred participation in the many center-city parishes where fear of crime kept people home after dark. As for the lay members of the various preparatory commissions, they were majority male, almost all white, and mostly resident in affluent parishes; nearly every commission member, moreover, was a college graduate.[13] Nominated by the clergy and appointed by the chancery, lay commissioners had to meet high standards. Even the Commission on the Laity required that members possess "some qualities of leadership, a better than average knowledge of Catholic Doctrine and practice and a commensurate interest which has proved effective preferably on a diocesan level."[14]

"Synod '69" convened at a time of escalating polarization in the archdiocese. Although many Catholics locally were moved by the event and proud of their collective achievement, the synod almost certainly exacerbated existing divisions among the laity. Barriers to synod participation for less-educated Catholics, along with the synod's endorsement of progressive goals and programs, alienated a portion of working-class Catholics as well as affluent conservatives. Synod support for Dearden's racial initiatives caused particular bitterness for many of the disaffected, given the parlous state of race relations in Detroit. Self-styled progressive Catholics, including those deeply involved in synod preparation, had grievances as well. Championing reforms with no possible chance of synod endorsement, such as optional celibacy for the clergy and election of bishops, progressives perhaps unwittingly intensified the frustration that prevailed among them. Participation in pre-synod activities created new connections among progressives locally, enabling them to live and move in what amounted to an ideological microclimate, from which vantage point most conservative Catholics appeared simply to be racists. As for the majority of Catholics locally, who belonged to no ideological camp, feuding within the Catholic ranks was a painful reminder of eroded Catholic unity and the contested status of church authority. Ordinary Catholics, moreover, were often as resentful of lay activists who ignored the views of others as they were of overbearing clergy.

Bitter as divisions among the laity were by 1969 – and these would subsequently worsen – those among priests were more intense. Polarization among the clergy correlated strongly with age. Younger priests in the wake of the Council emerged as the principal dissidents, giving voice to grievances that their elders could sometimes barely comprehend. Given that priests in the archdiocese in the early 1960s could expect to wait twenty years and more to become pastors, it is hardly surprising that the junior clergy's initial complaints centered on rectory life and authority relations in the parish. Many younger priests felt stifled by pastors who made decisions on their own (or even, in certain storied cases, in consultation with the rectory housekeeper), thus preventing their curates, some of whom were men in their forties, from exercising pastoral initiative. Typically moved to a new parish every five years, junior clergy sometimes felt like unwelcome transients in the rectory.[15] Nothing in church law prevented a pastor from such outrages as declaring the rectory living room off-limits to his curates, as a prominent monsignor in Detroit was allegedly wont to do.[16] Grievances such as these were not new. But they were articulated publicly in the mid-1960s, as had not earlier been the case, and with a vehemence that breached what many older priests regarded as the canons of clerical etiquette. Giving voice to such long-standing frustrations, moreover, seems to have endowed young priests with a taste for debate on questions not previously open to dispute.

Chief among these was the meaning of priesthood itself, an issue that the Council addressed in fairly perfunctory fashion. What did the priest do that was distinctive? Had he been adequately prepared for what younger priests insisted on calling his "professional role"? Many older priests were angered by such ruminations, such as the pastor who opined at a 1967 priests' retreat – one that had exploded into emotional confrontation across generational lines – "that there was something wrong with a priest who had to begin searching for his identity." Younger men, for their part, were outraged by the blindness of their elders – "'shocked' at the seeming unawareness of the older men of the real problems of today's Church," according to a participant in the retreat just mentioned.[17] More radical questioning quickly followed.

Was Christian witness in today's world not most authentically conveyed outside the sanctuary and in ecumenical settings, such as civil rights or antiwar activism? And what about mandatory celibacy? Did it not truncate a priest's emotional development and erect an unbreachable barrier between him and the laity? Reaffirmed in a papal encyclical in 1967, the discipline of mandatory celibacy served into the 1970s and beyond as a source of division among local priests, as well as a vehicle for a host of other grievances. "The rationale for mandatory celibacy given by the pope and bishops is simply not accepted by any except the oldest priests," as Father Joseph Gagnon summarized the sentiment prevailing in the suburban parishes west of Detroit in 1980, when he headed the local vicariate. He continued, "It would be difficult to overestimate the gap of viewpoint on this subject, and the resulting sense of distance and separation from the bishops that results."[18]

Conflicts such as these were not peculiar to the Archdiocese of Detroit in the post-conciliar years. But they unfolded there with an unusual degree of visibility, to which laity as well as priests were privy. This had to do in part with Dearden's tolerance for dissent; his clergy, by and large, were not afraid to speak their minds and growing numbers did so publicly. Detroit was among the first American dioceses, at the end of 1966, to establish a priests' senate – a reform that stemmed directly from the Council; elected by age group, the Detroit Priests' Senate was characterized from the first by free-wheeling and sometimes contentious debate. Dearden's chancery appointments signaled his reform sympathies with particular vividness, which encouraged openness on the part of his younger clergy and sometimes resentment among their elders. The chancery staff included youthful progressives such as Thomas Gumbleton and Walter Schoenherr, both of whom were named auxiliary bishops in 1968, and Kenneth Untener, later bishop of Saginaw. The breadth and sophistication of local programs for clergy education were a factor, too. Detroit's priests were exposed early on to the likes of Bernard Cooke, SJ, Bernard Haring, Charles Curran, and scripture scholar Raymond Brown. Since not all priests took advantage of such offerings, the unintended effect was to further clerical polarization and sometimes the alienation of priests from their congregations. "One of the priests felt that the more seminars that he went to on theology the wider the gap between him and his people," a member of the Priests' Senate reported in 1971, having recently met with members of the ordination classes of 1953 and 1954.[19]

Differences over sexual questions proved among the most vexing. Many younger priests moved in the mid-1960s toward a liberalized stance on birth control, typically advising married penitents to follow their consciences in the matter. For other priests, this amounted to collusion in sin. Matters came to a head with the issuance of *Humanae Vitae* in 1968, a crisis that by most accounts Dearden handled masterfully. Although he had previously endorsed a change in the teaching as a member of the papal birth control commission, Dearden declined to dissent from the encyclical either publicly or privately. Meeting with priests in small groups throughout the archdiocese, Dearden pointed to the positive aspects of *Humanae Vitae* – "the values of conjugal love and responsible parenthood are well presented by the Holy Father" – and urged compassion for struggling penitents. Above all, he counseled, the rights of conscience had to be respected. "The Archbishop expressed agreement with the statement of Cardinal Heenan that persons conscientiously unable to observe the papal doctrine nevertheless should not refrain from receiving the Sacraments," according to the minutes of a Priests' Senate meeting devoted to the issue.[20] Dearden thus addressed both the outrage of those many priests who regarded *Humanae Vitae* as a pastoral disaster and the fears of those for whom deference to papal authority was the ground of their priestly being. "He freed us up an awful lot," in the words of young Father Lawrence Jackson.[21]

In the wake of *Humanae Vitae*, the birth control question went underground. With fewer and fewer penitents in the confessional and these less likely than heretofore to confess to the sin of contraception, priests were seldom confronted by an issue that a few years earlier had been among their most serious pastoral problems. But birth control was quickly superseded as a source of division among the clergy by remarriage after divorce. The divorce rate rose for Catholics in the 1960s, as it did for other Americans. By the latter part of the decade, divorced Catholics were increasingly asking their priests whether they might remarry in the church – something they had not done before, simply because it would have been pointless. Dearden responded by expanding the staff of his marriage tribunal and, insofar as canonically possible, liberalizing the grounds for annulment. The tribunal, however, was quickly overwhelmed by petitioners, even as it struggled, in the words of its director, "to make the annulment process as painless and as swift as possible for all concerned."[22] In the circumstances, growing numbers of priests opted to resolve marriage cases at the parish level, presiding at marriages for the previously divorced and encouraging such couples to receive the Eucharist. Dearden was troubled by this development, as were many of the older clergy. While recognizing the acute pastoral difficulties created by divorce, Dearden told a group of dissident priests, he could not see how, as men who were "sent" by the church, priests could thus ignore its teaching: "In reference to the man who leaves his wife to marry another, the blunt remarks of Christ in Sacred Scripture are hard to evade."[23]

Dearden never disciplined any priest who embraced the "pastoral solution" to remarriage after divorce, presumably aware that such men were responding to a genuine pastoral crisis. "We are talking about an overwhelming problem," as the Priests' Senate noted in 1979.[24] Discrepant practice among the clergy – some pastors would not even refer parishioners to the tribunal – was an ongoing source of tension and anger, not only for clergy but laity, too. Uniformity had been an odd source of consolation for many Catholics as they coped with their church's hard teaching on marriage and sex. To have that teaching applied in seemingly arbitrary fashion made the discipline harder to respect. Many priests by the 1970s were uneasily aware of growing lay autonomy when it came to sexual morality. The flight from confession attested to it, as did growing defections among the young. "Priests are quite aware of declining mass attendance and of the numbers of alienated Catholics around them," as Father Charles Irvin, a former president of the Detroit Priests' Senate, wrote in 1976, "This adds to the sense of powerlessness and defeat. With each passing day the numbers of 'drop-out' Catholics add to the feeling of failure."[25] However a man chose to explain these developments, his morale was bound to be affected.

Most subversive of priestly morale, however, was a wave of resignations from the priesthood that began in 1967, when thirteen men requested leaves of absence. The numbers accelerated thereafter – twenty in 1968, twenty-eight each in 1969 and 1970 – before diminishing significantly in the later 1970s.[26] Most priests in the archdiocese agreed that those who left were unusually talented men. But there consensus ended. Since many who left did so to marry, younger priests generally regarded them as victims of the hierarchy's unhealthy fixation on celibacy. Older priests disagreed. "Defectors," as they insisted on calling them, had in their view reneged on a sacred promise; they objected to Dearden's compassionate approach to these men, whom he typically provided with interim health insurance, assistance in petitioning for a dispensation from the vow of celibacy, and limited financial help. For a group of pastors ordained between 1929 and 1932, such treatment was "somewhat equivalent to asking our people to subsidize married men who desert their wives and families."[27] Coupled with a collapse in new vocations to the priesthood, the resignations created an acute clergy shortage in the archdiocese, which made the lives of all priests harder. (According to guidelines published in 1976, only one priest would be assigned to a parish with as many as 1,500 families.[28]) The laity were negatively affected too, despite lay opinion moving decisively in favor of a married priesthood. "We have repeatedly noticed the harm done by abrupt, melodramatic or surreptitious departures from the priesthood," as a synod implementation subcommittee noted in 1971.[29]

"Wounded Communities"

The clergy shortage in the archdiocese was eased to some extent by the advent of new forms of ministry. Detroit's first permanent deacons were ordained in 1971, with a class of 13; there were 108 permanent deacons serving the archdiocese by 1980, the year that Dearden stepped down.[30] The archdiocese also pioneered a program by which African American men were commissioned to serve as liturgical and social leaders in certain parishes after a relatively brief period of training. "Ministers of Service," as such men were known, were installed in twenty-eight Detroit parishes as of 1976, by which time numerous women religious were also serving as pastoral associates.[31] That so much enthusiasm was evident among lay Catholics for parish ministries that were either unpaid or compensated poorly suggests that Detroit's post-conciliar church was not without vitality. One can easily overstate the extent to which polarization and bitterness were dominant themes in local church history after the mid-1960s. But at the time, a great many Catholics were more conscious of these darker themes than buoyed by evidence of new growth and energy. "Everywhere I went I found wounded communities," Father Ken Untener noted of his return to the archdiocese in 1971 after an interval of Roman study.[32]

Much of this "woundedness" had to do, directly or indirectly, with race. The 1960s saw escalating racial tensions in Detroit, culminating in 1967 in what was then the deadliest urban rioting of the American twentieth century. Since Catholics were relatively slow to leave the city, which had been losing white population since the late 1940s, the black-white conflict of the era was, as Dearden noted, "in great part a Negro-Catholic confrontation," with housing as the most frequent flashpoint.[33] Detroit had sustained heavy black in-migration during the Second World War, when an acute housing shortage in the city led to interracial violence, which helped fuel the postwar out-migration of whites. With escalating white flight and continued black migration from the South, Detroit was roughly 30 percent black at the start of Dearden's episcopate. By that time, numerous once all-white neighborhoods, many of them centered on extensive Catholic parish plants, had become majority or exclusively black, despite sometimes violent efforts on the part of whites to defend their once-segregated turf. "What originally was a situation facing a handful of parishes [served] by priests of religious communities and a few diocesan men has now arrived at the point where more than a hundred diocesan priests must face conditions which originally were the major obligation of only a few," Msgr. Harold Markey explained in 1960 with reference to the problem of diminishing Catholic populations in the

center city parishes.[34] Although most white Detroiters preferred to think
otherwise, it was clear that the process would continue. The black population was still growing and many black neighborhoods were severely over-
crowded. White flight continued apace over the course of the 1960s,
accelerating after the July 1967 riot. Detroit was a black-majority city by
the early 1970s.

Dearden moved to address the problem shortly after his arrival in Detroit,
motivated in good part by financial worries. The depopulated parishes in the
city core would eventually need subsidizing, at least if they were to remain
open, even as money was flowing to ever more rapacious suburban building
projects – to the churches, rectories, schools, and convents required by
a newly mobile Catholic population. But Dearden also saw a social justice
dimension to the project, although he knew relatively little at this point
about conditions of life in black Detroit or even about the extent of segrega-
tionist practices in the institutions of his own archdiocese. The initiative he
announced in March 1960, the Archbishop's Commission on Human
Relations (ACHR), had a dual thrust. For those many parishes where whites
were a rapidly diminishing minority, the ACHR emphasized convert making among local African Americans. Parish schools were a valuable resource
in this campaign, since those that accepted non-Catholic students required
their parents to take a course in Catholic doctrine. Children wishing to
convert, if only to be more like their classmates, sometimes led their parents
to embrace the church as well, despite difficulties not infrequently imposed
by the Catholic prohibition on remarriage after divorce. "Marriage entan-
glements have proved a big obstacle among the [N]egroes," as the pastor of
St. Edward's parish explained, artlessly revealing the mind-set of many in his
generation by his reference to the importance of visual aids in convert work
as being "more simple and attractive to the [N]egro mentality."[35]

The second, and more enduring, thrust of the ACHR was directed toward
parishes in the early stages of racial transition or likely to be so in the near-
term future. The focus on convert making did not disappear: priests and lay
leaders in these parishes were encouraged to invite black residents to visit the
church and perhaps consider its school for their children. But the primary
focus was on leadership training – on creating a cadre of white parishioners
who would work to calm the alarm that invariably greeted the movement of
blacks into a given neighborhood, stem the resultant panic selling, and
promote harmonious relations among neighbors. Although this stage of the
ACHR's work predated the Second Vatican Council, its programs were
ecumenical. Priests in the targeted parishes were urged to work with other
religious leaders locally to reach the broadest population possible. Typical

public programs featured denominationally diverse panels that stressed the un-Christian nature of racial prejudice and attempted to defuse the fears most often articulated by whites, namely that the presence of blacks would mean falling property values, rising street crime, and eventual marriage across racial lines. Group discussion at such gatherings was apparently limited. "These people are here to be educated in facts, to back up their right attitudes," a laywoman active in the ACHR told the chair of a Human Relations Group at an Eastside Detroit parish. She stressed the importance of a program's opening "with a brief statement of intent, on a moral basis which will not leave room for discussion."[36]

This early stage of ACHR programming was surprisingly ambitious. More than 6,000 people had attended an ACHR-sponsored panel during the campaign's first six months, Dearden told a meeting of the Detroit Urban League in March 1961. The message of racial brotherhood had also been preached in Catholic schools throughout the archdiocese, as well as by means of four programs on local radio.[37] If the ACHR initiative was not unique to Detroit in the early 1960s, as Dearden believed to be the case, it was certainly pioneering. Given local circumstances, it was also controversial. Some Catholics reacted with pride and a sense of relieved gratitude, delighted to find a venue where their own racial liberalism might be safely expressed and definitively endorsed. Others saw in the program an overdue source of hope for a city they had no wish to leave, despite the creeping ravages of deindustrialization. Whatever optimism he entertained for the future of his own and the surrounding Eastside parishes in Detroit, Father Joseph Srill told Dearden in 1962, was due to his having witnessed "the endless good will and fervent desire of simple people."[38]

Father Srill was guarded in his assessment, however. Many of his own parishioners, along with others on Detroit's heavily working-class Eastside, were apparently immune to the message of the ACHR. A few parish programs were disrupted by angry protests; many more suffered from widespread lay apathy. "I am only partly sanguine," in Srill's words, "because I see the appalling ignorance of, the scornful indifference and stiff resistance to the social message of the Gospel." Numerous letters received at the chancery provide specifics. "We lost between $4 to $5000 when Negroes started moving in our neighborhood," ran a typical complaint, one with particular resonance for a working-class population that tended to save in the form of home ownership.[39] With street crime rising rapidly and made even more threatening by rumor-fed exaggeration, some correspondents virtually accused Dearden of conspiring to keep them prisoners in their own homes. "I dare no longer go to mass in the morning, much less attend the services or functions I used to enjoy in the parish hall," according to one angry resident of what she called a "mixed neighborhood."[40] Catholics were apparently prominent among those who petitioned to have an initiative placed on the Detroit ballot in 1964 that would protect homeowners who refused to sell to blacks or other minorities. Despite editorial opposition by the *Michigan Catholic* and a vigorous campaign by the ACHR, the measure passed with substantial Catholic support. There were certainly priests who voted for it, given opposition among a number of pastors to the ACHR's agenda. Many feared for the future of their often indebted parish plants; a few were outright racists.

As civil rights activism and racial tension increased in the nation as a whole, Dearden grew more proactive, a response quite possibly prompted by his transformative experience at the Council. He personally endorsed passage of the 1964 Civil Rights Act and urged his priests to do the same. He permitted, indeed encouraged, his clergy's participation in civil rights demonstrations both locally and outside the archdiocese; priests and sisters from Detroit marched in Washington in August 1963 and in Selma in 1965, as the *Michigan Catholic* proudly reported. Dearden also authorized a major expansion in the parish-based educational work of the ACHR, which got underway in 1966. Under the aegis of "Project Commitment," thousands more Catholics in the archdiocese participated in antiracism programs and were urged to work for racial peace in their neighborhoods. The goal, never realized, was a human relations commission in every parish. Pastors as of 1966 were asked to direct at least 10 percent of their budgets toward support of the center-city parishes, with lay organizations encouraged to contribute their time and talents to assist the same.

Dearden was a moderate man by temperament. Even in the mid-1960s, he tried as best he could to stay above the racial battle, allowing his chancery subordinates to do most of the talking when it came to this highly charged matter. While there was no doubt in Detroit about where he stood on open housing legislation, for example, Dearden did not personally testify in favor of such until after the Detroit riot of July 1967. That tragic event, in which forty-three died and broad swaths of the city were reduced to rubble, appears to have radicalized the archbishop.

Shortly thereafter, he testified in favor of an open housing ordinance before the Detroit City Council. He endorsed the findings of the Kerner Commission on the causes of urban rioting and dispatched a specially trained corps of priests to do the same in pulpits throughout the archdiocese. In Dearden's view, the commission had been right to attribute recent urban violence to white racism, even though whites themselves were generally inclined to deny it. "We cannot leave [our people] contentedly in this state," he told his priests, "Whether they like it or not they must hear it."[41]

Most controversially, Dearden announced in the wake of the riot that most of the money collected in 1968 for the Archdiocesan Development Fund, hitherto directed toward support and expansion of local Catholic institutions, would be devoted to projects in Detroit's poor black neighborhoods, some of them under non-Catholic auspices. In conjunction with this announcement, Dearden pledged his support for the inner-city Catholic schools, most of which now enrolled numerous black students, many of them non-Catholic. (Compulsory classes in doctrine for their parents had by this time gone by the boards.) He stuck to this commitment in subsequent years, even after financial pressures forced the closure of scores of parochial schools throughout the archdiocese. When the prospect of city-suburban busing loomed in metro Detroit in the early 1970s, Dearden forbade his priests to accept pupils in their schools whose Catholic parents were apparently seeking to evade the busing order, even when enhanced enrollment might have saved the school in question.

Dearden's newly proactive stance put him at odds with a great many Catholics locally. Contributions to the Archdiocesan Development Fund fell sharply in 1968 in explicit reaction to its apparent new purposes and remained at low ebb for some years thereafter. Matters came to an excruciating head in the fall of 1970, with the approval of a referendum in Michigan that prohibited state aid to nonpublic schools. Some 40 percent of the Catholic schools in Detroit were at this point operating at a deficit; a great many more, in the suburbs as well as the city, had almost no cash reserves. The problem had multiple origins. Suburban Detroit's rapid growth had resulted in an overextended Catholic system, the financial consequences of which were exacerbated by the flight of many teaching sisters from vowed religious life. Fully half of the teachers in the schools of the archdiocese by 1970 were lay; Detroit's lay salaries, moreover, were the highest in the nation.[42]

It had long been clear to those paying attention that many Catholic schools would eventually have to close. A subset of progressive Catholics, most of them suburban, regarded this as a positive development, since in their eyes Catholic schools were both unecumenical and sometimes bastions of white privilege. "It is almost impossible in some circles to be a liberal on the subject of racial justice and poverty and be an advocate of aid to parochial schools," as a member of one Detroit parish testified in 1968.[43] But many others, not necessarily illiberal in their views on poverty and race, regarded the city's Catholic schools as critical to its future. "The school is an anchor and has a stabilizing effect on a community that is fighting desperately to maintain its integrated character," an Eastside parish reported.[44] "These people are not 'the rich,'" a reform-minded pastor reminded Dearden with regard to his mostly white parishioners: "Since ALL the people know that the value of their property is secured by the presence of this school, I truly fear that the closing of the school would bring about such a collapse of morale and such sourness that useful pastoral work would be nearly impossible for the future."[45]

When the Michigan legislature approved a program to subsidize the teaching of nonreligious subjects in the state's private schools in 1969, supporters of Catholic schooling statewide assumed that their cause had received a reprieve. The repeal of this program by popular vote in 1970 meant immediate crisis in Detroit, the Michigan diocese with by far the largest number of schools. Dearden moved swiftly after the November election. For a school to remain open, the chancery instructed pastors, it had to meet stringent financial criteria, including the ability to contribute to support of the remaining center-city schools: "We will not allow parishes to continue to operate schools, if at the same time they show little or no concern for the poor."[46] Dozens of schools were soon slated for closure as of June.[47] Decisions in this regard were made with almost breathtaking rapidity, with much of the action transpiring over the Christmas holidays. The predictable result was widespread lay outrage at the perceived lack of consultation. "The parish is in an uproar about 'sneaky meetings' being held about the fate of our school," an indignant mother wrote from suburban Warren, holding Dearden responsible for the situation.[48] Dearden's personal pledge to continue subsidizing at least some inner-city schools had predictable results as well. "Very many . . . are blaming the Archbishop for deliberately closing our schools for 'civil rights' or 'racial' purposes, feeling that the schools could have somehow stayed open if only he had kept out of things," according to a layman from suburban Grosse Pointe: "We have all heard these views in our office, at parties, at parish affairs and on the street."[49]

While the schools crisis undoubtedly constituted the high-water mark of alienation in the archdiocese, Dearden was not without supporters. Some Catholics locally regarded his as a brave and principled stance, while a good many priests were frankly relieved to be out of the business of running a school. Interestingly, people on both sides of the divide invoked Vatican II in their defense. Those hostile to Dearden's racial initiatives – his school policy was typically seen in this broader context – championed the rights of the laity against a heavy-handed chancery.

Invoking the Council's *Declaration on Religious Freedom*, one indignant correspondent charged that Dearden had violated parents' fundamental right to choose "the kind of religious education their children are to receive." Since the state permitted the existence of nonpublic schools, "we do not accept the Church's right to deprive us of this freedom."[50] Dearden's supporters, for their part, spoke in terms of a church open to the world, prioritizing the needs of the poor over the claims of fellow Catholics. Such, in their view, had been the principal message of the Council documents. Indicative of this division, which was not just between members of the laity but increasingly between many laity and their priests, were survey results from the fall of 1970. Asked whether "sermons should deal with the word of God and not with current social issues," 58 percent of the laity agreed as compared to only 28 percent of the clergy.[51]

Often intemperate in their language and sometimes sounding like racists, Dearden's critics are best understood as accusing him of communal betrayal. "As a result of this final crisis they feel they have been had," Father Thomas Hinsberg told Dearden at the height of the schools controversy: "They still accept the old values and they perceive the Cardinal as the enemy."[52] Racism was central to "the old values," as the avowedly radical Hinsberg saw it, and there was reason for him to think so. Some local Catholics were in fact so consumed by racial animosity that the label is appropriate. But probably a majority of Dearden's opponents are most usefully characterized in terms of an embattled parochialism. Schooled by experience and indeed by their church to valorize family and neighborhood loyalty, such Catholics were often bewildered by what seemed to them an abrupt shift in values on the part of local Catholic leaders.[53] "How the situation on education has changed when, but a few decades ago, parents could be excommunicated for not sending their children to Catholic Schools!" one pastor quite correctly noted.[54] If Catholics such as these were implicated in the historical processes currently upending their lives, they frequently did not understand them.

Catholic progressives, for their part, were increasingly repelled by anything that hinted at tribalism. By the mid-1960s, indeed, some were embarrassed by the chancery's encouragement of evangelization in the black community, fearing that it smacked of Catholic triumphalism and implied disrespect for black culture. Did Catholics not have much to learn from black civil rights activists, whose roots were typically in the black Protestant churches? Had they not modeled virtue in a way few Catholics could equal? Not surprisingly, evangelization was something of an afterthought in diocesan programming by the later 1960s.

The divisions that hardened in the course of the schools fight did not diminish perceptibly over the next few years. Local Catholics were inclined to read chancery decisions in light of the preconceptions that the struggle over schools had so vividly confirmed. Dearden, for example, was criticized by many in the antiabortion movement for doing too little to help their cause when Michigan voted in 1972 on a referendum to liberalize the state's abortion law. Although the Dearden chancery came late to the campaign, its resources were in fact critical to the referendum's defeat. Dearden himself urged a "no" vote on a number of public occasions; a taped message to this effect was sent to every parish to be played on the Sunday before the election. But many in the antiabortion movement were fundamentally suspicious of the cardinal. As they saw it, he had failed to speak out on abortion with the clarity and vigor he brought to civil rights and failed as well to grasp the singular urgency of the abortion issue. "I realize that Racial Justice – Drugs – Poverty are vital issues but they have been & will continue to be for years. THE most important issue in the state right now is the 'Abortion Reform' Referendum," as one lay activist wrote.[55] That clergy long associated with Dearden's racial initiatives sometimes expressed doubts about Catholic teaching on abortion helps explain this well of mistrust. More fundamental, however, was the makeup of the movement itself. Antiabortion activists came disproportionately from the ranks of the "parochially minded," whose view of the world had been so thoroughly challenged by Dearden's racial initiatives. Ironically, their antiabortion activism propelled many of them toward a new ecumenism, centered on a growing sense of kinship with non-Catholics who placed a high priority on family and conventional gender roles.

Passions Cool; Dearden's Legacy

Passions cooled in the second half of the 1970s. Although a black-majority Detroit meant that the city was more segregated than ever, race ceased to be an overtly divisive issue among local Catholics. With the city governed by a black mayor and "black power" ideology in the ascendance, further racial initiatives under chancery leadership were frankly unwelcome to local black leaders. None were forthcoming, although Dearden remained genuinely concerned about the future of his See city. He closed few Detroit parishes during his tenure, despite their dwindling populations and increasingly parlous finances. Indeed, many of his most talented priests chose, with their cardinal's blessing, to devote themselves to urban ministry. The parishes over which they presided were often success stories, oases of hope in an increasingly poor and violent city. Certain of these churches drew a stream of admiring visitors from the suburbs, while thousands turned out annually to march in support of Focus: Hope, an ambitious Catholic-led organization whose programs ranged from food pantries to job training. Presided over by the charismatic Father Bill Cunningham, Focus: Hope also meant new life for Detroit's Madonna parish, where he served as pastor. For many in Catholic metro Detroit, the devastatingly handsome Father Cunningham was something akin to a clerical rock star.

African American Catholics, for their part, generally experienced the 1970s in terms of personal liberation. Almost certainly better educated than the average city resident, Detroit's black Catholics found in that decade signifi- cantly enhanced economic opportunity in both the public and private sectors. A black majority city meant an intensified sense of group agency and racial pride, despite growing fears among the black elite about the city's accelerating population loss and growing rates of poverty. White-ruled Detroit in its economic heyday had been a repressive place even for affluent African Americans, who had reason to fear the local police and were regularly insulted by whites attempting to protect their segregated turf, particularly when it came to housing. The resulting wounds went deep. It was no accident that nearly all black Detroiters referred to the violent upheaval of July 1967 as a "rebellion" rather than a riot, the term employed – then, as now – by nearly every white.

Increasingly a majority in growing numbers of city parishes, more and more African American Catholics assumed positions of leadership at the parish and even diocesan levels. An Office of Black Catholic Affairs was established in 1972, the first such concession to "ethnic" Catholicism in the history of the archdiocese.[56] A number of Detroit parishes established gospel choirs in the late 1960s or early 1970s, moving toward a warmer, more exuberant and self-consciously "black" mode of worship. St. Cecilia's parish, on the city's near-northwest side, offers an engaging example. Founded in 1921 on the then-fringes of Detroit, St. Cecilia's had an all-white congregation as late as 1960. Ten years later, the surrounding neighborhood was almost totally black. Led by an innovative and charismatic priest, himself of Syrian descent, parish leaders embraced the new reality, welcoming children of all religious back- grounds to the parish school and introducing African American music and motifs into Sunday worship. St. Cecilia's garnered national attention in 1968 when parishioner DeVon Cunningham created an apse mural in the church featuring a black Christ surrounded by multiethnic angels and a sprinkling of mostly non-Catholic heroes ranging from Gandhi to Malcolm X. In the wake of a black student strike at the parish high school that culminated in the burning of allegedly racist religion textbooks, Pastor Raymond Ellis had come to believe that young African Americans "could not envision Jesus as black." Or so a later parish history explained the mural's genesis.[57]

Despite its successful outcome, racial transition at St. Cecilia's was painful. "During the past few years, we have experienced divisions which have caused much suffering," parish leaders confessed in 1973.[58] The divisions were based in good part on race, as many of the remaining whites in the congregation came to feel, often resentfully, like outsiders. But older African Americans were sometimes alienated, too, if not by the innovative liturgy – although this was not uncommon – then certainly by rising crime in the vicinity of the church. Unsafe streets made it hard to sustain any evening programs, according to the priest who briefly succeeded Father Ellis, whose death in 1971 was a serious blow to parish progress.[59] Over the course of the 1970s, however, the now mostly black congregation began to grow and thrive, in no small part the result of the talents of longtime pastor Thomas Finnegan, who arrived in 1973. Enrollment at St. Cecilia's elementary school – the high school was closed in 1969 – had once again reached capacity by 1985. Classroom religious instruction, according to the Detroit *Free Press* in that same year, was "not strictly Catholic since only about 25 percent of the students are Catholic."[60] The parish sports program, inaugurated in the wake of the 1967 riot, enjoyed citywide recognition in the 1970s and after, while Sunday worship was locally renowned for its warmth and vitality.[61]

In Detroit's suburbs, many of which were still growing, Catholic life in these same years continued with something of its former vigor. Mass attendance was significantly lower than it had been in the 1950s, but most churches were reasonably full on Sundays, and many parishes continued to function, especially for older adults, as an important locus of social life. A sharp decline in observance among the young was a worrisome portent, however, especially when coupled with a rising rate of religious intermarriage. Given the rapidity of Detroit's demographic transition, its suburbs were filled with Catholics whose roots were in the city – a place that large numbers were now afraid to visit. Grieving and angry, for many in this situation the continued Catholic presence in the city came as an odd sort of balm. Media coverage of Detroit's priests and the services rendered through its parishes and Catholic charitable agencies found an appreciative suburban audience, as if such images somehow redeemed a portion of the painful past. Portrayals of African Americans in explicitly Catholic settings were popular, too. Many Catholics continued to be burdened by racial fears and resentments, but their views on integration were significantly more liberal by the early 1970s than had been the case a decade earlier.[62] Dearden's efforts at racial enlightenment should arguably be counted among the many causes of this transformation.

Dearden tendered his resignation to the Holy See in 1980, although he was two years shy of the mandatory retirement age. He was not in good health, having suffered a major heart attack in 1977. Detroit's health was precarious by this time, too. The city saw a population decline of 20 percent over the course of the 1970s, dwarfing the population out-flow of the two previous decades. Despite the affection on generous display at a public farewell ceremony in October, Dearden was probably tempted to regard his Detroit episcopate as a failure. "Here in the Archdiocese we must give priority to every effort that can help to resolve the problems of racism, poverty, and injustice," he had told the chancery staff in 1968.[63] Detroit in 1980 was poorer, more segregated, and more violent than ever before in its history. Firmly committed to Catholic education at the outset of his tenure, Dearden had presided over an unprecedented wave of parochial school closings. And he surely knew that he was bequeathing to his successor the immensely difficult task of closing numerous city churches.

A balanced appraisal of the Dearden years, however, must deal in other than stark categories of failure and success. The church in Detroit did indeed experience institutional decline over the course of Dearden's tenure. But Catholics in the archdiocese also became more socially conscious, tolerant, and open to experience – in a word, less tribal – and here Dearden's leadership was important. He also introduced a measure of collaborative decision making into an archdiocese that had previously been governed strictly from the top. With parish councils the norm by the early 1970s and an archdiocesan pastoral council established in 1973 with an elected lay majority, local Catholics increasingly experienced church in ways not radically incongruent with their democratic values. Even women had reason to believe that their church was more genuinely participatory, given the number of female lectors, Eucharistic ministers, and altar servers in local parishes by the mid-1970s and the women employed in parish ministry. Dearden gave quiet support to each of these developments.

In 1971, reflecting on what remained to be done to realize the Council's reforming vision, Dearden singled out the social attitudes of the laity: "The uncertainties and confusions that exist about the Church's mission to the human community must be dispelled. Somehow the message of 'Gaudium et Spes' in all its implications must come through."[64] If Detroit's Catholics were still a stubbornly imperfect lot, they were nonetheless closer to understanding that message at the close of Dearden's episcopate than they had been at its halcyon outset.

NOTES

1. Gerhard Lenski, *The Religious Factor: A Sociological Study of Religion's Impact on Politics, Economics, and Family Life* (Garden City, NY: Anchor Books, revised edition, 1963), p. 49

2. The figure was 56 percent in 1958. Msgr. Vincent Horkan to Cardinal Edward Mooney, June 23, 1958, Archives of the Archdiocese of Detroit (hereafter AAD), Chancery. records, Schools Office.
3. "Sermon 2: Mass Is a Family Meal and Sacrifice," to be preached on Sunday, November 8, 1964. AAD, Worship Department, box 1, folder Liturgical Commission sermon outlines 1959–1966.
4. For initial responses to the liturgical changes on the part of both clergy and laity, see "Preliminary Tabulations, Survey of the Liturgy," undated but 1965, AAD, Worship Department, box 1, folder Liturgical Commission 1965.
5. Sister Mary Timothy, CSFW, to Dearden, February 15, 1967, AAD, Worship Department, box 1, folder Liturgical Commission 1966–1968.
6. "Archbishop's Meeting with Priests, Thursday, March 14, 1968." AAD, John F. Dearden papers (partially catalogued), box 23, not yet in folder.
7. Sermon for the 16th Sunday after Pentecost, undated but 1967. The text was sent to the priests of the archdiocese by the Chancery's Sermon Commission, though its use was not mandatory, AAD, Worship Department, box 1, folder Liturgical Commission 1966–1968; quote from Rev. Patrick Cooney to Bishop Thomas Gumbleton, March 30, 1970. AAD, Worship Department, box 1, folder Gumbleton (Vicar for parishes) 1969–1971.
8. The Archdiocese of Detroit's Office of Planning and Research's *Insight: Our Faith Today* (Detroit: Archdiocese of Detroit, 1971) summarizes the survey findings; for opinions on the liturgy, see page 17. The survey was done in the fall of 1970.
9. Progress Report on Pre-Synodal Activities, undated. The unnamed author quotes Dearden speaking at a clergy conference in 1966. AAD, Synod Implementation Committee, box 2, folder 14.
10. The synod gave eventual rise to the Archdiocesan Pastoral Council, which dates from 1973.
11. "Report of Registration for parish Participation Plan," August 4, 1967, AAD, Synod Implementation Committee, box 2, folder 11.
12. "parish Operation, parish Coordinating Committee Sub-Committee, Balloting – Election," undated but 1968, AAD, Synod Implementation Committee, box 2, folder 12.
13. Numerous nominations for the various commissions are found in AAD, Synod Implementation Committee, box 1, folders 4–7. The typical nominee had a college education and a white-collar job.
14. Form letter from the Dearden Chancery to "Dear Father" with regard to nominations for lay members of the synod commissions, unsigned and undated, but probably 1967, AAD, Synod Implementation Committee, box 2, folder 16.
15. Evidence of discontent over such matters is found in many collections in the AAD, particular the papers of the Priests' Senate and those of the Association of Detroit Priests. Confirmation is also found in the results of an August 1965 survey of the priests in the archdiocese, appended to Thomas J. Gumbleton [vice chancellor] to "Dear Father," January 1966, pages 5–7.
16. Author interview with Fr. William Pettit, December 10, 1998.
17. Memo, Fr. Kenneth Untener to Msgr. Thomas Gumbleton, February 27, 1967, in re a Priests' Retreat held February 20–23 at St. John's Seminary, Plymouth, MI, AAD, Chancery collection, box 22, folder 26.

18. Rev. Joseph A. Gagnon [vicar Western Wayne Vicariate] to Rev. Dale Melczek, April 29, 1980, AAD, Dearden papers, box 12, folder "Clergy Shortage Committee." Gagnon was ordained in 1961.

19. "Constituent Meeting, Classes of 1953, '54," May 23, 1971, no author given, AAD, Priests' Senate, box 2, folder 22.

20. Minutes, Priests' Senate meeting of September 3, 1968, from which both quotes are taken. The recorder was John Schwartz, SJ, AAD, Priests' Senate, box 4, folder 12.

21. Author interview with Father Lawrence Jackson, October 15, 1998, in Sterling Heights, MI.

22. Quoted in the *Archdiocesan Newsletter for Priests*, April 6, 1977, AAD, archdiocesan newsletter, box 2, folder Priests Newsletter 1977.

23. Dearden to Rev. Michael O'Connor, August 28, 1970, AAD, Non-Chancery records, box 11, Association of Detroit Priests, folder 5.

24. Minutes, Priests' Senate meeting of March 20, 1979, enclosure B, AAD, Priests' Senate, Box 1, folder 17.

25. "Expectations and Hopes," Rev. Charles Irvin (ed.), January 1976, p. 3, AAD, Dearden papers, box 9, folder Michigan Federation of Priests' Councils.

26. Leaves of absence were reported periodically in the *Archdiocesan Newsletter for Priests*. See especially issues of March 19, 1975, and July 10, 1978.

27. "Proposals to the Archdiocesan Synod by the Priests' Senate Group, 1929–1932," undated but late 1967, AAD, Synod Implementation Committee, box 2, folder 20.

28. "Criteria for Distribution of Priests in parishes," *Archdiocesan Newsletter for Priests*, March 29, 1976. Two priests would be assigned to parishes with from 1,500 to 2,700 families. AAD, archdiocesan newsletter, box 2, folder Priests' Newsletter 1976.

29. "Recommendations from Sub-Committee on Priestly Life Style and New Ministries," no author given, undated but mid-1971, Archives of the University of Notre Dame (hereafter AUND), Thomas Gumbleton papers (CGUM), box 14, folder Synod I.C. Sub-Committee, Priestly Life and Ministry 2.

30. "Archdiocese of Detroit: The Permanent Diaconate Program, Program Policies," September 1971, Office of the Permanent Diaconate, AAD, Priests' Senate, box 2, folder 5; *Archdiocesan Newsletter for Priests*, December 1, 1980, AAD, archdiocesan newsletter, box 2, folder Priests' Newsletter 1980. The Archdiocese of Detroit was a pioneer both with regard to its embrace of the permanent diaconate and the creation of Ministers of Service.

31. Thomas C. Fox, "Detroit Married Men: Some Minister, Some Seek Orders," *National Catholic Reporter*, 1976 (undated clipping) in AAD, Dearden papers, box 13, folder Ordaining Married Men to the Clergy. The Ministers of Service program began in 1969, as did the archdiocesan program for training candidates for the permanent diaconate.

32. Rev. Kenneth Untener to Father Jim Wright, June 11, 1972, AUND, CGUM, box 15, folder Synod: Spirituality of Priest Study.

33. John F. Dearden, "Challenge to Change in the Urban Church," an address to the National Catholic Conference for Interracial Justice, August 1967, copy in AAD, Archbishop's Commission on Human Relations (hereafter ACHR), box 6, folder 13.

34. Msgr. Harold Markey, transcript of an untitled talk presented at an archdiocesan clergy conference, undated but September 1960, AAD, ACHR, box 7, folder 31.

35. Fr. G.H. Kerby, responses to the "Apostolate of the Negro parish Questionnaire," July 23, 1962, AAD, ACHR, box 1, folder 5.

36. Mrs. Foster J. Braun to Joseph M Goetz, January 23, 1962, AAD, ACHR, box 3, folder 20.

37. Archbishop John Dearden, "Program for Better Human Relations," address to the Detroit Urban League, March 9, 1961, AAD, ACHR, box 6, folder 13.

38. Fr. Joseph A. Srill, OSA, "Evaluation of Human Relations Program conducted by the Archbishop's Committee at St. John Berchman's parish," October 25, 1962, AAD, ACHR, box 3, folder 20.

39. "A Practical Catholic" to Fr. James Shehan (chairman, ACHR), December 7, 1966, AAD, ACHR, box 3, folder 12.

40. "Sad Catholic Detroiter," to Dearden, June 25, 1963, AAD, ACHR, box 7, folder 18.

41. Cardinal John Dearden, "Talk to Clergy re: Kerner Report," undated typescript but March 14, 1968, AAD, Dearden papers, box 23 (temporary cataloging), not yet in folder.

42. Minutes, "USCC Emergency Conference on School Problems," Mundelein, IL, December 17–18. AUND, CGUM, box 48, folder 12.

43. Anonymous "request to speak" form, Archdiocese of Detroit, pre-synodal feedback session, undated but 1968, AAD, Synod Implementation Committee, box 2, folder 15.

44. Memo to school task force from St. Martin/St. Philip Elementary School, December 4, 1970, AUND, CGUM, box 48, folder 9.

45. Msgr. William Sherzer to Dearden, November 25, 1970, AAD, Dearden papers, box 13, folder School Closings.

46. Bishop Thomas Gumbleton to pastors, parish Council presidents, and school principals, December 23, 1970, AAD, Dearden papers, box 13, folder School Closings.

47. A total of 56 schools were closed in 1970.

48. Rita Karras to Dearden, January 7, 1971, AAD, Dearden papers, box 13, folder Task Force: School Closings.

49. Ed Rooney, "Some Thoughts on the School Closings," undated but 1971, prepared for the parish Council of St. Paul's, Grosse Pointe, AAD, Dearden papers, box 13, folder School Closings.

50. Anonymous to Dearden, undated but late 1970 or early 1971. AUND, CGUM, box 48, folder 11.

51. *Insight: Our Faith Today*, 10.

52. Fr. Thomas f. Hinsberg to Dearden, November 27, 1970, AUND, CGUM, box 48, folder 9.

53. This line of argument is brilliantly developed in John T. McGreevy, *parish Boundaries: The Catholic Encounter with Race in the Twentieth-Century*. Urban North (Chicago: University of Chicago Press, 1996). Also relevant, if less attentive to religion: Ronald P. Formisano, *Boston Against Busing: Race, Class, and Ethnicity in the 1960s and 1970s* (Chapel Hill: University of North Carolina Press, 1991); Thomas J. Sugrue, *The Origins of the Urban Crisis: Race and Inequality in Postwar Detroit* (Princeton: Princeton University Press, 1996); and Kenneth D. Durr, *Behind the Backlash: White Working-Class Politics in Baltimore, 1940–1980* (Chapel Hill: University of North Carolina Press, 2003).

54. Fr. Robert J. Burroughs to Dearden, December 7, 1970, AAD, Dearden papers, box 13, folder School Closings.

55. Shirley A. Watt, response to an "activities survey" from the Human Relations Commission, Department of Christian Service, Archdiocese of Detroit, April 26, 1972, AAD, ACHR, box 7, folder 33.

56. Dating is a bit tricky, since the "black secretariat" initially operated out of St. Bernard's parish on Detroit's Eastside. Presumably as a result, the surviving record is spotty.

57. *Pantocrator: The 'Black Christ,'* undated but 2008, no author given. See also Rev. Raymond Ellis, "From the Desk of the Pastor," *The Beacon*, March 24, 1968, p. 8. Both in AAD, St. Cecilia, Detroit parish file, box 1, folder 10.

58. "St. Cecilia's parish Profile," undated but 1973. Of this document, pastor Thomas Finnegan writes: "The parish Council worked long and hard on this and I feel it is an honest and accurate description of the parish." AAD, St. Cecilia's, Detroit parish file, box 1, folder 9.

59. Rev. Edward Olszewski, "parish Description," 1971, AAD, St. Cecilia's, Detroit parish file, box 1, folder 9.

60. Cassandra Spratling, "St. Cecilia's Courts Pupils with Sound Basics," Detroit *Free Press*, undated clipping but February 1985, copy in AAD, St. Cecilia's, Detroit parish file, box 1, folder 9.

61. The radical depopulation of Detroit in recent years has threatened the future of St. Cecilia's, which was merged with St. Leo's parish in 2013 and renamed St. Charles Lwanga. St. Cecilia's elementary school closed in 2010.

62. Andrew M. Greeley and Paul B. Sheatsley, "Attitudes toward Racial Integration," *Scientific American* 225:6 (December 1971), pp. 13–19; Andrew M. Greeley, William C. McCready, Kathleen McCourt and Shirley Saldanha, "American Catholics," *The Critic* 33:2 (1975), 19.

63. Dearden, memo to "all Departments, Agencies and Offices," March 4, 1968, AAD, ACHR, box 6, folder 13.

64. Dearden, Talk Given at the University of Louvain, June 20, 1971, AAD, Dearden papers, box 23, not yet in folder.

6

LAY WORKERS IN THE RURAL CHURCHES OF NEW MEXICO: VATICAN II, MEMORY, AND MINISTRY

Kathleen Holscher

This chapter considers Vatican II in the lives of Hispanic Catholics in the Archdiocese of Santa Fe. New Mexico's poverty and the irregular presence of priests in rural villages shaped how reform happened there in the sixties. Today those circumstances inform how Nuevomexicanos remember the Council and construct its meaning.

THE UNITED STATES CATHOLIC CHURCH PRESENTED ITSELF TO the international audience monitoring the Second Vatican Council as a network of large urban and suburban dioceses. Although 240 American bishops attended its sessions, big city cardinals such as Francis Spellman of New York and James Francis McIntyre of Los Angeles dominated headlines for the outspoken parts they played there.[1] Observers following U.S. activity at the Council had little reason to pay attention to a dusty, sparsely populated place such as New Mexico. Although the Archdiocese of Santa Fe had enjoyed diocesan status for more than a century in 1960, it remained one of the most rural outposts of the North American church. The archdiocese was home to approximately 275,000 Catholics scattered over nearly 75,000 square miles.[2] While many of them lived in the growing urban hub of Albuquerque, with a population of 200,000 in 1960, and the smaller state capital of Santa Fe, most of the rest inhabited subsistence farming, ranching, and mining communities, isolated by arid and mountainous topography and served by a single church or mission *capilla*.[3]

These villages, populated mainly by Hispanos who traced their families' presence in the region to the Spanish colonial period, were some of the poorest Catholic communities in the United States at midcentury. The poverty rate in Rio Arriba County, in the heart of rural northern New Mexico, hovered near 60 percent in 1960.[4] These New Mexican villages were also among the most priestless pockets of the U.S. church. In a nation that had more priests than ever before, rural New Mexico was – as it had

often been – short in Catholic clergy. The Archdiocese of Santa Fe ranked
fifth among all U.S. dioceses in physical churches in 1960, with some
370 buildings, but less than a quarter of those churches had resident pastors,
a number that put the archdiocese well behind most of its national
counterparts.[5] The vast majority of its churches were missions, visited by
a priest once a week or, in the case of more remote *capillas*, once a month (or
sometimes less). For the Nuevomexicanos who belonged to rural parishes
and their missions, religious life followed patterns informed both by difficult
material conditions and by this on-and-off priestly presence.

This is a study of the Second Vatican Council in the lives and memories of
Catholic Nuevomexicanos in rural parts of the Archdiocese of Santa Fe.[6]
The archdiocese is an ecclesiastical district that overlies a region, and here
I consider that region – all the interrelated qualities of landscape, history, and
culture that distinguish New Mexico from other places in the world – as
a contributor to Vatican II history, as something that shaped how men and
women learned about the Council, and also how they made sense of it,
assessed its value, and put it into practice. The prevalence of rural villages in
New Mexico, the hard material conditions in them, and their history of
irregular priestly presence are all regional qualities that matter to a local story
about Vatican II. Together they explain why the Council arrived in New
Mexico in the manner it did. The Council's reforms, liturgical and otherwise, happened unevenly in the Archdiocese of Santa Fe. By the mid-1960s,
New Mexico was home to pockets of conciliar enthusiasm, and it was also
home to parishes where the Council and its instructions remained unknown.

New Mexico's rural setting, its poverty, and the movement of clergy in
and out of its villages also inform how Catholic Nuevomexicanos today
remember the Council and give it meaning. Memory is a product of complex
and multiple presents. As Joan Tumblety writes in her introduction to
Memory and History:

> We do not have memory as much as ... performances of remembering,
> where what we remember is shaped fundamentally both by the meaning of
> the initial experiences to the individual ... and by the psychological – and
> inextricably social – circumstances of recall. Just as significant is the way that
> intervening presents shape what is recalled.[7]

New Mexicans' memories of the Second Vatican Council, like those of
Catholics around the world, are informed by what happened in Rome in
the 1960s, and by what went on in their archdiocese as a result. They are
also formed from other religious and nonreligious circumstances of their
lives – other things that happened fifty years ago, and other things that

have mattered to them in the decades since. For some Nuevomexicanos, the memory of Vatican II is shaded by, and inextricable from, powerful recollections of priests from that period. The Council coincided with a surge in the number of priests working the archdiocese – a 78 percent increase in clergy in less than twenty years.[8] As unfamiliar priests took up residence in rural places through the second half of the century, they brought the Council's messages with them. But they also did things to reorder – and sometimes disrupt – local life. For Catholics who experienced new priests in these ways, recollections of disruptive clergy can and do predominate over memories of the Council.

Other rural Nuevomexicanos remember differently, recalling Vatican II as the towering event of midcentury Catholic life. Over time, liturgical change and – more importantly, for this group – the Council's emphasis on lay ministry, settled into the fabric of rural Catholicism.[9] Men and women I spoke with told me the Council's call to ministry changed them, and changed how they understood their duty to church and to community. In their accounts of the era, priests are less relevant than their own, newfound ability and responsibility to do God's work directly.

Though most New Mexicans have never read the Council's document *Apostolicam Actuositatem*, today many inhabit the world it called into being – one where ordinary Catholics exist in "living union with Christ," and where believers have "the right and duty" to use gifts derived from that union "in the world for the good of men and the building up of the Church."[10] In their telling of it, Vatican II's affirmation of lay ministry resonated especially powerfully in poor, rural places where, absent a regular clerical presence, generations of Catholics had privileged local forms of lay religious work. For these Nuevomexicanos, the Council laid a profound new spiritual groundwork – a new apostolic orientation – for imagining and for doing this type of local, community-based work.

Of course these Vatican II remembrances are also created from "intervening presents" and other "circumstances of recall."[11] Many Nuevomexicanos who are active in their churches assess the Council's import in light of subsequent developments within Catholic life – changes that happened not only in the Council's immediate aftermath but also through the late twentieth and early twenty-first centuries. These include everything from the spread of the spiritual-renewal-focused Cursillo and Charismatic movements to Pope John Paul II's emphasis on a New Evangelization. Together these interventions have inflected a Nuevomexicano conversation about the Council that, while deeply embedded in the region in all the ways I have described, also references an individualized, evangelical spirituality.[12] As I talked with Nuevomexicanos about their memories of Vatican II and its importance to them, they described joys and challenges that are part of rural New Mexican life. But they also talked – a lot – about God's caring presence in their own lives, and they told me stories of personal transformation, born out of their loving relationship with that presence. Today some Catholics in New Mexico, as elsewhere, describe Vatican II as the catalyst for a profound reorientation – a coming to know God in intimate terms, from the inside out. For them, this new way of knowing God is the critical foundation for lay ministry. These stories of transformation are a part of the history of Vatican II in New Mexico. To listen to men and women remember the Council, and to take seriously how it *feels* in their lives, sometimes requires stepping away from the overlapping frameworks of diocese and region to consider other types of spaces – personal, individual, interior – ones where many Vatican II Nuevomexicanos locate their encounters with God, and out of which they know their lives and communities are remade as a result.

Vatican II in a "Do-Nothing" Diocese

The Second Vatican Council spanned the prelateships of two archbishops of Santa Fe: Edwin V. Byrne and James P. Davis. Both men dutifully attended the Council's sessions, accompanied by their chancellor, Msgr. Manuel Rodriguez. A graduate of the Pontifical North American College and the recipient of a doctorate in canon law from Catholic University in Washington, DC, Rodriguez was invited by Pope John XXIII to serve the Council as an expert – a great honor for any priest, and a special and unusual one for a Spanish-speaking native of a rural American diocese.[13] Neither Byrne nor Davis distinguished himself at the Council. On the eve of his departure for Rome, in October 1962, Byrne issued instructions that priests incorporate a prayer for the success of Vatican II into all Masses celebrated in the archdiocese, and that novenas for the same intention be held in parish churches.[14] Despite these supportive gestures, however, the Council's debates remained a world away from Byrne's own episcopal priorities, which included drumming up vocations and working amid scarce resources to strengthen New Mexico's parochial schools.[15] Fr. Wilbur Perea, a priest who worked closely with both Byrne and Davis during the 1960s, recalled that Byrne was distracted from the Council's work. As Perea remembered it, Byrne's attitude was "we have more important work to do [than focus on the Council]; let somebody else do it."[16]

Archbishop James Davis, by comparison, did invest himself in the Vatican II vision. Davis came to New Mexico following Byrne's sudden death in 1963. The new prelate used his installation ceremony to call attention to the Council and emphasize its importance for his episcopacy. "I can think of no better testimony to the resurrection of Christ," Davis announced, "than to dedicate ourselves anew to the pursuit of the objective of the Council." "Our acceptance of the apostolic mandate," he continued, "includes a ... persistent and progressive effort to involve the church committed to our care in the constant renewal of Christian living ... in the family, in business, in the farms and factories, in the parish, in the state."[17] On his return from the Council's fourth session, Davis showed initiative, promoting the conciliar theme of ecumenism within the archdiocese. In late 1964, the Archdiocese of Santa Fe joined the New Mexico Council of Churches (NMCC) – the first U.S. Catholic diocese to sign on to an interdenominational council.[18] Over the next year, the archdiocese collaborated with the NMCC on a series of events, including an interfaith worship service and a parish "open house."[19] Held at Our Lady of Fatima parish in Albuquerque, "Operation Understanding" attracted 6,000 Protestant visitors. The *New Mexico Register*, official newspaper of the archdiocese, described the open house with obvious pleasure:

> Informed lay guides ... explained various Catholic beliefs, practices, and furnishings ... The Dominican Sisters ... guided guests through the convent and answered questions concerning convent life ... Particular interest was shown in the confessional – the fact that the priest cannot see the penitent – and in the other sacraments. Also of interest were ... rosaries, holy water, and medals ... One of the Protestant ministers became so enthusiastic that he picked up a hymnal and joined in the singing of the inter-parochial choir.[20]

Eight of the city's Protestant churches returned this show of ecumenical goodwill, inviting area Catholics to tour their facilities two months later.[21]

Despite his early excitement, Archbishop Davis, like his predecessor, found himself caught up by the day-to-day responsibilities of his episcopacy, with neither time nor resources to develop a Vatican II agenda for New Mexico. Reflecting on the failure of both bishops to prioritize the Council, Perea described Byrne and Davis as desperately overextended in a poor diocese. "They didn't have personnel," he put it simply.[22] In the absence of archdiocesan guidance, most decisions about Vatican II's implementation happened within parishes and were made by priests who pastored there.[23] For some clergy, the Council – and especially its recommendations for liturgical renewal – quickly became foundational to ministry. Most, but not all, of these conciliar-minded priests worked in Albuquerque and Santa Fe. In January 1964, several archdiocesan clergy, representing urban and rural parishes, attended the first meeting of the Southwest Liturgical Conference in San Antonio.[24] While there, they were reminded of their responsibility, as pastors, to bring the Council's liturgical innovations to the Catholic community. "It would be futile to entertain any hopes for realizing active participation of the laity in the liturgy," a conference leader admonished them, "unless the pastors themselves . . . become thoroughly imbued with the spirit and power of the liturgy and undertake to give instruction about it."[25]

Many New Mexican priests explored that "spirit and power." A former seminarian reflected on the emotions percolating among his teachers at the Immaculate Heart of Mary Seminary in Santa Fe during the early-to-mid-1960s. "Overall . . . there was an excitement for the changes that were coming," he recalled.[26] In December 1964, the editor of the *New Mexico Register* expressed his own excitement on attending an updated Mass at St. Catherine's Indian School, also in Santa Fe: "Very noticeable . . . was the enthusiastic way in which the students participated. The students sang songs . . . and a boy and a girl, attired in their traditional tribal dress, carried the Offertory gifts down the aisle to the celebrant."[27] Liturgical fire also swept through Santa Fe's Cathedral Basilica of St. Francis of Assisi that fall. "Within a single week," the *Register* reported, the cathedral "removed its altar, dating to the days when stage-coaches still rumbled along the Santa Fe Trail." "For a short time," the author added with flourish, "the dismantled altar lay in pieces, as if the Cathedral had fallen prey to another Indian attack such as destroyed the church of St. Francis that once stood there."[28]

The height of liturgical renewal in the archdiocese came six years later, when Dominican priest and native New Mexican Blase Schauer founded Liturgy in Santa Fe (LSF), which developed out of Schauer's work with students at New Mexico State University in Las Cruces (then part of the Diocese of El Paso) in the early-to-mid-1960s. As pastor of the university's Newman Center, the priest had encouraged students to deepen their relationship with the liturgy through evocative symbolism and hands-on activities. Together they quarried rock from the nearby Organ Mountains for an altar, chopped wild palms for Palm Sunday, and visited the bees that made their candle wax.[29] On a spring day, pastor and parish celebrated the Feast of the Ascension with missiles from the nearby White Sands Missile Range pointing skyward at their church's entrance.[30] With this same inventive spirit, Schauer organized the LSF in 1970 as a resource to help "those who have directive roles in worship" explore liturgical possibilities via creative use of symbolism and an innovative, multimedia approach. His goal (never fully realized) was to establish a national "liturgical laboratory and research facility" in Santa Fe.[31] For Schauer, New Mexico presented an ideal setting for liturgical experimentation. As the LSF steering community put it, "the land, the people, the land forms, the sun, and the mountains and valleys, touch the heart and fill the senses."[32]

Despite Liturgy in Santa Fe's assertion that New Mexico, a place "permeated with symbolism," offered a natural home for the work of Vatican II, the organization's all-out enthusiasm for the Council was an exception in the archdiocese.[33] By the mid-1960s, at least some Catholic leaders in New Mexico had become frustrated, complaining that too little was happening in the Council's name. In October 1966, the Register's editor called for letters from readers, to "convince the Archbishop that his flock wants to see the recommendations of Vatican II put into practice – here and now."[34] "Obviously we believe there is considerable latent desire for action," the editor continued, "[The question that] is in the minds of many people is a question [that] goes something like this: 'Why should our diocese, which is ... small in numbers – not nearly so vast and unwieldy as some – sit quietly by and become known as a sort of "do-nothing" diocese!'"[35] Without direct pressure from the archbishop, many New Mexican clergy had dragged their heels on liturgical reform. Nuevomexicanos who belonged to rural parishes, where priests were overextended, and where turnover among pastors was frequent, often remember the new liturgy arriving late. Others recall their pastor's failure to teach them about the Council. One man I spoke with, who grew up attending a mission outside of Villanueva, only learned about Vatican II when he relocated to Albuquerque after high school. "I graduated in 1967," he recalled, "Even then, nothing had changed [at the mission]. What I do know is that I didn't know anything about Vatican II."[36] A man from rural northeastern New Mexico offered a similar story: "We knew very little about the ... Council at the time." When liturgical changes happened they were traumatic, he added, "[The people] could not understand why the church had done this."[37] Fr. Carlos Garcia, who worked as a pastor in Santa Fe during the 1960s, recalled situations like this in other rural parishes. "Those people didn't hear much about Vatican II," he remembered. "To the extent that [those rural parishes] did not implement that change was due," he stressed, "to the priest."[38]

Laity, Priests, and Rural Life

Celine Gomez and her husband Arturo welcomed me to their home in Albuquerque's upscale Northeast Heights. Celine had extended the invitation, offering to share memories of the Second Vatican Council and her early life on the Tijeras land grant east of the Sandia Mountains.

Another East Mountains couple, Joanne and Michael Sheen, joined us. Celine kicked off the conversation by recalling her childhood at the Tijeras mission, and her earliest memories of the Council. "We didn't get exposed to it like the big cities did," she said, "We didn't realize [Vatican II] was happening . . . But a lot of beautiful music came out of the Spanish community," she continued.[39] Celine's mention of the music that accompanied liturgical change in Tijeras got the group talking. Soon the friends had moved from discussing the gains of Vatican II to lamenting things lost around Tijeras in the decades since the Council. Over the next hour, the four helped one another recall Catholic life in the old mission, and they shared their bitterness over what changed when Tijeras became a parish in the late 1960s. Again Celine led with her reminiscence of the early days. "My . . . padrino," she explained, "would go get the saints from the various [missions], and put them in his truck. The Santo Niño . . . they'd put him in the back of the pickup and go down the road, and take him into the homes . . . You should see how beautiful the ladies have the homes!" she stressed, settling into her recollection: "They'd put an altar, and dress it with white linen, and they'd burn incense – they made it out of flowers from their own gardens, the rose petals. My God, I can still smell it! They would bring in the saints, and they'd say a rosary. And we'd go from house to house."[40]

Life changed in the East Mountains, the group told me, after the archbishop created the new parish and assigned a series of priests to pastor it. "There were a couple of priests who were very, very controlling," Michael recalled.[41] The couples remembered one priest who removed the choir director, replacing him with an outsider who, as Joanne put it, "doesn't play the music of the East Mountains."[42] The same priest renovated the church's interior; in doing so, he covered a local artist's depictions of the Santo Niño de Atocha and the Virgin of Guadalupe. "The first thing he did was to hang a sheet over [the images], like a drape," Michael remembered angrily, "We went down . . . to see what condition they were in, hoping to . . . save them. We lifted up the sheet to look and he had painted over them – without telling anybody. He destroyed them."[43] His voice trailed off. "It was not right," Arturo added with emotion.[44]

* * * * * *

AS VATICAN II CAME TO NEW MEXICO'S RURAL COMMUNITIES DURING the mid-twentieth century, its arrival coincided with a larger priestly presence. The Archdiocese of Santa Fe had just 200 priests (diocesan and religious) in 1950, but by 1968 it boasted 356. More priests on the ground meant more parishes, and fewer missions – the archdiocese's parishes increased from 71 to 90 during this eighteen-year period, while its missions decreased from 374 to 278.[45] Although still overextended, a new cadre of rural pastors enjoyed enormous latitude within the parishes, including in decisions about the Council's implementation. One diocesan priest, familiar with New Mexico's rural churches, summed up the attitude that prevailed among these clergy during the 1960s, 1970s, and 1980s as a "Lone Ranger mentality."[46] In communities such as Tijeras, the regular presence of a pastor meant changes in addition to a new liturgy. As Celine and her friends told it, Vatican II's arrival in rural New Mexico happened against a backdrop of jeopardized lay traditions – institutions and rituals cultivated by generations of Nuevomexicanos in the absence of priests, and disrupted by the changing, increasingly clerical character of the archdiocese at midcentury. For some young people, it is necessary to add here, the arrival of priests resulted in interactions more painful than these cultural disruptions. The new population of priests at work in New Mexico included a small but damaging group of men who had abused children in other dioceses whom archdiocesan officials nonetheless returned to ministry within the Archdiocese of Santa Fe.

From the time New Mexico was claimed as a diocese by the U.S. church, many of its Catholic communities lacked priests. When Santa Fe's first bishop, Jean Baptiste Lamy, arrived in 1851, there were seventeen clergy in all his immense new territory.[47] Lamy made correcting this dearth in church leadership (as he saw it) a priority, importing priests and women religious from Europe and the United States to work in New Mexico. His successor bishops did the same.

In the meantime, New Mexico's Hispano communities cultivated their own formal and informal institutions of lay leadership. In villages without a resident pastor, or where the local priest was responsible for several difficult-to-reach missions, Nuevomexicanos carried out the day-to-day, non-sacramental work that supported Catholic life. This included everything from educating children and maintaining church property to organizing Holy Week devotions and fiestas for *santos*. It was work that happened mostly out of view of pastors and other archdiocesan-assigned personnel, and that continued in its dominant forms into the twentieth century (and in various locales continues today).

Two lay institutions distinguished rural New Mexican Catholicism before the Second Vatican Council – the *Hermanos Penitentes* and church and fiesta *mayordomos*.[48] The *penitentes* have been active in northern New Mexico since at least the early nineteenth century.[49] Despite statements by Lamy and his successors suppressing the *cofradía*, its members performed a broad set of charitable, social, and devotional services in Hispano villages through the territorial period. Though especially known for their Holy Week rituals, *hermanos* managed fiestas, provided material assistance to the sick and to families of the deceased (work that included preparing corpses, managing wakes, and digging graves), and arbitrated community disputes.[50] Today *hermanos* commit to similar types of service, although the brotherhood now works closely with priests in many locales, and with the approval of the archdiocese. Describing the brotherhood's present responsibilities, one *hermano* told me, "We do a lot of praying, and when people die, we're called to do the services [and especially the singing]. Priests depend a lot on [us], especially in the missions. The priest calls us to do a lot of things when he needs help."[51] According to anthropologist Marta Weigle, "a sizable majority of Hispanic males . . . maintained [*penitente*] *moradas* [meeting houses]" in northern New Mexico through the early 1900s. By the mid-twentieth century, however, membership in the brotherhood had waned.[52] Weigle attributes this decline in part to deepening rural poverty, which depleted community resources and forced a migratory male population.[53] The growing number of priests and religious working in rural villages also solidified a parallel church authority structure that qualified, if it did not always directly challenge, the brotherhood's role in village religious life. By Weigle's estimate, only 1 to 2 percent of Hispanic men in the state were participating in the brotherhood by 1960.[54]

On the eve of Vatican II, *mayordomos* existed alongside *penitentes* as a second lay institution important to rural New Mexican religious life. While the Eucharist remained out of lay hands, day-to-day responsibilities of maintaining the local church were managed by *mayordomos*. Especially in missions, these men and women (usually a husband and wife team) had broad duties. In Hispano New Mexico, the term *mayordomo* is common. It translates loosely to "custodian" or "caretaker," but it also suggests a person who makes decisions in the interest of a community. In rural villages, the same term designates a "ditch boss" – a person elected to manage the *acequias* (irrigation canals) on which life and livelihood depend. *Acequia mayordomos* were (and are) responsible for organizing workers to clear brush and shore up eroding banks, delegating water to needy *parciantes* (share holders), and resolving inevitable and often high-stakes disputes over water portions.[55] In northern New Mexico, *mayordomo* is a position that comes with social power and status.

Ditch *mayordomos* and church *mayordomos* shared more than a name at midcentury.[56] Robert Baca, a former *mayordomo* at the Velarde mission, reflected on why the term is applicable to ditches and churches alike.

"In the ditch, there's somebody who's in charge of the operation of it," he explained, "In the church, [it's] the same way."[57] In rural churches, *mayordomos* shared responsibility for everything from mundane cleaning to large-scale interior renovations. Like their counterparts in the ditches, church *mayordomos* also acted as community leaders, keeping their neighbors abreast of important happenings, and putting pressure on them to give time and labor to the church. Dorothy Archuleta, who grew up outside Taos, recalled the work shared by her parents, who served as *mayordomos* at the local *capilla*:

> They were responsible for upkeep; keeping it clean, maintaining it, opening it up when services were held . . . They had it wired for electricity; up [until] then they'd just used gas lamps. And of course walking around the neighborhood and inviting [neighbors] to come to the parish event, the *función*. Also they used to *doblar*; when someone in the community died, they let people know with the bell. When you'd hear the bells you'd say, "Somebody passed away!" That was the way they'd get messages across.[58]

Mayordomos were also chosen within communities to lead religious celebrations, and these men and women bore special responsibility for a village's saints. In some villages, a highlight of the annual fiesta was the *entrega* – a ceremony during which outgoing *mayordomos* passed on the *santos* to their incoming counterparts, accompanied by an *entregador* who composed and sang songs in their honor.[59] People I spoke with emphasized all it meant to be selected as *mayordomo*. Celine Gomez recalled when she served as *mayordomo* alongside her brother at the Tijeras mission: "It was an honor."[60]

Rural – and formerly rural – Catholics like Celine Gomez recall the increased priestly presence that ran parallel to Vatican II in New Mexico as a story of cultural disruption and loss. Their memories are marked by longing for lay traditions – the fiestas, the *penitentes*, the *mayordomos* – that still exist, but only in diminished forms, in most post–Vatican II parishes.

Tijeras no longer has *mayordomos*, Michael Sheen told me ruefully, just like it no longer has its *santos* on display, nor its East Mountains religious music.[61] Other factors that contributed to these disruptions, including the movement of Gomez and thousands of other young Nuevomexicanos out of villages and into urban centers during the period, hardly matter in the way these men and women talk about the past. As they remember it, new priests stepped in and made the decisions that put an end to traditional religious life. Tijeras's transition from a priestless mission to a pastor-staffed parish came at a dear cost.

For one group of New Mexicans, the cost of having new priests around was far higher. The Archdiocese of Santa Fe met its priest shortage at midcentury, in small part, by accepting men who had troubling records in other dioceses. Beginning in 1948, clergy from across the United States who had "fallen a prey to . . . insidious snares of evil" arrived in New Mexico for treatment at the Via Coeli Monastery in Jemez Springs, run by the Servants of the Paraclete.[62] Over time, more and more of these monastery residents were men who, according to the Paraclete's founder Fr. Gerald Fitzgerald, "have been addicted to abnormal practices" including "sins with the young."[63] On his installation, Archbishop Davis – an advocate of therapeutic rehabilitation – committed himself to helping "guest-priests" of the Servants of the Paraclete return to active ministry. At a private meeting with representatives of the order and a consulting physician in 1967, Davis agreed to allow clergy under the congregation's care to begin parish work in his archdiocese "as a final step in the graduated program of rehabilitation."[64] Although it is not known how many abuser priests began work in the archdiocese as a result of Davis's initiative, at least forty-four clergy were publicly accused of sexually abusing minors in the archdiocese during the second half of the century.[65] Several of these men arrived in New Mexico via Via Coeli, and others were accepted into the archdiocese despite accusations of abuse in other dioceses.[66]

The arrival of new priests, and local forms of disruption they caused, is one narrative Nuevomexicanos draw on to recall the Vatican II era. That said, painfully controlling priests were not typical in the archdiocese, and abusive priests less so. Many clergy, urban and rural, respected local traditions and local residents, and many laity experienced their pastors – whether old or new – in positive ways. Many women and men I spoke with described the Vatican II era – the 1960s, 1970s, and 1980s – as a period that, above all, brought good opportunities to rural communities. These opportunities, grounded directly in the Council and its affirmation of the role of the laity, were part of a process by which these Nuevomexicanos came to reimagine the parameters of religious work. People I interviewed talked about knowing God in a new way because of Vatican II. This emergent sense of oneself in a close relationship with God changed what it meant to serve one's community as a Catholic. Vatican II urged Catholics to perform service not just as penance, and not just on behalf of one's priest or to honor one's saints, but as a direct extension, a *manifestation*, of a loving relationship. This is how people I interviewed know ministry. They see ministry as complementing – not supplanting – traditional forms of lay religious work. They understand its value as standing apart from the absence *or* presence of priests. They credit it with enabling ordinary Catholics, like themselves, to meet the many needs of their neighbors in compassionate new ways.

Vatican II and Rural Ministry

I met Deacon Fred Argenta for coffee at a diner in Springer, a town of 1,300, on flat land stretching east from the Cimarron Mountains. Deacon Fred is a former correctional officer. He has lived in Springer his entire life and for the past thirty-five years he has served as deacon in his parish and its missions. We sat in an out-of-the-way corner, away from the diner's fluorescent lights, and Fred told me first about living Cursillo in the 1960s, and then about his diaconate training more than a decade later. The two experiences are joined closely in his memory.

Cursillo, he explained to me, "gives you a spirituality that you can put a handle on and utilize in your life."[67] Preparing for the diaconate made him aware, more precisely, of the ways he could employ his spirituality to serve his community. I queried him about the work of a deacon in a rural parish, and Fred began to describe the weekly routine of baptismal studies, marriage preparations, and liturgical services. Then he mentioned that he'd served as president of the New Mexico Wildlife Federation. My ears perked. Fred's presidency, I learned, was one chapter in a nearly half-century-long second career in land advocacy – a career marked, most importantly for him, by a decades-long fight to preserve public access to a wilderness area west of Springer.

"This big rancher, he's from Texas," he explained, "And he closed access to the public lands, 41,000 acres."[68] He went on to describe litigation, letter-writing campaigns, and on-site showdowns over signs and barricades. Fred is an absorbing storyteller, and it was a minute before I realized he was still discussing his work as a deacon. One day during diaconate study, he recalled, the presiding pastor pulled out a full-page article about the land dispute, published in the *Albuquerque Journal*. The article featured a photo of Fred. "This is what the diaconate is about," he remembered the priest saying to the men gathered, "protecting the needs of the people." Fred went on, in his own words: "Who hunts and fishes in our public lands if it isn't the poor? . . . We have to protect the rights of the people." "This is what the diaconate is about," he repeated, "It may not look like a spiritual situation, but it is, in the long run. It is."[69]

FOR MOST NUEVOMEXICANOS, LITURGICAL CHANGE – WHENEVER and however it happened in their churches – was their introduction to Vatican II. For many who are active in their churches today, however, other changes are more important in their memory of the Council. For

Catholics I spoke with, the process of coming to know themselves as ministers and the reorientation of religious work that came with it figure especially prominently. The same individuals who had difficulty – as several of them did – remembering whether the language of the liturgy changed in their churches into English or Spanish spoke at length about knowing God in a new way, and acting differently in the world. Deacon Fred, reflecting back over his adult life, emphasized a new *spirituality*, one through which he reimagined service in his community. Other people emphasized the same. For these rural Catholics, the Council is important because it taught them their capacity to not only serve God but to also deliver God's Word, and because it directed them toward the open-ended responsibilities this capacity entailed.

Although closely associated with Vatican II in the memories of people, this new spirituality was not only a result of the Council. Many men and women, Deacon Fred included, encountered this spirituality first during Cursillo. Cursillo in New Mexico complemented Vatican II, but it also predated it. Cursillo, a movement built on intense, weekend-long lay retreats, began in Spain during the mid-1940s. The movement's founder, Eduardo Bonnín Aguiló, was inspired by the early twentieth-century Catholic Action movement and by the emergent discussion of a "theology of the laity" within the church.[70] From its inception, the purpose of Cursillo was to provide a place "to experience Christ and the Holy Spirit and a setting where . . . spirituality could grow." "The goal of the movement," writes Kristy Nabhan-Warren, "was for Catholic men to . . . take ownership of their faith, to renew not only themselves but their Church."[71] Benedicto Cuesta, a Spanish-born priest, introduced Cursillo to the Archdiocese of Santa Fe in 1961. Within three years, more than 900 men and women in the state had completed a Cursillo weekend.[72] While most of the movement's early Nuevomexicano leaders came from Albuquerque and Santa Fe, rural areas were represented among the leadership as well.[73]

By the mid-1960s, Cursillo was encouraging lay ministry in New Mexico by, among other things, introducing its participants to Vatican II. In 1964, the archdiocese's annual Cursillo conference was dedicated to exploring lay opportunities offered by the Council's documents.[74] The year following, *cursillistas* heard presentations on the Council's purpose and the new liturgy. The priestly capacity and responsibility of ordinary Catholics were dominant themes. As one speaker told participants, "The people of God share in the priesthood of Christ. The common priesthood of the faithful and ministerial or hierarchical priesthood are interrelated."[75] The Santa Fe Secretariat of Cursillos promoted this idea of the "common priesthood of the faithful" in its literature as well, encouraging *cursillistas* to involve themselves in the sacrifice of the Mass, and to read the Bible for themselves, "along with good commentary," for at least fifteen minutes every day.[76]

Through living Cursillo, ordinary women and men learned they, like their clergy, had the ability and responsibility to be bearers of God's presence. Donald Anaya, who grew up on a farm outside Santa Cruz de la Cañada, and who completed one of the first archdiocesan Cursillos in 1962, summed up his experience as a *cursillista* by describing his personal duty to serve God and the church, a duty that entailed carrying God's Word into the world in the best ways he knows how. Cursillo and Vatican II together taught him this duty. "Cursillo made a big change in me, because ... I understood more what Vatican II was trying to do," he explained, "[that it was] about having a duty and responsibility in the church." Reflecting on this responsibility, he invoked his rural upbringing. "I felt like ... I belonged to a family," he remembered. "Growing up on the farm, we were thirteen brothers and sisters and we all had a job. So I saw that in the church. I belonged to a church that's family, so I had a job." He returned to the themes of family and shared responsibility at the end of our talk: "When we're baptized we come into a family, and to me that meant so much ... I can't imagine my father doing everything he had to do. I had my own chores, and everyone depended on everyone. We're interdependent. You can never be independent – never, never, never."[77]

Together Cursillo and Vatican II taught Donald Anaya that he was integral to God's mission for and in the world. For him, and for many men and women in rural places, this knowledge opened up new possibilities for lay service as *ministry*, possibilities that added to, and also complicated, older traditions that cast lay religious work in other ways. Donald has lived his adult life as both an active *cursillista* and as a *penitente*, a leader within his *morada*. He sees the two roles as different, but never in conflict. Rather, he thinks of them as running in easy parallel. Both, he reminded me, are forms of service, but for the *penitentes*, "it's about the sacrifice that's involved, and our commitment to the church, to help out in whatever way we can." For Anaya, cursillo, carries forward the evangelical message of Vatican II – the message that laity can and should not only support the church and its clergy as they work to deliver God's Word, but get at that primary work themselves. "As a result of Vatican II, we have so many ways of evangelization," Donald concluded. "And it started really with Cursillo."[78]

For Deacon Fred, Cursillo spirituality was enhanced and made into community service through the diaconate. In *Lumen Gentium*, the Council called for the restoration of the permanent diaconate.[79] The first permanent deacons were ordained in the Archdiocese of Santa Fe in 1973.[80] The diaconate offered a way for men to pursue a vocation in ordained ministry – one that required extensive training and entailed extensive responsibilities but also allowed them to honor commitments to spouses, families, and local communities. Men who trained for the diaconate in New Mexico during the 1970s and 1980s attended classes in Albuquerque once or twice a month, year round, for several years – a course of study that entailed a heavy commitment of time and money.[81] Deacon Fred recalled how his battered company truck, which he depended on to make the 380-mile drive to Albuquerque and back, miraculously held up through his training and finally broke down right before his ordination.[82] After ordination, rural deacons usually returned to work in their home parishes, where their local roots and their "stay putted-ness" distinguished them from the pastors with whom they served. Deacon Walter Luces, former diaconate director for the archdiocese, and himself a rural deacon, laid out the contrast between the mobility of priests and the permanency of deacons in New Mexico. "New priests [are assigned] to rural parishes, and they spend a year and a half, and they're reassigned closer to Albuquerque," he told me. As for deacons, "They're there. The priest comes and goes. [Deacons] are the continuity."[83]

Today the Archdiocese of Santa Fe has more than twice as many deacons, per capita, as the U.S. church as a whole.[84] Within the archdiocese, the restored diaconate has both strengthened institutional leadership in parishes still – and more so, again, in recent decades – facing a lack of priests. Permanent deacons have also demonstrated a new capacity within church leadership for local, place-based ministry. As Deacon Walter put it, deacons are "supposed to carry [their ministry] into the marketplace."[85] Another deacon I spoke with, from San Juan (Ohkay Owingeh) Pueblo, located his ministry in this way as he discussed his work directing a northern New Mexico health care system. Highlights of Deacon Gilbert Rodriguez's ministry, as he described it to me, included taking local pilgrims on tours of the Holy Land *and* writing a book to train local health care professionals in Spanish.[86] For rural deacons such as Gilbert and Fred, the parish-centered responsibilities of their work – witnessing marriages, assisting at the altar, preaching, and so on – are pieces in a broader life of ministry, one that is open ended in its possibilities, while always rooted in the places they live and the spiritual and material needs of the people in their communities. As Fred suggested, there's no distinction between them. His land fight "may not look like a spiritual situation, but it is."[87]

Vatican II and Personal Transformations

Clara Rodriguez and I sat above the rectory at St. John the Baptist Church on the San Juan (Ohkay Owingeh) Pueblo north of Española. Clara, like most of the parishioners at St. John the Baptist, is Hispano, and she grew up in a farming village, also outside Española. She told me how she came to ministry on the heels of Vatican II. For her, it was a pair of experiences – becoming a catechist and reading the Bible for the first time – that made her realize she could speak God's Word. Thinking back to her childhood, Clara was matter of fact: "We were told we weren't supposed to read the Bible, because we would misinterpret it ... We didn't own Bibles; we didn't understand them."[88] That changed for her in the mid-1960s; today her Bible is "almost in pieces ... In 1985 I said, 'Why don't I read the Bible, page by page, and see how long it takes me?' I read one chapter a night, and it took me over a year to read the whole Bible."[89] Clara described how she brings her Bible along when she meets children preparing for First Communion, and also their parents. "I don't call it teaching," she explained to me with a smile, "I just call it refreshing their memories." She shares it with them and explains its importance: "I take my Bible with me, and I say ... 'Look at it; it's taped together.'"[90]

Two hours later I met Freddy Griego at a senior center in Chimayó. Over a cafeteria-style lunch of hard-shell tacos and cartons of milk, we talked about how Vatican II had changed his life. With great feeling, Freddy described the decades following the Council as a process of awakening – of coming to know that he mattered to the church and to God. He recalled the new liturgy, and what it did for him. "That's when I started lectoring," he told me, "I could understand [the Scripture] – I could really feel what it's saying. I remember when I went to lector training they told me, 'You've got to realize that you're not talking for yourself. You're speaking God's Word. So ... don't worry about what you say or how you say it, your accent – just go out and proclaim!'" The instructor "wanted us to be as good at proclaiming the Word as any priest," he emphasized.[91] Freddy went on to live Cursillo, participate in ACTS (Adoration/Community/Theology/Service) retreats, and join the Charismatic movement. Today he thinks of himself as a full-time minister to his peers and even, on occasion, to his own priest, who he views as "a child in formation, although he's got a lot more religious formation than I do." He loves John XXIII as a saint. "Basically he was a man alone," he remembered of the pope, "His concern for all us little ones; all of a sudden we mattered ... to someone important." Freddy lingered on John XXIII's decision to convene the Council. He looked hard at me, and his eyes had tears: "What has happened since Vatican II, to me? God has acknowledged my existence." His voice cracked, "It's not anything spectacular, but it's how I know personally that God loves me."[92]

BESIDES CURSILLO AND THE DIACONATE, THE DECADES DURING and after Vatican II brought other ways for rural Catholics to engage their faith. Men and women who grew up surrounded by *penitentes, mayordomos,* and other traditions of lay religious work began, as adults, to serve as catechists, and to participate in the liturgy as musicians, lectors, and Eucharistic ministers. Over time, some like Freddy Griego discovered the Charismatic Renewal and/or were inspired by late-twentieth-century church efforts toward the New Evangelization. Founded in San Antonio in 1987, ACTS Missions is a movement based on Cursillo and directed at the New Evangelization. "We're *finally* doing [ACTS] here in New Mexico," Freddy told me.[93]

Like deacons, these men and women understand their new ministries as being of and for the places they live and the people they live alongside. Their work draws on the cultural resources of rural New Mexico. As Celine Gomez remembered, the new liturgy in Tijeras allowed East Mountains musicians, albeit briefly, to bring local instruments and playing styles into the Mass. Their ministries also respond to the difficult parts of life in New Mexican towns and villages. Today these challenges are myriad; they include everything from restricted public lands access and unreliable medical care to – especially in the Española Valley of Rio Arriba County – poverty and widespread drug addiction. As of 1990, Hispanos in Rio Arriba County earned less than half as much, per capita, as their non-Hispanic white American counterparts, and the county had the highest rate of drug overdoses in New Mexico. Fifteen years later, the valley had the most per capita heroin addicts in the nation.[94] For Clara Rodriguez, her life and her ministry are here. Her knowledge of the Bible gave her the means to minister, not only to children in need of catechesis, but also to their parents and to other Española Valley residents who make their own lives amid these difficult circumstances. As she talked to me about the Bible, and its importance to her, Clara thought of a nephew: "We all have problems," she said, "but one of my nephews, his trailer burned down, and my [Scripture] reading that day had something to do with that, so I . . . sent it over. God is good; he puts things in front of me."[95]

In this way, the Vatican II story in New Mexico is rooted firmly in region, in particular qualities – historical and material – that bear on what it means to live a Catholic life in the village of Tijeras, or Springer, or Chimayó, or the communities around Española. But at the same time, the stories that Clara Rodriguez, Freddy Griego, and other Nuevomexicanos shared with me also locate Vatican II and its importance somewhere else. To listen to Clara and Freddy, and to consider the ways they remember the Council, means positing that some of the spaces that matter to the "lived" Vatican II experience are private and interior ones. To return to Clara's account, the quiet bedroom, the pages of Scripture, and ultimately the human heart are privileged locations where she, as an individual, came to know and participate in an intimate relationship with God. Her ministry in the world has come as a result. Like Clara, Freddy also talked with joy about ministering to his parish and his peer group, but the emotional center of his remembrance was his new awareness of himself as someone loved by God "personally" and directly, and as "mattering" to God's church. For Freddy, God's love filled him – and transformed him – from the inside out; God holds him so close that when he reads Scripture he is "no longer talking" for himself.

Clara and Freddy, like other Nuevomexicanos and like Catholics all over the world, inhabit a region as well as a diocesan institutional structure, and their religious experiences are indelibly marked by their located-ness within both. But they also know themselves as individuals suspended in a personal encounter with God. Listening to their accounts means acknowledging that the Second Vatican Council, and its emphasis on the immediacy of God's presence in the lives of ordinary Catholics, helped reorient lay spirituality. Developments in Catholic life in the half century since the Council have done the same. Today Catholic spirituality in New Mexico includes an evangelical strain, one that refuses to be summed up as the product of external intermediaries, whether they are the rules and leaders of a diocese or the customs of a region. For men and women I talked with, where they live and the institutions and communities they live among continue to matter immensely. But their spirituality is constantly calling them to listen for God, and to engage Him, as individuals who are – in God's eyes – *more* than those environments. I went into the conversations that inform this chapter expecting to hear stories that were distinctly New Mexican, and distinct to the Archdiocese of Santa Fe. I heard plenty of them, but men and women wanted to tell me other kinds of stories as well. Moving away from the frameworks of diocese and region – or at least drawing attention to categories of personal experience they conceal – makes necessary space for the narratives of transformation these people want to tell.

The Archdiocese of Santa Fe, with its poor, rural, largely Spanish-speaking Catholic population, was the furthest thing from a "typical" American diocese during the Second Vatican Council. Both the difficulties the archdiocese faced implementing the Council's documents, and the ways the Council's messages resonated within historically priestless villages, make New Mexico's Vatican II story a regional variant in a midcentury national narrative dominated by big city themes. Even so, the lived history of the Council in Hispano New Mexico reveals a great deal about how Catholics in rural places applied the Council's teachings over time. Vatican II happened alongside, and interacted with, other changes – some of them welcome, some of them disruptive – to New Mexican Catholic life in midcentury. In the memories of laity who value it the most, however, the Council brought important opportunities for rural ministry. For many Nuevomexicanos, these new opportunities derived directly from a transformed understanding of the self in a relationship with God. Together these opportunities and that relationship mark the lived importance of Vatican II for people across Catholic New Mexico.

NOTES

1. James P. McCartin, "Vatican II," *Dictionary of American History*, 3rd ed. (New York: Charles Scribner's Sons, 2003), pp. 308–309.
2. Dave Baker, Maryellen Schaub, James Youniss, and Life Cycle Institute at The Catholic University of America, principal investigators, "System For Catholic Research, Information and Planning (1960), 1990," *The Association of Religion Data Archives*, www.thearda.com, accessed February 27, 2013. In 1960, parts of the state of New Mexico also fell under the ecclesiastical jurisdiction of the dioceses of Gallup and El Paso.
3. U.S. Bureau of the Census, *Census of the Population: 1960, Volume 1: Characteristics of the Population, Part 33: New Mexico*, p. 10.
4. U.S. Bureau of the Census, Poverty: 1960, 1970, 1980, and 1990 censuses, www.census.gov/hhes/www/poverty/data/census/1960/, accessed April 21, 2014. Thirty percent of New Mexicans fell below the poverty line in the 1960 census. The state's poor were disproportionately Hispano and Native American and lived disproportionately in rural areas. Rio Arriba County, which is home to many of the villages mentioned in this chapter, had a 61 percent poverty rate in 1960.
5. Baker et al., "System For Catholic Research." Twenty-seven of those parishes, and more than two-thirds of the archdiocese's clergy, were concentrated in Albuquerque and Santa Fe; "Diocese Lists 223 Priests," *New Mexico Register*, p. 1. In 1940, the Archdiocese of Santa Fe ranked last among all U.S. archdioceses in number of priests per capita, with one priest per 1,047 Catholics. By 1955, five archdioceses had fewer priests per capita than Santa Fe, but all of them (Detroit, Hartford, Los Angeles, Newark, and New Orleans) were more urban and the Archdiocese of Santa Fe continued to far outnumber them in number of missions. In 1955, Santa Fe had 308 missions, compared to 16 in Detroit, 20 in Hartford, 53 in Los Angeles, 12 in Newark, and 103 in New Orleans. *The Official Catholic Directory, Anno Domini 1940*

(New York: P. J. Kenedy & Sons, 1940), pp. 12–236; *The Official Catholic Directory, Anno Domini 1955*, pp. 10–260.

6. I use to term Nuevomexicano in this chapter to describe men and women who identify as Hispano (of Spanish ancestry), and who grew up speaking Spanish as their first language or bilingually. Most rural Catholics in New Mexico at midcentury were Nuevomexicanos, although the archdiocese also included a significant number of Native Americans and a growing number of Anglos.

7. Joan Tumblety (ed.), *Memory and History: Understanding Memory as Source and Subject* (New York: Routledge, 2013), p. 7.

8. *The Official Catholic Directory, Anno Domini 1950* (New York: P. J. Kenedy & Sons, 1950), p. 216; *The Official Catholic Directory, Anno Domini 1968* (New York: P. J. Kenedy & Sons, 1968), p. 781.

9. For this project, I interviewed fifteen men and women about their memories of Vatican II in the Archdiocese of Santa Fe. These men and women are mainly Nuevomexicano (twelve of them grew up speaking Spanish or bilingually). All but one have spent time living in rural parishes, and most are laity, although my interviewees also included four deacons and two priests. The lay people I spoke with are all active members of their parishes; thus, the stories included here do not speak to how Vatican II is remembered, or not remembered, among New Mexican Catholics broadly. Rather, these stories indicate the importance of the Council for rural Nuevomexicanos who remain, or have grown, active within their churches.

10. *Apostolicam Actuositatem* (*Decree on the Apostolate of the Laity*), online archive of the Vatican, accessed April 15, 2014, www.vatican.va/archive/hist_councils/ii_vatican_council/documents/vat-ii_decree_19196511118_apostolicam-actuositatem_en.html

11. Tumblety, *Memory and History*, p. 7.

12. See Kristy Nabhan-Warren, *The Virgin of El Barrio: Marian Apparitions, Catholic Evangelizing, and Mexican American Activism* (New York: New York University Press, 2005), on evangelical narratives of personal transformation among Hispanic Catholics in the Southwest. See also Benjamin Bennett-Carpenter, David R. Maines, Michael J. McCallion, "Individualism and Community as Contested Rhetorics in the Catholic New Evangelization Movement," *Review of Religious Research* 54:3 (2012), 291–310.

13. Fr. Wilbur Perea, personal interview, January 2013. I refer to interviewees by pseudonyms throughout this chapter.

14. "Archbishop Asks Prayer for Council," *New Mexico Register*, September 28, 1962, pp. 1, 3.

15. Perea interview.

16. Perea interview.

17. Quoted in "Archbishop Urges Active Witness In Renewal of Christian Life," *New Mexico Register*, February 28, 1964, p. 1.

18. "Historic Event in Ecumenical Action in U.S.," *New Mexico Register*, December 25, 1964, p. 1.

19. "Archbishop Urges All Catholics to Attend Inter-Faith Scripture Service January 3," *New Mexico Register*, January 1, 1965, p. 1.

20. "Another Step Toward More Understanding," *New Mexico Register*, January 1, 1965, p. 1.

21. "Protestants Invite Catholics to 'Open House' on Feb. 28," *New Mexico Register*, February 26, 1965, p. 1.

22. Perea interview.

23. In March 1962, Byrne did initiate an archdiocese-wide program to educate laity on their role in the liturgy. As part of his initiative, "detailed instructions were sent to all pastors and school authorities outlining the various methods of lay participation in the Mass." The archbishop directed priests and religious that these instructions be given "at the earliest convenience in place of the regular Sunday homily," and as part of religion courses in all Catholic schools. "New Program to Teach Liturgy to Faithful," *New Mexico Register*, March 23, 1962, p. 1.

24. Rev. Lucian C. Hendren, "We 'Must Catch Spirit' of Revival in the Liturgy," New Mexico Register, February 14, 1964, p. 1.

25. Rev. Lucian C. Hendren, "Pastors Must Be Leaders in Liturgy," *New Mexico Register*, February 21, 1964, p. 1.

26. Personal interview with Frank Ortiz, Taos, New Mexico, January 29, 2013. The first English Mass was offered to the Albuquerque public in October 1964. The first English Mass in Santa Fe happened nine days later. "English Mass Set in Albuquerque Oct. 12," *New Mexico Register*, September 18, 1964, p. 1; "1st Santa Fe English Mass Set Oct. 21 At Cristo Rey," *New Mexico Register*, October 2, 1964, p. 1.

27. "Indian School," *New Mexico Register* editorial, December 18, 1964, p. 2.

28. "'Aggiornamento' in Cathedral," *New Mexico Register*, November 20, 1964, p. 1.

29. Geraldine Carrigan, "The Las Cruces Experiment: Temple in the Desert." *Reporter*, 6:45, October 15, 1965, n.p., Liturgy in Santa Fe file, collections of the Archdiocese of Santa Fe, Santa Fe, New Mexico. See also "Aggiornamento on the Campus," *America* 112:4 (January 23, 1965) n.p., Liturgy in Santa Fe file, collections of the Archdiocese of Santa Fe.

30. "Aggiornamento on the Campus."

31. Case statement, Steering Committee, Liturgy in Santa Fe, Pentecost 1976, Liturgy in Santa Fe file, collections of the Archdiocese of Santa Fe.

32. Case statement, Steering Committee, Liturgy in Santa Fe, Pentecost 1976.

33. Case statement, Steering Committee, Liturgy in Santa Fe, Pentecost 1976.

34. *New Mexico Register* editorial, October 28, 1966, p. 1.

35. *New Mexico Register* editorial, October 28, 1966, p. 1.

36. Personal interview with Robert Baca, Velarde, New Mexico, January 27, 2013.

37. Personal interview with Dcn. Fred Argenta, Springer, New Mexico, March 18, 2014.

38. Personal interview with Fr. Carlos Garcia, Santa Fe, January 14, 2013.

39. Group interview with Celine Gomez, Albuquerque, New Mexico, March 14, 2014.

40. Group interview with Celine Gomez, Albuquerque, New Mexico, March 14, 2014.

41. Group interview with Michael Sheen, Albuquerque, March 14, 2014.

42. Group interview with Joanne Sheen, Albuquerque, March 14, 2014.

43. Michael Sheen interview.

44. Group interview with Arturo Gomez, Albuquerque, March 14, 2014.

45. As in other U.S. dioceses, the late 1960s represented a high point in priest numbers; by 1979 the number of priests in the archdiocese had dropped down to 251. The number of parishes and missions, however, stayed relatively constant. *The Official Catholic Directory, Anno Domini 1950*, p. 216; *The Official Catholic Directory, Anno Domini 1968*, p. 781; *The Official Catholic Directory, Anno Domini 1979*, p. 863.

46. Personal interview with Fr. Joe Ingard, Albuquerque, January 4, 2012.

47. Robert E. Wright, OMI, "How Many Are 'A Few'?: Catholic Clergy in Central and Northern New Mexico, 1780– 1851" in Barbe Awalt, Paul Rhetts, and Thomas J. Steele, SJ (eds.), *Seeds of Struggle, Harvest of Faith* (Albuquerque: LPD Press, 1998), p. 238. Wright offers important evidence to qualify the prevalent historical assumption that during its late Spanish colonial and Mexican periods, New Mexico was a "church without clergy," p. 228. As a U.S. diocese, however, the number of clergy per capita in the Archdiocese of Santa Fe did lag well behind its counterparts through the middle of the twentieth century (see note 5).

48. These institutions functioned alongside informal traditions of lay leadership – most notably the religious education of children, which took place mainly in the home, especially in communities without Catholic schools, and was overseen by women. On the role of Nuevomexicano women in preserving the Catholic faith in rural villages in the late nineteenth and early twentieth centuries, see Pauline Chávez Bent, "The Faith, Courage, and Spirit of New Mexico's Hispanic Pioneering Women: A Profile in Rural Catholicism," in *Seeds of Struggle, Harvest of Faith*.

49. On the history of the *penitentes* (formally *Los Hermanos de la Fraternidad Piadosa de Nuestro Padre Jesús Nazareno*) in New Mexico, see Marta Weigle, *Brothers of Light, Brothers of Blood* (Albuquerque: University of New Mexico Press, 1976).

50. Weigle, *Brothers of Light*, pp. 150–152.

51. Personal interview with Donald Anaya, Santa Fe, March 17, 2014.

52. Weigle, *Brothers of Light*, p. 96.

53. Weigle, *Brothers of Light*, pp. 95–101.

54. Weigle, *Brothers of Light*, p. 98.

55. On acequia culture, see Sylvia Rodriguez, "Honor, Aridity, and Place" in Phillip B. Gonzales (ed.), *Expressing New Mexico: Nuevo Mexicano Creativity, Ritual, and Memory* (Tempe: University of Arizona Press, 2007).

56. The social capital attached to the former helped build the reputation of the latter, especially in small villages where the positions were shared by the same individuals and families. Rodriguez, "Honor, Aridity," p. 37.

57. Interview with Baca.

58. Personal interview with Dorothy Archuleta, Taos, New Mexico, January 28, 2013.

59. Interview with Michael Sheen. See also Rodriguez, "Honor, Aridity," p. 39.

60. Celine Gomez interview.

61. Michael Sheen interview.

62. "Pope John XXIII's Apostolic Blessing for the Servants of the Paraclete," bishopaccountability.org, www.bishop-accountability.org/docs/sP/SERVANTS_569 41959_09_14_John_XXIII_to_Fitzgerald.pdf, accessed May 25, 2014.

63. In founding the congregation and the monastery, Fitzgerald had a vision of helping priests who struggled with alcohol. Though Via Coeli did count alcoholics among its residents, Fitzgerald increasingly – and reluctantly – found himself receiving priests who had been accused of abusing minors. "Letter by Fitzgerald to Pope Paul VI," August 27, 1963, bishopaccountability.org, www.bishop-accountability.org/docs/sP/ SERVANTS_0024_00281963_08_27_Fitzgerald_to_Pope_Paul_VI.pdf, accessed May 25, 2014.

64. Minutes of the meeting, February 13, 1967, bishopaccountability.org, www.bishop-accountability.org/docs/sP/SERVANTS_6793_67961967_02_13_Minutes.pdf accessed May 25, 2014.

65. This number is as of 2004, as self-reported by the Archdiocese of Santa Fe. Most Rev. Michael Sheehan, "Report on the Archdiocese's Compliance and Implementation of the Charter for the Protection of Children and Young People," bishopaccountability. org, www.bishop-accountability.org/usccb/natureandscope/dioceses/santafenm .htm, accessed May 25, 2014.

66. According to case notes available on bishopaccountablity.org, at least six accused priests in the archdiocese were former patients with the Paracletes, and others arrived after facing accusations of abuse in other dioceses. "Database of Publicly Accused Priests in the United States," bishopaccountability.org, bishop-accountability.org/member/psearch.jsp, accessed May 25, 2014. See also Brian Fraga, "Fall River Predator-Priest Father James Porter: A Timeline," bishopaccountability.org, www.bishop-accountability.org/news2013/05_06/2013_06_25_Fraga_FallRiver.htm, accessed May 25, 2014.

67. Interview with Argenta.

68. Interview with Argenta.

69. Interview with Argenta.

70. Kristy Nabhan-Warren, *The Cursillo Movement in America* (Chapel Hill: University of North Carolina Press, 2013), p. 91.

71. Nabhan-Warren, *Cursillo Movement in America*, pp. 30–31.

72. "Cursillos Plan 3rd Anniversary," *New Mexico Register*, January 10, 1964, p. 1.

73. "Cursillos: Publ. of the Secretariate of Cursillos de Cristianidad, Archdiocese of Santa Fe," vol. I, no. 11 and 12, pamphlet, collections of the Archdiocese of Santa Fe.

74. "Fourth Anniversary of Cursillos," *New Mexico Register*, January 29, 1964, p. 1.

75. "Cursillo Conferences Explore 'His Church,'" *New Mexico Register*, February 12, 1965, p. 1.

76. "Cursillos: Publ. of the Secretariate."

77. Interview with Anaya.

78. Interview with Anaya.

79. Pope Paul VI followed through on the Council's call to restore the permanent diaconate in his 1967 apostolic letter *Sacrum Diaconatus Ordinem*.

80. Dcn. Walter Luces, personal interview, White Rock, New Mexico, January 24, 2014.

81. Interview with Luces; interview with Argenta.

82. Interview with Argenta.

83. Interview with Luces.

84. As of 2010, the Archdiocese of Santa Fe had 216 deacons, or one deacon for every 1,455 Catholics. This is more than double the 2012 national average of one deacon for every 3,856 Catholics. Archdiocese of Santa Fe, www.catholic-hierarchy.org, *Frequently Requested Church Statistics*, Center for Applied Research in the Apostolate, accessed April 20, 2014.

85. Interview with Luces.

86. Interview with Dcn. Gilbert Rodriguez, Albuquerque, March 20, 2014.

87. Interview with Argenta.

88. Personal interview with Clara Rodriguez, Ohkay Owingeh Pueblo, New Mexico, January 28, 2013.
89. Interview with Rodriguez.
90. Interview with Rodriguez.
91. Personal interview with Freddy Griego, Chimayó, New Mexico, January 28, 2013.
92. Interview with Griego.
93. According to its mission statement, "ACTS Missions provides the spark that ignites Catholics, worldwide, with the true eternal flame of the Holy Spirit. As an instrument of God, ACTS is the light that will bring about the New Evangelization to the entire world." *Mission Statement*, ACTS Missions, accessed June 12, 2014.
94. Michael L. Trujillo, *Land of Disenchantment: Latina/o Identities and Transformations in Northern New Mexico* (Albuquerque: University of New Mexico Press, 2009), pp. 3, 11; Angela Garcia, "Land of Disenchantment," *High County News*, April 3, 2006, accessed April 20, 2014.
95. Interview with Rodriguez.

7

BLACK AND CATHOLIC IN ATLANTA: CHALLENGE AND HOPE

Andrew S. Moore

The Second Vatican Council coincided with the height of the American civil rights movement, and the implementation of conciliar reforms raised questions about racial integration and the position of African Americans in the local church. In the diocese of Atlanta, blacks felt as if they were problems to be solved, rather than key actors and decision makers in their own future; however, by two decades after the Council, social, liturgical, and administrative changes rendered the Atlanta church no longer entirely "white."

T HE CONVERGENCE OF THE SECOND VATICAN COUNCIL AND THE civil rights movement electrified many U.S. cities. Many Catholics interpreted the Council's emphasis on the church as the "people of God" and the spirit of *aggiornamento* as legitimating their racial justice activism.[1] In this view, by opening up the church to the "modern world," the Council reinforced the freedom struggle's efforts to usher in a color-blind society. For its part, the church would finally welcome everyone, regardless of skin color. This was an extraordinary turn of events given the existence of separate parishes that had been established to comply with the South's Jim Crow system for much of the twentieth century. Those parishes played important roles in local black communities. In Atlanta, Georgia, the oldest African American parish – Our Lady of Lourdes, established in 1912 – was located in the predominantly black Sweet Auburn neighborhood. There a shared racial identity led to a de facto ecumenism between Catholics and Protestants that made Our Lady of Lourdes an integral part of the community.

Janis Griffin and her family illustrate the relationship between Atlanta's African American population and the Catholic Church. Griffin was born in 1948 and reared approximately a mile from Our Lady of Lourdes. Her parents were active members of Ebenezer Baptist Church, the spiritual anchor of the Sweet Auburn neighborhood and church home to many of the city's African

American middle class. Ebenezer's senior pastor was Martin Luther King
Sr. ("Daddy King"), and Martin Luther King Jr. was born and raised in the
area. Our Lady of Lourdes is down the street from Ebenezer, and a young
Martin Luther King Jr. ("Mike") could often be found playing on the parish
grounds. Like the children of many other Baptist families, Griffin and her
brother enrolled in Our Lady of Lourdes School in the early 1950s. At the
time, Daddy King complained about Griffin's father sending his children to
"that white church." Undeterred, the elder Griffin allowed his children to be
baptized Catholics.[2] Within ten years of the Griffins entering Our Lady of
Lourdes, the Second Vatican Council intersected with local civil rights
demonstrations and the phenomenon of white flight, the movement of
whites out of urban Atlanta to escape pressure to desegregate. For black
members of Our Lady of Lourdes (and later Saint Paul of the Cross,
established in 1955), their identity as "black Catholics" had been rooted
in the local parish. This was where they were accepted by white priests and
sisters, where their children went to school, and where they could comfor-
tably practice their Catholicism without the shadow of racial prejudice.
Vatican II disrupted that identity. Indeed, it exposed Daddy King's critique
as a reality. The Catholic Church was a "white church."

Despite claims that it was a global gathering, the Second Vatican Council
was a predominantly European affair; its documents gave little consideration
to racial and ethnic issues. In the United States, the reforms called for were
mediated through white priests and bishops, working in tandem with a
predominantly white diocesan lay leadership. Local Catholic leaders in
Atlanta gradually realized that they did not have a handle on the post–civil
rights movement's "race problems" and that a color-blind approach was
complicated at best and even undesirable for some blacks and whites alike.
Conciliar reforms effectively encouraged white Catholics to continue to treat
African Americans as problems still to be solved. In this way, Vatican II
exacerbated forces already at work and did nothing to address the roots of
long-standing racial problems. Separate parishes had provided the means by
which white Catholics could ignore African Americans within the archdiocese. Vatican II did little to correct that. Whites continued to see blacks as not
fully equal members of the churches and wider church they shared.

Archbishop Hallinan and Racial Reform

When the Second Vatican Council convened in 1962, Atlanta had just been
elevated to an archdiocese. Paul J. Hallinan arrived from South Carolina to
serve as the diocese's first archbishop. Hallinan, an Ohio native who "had

a knack of being on the cutting edge of things,"[3] was sympathetic to the civil rights movement. Indeed, he believed that liturgical reform in the church and racial reform in the city at large should be embraced together. It was the "effect on the lives of our people" of the "living" liturgy, Hallinan wrote, "that is the reason for the renewal." For the people of God, "the need of our time is love, human love shot through with the splendor of divine love." That love came through liturgy.[4] Not surprisingly, Hallinan's fellow American bishops selected him for the Council's liturgical commission.[5] At first, Hallinan made himself chiefly responsible for communicating the conciliar reforms to the people of Atlanta through pastoral letters, columns in the Georgia *Bulletin*, and in a pamphlet *How to Understand Changes in the Liturgy*. Under his guidance, the structure and substance of liturgical reforms would be communicated via a top-down approach. This meant that liturgical changes were handled on a diocesan-wide basis. The liturgy commission initially did not consider any parish-specific changes, and no requests to deviate from the diocesan-wide norms were made.[6] The expectation was that liturgical reforms would unfold in similar fashion across the diocese, and no distinctions between black and white parishes would be made.

Indeed, the possibility that there might be differences among these churches did not seem to occur to anyone. When reform began in 1962, the initial instructions from the archbishop to the people were about lay participation in the Mass, which was to be a "dialogue" between priest and people, an extension of pre-conciliar liturgical reform efforts. The Gospels would be read in English, and congregants were to be taught the proper responses – in either Latin or English.[7]

More dramatic changes followed in 1963 and 1964, with the priest celebrating Mass facing the people and then an entirely English Mass. According to members of the Sisters of the Blessed Sacrament, who staffed the school at Our Lady of Lourdes, when the priest first faced the people, "the Congregation seemed to like it, if we can judge by the intense concentration, and Father McKeever liked it very much."[8] The first Sunday in Advent, November 29, 1964, brought an entirely English Mass – "at last," the sisters celebrated. Rev. William Calhoun, a former parishioner of Our Lady of Lourdes and the archdiocese's first black priest (ordained the year before), had instructed the members of the parish in the new English Mass, "so everyone participated."[9] Janis Griffin, who was in high school at the time, recalled, "For me personally, it was great." English removed barriers and made it easier for her to invite her non-Catholic family and friends to Mass with her.[10] Not everyone was pleased, however. Parishioner Sandra Criddell recalled that one friend's mother suffered a "holy fit" over the change.

Another woman left for Sacred Heart as soon as an alternative Latin Mass was offered there and never returned to Our Lady of Lourdes.[11] Although she remembered that the transition to the English Mass brought a handful of new converts, parishioner Karen Allen felt that the new liturgy "didn't seem as reverent" as the Latin. It "didn't seem like church at all to me."[12]

Hallinan expected liturgical reform to lead to racial reform; the consistency of the liturgy across racial boundaries no doubt was his intention. But a color-blind liturgy continued to disguise the most pressing problem for the Archdiocese of Atlanta, as well as for the entire city, namely, the persistence of residential segregation and the difficulty of achieving true racial integration. Although this was not legally mandated, Atlanta's churches followed the pattern of racial segregation that characterized the rest of the city. Minorities in a predominantly Protestant region, Catholics believed they had little choice but to comply with the region's racial status quo.

Since the late nineteenth century, ministering to African Americans meant establishing separate parishes and schools such as Our Lady of Lourdes, which enjoyed a special position in Atlanta's black community. The school was an important vehicle of evangelization. "Mixed marriages" between Catholics and Protestants – and even "mixed" families, meaning Protestant parents and children who had been baptized into the church, were common. One member of the Sisters of the Blessed Sacrament who taught at the school from 1955 to 1968 recalled that rarely was the school enrollment more than 51 percent Catholic, with the percentage of Catholic parents even less than that. Yet parents cooperated with the sisters, and this "played an important role in breaking down the hostility towards the Church in what was a strongly Baptist Black Community."[13]

In the late 1940s and 1950s, Atlanta was a city literally on the move. African Americans relocated into formerly all-white neighborhoods and pressed for the desegregation of schools, and white residents, in turn, moved out of the city altogether.[14] With blacks increasingly dispersed throughout greater Atlanta, the archdiocese followed them. In 1955, Saint Paul of the Cross parish and school opened in a western part of the city that had transitioned quickly from white to black in the early 1950s.[15] In 1961, Drexel High School opened on the campus of Saint Paul of the Cross. Parochial schools had ostensibly been desegregated since the 1962–1963 school year, but persistent residential segregation hindered the actual integration of the city's Catholic schools. On the eve of Vatican II, then, archdiocesan officials believed they were serving their black Catholic population, when, in fact, their actions inadvertently reinforced white Atlantans' resistance to attempts to desegregate schools and neighborhoods.

Direct racial conflict in Atlanta intensified in March 1960, when student protesters targeted Rich's department store and other downtown businesses. Protests and negotiations with members of the Chamber of Commerce continued into 1961. Even then a tentative agreement did not include increases in black hiring, something that protesters were still pressing for in 1963 and 1964.[16] Members of Our Lady of Lourdes, including sisters, participated in those demonstrations.

Carolyn Long Banks (a convert whose parents were Episcopalians) used her home as a meeting location for demonstrators, although she kept details from her parents "because I didn't want to jeopardize their jobs."[17] The parents of one woman, Karen Davenport Allen, whose mother was raised in Our Lady of Lourdes, discovered in 1964 that their daughter was active in the demonstrations when they saw her on television. They sent her away to Houston, Texas, for her own safety. She finished college there, encountered the black power message of Stokely Carmichael, and then returned to Atlanta. She and Sandra Criddell (a convert, whose family attended Ebenezer Baptist Church) remembered later that "everybody was [active] really, if you were of age."[18] For their part, in 1965 all seven of the Sisters of the Blessed Sacrament joined sixty-five African American Catholic high school students and some 2,000 people total in a "sympathy march to protest the recent violence in Selma, Alabama."[19]

In Hallinan's understanding, the Council had de-emphasized the bishop and increased the responsibility of the laity in church leadership. When the Council's final session adjourned in 1965, the archbishop set in motion events that would increase the collaborative leadership that he believed Vatican II had called for. In January 1966, he announced that the first archdiocesan synod would be held the following November. The synod would "be a reflection of the great Vatican Council just ended, but it will be local, not universal in its purpose. With God's grace, it . . . will preserve the deposit of the faith, and at the same time, meet the challenge of today's world."[20] Hallinan also convened a congress of religious and a lay congress to meet during the spring. Delegates to the lay congress would be chosen at the parish level, with the number of parish delegates depending on the size of their respective congregations. The laity and sisters were to advise the priests' synod on how best to implement conciliar reforms relevant to them.[21] Delegates received training at a series of workshops.[22] One couple, Jack and Alice Cawley, recalled an early meeting between Hallinan and thirty lay leaders. When asked what he expected of the laypeople at the congress, Hallinan replied, "I want you to decide what shall be done, how it shall be done, and by whom it shall be done."[23] Hallinan was pleased with the result: "A new

departure was being examined, carefully, individually, even painfully ...
Authority and obedience in the proper areas are still of the essence of the
faith." This would not be "business as usual," the archbishop continued.
"We are all (you and I) searching for ways and means to translate these fine
phrases 'hour of the laity,' 'emerging layman,' etc., into reality and action."[24]
For their part, the sisters demonstrated concern for parochial education and the
social justice mission of the archdiocese, as well as "a more positive movement
towards integration of both White and Negro schools."[25]

According to the synod participants, conciliar reforms required greater lay
involvement in parish and archdiocesan leadership, with lay "jurisdiction
enlarged, under the influence of the recent Council, by a true consultative
process."[26] Each parish should develop "imaginative ways" of achieving
a sense of community. That sense of community would require eliminating
separate parishes for African Americans. "In an earlier day," the synod
declared, separate black parishes "resulted in segregation due to human
weakness on the part of white Catholics. The time is far overdue for us to
eliminate any parish boundaries that might even appear to perpetuate 'Negro
parishes.'"[27] A preliminary committee report had gone even further, calling
for an end to segregated housing, and encouraging fully integrated youth
activities and "home visiting between the races." In short, "The Negro must
feel welcome in all parish activities."[28] Over the course of the next few years,
archdiocesan officials wrestled with how to implement this vision. This
desire to eliminate racially distinct parishes and integrate schools came from
a well of good intentions fed by conciliar reforms, but discussions of eliminating all-black parishes ignored the special place that those parishes and
schools such as Our Lady of Lourdes played in the black community, in
African American history in Atlanta, and in the civil rights movement.

"Integration" and Parish Consolidation

Early in 1967, Auxiliary Bishop Joseph Bernardin convened a series of meetings with priests from downtown Atlanta parishes, particularly Our Lady of
Lourdes, Sacred Heart, and the Shrine of the Immaculate Conception.
Bernardin intended the meeting as recognition of the importance of coordination among urban parishes. The group talked in general about the need
to rearrange parish boundaries, but Bernardin said the main issue was what
to do with Our Lady of Lourdes. There were two sets of problems,
according to Bernardin: those having to do with the inner city (such as
demographic changes in downtown neighborhoods) and parish issues. Our
Lady of Lourdes's pastor, Rev. Dale Freeman, warned against unilateral

decisions. He urged the chancery to consult members of the African American community; their opinions must be "seriously considered." Bernardin suggested that a dialogue begin in each parish, in particular Our Lady of Lourdes.[29]

The group met again two weeks later. This time the members agreed that the ultimate goal was "the elimination of personal parishes based on race because such parishes are inconsistent with Catholic principles." Nevertheless, the committee delayed any decision about closing Our Lady of Lourdes. Bernardin and the inner-city pastors agreed on a plan to convince African Americans to willingly join the territorial parishes where they lived. In proposing this, the group considered three factors. First, they must prepare whites in the parishes that blacks from Our Lady of Lourdes would join. Second, they must address the fact that blacks at Our Lady of Lourdes – for a variety of legitimate reasons – were reluctant to leave. Finally, the committee acknowledged the "obligation of the Church to work toward an integrated parish community and to educate both whites and Negroes as to the long-term advantages of this."[30]

The proposed plan involved a pastoral approach. Priests at Our Lady of Lourdes and the parishes where the African Americans should attend "would try instead to convince the Negro parishioners that they truly belong to the territorial parishes in which they live … and that they will be welcome in those parishes." Priests were to contact parishioners directly and add them to their parishes' mailing lists. Priests were also urged to "establish some contact between the white and Negro Catholics" outside regular parish times. One proposed method for accomplishing this – "through Mass in the home" – would not have been considered prior to Vatican II. There is no evidence such liturgical gatherings ever took place. Bernardin and the priests involved decided to make no decisions right away about closing Our Lady of Lourdes. They decided instead that Saint Paul of the Cross church be designated a territorial parish "as soon as possible."[31]

That would not be soon at all. In 1968, the pastor of Sacred Heart, Rev. John J. Mulroy, offered to send his parish's bulletin to Our Lady of Lourdes parishioners. "As I understand [it] the negro catholics living within the boundaries of this parish are free to attend either Sacred Heart or Our Lady of Lourdes," Mulroy wrote Bernardin in February 1968. He needed parishioners' addresses, and he sought Bernardin's permission before contacting the pastor of Our Lady of Lourdes. Bernardin told him to wait until they could have another meeting.[32] That next meeting took place over a year later, this time to discuss the two African American parishes, not the urban neighborhoods themselves. A month later, in March, a different group of priests again determined that Saint Paul of the Cross would be reclassified as a territorial parish. One roadblock, however, was that the mission of the Passionist priests who staffed the parish did not include the supervision of regular diocesan parishes. Nevertheless, the priests concluded, converting Saint Paul of the Cross "would not substantially change the nature of their work, at least for the foreseeable future."[33]

At that same meeting, it was decided to implement the plan discussed the previous year. Pastors of territorial parishes would "quietly and informally" contact African Americans living within their parish boundaries "to let them know that they really belong to the territorial parishes and may go there if they wish." A day was anticipated when the number of people who attended Our Lady of Lourdes "drops substantially" enough for it to cease to be a viable parish. Before that happened, however, it was recognized that "plans must be made ... to reorientate our program at Our Lady of Lourdes to the needs of the total community and not just the Catholics." Perhaps, the priests imagined, Our Lady of Lourdes could "continue as a center for specialized Inner-City apostolate." The group planned to reconvene in three months to determine how effectively its strategy for reorienting Our Lady of Lourdes's members had been implemented. If that meeting happened, any archival evidence of it has not survived.[34]

Clearly a disconnect existed between the 1967 and 1968 meetings to discuss the future of Our Lady of Lourdes. The available archival evidence does not shed enough light on matters to fully explain the false start of the 1967 meeting, but some things are clear. For one, Atlanta itself was still sorting out its racial future. Continuing demonstrations and conflict between police and African Americans led to the arrest of Stokely Carmichael there in September 1966. Black power activism split the moderate political coalition that had controlled the city, just as African Americans' proportion of the city's population was rising to almost half by the end of the decade.[35] This shift in demographics had ramifications for the black Catholic population in urban parishes. By 1967 – five years into archdiocesan efforts to integrate its schools – Drexel High School had only 156 students, all of them African Americans. In March 1967, Hallinan announced that Drexel would close at the end of the academic year. The school remained unaccredited and the library and academic programs were inferior to the two other better-attended Catholic high schools, Saint Pius X and Saint Joseph. Surprised by the backlash this announcement provoked, Hallinan delayed the decision until he could hold meetings with African American parents and students.

At a meeting in April 1967, one parent spoke for many others when he complained that "Negroes have been planned for, not planned with." Another parent asked rhetorically, "Does integration always have to be black into white?"[36] For George Coleman, a member of Saint Paul of the Cross, the decision to close Drexel "shows you still just can't see us." Whites, Coleman concluded, "must do as much of this integrating as Negroes."[37] Ultimately, Hallinan's original decision stood, and Drexel's students would be admitted to Saint Pius X or Saint Joseph high schools.[38] Wounds healed slowly. As late as 1969, the priest at Saint Paul of the Cross, Rev. Richard Leary, CP, reported to Archbishop Thomas Donnellan, who had replaced the late Hallinan in 1968, that efforts to create a liturgical committee in the parish were proving difficult. The parish suffered "critical problems with our choir membership," and "areas of tension in the black community and in the parish" hindered liturgical reform for the time being.[39] Leary did not elaborate on those tensions, but the conflict over closing Drexel High School left many black Catholics feeling as if they were not equal members of their church. To them, Daddy King's charge that it was a "white church" still rang true.

The hard feelings did not go away, and the bishop and priests were aware of it as discussion of parish boundaries – and even consolidating parishes – continued into the 1970s. Given the nature of authority in the Catholic Church, archdiocesan officials could have simply compelled parish realignment and racial mixing. But according to the archdiocesan pastoral council, integration achieved this way would reveal "our attitude and our practices toward our Christian brothers."[40] It also would have involved a level of coercion that archdiocesan leaders were not eager to enforce. Their reluctance stemmed from the opposition they knew they would face, especially from white Catholics. Rev. William Headley was a priest of the Congregation of the Holy Spirit and graduate student at Atlanta University. Stationed in Charleston, South Carolina, Headley lived in the Sacred Heart rectory while he pursued his graduate studies.[41] His master's thesis compared attitudes toward desegregation among Sacred Heart and Our Lady of Lourdes parishioners. Sacred Heart's boundaries included most of downtown Atlanta and several distinct white and black neighborhoods. Our Lady of Lourdes was situated within Sacred Heart's territorial boundaries. The interstate highway system separated each parish's surrounding neighborhood; this element of urban geography made the mile-and-a-half between the two racially distinct parishes seem only greater. What Headley found gave archdiocesan decision makers pause. There was ambivalence, he discovered, if not outright resistance to eliminating parish boundaries and consolidating parishes.

At the time of Headley's research, Sacred Heart was several times larger than Our Lady of Lourdes. Surveys of the 205 participants (roughly half of those from each parish) revealed, contrary to Headley's initial hypothesis, that there was no widespread support for desegregation. Rather, Headley concluded, "stimuli to alignment on a racial basis seemed so natural and strong that other stimuli such as religious affiliation are somewhat overlooked."[42] Racial identity trumped Catholic identity, in other words, especially for white Catholics from Sacred Heart. Our Lady of Lourdes parishioners, especially its young adults, were more favorable to desegregation and to the idea of merging the two parishes. Surprisingly, Headley found a connection between attitudes toward desegregation and those toward liturgical renewal. The greater social interaction called for by the liturgical changes of Vatican II would make it more difficult to achieve desegregation, he argued, especially among the non–college educated and lower classes in both parishes. Sacred Heart and Our Lady of Lourdes had heterogeneous memberships, which might mitigate the opposition to integration among certain segments of the population.[43] Based in part on Headley's thesis, the archdiocesan pastoral council decided that "not enough facts were available to make any worthwhile recommendations." They would continue to study the issue.[44]

Whatever the reasons, by 1972 Our Lady of Lourdes was still a parish without territorial boundaries; but, at least according to its pastor, Matthew Kemp, this was possibly an advantage: "That way we can exclude no one." Kemp had become pastor at Our Lady of Lourdes in June 1971, after serving as assistant pastor there in the mid-1960s and then on the staff at Sacred Heart. By the time he assumed the pastorate, "both church membership and attendance had dwindled tremendously."[45] Many parishioners had followed the beloved Rev. Michael McKeever to his new appointment at Saint Anthony of Padua parish in the West End neighborhood of Atlanta. Founded by the wife of white author Joel Chandler Harris, Saint Anthony was in the process of becoming a predominantly African American parish. Other parishioners left St. Anthony's after Rev. Alan Dillman, who preceded Kemp, announced that they were required to attend the parish closest to where they lived.[46] The migration away from Our Lady of Lourdes stopped after a few years, for the time being, at least. In the year after Kemp became pastor, the parish added sixty new families. Many no doubt came from other parishes; others had returned to the church "after years of absence," in Kemp's words. Overall half of the then-current members were converts to Catholicism. Indeed, in March 1972, a dozen or so potential converts were receiving instruction from Kemp, and nine had been baptized into the church the previous Christmas.[47]

Although the turnaround proved to be temporary, at the time Kemp and the principal of the school, Sr. Judith McGinley, SBS, attributed it to a change in Our Lady of Lourdes's "image" and the new "sense of 'family'" among parishioners. Kemp actively sought to capture the spirit of Vatican II by encouraging lay involvement in running the parish. The local parish Council "had been practically abandoned," when he had arrived there. He opened the rectory for "parishioners interested in the well-being of the parish," and many responded: "The people are very happy that they can invade the privacy of a priest and get together with him to talk about problems of the parish." Whites and blacks were still divided, Kemp believed. Few black Catholics lived in the neighborhood anymore. Still, they returned, because, as Kemp recalled, "they feel that they belong." They "feel very comfortable here and . . . their roots are here. Many of them grew up in the area, but since have moved away." They had a history there. For Kemp, there was "so much black culture . . . people-wise." "I never forget that the parishioners are black, " Kemp said in 1972, "but sometimes I forget that I am white."[48]

Caught up in this internal debate over territorial boundaries and demographic change were the Sisters of the Blessed Sacrament. Having served there since the school's inception, the sisters knew the parish and neighborhood better than anyone. Under their leadership, the school served as a "bridge" between the church and the community. According to one of the sisters, Mary Patrick Lynch, the school also proved to be "a source of identity for Black Catholics, even, and perhaps especially, after integration."[49] Discussions in the early 1970s over the sisters' continuing presence in the parish revealed both the special place of Our Lady of Lourdes in the spiritual life of the city's black Catholics and how much the parish and Sweet Auburn had changed in recent years. Between 1969 and 1973, the school's enrollment decreased from 267 to 220. At the beginning of the 1973–1974 school year, the number dropped again to 187. Most of the students came from elsewhere in the city, and most of them were not Catholic. In May 1973, Sister Maureen Immaculate, SBS, reported to Mother Mary Elizabeth that only 73 of the school's 220 students were Catholic. Only two of the twenty-five eighth-grade students walked to school. The rest arrived by car or bus. What was more, most children in the school did not attend Mass at the church on Sundays. Sr. Maureen Immaculate observed that "their spiritual needs are being served elsewhere."[50] At the same time, tuition increased, leaving an Our Lady of Lourdes education unaffordable to many of the African American children still in the neighborhood. The students who lived elsewhere could afford to attend the parish schools located nearer their homes. "We are continuing segregation," Sister Mary Judith, SBS, commented in 1972, "by accepting such a great subsidy from the archdiocese to keep this school open."[51] At last, citing decreasing enrollment, rising tuition, the availability of other educational opportunities, and the reality that "we are obviously not serving the poor in the school," Mother Mary Elizabeth, SBS, announced that the sisters would withdraw at the end of the 1973–1974 school year.[52]

Archbishop Donnellan reminded Mother Mary Elizabeth in 1973 of the prominent place of Our Lady of Lourdes school in the black community. Most African Americans in the area encountered Catholicism through the school. The archbishop acknowledged that students who attended there could attend a school closer to their homes, but they did not, the Bronx-born prelate wrote, because Our Lady of Lourdes "has a certain mystique in the Black Community."

He conceded that without the SBS sisters and the school they ran, the church would not enjoy the reputation it did among African Americans. Black Catholics still resented the closing of Drexel High School. Rumors circulated that Saint Joseph's High School would be next "because it has a high Black registration," Donnellan wrote to Mother Mary Elizabeth in October 1973: "I dread to think what interpretation will be placed on the closing of Our Lady of Lourdes."[53] The school did not close just then, but the archbishop recognized that the church had not done enough to meet the needs of black Catholics.

As Donnellan had said, Our Lady of Lourdes enjoyed a favorable reputation among African Americans, even if the Catholic Church itself did not. Through the 1970s, despite talk of changing territorial boundaries and eliminating parishes specifically for African Americans, Our Lady of Lourdes continued to emphasize its racial heritage and to connect itself to the history of its neighborhood and to the legacy of Martin Luther King Jr. The 1969 curriculum included the "study of the Black American," especially "the hopes and dreams of the Black People today as well as the contributions of the Negro Americans of the past."[54] In 1972, Fr. Kemp gauged interest in an "African Free School training youngsters in the important elements of our African Heritage."[55] The parish collaborated with and supported local black Protestant churches. Choirs from other churches performed concerts in the Our Lady of Lourdes sanctuary, the parish recognized Black History Month, and Our Lady of Lourdes members participated in special worship services to raise money for black Protestant congregations.[56] The most popular ecumenical efforts came in celebration of Martin Luther King Jr.'s birthday and on behalf of the MLK memorial across the street. Church bulletins publicized neighborhood ceremonies celebrating King each January. In 1975, University of Notre Dame president Theodore Hesburgh was the principal speaker at the service held at Ebenezer Baptist Church. Contributions from Our Lady of Lourdes parishioners to the King Center showed that "our vision must be larger than our own needs," an article in the parish bulletin in 1975 maintained, "and must have a sense of history and destiny for all people everywhere." Fr. Terry Kane praised parishioners a year later for contributing $216 at weekend Masses for the center (the regular offering was $265). "Once again," he declared, "the Parish family of Our Lady of Lourdes has joined together to respond to the vision of a larger community about us – the spirit is moving!"[57] At a special ceremony dedicating King's tombstone the following year, Fr. Kane delivered the opening prayer. Later in the decade, Our Lady of Lourdes was used as a gathering place for associated marches for full employment and against the death penalty.[58]

Evolution of a Black Catholic Identity

The parish's celebrations of its own history recognized the special place that it played in the Atlanta black community and in Sweet Auburn in particular. Down the street from Ebenezer Baptist Church, members of the King family (including Daddy King and Coretta Scott King) participated in special services at Our Lady of Lourdes. The ecumenical service celebrating the church's sixty-fifth anniversary in 1977, organized around the theme "Unity of God's People," drew African American Protestants from across the city. The Methodist president of the Interdenominational Theological Center delivered the invocation, a representative from the King Center read the scripture, and a bishop of the African Methodist Church offered the benediction after a candlelight procession to the gravesite of Martin Luther King Jr.[59] A decade later, at the seventy-fifth anniversary, civil rights activist Andrew Young, mayor of Atlanta and former ambassador to the United Nations, was the featured speaker.

In early 1979, Rev. Frank Giusta was named pastor of Our Lady of Lourdes. He inherited a parish in disrepair that was still not self-supporting. In the spring of that year, Giusta wrote the archdiocesan chancellor, Monsignor Jerry Hardy, that his goal was to make the parish self-sufficient, adding ruefully, "if and when it will happen I do not know." In the meantime, bills had not been paid and were it not for financial help from the archdiocese, a wall behind the rectory would have collapsed. The archdiocese also helped cover the replacement of church water pipes. Giusta lowered the expense of that project by hiring "workers off the street, as the Gospel says to do" for the digging. He economized further by eliminating the school of religion's separate office and shifting as much parish work as possible to volunteer and temporary labor. The archdiocese subsidized his salary, too. Although this was meant to be temporary, Giusta explained to Monsignor Hardy that the subsidy amount – $270 – "constitutes ¾ of a Sunday collection." Archdiocesan officials changed their minds and decided to continue it.[60]

According to Giusta, one hundred additional families added to the rolls "would have the problem solved, and other ones as well." In October 1979, Giusta and Our Lady of Lourdes launched an evangelization campaign to attract seekers to their parish. A flyer for the campaign noted that the parish "is no longer an all Black Catholic Church," though that was certainly part of its history as "a pilgrim people." But now the parish welcomed "people of all races and economic backgrounds to our celebration of the good news of Jesus Christ."[61] The evangelism campaign did not target any particular racial group, but Giusta later acknowledged that the neighborhood's remaining black population was the focus of the campaign.

Nevertheless, the parish's racial composition had not changed much since the 1960s. The neighborhood was changing, however. In December 1979, Giusta drafted a memo to Archbishop Donnellan about the size and composition of Our Lady of Lourdes, which, Giusta told Donnellan, remained "an ethnic parish." The number of parishioners had declined to "189 registered units" (presumably a combination of families and single people)." Giusta counted only four families with children for whom Our Lady of Lourdes was the parish closest to where they lived. Most former parishioners "attend services at the church nearest their present homes." Those who remained did so "because of the school and because of the emotional attachment they have to this church." He concluded that Our Lady of Lourdes was "no different from most Protestant churches in the area, which draw the majority of their congregations from other areas of the city and from Decatur."[62]

The reality was that the neighborhood around Our Lady of Lourdes was in transition. It was decreasingly residential, with office space and memorials to Martin Luther King Jr. dominating the area. The housing that was still available was "undesirable," and African Americans moved out as soon as they could afford it. Areas that had been redeveloped and upgraded appealed more to "middle-class Whites, including Catholics," who might not be inclined to choose Our Lady of Lourdes as their home parish. For these reasons, Giusta predicted a day when Our Lady of Lourdes would be "an empty church with a great past and a very privileged location . . . with a lot of emotional appeal to people and near to areas of the city which have been enormously upgraded."[63]

Even a successful campaign would not have been enough to change the parish's outlook. Giusta listed three options in these circumstances. The first was to close the parish in a few years. Most of the parishioners would be gone by then, he thought, but the "repercussions are obvious ones and will be felt nation-wide because of tourist publicity." The second option was a direct appeal to all Atlanta-area African American Catholics to return to Our Lady of Lourdes. Either they or their parents more than likely became Catholics at Our Lady of Lourdes. Giusta underestimated the influence of the city's other predominantly black parish – Saint Paul of the Cross – but his appeal was no less rooted in racial pride and Catholic heritage.[64]

Giusta favored a third option. This would be to assign boundaries to Our Lady of Lourdes and eliminate its racial status. The consensus of the current parishioners seemed to be that this was "an idea whose time has come." Such a redefinition would change the nature of the parish, of course, and increase the workload of the priest; it might also create the need to compete with area Protestant churches in evangelization. But Our Lady of Lourdes was prepared for this; the school "offers an excellent opportunity for evangelization." Since only two of the eleven teachers there were Catholic, relying on it for that purpose, however, also increased the burden on the priest.[65]

Giusta's concern about the likely additional duties he might have to assume is understandable in light of his and other area priests' perception of their diminished status in an increasingly suburbanized archdiocese. In 1980, Giusta and the priests of two other south Atlanta parishes, Rev. John Adamski of Saint Anthony and Rev. Henry Gracz of Saints Peter and Paul in Decatur, met with an archdiocesan official (unnamed in the memo, although probably Chancellor Jerry Hardy) to discuss their "isolation ... from a Church awareness point of view." The "economic character and racial make-up" of these three parishes set them apart from the "northside and suburban parishes which tend to be more homogeneously affluent and white." The differences were stark. Wealthier white suburban parishes constructed new buildings, while these isolated parishes had trouble staffing essential positions like secretaries and religious education coordinators. The archdiocese did little to counter this isolation and to offset an "attitude of indifference from the larger segment of the Church of Atlanta which is white and middle class."[66]

At the same time, the archbishop approved financing for a long-range renovation project at Our Lady of Lourdes. In April 1980, Giusta proposed a plan that would improve maintenance and the aesthetics of the parish and school. An architect's report noted that the Martin Luther King Jr. historical site continued to add new buildings, and the "general neighborhood is part of a revitalization program." "In keeping with the neighborhood spirit," Our Lady of Lourdes needed to "improve its aesthetic impression." This included renovations to give the church, school, and rectory a more uniform exterior – "to give the impression that they belong together and are part of the same project." Giusta called for landscaping improvements, additions and improvements to the church and rectory, and the general updating of the interior of all three buildings. The parish had some savings – approximately $10,000 – to put toward the $35,000 project, and the rest would come from an interest-free loan from the archdiocese.[67]

Neighborhood changes and church and school renovations improved the outlook for the parish, along with Giusta's attitude. In August 1982, he resubmitted his 1979 report to Donnellan. He and the archbishop had discussed its contents in the intervening three years, but nothing official had been done in response. Now "the situation both at the church and at the school has improved considerably, thank God," he wrote to the archdiocesan chancellor. Giusta revised the previous report by crossing out details that were no longer relevant. Amid the changes, Our Lady of Lourdes's role in its revitalized neighborhood appeared more secure.[68]

Meanwhile, discussions about Our Lady of Lourdes's racial status and boundaries continued. The archdiocesan consultors took up the question again in September and October 1982. At its October 4, 1982, meeting, Our Lady of Lourdes's parish council called on the archdiocese to remove the parish's "ethnic connotation," without assigning territorial boundaries. The reason for making that distinction, Giusta explained, was that Our Lady of Lourdes's parishioners "have long memories." They did not want to be pressured to join territorial parishes closer to where they lived. This was what happened – "talks from the pulpit and letters to each parishioner" – when Saint Paul of the Cross was established from Our Lady of Lourdes. Now they did not want to be "forced to join the parishes of their neighborhood." This was what archdiocesan leaders and area pastors had discussed doing in the late 1960s. Giusta had not been part of those earlier conversations. Now he recommended assigning boundaries "without any big publicity about it."[69] This would not happen until 1996.[70]

A few years before Giusta arrived at the parish, Janis Griffin returned to Atlanta and Our Lady of Lourdes. The parish she returned to "was dying," she remembers. The neighborhood had changed, and the drop in membership reflected in part the dispersal of the black population throughout the city. For Griffin, though, the problem also was the music. The choir was "struggling" and the music was "so dead." Griffin had left Atlanta for Howard University in 1966. Back then, in the wake of Vatican II, Hallinan was leading the archdiocese through musical as well as liturgical changes. In 1967, interpreting the pope's instructions on the use of music in liturgy, Hallinan told Atlanta's Catholics, "Don't throw away your guitars, boys – the strings may rise again." The pope had not ruled any type of music necessarily sacred. Rather, music used in worship was intended to evoke an authentic

"God-oriented" emotional response; it should "put us in God's presence in a special, praiseful way," and at the same time it should be "in keeping with the spirit of the Mass." As it happened, music was even more divisive than the use of the vernacular. Hallinan warned that the pope's instruction on music "might well be our last great hope for peace in the cold liturgical war now being waged."[71] In 1968, Auxiliary Bishop Bernardin complained that across the archdiocese "our music needs much improvement." He called for the use of a variety of musical forms, adapted to best serve the people in each individual parish. While "folk-style music" was not the only musical style appropriate for the "renewed liturgy," it was "good because it means something to many people, especially the young." He also called for "the development of good choirs" balanced with "congregational singing," something that Protestant churches "seem to have been able to work out."[72]

As Griffin learned, then, at Our Lady of Lourdes the musical transition to the post–Vatican II liturgy was not smooth. While at Howard, she mastered the guitar, and she learned many of the songs associated with the folk Mass movement, especially those by Ray Repp. She was responsible for performing at a weekend "coffee house" in the basement of Howard's Newman Center. When she went home to Atlanta during the summers of 1967 and 1968, she wanted to bring her guitar and the folk Mass to Our Lady of Lourdes. The parish only had an organ, and there was opposition to her guitar. She and three or four others "dug our heels in," and they were eventually allowed to play at Saturday Mass.[73] The folk Mass style was certainly different from the formal music of the pre–Vatican II liturgy. But little distinguished this musical worship style from what was sung at any other parish in the archdiocese. For Griffin, the fruits of this were evident in the 1970s. There was still no distinctive black liturgical experience and nothing unique about the parish other than its location and its history. There was nothing, Griffin concluded, to keep blacks there: "The music didn't reach you. It didn't appeal to our community. It wasn't soul-stirring." The parish finally replaced its organ with an upright piano, and a series of experienced lay choir directors pointed the congregation toward the important role music played in liturgy. Griffin saw a process that had come "full circle." Vatican II created opportunities for composers to write music for the new liturgy. The new compositions demonstrated the need for music that enhanced the liturgy without overshadowing it. According to Griffin, "black Catholics finally started to realize that" for themselves, and worship at Our Lady of Lourdes eventually reflected the fullness of its racial heritage. Beginning in the early 1980s, an "alive" choir and "engaging" music gave "people a reason to come to church." Those drawn to Our Lady of Lourdes included whites, who were "getting something there they weren't getting elsewhere."[74]

Atlanta Catholics continued to identify Our Lady of Lourdes as an African American parish, but now that designation had meanings different from those it had twenty years earlier. A distinctive black liturgy and a sense of purpose in its home neighborhood gave Our Lady of Lourdes new life. In March 1982, the Archdiocesan Commission on Black Catholic Concerns held its first meeting in Atlanta, with nineteen representatives from five parishes. This commission's purpose was to communicate to the archbishop the special needs of the black community.[75] For the history of African American Catholics in general, this paralleled developments in the larger church. In 1984, the ten black bishops in the United States issued a pastoral letter, "What We Have Seen and Heard." The black Catholic community, the bishops wrote, was no longer marginalized in the Catholic Church. African Americans had finally moved beyond separate but equal to a place where their contributions were distinct and measurable.[76] African Americans remained overwhelmingly urban in an increasingly suburban archdiocese, and their numbers suggested they still were an open mission field.[77] Nevertheless, two decades past the Second Vatican Council, the church in Atlanta was no longer a "white church." Black Catholics were finally better positioned to engage that ministry – and craft their identity as Catholics – on their own terms.

NOTES

1. See John T. McGreevy, *Parish Boundaries: The Catholic Encounter with Race in the Twentieth-Century Urban North* (Chicago and London: University of Chicago Press, 1996), especially chaps. 7–9; and Andrew S. Moore, *The South's Tolerable Alien: Roman Catholics in Alabama and Georgia, 1945–1970* (Baton Rouge: Louisiana State University, 2007), especially chaps. 4 and 6.
2. Personal interview with Janis Griffin, February 20, 2014. Griffin's father would have converted, too, if he had not been a Mason. The parish priest at the time, however, would not accept him as a Mason.
3. Thomas Shelley, *Paul J. Hallinan: First Archbishop of Atlanta* (Wilmington, DE: Michael Glazier, 1989), p. 40.
4. Hallinan quoted in M. Elise Schwalm, RSM (ed.), *In His Own Words: Paul J. Hallinan, Archbishop of Atlanta, 1962–1968*, unpublished manuscript in possession of author, p. 53–54.
5. Shelley, *Paul J. Hallinan*, pp. 165–166.
6. On the exception, the Community of Christ Our Brother, see Andrew S. Moore, "Christian Unity, Lay Authority, and the People of God: The Community of Christ Our Brother in the Archdiocese of Atlanta, 1967–1969" in Jeremy Bonner, Mary

Beth Fraser Connolly, and Christopher Denny (eds.), *From Catholic Action to the People of God: American Lay Apostolates Before and After Vatican II* (New York: Fordham University Press, 2013), pp. 274–298.

7. See pastoral letters from Hallinan, May 24, 1962, November 8, 1963, and other documents in Archdiocesan Commission for Liturgy, folder 1, Archdiocese of Atlanta Archives (AAA).

8. Annals, March 1, 1964, entry, Our Lady of Lourdes (OLL), box 1, folder 5, annals January 1962–August 1973, Sisters of the Blessed Sacrament (SBS) archives. For a personal response, see author interview with Karen Allen and Sandra Criddell.

9. Annals, November 29, 1964 entry, OLL, box 1, folder 5, annals January 1962–August 1973, SBS archives.

10. Author telephone interview with Janis Griffin.

11. Personal interview with Karen Allen and Sandra Criddell, Our Lady of Lourdes parish, Atlanta, Georgia, July 12, 2012.

12. Author interview with Karen Allen and Sandra Criddell.

13. Sr. M. Patrick Thomas Lynch, Baton Rouge, LA, to Mother Mary Elizabeth, May 2, 1973, Our Lady of Lourdes, folder 11, correspondence, 1970–1974, SBS archives.

14. See Kevin M. Kruse, *White Flight: Atlanta and the Making of Modern Conservatism* (Princeton and Oxford: Princeton University Press, 2005).

15. On the transition of the neighborhood from white to black, see Kruse, *White Flight*, pp. 97–103.

16. See Gary Pomerantz, *Where Peachtree Meets Sweet Auburn: The Saga of Two Families and the Making of Atlanta* (New York: Scribner, 1996), pp. 251–275; and Ronald H. Bayor, *Race and the Shaping of Twentieth Century Atlanta* (Chapel Hill: University of North Carolina Press, 1996), pp. 115–116.

17. Suzanne Haugh, "Catholic Councilwoman Recalls Civil Rights History," *Georgia Bulletin*, January 21, 2010. Banks would go on to be the first African American woman on the Atlanta city council.

18. Author interview with Karen Allen and Sandra Criddell.

19. Annals, March 1965, folder 5, annals January 1962–August 1973, Our Lady of Lourdes box 1, SBS archives.

20. "A Decree Convoking the First Archdiocesan Synod of the Archdiocese of Atlanta," January 6, 1966, Archdiocese of Atlanta Synod (First), AAA.

21. "The Church of Christ: Decree Enacted by the First Synod of Archdiocese of Atlanta, 1966," Archdiocese of Atlanta Synod (First), AAA.

22. "Capsule History of the 1966 Lay Congress, Archdiocese of Atlanta," May 1966, Archdiocese of Atlanta Synod (First), AAA.

23. Jack and Alice Cawley, Atlanta, Georgia, from "As I Remember Him," the newsletter of the Cleveland Newman Alumni Association, June 1968, 10–11, quoted in Schwalm (ed.), "In His Own Words," p. 63.

24. From Hallinan to Dear Committee Member, July 1, 1965, Archdiocese of Atlanta Synod (First), AAA.

25. Sisters' Congress, preliminary meeting, December 18, 1965, Archdiocese of Atlanta Synod (First), AAA.

26. "The Church of Christ: Decree Enacted by the First Synod of Archdiocese of Atlanta, 1966," Archdiocese of Atlanta Synod (First), AAA.

27. "The Church of Christ: Decree Enacted by the First Synod of Archdiocese of Atlanta, 1966," p. 29, Archdiocese of Atlanta Synod (First), AAA.

28. Summary of committee reports to date, area chairmen meeting, April 4, 1966, Box 006/5, Synod (First 1966), 1964–1966, folder 1, Archdiocese of Atlanta Synod (First), 1964–1966, AAA.

29. Downtown parish meeting notes, January 11, 1967, OLL minutes boundaries, 1967, 1980.

30. Meeting notes, January 26, 1967, Our Lady of Lourdes correspondence, folder 1, AAA.

31. Meeting notes, January 26, 1967, Our Lady of Lourdes correspondence, folder 1, AAA.

32. Rev. John J. Mulroy to Bishop Bernardin, February 16, 1968; and Bernardin to Mulroy, February 19, 1968, in Sacred Heart Correspondence, folder 1, AAA.

33. Memorandum from Bishop Bernardin, RE: Parishes of Our Lady of Lourdes and Saint Paul of the Cross, [n.d.], AAA.

34. Memorandum from Bishop Bernardin, RE: Parishes of Our Lady of Lourdes and Saint Paul of the Cross, [n.d.], AAA.

35. See Kruse, *White Flight*, pp. 234–5.

36. "Arguments On Closing Of Drexel Aired at Education Board Meet," *Georgia Bulletin*, April 6, 1967, p. 1, 2.

37. "Drexel's Death Shows You Still Just Can't See Us," *Georgia Bulletin*, March 30, 1967, p. 5.

38. "Drexel Closing Final," *Georgia Bulletin*, April 20, 1967, p. 1.

39. From Richard Leary, CP, to Donnellan, August 20, 1969, Archdiocesan Commission for Liturgy, 1959–1984, folder, Atlanta, liturgy, 1959–1975, AAA.

40. From Michael A. Doyle, executive secretary, Archdiocesan Pastoral Council, to Donnellan, May 19, 1970, Archdiocesan Pastoral Council, folder 2, January–May, 1970, AAA.

41. From Rev. John J. Mulroy to Archbishop Thomas A. Donnellan, October 4, 1968, Sacred Heart correspondence, folder 1, AAA.

42. William R. Headley, "A Study of Attitudes Concerning Desegregation of Catholic Parishes Among Northeast Atlanta's White and Negro Catholics," a private report, June 1970, Our Lady of Lourdes reports and minutes, folder 2, AAA.

43. William R. Headley, "A Study of Attitudes Concerning Desegregation of Catholic Parishes among Northeast Atlanta's White and Negro Catholics," M.A. thesis, Atlanta University, 1970, pp. 56–70; also, William R. Headley, "A Study of Attitudes Concerning Desegregation of Catholic Parishes Among Northeast Atlanta's White and Negro Catholics," a private report, June 1970, Our Lady of Lourdes reports and minutes, folder 2, AAA.

44. Minutes of meeting of executive committee, June 10, 1970, Archdiocesan Pastoral Council, Archdiocesan Pastoral Council, folder 3, June–December 1970, AAA.

45. "Parish Profile: Our Lady of Lourdes," *Georgia Bulletin*, March 2, 1972, online archives.

46. Interview with Criddell and Allen.

47. Interview with Criddell and Allen; "Parish Profile: Our Lady of Lourdes," Our Lady of Lourdes new articles, AAA. On St. Anthony of Padua becoming an African American parish, see Thea Jarvis, "St. Anthony's: A History and a Homecoming," *Georgia Bulletin*, November 25, 1982, online archives.

48. "Parish Profile: Our Lady of Lourdes," *Georgia Bulletin*, March 2, 1972 online archives.

49. Sr. Mary Patrick Thomas Lynch, Baton Rouge, LA, to Mother Mary Elizabeth, May 2, 1973.

50. Sr. Maureen Immaculate, SBS, Atlanta, to Mother Mary Elizabeth, May 6, 1973. For figures from earlier years, Sister M. Judith, Observations Concerning Our Lady of Lourdes School, [n.d. – ca. 1973]. Both are in OLL, folder 11, correspondence, 1970–1974, SBS archives.

51. Sister M. Judith, Observations Concerning Our Lady of Lourdes School, [n.d. – ca. 1973].

52. Mother Mary Elizabeth, president, SBS, to Most Rev. Thomas A. Donnellan, Atlanta, October 12, 1973, OLL, folder 11, correspondence, 1970–1974.

53. Archbishop Thomas A. Donnellan to Reverend Mother Mary Elizabeth Fitzpatrick, SBS, October 24, 1973, OLL, folder 11, correspondence, 1970–1974.

54. "Study of Black America Featured in Curriculum," February 13, 1969, news clipping [uncertain publication], Our Lady of Lourdes Parish Files, AAA.

55. Our Lady of Lourdes parish bulletin, March 11 and 12, 1972, Our Lady of Lourdes bulletins, folder 4, AAA.

56. Our Lady of Lourdes bulletin, January 9, 1977, OLL bulletins, folder 6, 1977, AAA.

57. Previous quotation, Our Lady of Lourdes bulletin, December 28, 1975, OLL bulletins, folder 5, AAC; Our Lady of Lourdes bulletin, January 18, 1976, OLL bulletins, folder 5; for above examples see other bulletins in folders 5 and 6, AAA.

58. Our Lady of Lourdes bulletin, January 9, 1977, OLL bulletins, folder 6, 1977, AAC.

59. Our Lady of Lourdes Parish, 65th Anniversary Celebration, 1912–1977, OLL parish files, AAA.

60. From Fr. Frank J. Giusta to Monsignor Jerry Hardy, May 28, 1979 and June 16, 1979; Hardy to Giusta, June 25, 1979, for archdiocese continuing the subsidy; Our Lady of Lourdes correspondence, folder 1, AAA.

61. Evangelization flyer, October 1979, Our Lady of Lourdes correspondence, folder 1, AAA.

62. Memo from Fr. Frank J. Giusta to Most Rev. Thomas A. Donnellan, December 5, 1979, parish files, Our Lady of Lourdes, AAA.

63. Ibid.

64. Ibid.

65. Ibid.

66. Minutes of Meeting with Fathers Adamski, Giusta, and Gracz, September 23, 1980, Our Lady of Lourdes reports and missions, folder 1, AAA.

67. "An Architectural Review of Church Facilities," Our Lady of Lourdes Church, April 1980; and memoranda and correspondence in folder, Our Lady of Lourdes renovation project, 1980–1981, AAA.

68. Fr. Frank J. Giusta to Rev. Msgr. Jerry E. Hardy, August 9, 1982, with attached memo from Giusta to Most Rev. Thomas A. Donnellan, December 5, 1979 [revised 1982], in Our Lady of Lourdes boundaries, folder 2, AAA.

69. From Fr. Frank J. Giusta to Msgr. Jerry Hardy, October 5, 1982, Our Lady of Lourdes boundaries, folder 2, AAA.

70. See the letters and memoranda in Our Lady of Lourdes boundaries, folder 2, AAA.

71. "Archbishop Calls Music Instruction 'Up-To Date,'" *Georgia Bulletin*, March 16, 1967, p. 8.

72. Most Reverend Joseph J. Bernardin to Reverend John J. Mulroy, Sacred Heart Church, Atlanta, February 13, 1968, Archdiocesan Liturgical Commission, folder 4, 1968–1969, box 011/4, AAA.

73. Interview with Janis Griffin, February 20, 2014.

74. Interview with Janis Griffin, February 20, 2014.

75. Press release for March 23, 1982, folder, History-Blacks, AAA.

76. *What We Have Seen and Heard, A Pastoral Letter On Evangelization from the Black Bishops of the United States* (Cincinnati: St. Anthony Messenger Press, 1984), p. 2. On liturgy, see *In Spirit and Truth: Black Catholic Reflections on the Order of Mass*, Bishops' Committee on the Liturgy, National Conference of Catholic Bishops, 1988; *Plenty Good Room: The Spirit and Truth of African American Catholic Worship* (National Conference of Catholic Bishops, 1990).

77. "Black Catholic Ministry," Black Catholic ministry folder, AAA.

PART II

International Essays

8

CATHOLIC MOBILIZATION AND CHILEAN REVOLUTIONS, 1957–1989

Sol Serrano and Luz María Díaz de Valdés

This chapter examines the adaptation of Vatican II in the Archdiocese of Santiago, Chile, which legitimized and consolidated a social apostolate and grassroots organizations from 1957 through 1989. It explores Vatican II's new and participatory forms and language, which helped enact social and political transformations in Chilean society.

W HEN THE ARCHBISHOP OF SANTIAGO, CHILE, RAÚL SILVA Henríquez, initiated an agrarian reform on the ecclesiastical lands of his diocese in 1962, he informed Catholics, the clergy, and the wider society that his archdiocese would lead the renewal of the local church. He also noted that the church's opening up to the problems of the world in poor and underdeveloped societies would require a radical commitment to justice and to the poorest among them. The church of Santiago launched this initiative in the face of communism and capitalist conservatism, in the midst of the Cold War and three years after the Cuban Revolution. From the perspective of Silva and the Chilean context, the Second Vatican Council had political and pastoral dimensions: it called both for a structural reform inside of a democratic system and for bridging the gap between the church, the poor, and their social and economic problems.

The agrarian reform of 1962 and a process of general mission begun in 1963 were expressions that predated the social teachings promulgated at the Council. They were rooted in the experiences of social Catholicism as well as John XXIII's 1961 encyclical *Mater et Magistra*. But in the minds of the agrarian reform and general mission leaders, the Council also legitimized, expanded, and consolidated grassroots organizations, understood as Catholic organizations with a social and/or ritual nature working among the most vulnerable sectors of society: the peasants and the inhabitants of the urban slums. The leadership of Archbishop Silva put social ministry at the center of the archdiocesan mission, legitimizing what before had only been sporadic apostolic efforts in the social arena. In political terms, this shift sparked a huge upheaval that weakened the ecclesiastical hierarchy's historic alliance with the conservatives and strengthened links with the social Christians whose electoral power was rapidly increasing. The shift also made waves within the church and especially within the clergy.

Promoted by the institutional church, grassroots organizations responded to the pastoral call for Catholics to play a central role in politics and society and thus played an important role in the triumph of Christian Democrat candidate Eduardo Frei Montalva and in his government (1964–1970). What began as a font of optimism and boldness through the first half of the 1960s, however, by the end of the decade began to show serious signs of tension, confrontation, and polarization. This was made evident with the election of socialist Salvador Allende in 1970 and the enormous break it produced in the church of Santiago and in national Catholicism because of the participation and support for a Marxist government among a sector of the clergy, the lay leaders, and grassroots Catholics.

The coup d'état of 1973 abruptly ended this kind of Catholic association as the resulting military dictatorship of Augusto Pinochet (1973–1989) repressed free expression and political organization. Nevertheless, these same Catholic grassroots organizations were the only ones that were able to initially survive under the new regime. They became the space of solidarity among the poorest in their fight for the defense of human rights. In the face of the harshness of the regime's repression, priests and nuns worked to rebuild grassroots organizations in marginalized populations. The Archdiocese of Santiago became directly involved and led this process from the ground up, taking on the roles of articulating a message about human rights, coordinating defense actions for those persecuted by the regime, sheltering civil social organizations, and defending victims through the Vicariate of Solidarity. The Catholic hierarchy was arguably the only public body that had the legitimacy to play an active role in opening political dialogue, which would lay the foundation to bring about the transition to democracy at the end of the 1980s.

The reception and adaptation of the Second Vatican Council in Chile legitimized, expanded, and consolidated a new social apostolate and empowered the laity through different and dynamic grassroots organizations. In what follows, we examine a short history of the Archdiocese of Santiago and the Council encompassing the various conciliar sessions in Rome, the important participation of the archbishop of Santiago in those sessions, and the immediate reception of the Council, particularly the influence of the

1967 Synod of Santiago and the 1968 Medellín Conference of Latin American Bishops. We also explore a longer history of the archdiocese and the Council, spanning the era from the beginning of a broader social apostolate during the late 1950s to the period of the military dictatorship when the church and the grassroots organizations it supported prominently defended human rights.

Organizations before the Conciliar Era

Catholicism in Chile had strong roots in both the elite and the popular sectors. The Conservative Party was the political arm of the church until the opening decades of the twentieth century, when social Catholicism began to acquire political expression among the youth, especially those with a Jesuit education. The church hierarchy generally distrusted this group, the most emblematic case being that of the Jesuit Alberto Hurtado, who is now a saint. Beginning in the 1940s, the social apostolate was closely linked to the sociology of religion. In 1957, the Fédération Internationale des Instituts Catholiques de Recherches Socio-Religieuses was formed, with its headquarters in Freiburg, Switzerland. It included Latin American centers such as the Centro de Investigación y Acción Social (CIAS, the Center for Studies and Social Action), which Jesuits founded in Santiago to nourish the archdiocese with material for analysis, reflection, and pastoral planning.

The diocesan church continued with a ritual pastoral structure centered on the parish, while social Catholicism, principally through Catholic Action, created organizations for social development in working-class sectors. Especially relevant was the early presence of the church in the rural areas, which up until that time had languished in a practically colonial state.[1] The first rural organizations were small, but sufficiently visible so that conservatives accused them of participating in peasant demonstrations. These were the first groups to operate independently of the land owners. Among the urban dwellers, Juventud Obrera Católica (JOC, Catholic Youth Workers) was the most organized group. It developed recreational activities with a pastoral dimension. In the liturgy, Spanish, the guitar, and the participation of the laity in the readings were incorporated. In 1956, there were a total of seventy-eight JOC centers, at least one in each working class town.[2] The TECHO Foundation, also connected with the Jesuits, advised residents about building their own homes and trained women for professions in its Mothers' Centers. The Jesuit journal *Mensaje* noted in 1960 that TECHO had sixty-nine centers in twenty-two towns with an aggregate total of more than 3,000 members.[3]

This active participation in the formation and strengthening of working class organizations permitted the church to be present in the formation of the new *poblaciones callampas* ("mushroom colonies"), so named because they had sprung up overnight by occupying land on the outskirts of Santiago. An illustrative case is that of La Victoria slum district in Santiago. On October 30, 1957, at 6:30 in the morning, 1,200 families occupied an area of government land on the south side of Santiago. The church and the Communist Party were the strongest civil society institutions that participated in this occupation. A priest from the neighboring parish joined in the occupation. Catholic university students contributed toward housing and health care. Catholic welfare organizations arrived immediately. Caritas distributed food, clothing, and other basic necessities. The Jesuit organization Hogar de Cristo (Home of Christ) provided building materials and organized groups to assist in home construction projects. State repression was harsh, leading the then archbishop of Santiago, Cardinal José María Caro, to intervene with the Chilean president and mediate for the withdrawal of the police.[4]

Meanwhile, toward the end of the 1950s, a team of diocesan priests and religious officials began the meticulous organization of a general mission in the archdiocese, including consultation with French pastoral leaders who lent their expertise in pastoral learning processes. They studied the religious practices of the faithful, their perception of the church, and the needs and organization of the working-class sectors. These studies revealed alarming figures: 89 percent of those studied declared themselves to be Catholic, but fewer than 10 percent attended Mass regularly. The pastoral leaders of that time were concerned about preserving the faith, protecting the sacraments, and maintaining the discipline and influence of the church. But they also saw that it was necessary to reach the non-Catholic population and to provide a "systematic penetration and elevation of the structures of civil society."[5] The General Mission, designed in 1959, did not have enough support to accomplish its goals immediately. It would require an enormous mobilization. Suspicions from the conservative sectors of society also inhibited it.

The announcement of the Vatican Council and the first papal encyclicals of Pope John XXIII supported the claims of progressive Catholics that the social apostolate and the opening of the church to the world's problems were not peripheral concerns but rather were central to the magisterium and the wider church. The Council helped move social ministries from suspicion to legitimacy and also helped form a hierarchy in which reformers overshadowed conservatives. It also facilitated a shifted emphasis toward the social Christian center, represented by the Christian Democratic Party. Sudden change ensued from strong ecclesial leadership, both the new pope in Rome and the new archbishop in Santiago.

The Cardinal of the People

Raúl Silva Henríquez, a Salesian priest and bishop of the port of Valparaiso, was named archbishop of Santiago in 1961, apparently in part because he was the candidate neither of Catholic conservatives nor of social Christians. "Nobody was pleased with me," he recollected years later. Silva took over a complex archdiocese with 2,368,595 inhabitants, 154 parishes, 976 priests, and 2,517 women religious. "In every instant, one can see the agony of an era that is coming to an end," he observed in his inaugural homily. The announcement of the intent to hold a Council in January 1959 did not provoke an immediate reaction in Chile. In fact, Silva heard about it January the following year. It was *Mater et Magistra*, promulgated on May 15, 1961, that first marked his reformist vocation and in that sense also marked the beginning of the conciliar era in Chile: "For us, who believed that a complete revolution in the church with the desire for change was essential, that encyclical constituted, much more than a breath, a true cornerstone of the path that we would follow during the coming years."[6]

Silva reorganized the archbishop's secretariat, formed the Office of Planning, recruited a new cadre of young priest leaders, and promoted centers of religious sociology with their empirical studies serving as the basis of pastoral planning and change. Shortly after his appointment as archbishop, he announced the Plan for Pastoral Action for Santiago, which was later adopted by the episcopal conference for the whole country.[7] Silva also formed commissions of experts to study agrarian reform on church lands, self-construction of housing, and the general advancement of marginal peoples. Concurrently, he formed the theological commission, composed of renowned theologians from the faculty of theology at the Pontifical Catholic University of Chile, and charged them with studying the Vatican II documents.

One of the symbolic milestones that Silva launched was the agrarian reform of church lands two years before the state moved forward with such a process on both public lands and private estates. On being named cardinal in January 1962, Silva consulted with Pope John regarding his agrarian project. In his *Memoirs*, he recalls that the pope responded with a wink, "Do it. I will back you up."[8] When he returned to Chile, the Conferencia Episcopal de Chile, CECH (Chilean Episcopal Conference), with Silva's strong support, published the pastoral letter *La Iglesia y el problema del campesinado chileno* (The Church and the Problem of

Chilean Peasantry). In it, the bishops denounced rural poverty caused by the *latifundio* (large estates) and outlined an agrarian reform based on cooperativism.[9]

"Today on this land ends the system of *inquilinaje* [the institution of tenant labor on large estates]," Cardinal Silva proclaimed. *Inquilinaje* dated from the seventeenth century and was the backbone of an immovable agrarian social structure in which 80 percent of the land was composed of *latifundios*, an arrangement that had long been considered one of the most unjust in Chile. One Catholic newspaper deemed the cardinal's announcement on July 28, 1962, a "pastoral bomb." The decision outraged traditional Catholics, provoked mistrust on the left, and earned the praise of Catholic Christian Democrats. For the left, as Communist senator and future Nobel laureate in literature Pablo Neruda put it, this move was no more than "a few acres to obscure the ecclesiastical servility in the face of imperialism and oligarchy."[10] In fact, the lands reapportioned were smaller properties, but they would become a pastoral, political, and social bomb. One of the peasant farmers present commented incredulously, "And to think that we were the first."[11] He was just as surprised as the rest of Chilean society.

The shock of the July announcement was exacerbated when the same hierarchy assumed stronger leadership within the social apostolate. In September, the pastoral letter *El deber político y social de los católicos en la hora presente* (The Political and Social Duties of Catholics at the Present Hour) got to the heart of the matter. It defended the reforms and weighed in on the social problems of the country and region and on the ideological context of the moment. It denounced the *latifundios*, urban marginalization, homeless families, unemployment, unequal income distribution, and the selfishness of the owners of capital. After criticizing communism, it called on Catholics to participate in a structural reform inspired by humanist and Christian values.[12]

Many observers have attributed the change in the ecclesiastical hierarchy in 1962 principally to the international context of the Cold War and the Cuban Revolution of 1959, which led the United States government and the Vatican to turn their attention to Latin America. Domestically, analysts note the likelihood that the alliance on the left, which included the communists, would have gained control of the government, given the high voter turnout for the 1958 presidential election.[13] This context is essential for understanding the shift in the Catholic hierarchy's social action, but it ignores the religious dimension of the change that had been developing since the middle of the century in the social apostolate. The winds of change from the Council were blowing in the same direction, as the ecclesiastical hierarchy and the majority of Catholic Chileans saw it.

The Beginnings of the Council

Before his departure for Rome, Silva met with various groups and Catholic movements to explain the purpose of the Council, which he knew firsthand from his participation in the Council's Central Preparatory Commission. His message was short and clear: the church wanted to discern the needs of the present moment from the perspective of the Gospel, to open itself to society, to fight for justice, and to defend the path of social reform rather than revolution.[14] In this church, the laity would have a central role. Silva challenged university students to be reformers of the social structure in the pursuit of justice.[15] He also met with the 300 priests of the archdiocese to discuss the pastoral plan, the formation of grassroots communities, and the duties of the church to denounce injustice and to make the problems of the world its own. Silva and the Episcopal Conference clearly accentuated the aspect of the coming Council they found most urgent for the Chilean society, and that was social change.

At noon on October 11, the opening day of the Council, bells rang in all the country's churches. The Chilean delegation arrived in Rome enthusiastic about the Council as a result of the intense debate the preparatory documents had incited among them. Various Chilean and Latin American bishops, aware of the dynamics of the Roman Curia, were skeptical about the effectiveness of their participation; they believed they would ultimately have to approve the outlines the Vatican bureaucracy had already composed. But the first Council session increased their hope when the bishops voted for the creation of commissions to work on the schemata. Subsequently the episcopal conferences from Latin America worked in unison despite how marginal they were in a Council the European conferences tended to dominate.[16] One principal theme for the Chilean conference, over which Silva presided, was compassionate and welcoming pastoral care rather than a pastoral approach that was defensive and condemnatory. Silva spoke as the representative of the bishops of South America and criticized the notion that the church should be a punishing judge, alienating the faithful and causing dissent among Catholics.[17]

A Church That Goes to the Poor

The first period of the Council coincided with the beginning of the archdiocesan General Mission. Its organizers tried to link both events, but the Council seemed distant. "It was just a conference off in Rome," said a leader of the JOC who recalled that moment.[18] Nonetheless, the energetic social outreach of the mission was consistent with the emerging tone of the Council.

Under the slogan "Do you know that God loves you?" thousands of laity, women religious, and priests initiated a tremendous mission that addressed more than 2 million residents from both the rural and urban sectors.

The mission was unprecedented in its magnitude and style. For the first time, missionaries did not stay in the house of the land owners, but rather with the peasant farming families. They used the radio as a mode of pastoral communication, transmitting radio dramas with famous actors and episodes that dealt with themes of everyday life: marriage, educating children, workers' rights, participation, and solidarity. Sermons applied doctrine to daily life. Catechism classes featured slides depicting the life of Jesus and movies with religious themes. Popular songs and the use of some Spanish enlivened celebrations of the Mass. Leaders educated mothers as catechists and identified active Catholics to establish the first grassroots communities. All told the mission left an indelible mark in the popular Catholic memory among lower-class Catholics. New voices surfaced: that of women religious, whose warm approach to the people impacted the clergy; that of young seminarians with a marked vocation for service to the people; that of catechist mothers; and the voices of children and youth who would later become social activists.[19]

The growing Catholic presence among the organized lower-class sectors during the 1960s occurred simultaneously with competition between the left and the Christian Democrats for the support of these same sectors. In September 1964, the Christian Democratic candidate, Eduardo Frei, won the presidential election by a wide margin over his socialist contender, Salvador Allende. The support he received from the church was absolutely essential to his electoral success, and the convergence between the hierarchy and social Catholics was evident. Extensive and well-structured Catholic organizations poured out support for Frei. Church initiatives such as land reform, working-class advancement, and the social analysis of marginality and development were programmatic pillars in the new government, which got started under the slogan "Revolution in Freedom." Consequently, many among the clergy and lay consultants believed it was no longer necessary to maintain the Catholic social action network. The cardinal was opposed to such withdrawal, however, and insisted on maintaining a pastoral vision focused on the most vulnerable sectors of society.

A growing urban population imposed a tremendous pastoral challenge for the church. The General Mission had shown the vitality of marginalized populations and, at the same time, the difficulty of building a pastoral structure because of the scarcity of priests. To enhance the work among the poor sectors that archdiocesan officials had defined as a priority, in 1964 the archdiocese established the Vicariate of the Southern Zone.[20] The

Southern Zone was "a city within the city," a "poverty belt," with the highest unemployment rate in Santiago, and home to the poorest of the poor. In this context, and especially after the General Mission, an initiative emerged among some priests and nuns to live and serve among these slums and their inhabitants. This practice motivated "those Christians in the southern zone to take on responsibilities in the social sphere and in popular organizations."[21]

The experience of pastoral agents in the slums is illustrated in the work of the religious of the Congregation of the Sacred Hearts. Together with the celebrated Esteban Gumucio, mystic and poet, three young priests entered into this witness and ministry. They arrived from their novitiates with excellent education in the latest European theology, liturgical ministry, and ethics. According to one of the novices, Patricio Frías, this training made them feel sure of themselves. "We thought that we knew how to get along among the people, how to behave, and how to minister," Frías recalled in a 2012 conversation. One had to deliver a "living, real, authentic Gospel," with "neither sanctimony nor ritualistic formalities." The liturgy should be "within the reach of the people, very participatory, incarnated in the reality of the people, in the reality of the worker, the reality of the community." Frías and the other novices believed that they were "in line with Vatican II," with its search for the "transformation of structures" and "the promotion of social organizations." To achieve this, one had to reach "union leaders, community leaders, and the Mothers' Centers." The priest's life was to be the same as that of the rest of the population.[22] "They began to speak about another type of relationship," remembers one resident, Luis Medina, "in which we are brothers, where we must get to know each other." "The priest is no longer on a pedestal," Medina says, "He is a friend, a neighbor, on a first name basis."[23] These priests arrived without their cassocks but with a new pastoral focus. They, like others after them, took charge of pastoral work and the formation of parishes in the urban slums of the capital.[24]

This intense Catholic participation in social organizations blurred the lines of an old division between Catholics and militants from the left. What had been formulated on the theological level, particularly in some European intellectual circles, was lived at the experiential level in many areas of the Southern Zone of Santiago. A new stage was beginning for the Chilean church, inspired and reinforced by the Council, and connected to the profound ideological conflicts of society. Indeed, the Chilean church was an essential part of those conflicts.

Institutionally, the Council was received in Santiago with the synod Cardinal Silva convened in 1966. One indication of the new ideas brought from Rome was seen in the willingness to receive suggestions and comments from the faithful, who submitted more than 120,000 written comments when asked to do so as they left church after Mass. Approximately 400 people attended the synod, almost half of whom were laity. The final study, *Iglesia de Santiago, ¿qué dices de ti misma?* (Church of Santiago, What Do You Have to Say about Yourself?), synthesized the changes the diocese and society had experienced since the 1950s.[25] Its originality was in its use of language that was more pastoral than normative, in its inductive method, in the incorporation of opposing viewpoints, and especially for its dialogue between ecclesial ministry and society. It was an effort that mobilized Catholics as well as an encounter between various Catholic groups that confronted one another dramatically a few months later in 1968.

Revolution of Catholics

On Sunday, August 11, 1968, the doors of the Cathedral of Santiago were chained shut. From its towers, which looked toward the Plaza de Armas, hung a banner that read, "Por una Iglesia junto al pueblo y sus luchas" (For a Church united with the people and their struggles). The cathedral had been overtaken by a group of priests, nuns, and mostly laity from the union and working-class sectors in Southern Zone parishes, protesting the meager commitment of the Chilean and Latin American church to the poor and the scant participation of the laity in ecclesial governance. With this act, carried out days before the Second Conference of Latin American Bishops in Medellín, the church occupier group demanded a "poor, free, servant Church open to humankind." Cardinal Silva harshly criticized the occupation of the cathedral and immediately brought sanctions against the priests who participated. His words reflected the gravity of their actions: "The actions of a few out-of-control priests," he declared to the press immediately following the action, "have led a group of laypersons and youth to bring about one of the saddest actions in church history."[26]

The occupation of the cathedral and the group Iglesia Joven (Young Church) that emerged from the event marked the beginning of a period of turmoil for Catholicism and for Chilean society. Critics exhibited a growing dissatisfaction that the pace of change was not rapid nor broad and deep enough to meet the need. The breath of fresh air that the Council brought, received with hope and jubilation years before, was now triggering confusion, frustration, and internal crisis within some groups of the Chilean and also the Latin American church.

At the same time, the Second Conference of Latin American Bishops in Medellín, convened from August 26 through September 8, 1968, was a catalyst for Catholic progressive forces of the region, both reformists and those leftist forces that emerged at the end of the 1960s. The objective of Medellín was the adaptation and enactment of the conclusions of Vatican II to the specific Latin American reality. Intentionally or not, one result of Medellín was an internal ecclesial debate that lasted for the whole period of this chapter's study, even down to the present. For the architects of the Medellín conclusions, the Council would only be received and adapted in the region if it took charge of the continent's serious social problems, especially the injustice, marginalization, and oppressive structures that had plunged a large part of the population into a situation of extreme poverty. Along these lines, the concept of "institutionalized violence," used to describe the situation of structural injustice in the region, was essential, but also extremely controversial.[27]

From that point on, Medellín validated a whole new school of Catholic thought surrounding the issues of poverty and Latin American structures that had been in development since at least the beginning of the 1960s. The concepts of "dependence," the "poor," and "liberation" united all the new religious and political forces from the left and those who endorsed a revolutionary path. These were the pillars on which liberation theology was built, gaining ground after the Medellín conference. This theology, notwithstanding the many differences among liberation theologians, takes some elements of the Marxist thought and suggests that Jesus addressed his message to the poor and, moreover, that he had been one of them. Therefore, according to this line of thinking, the poor should be at the center of the church's teachings and ministry in a material sense, even to the point of supporting the struggles of the oppressed for life and justice.[28]

In Chile, a clergy progressively more committed to politics and socialism and a mainly social Christian, reformist hierarchy comprised the primary camps that debated the role of the church in the nation during these years. The election of socialist Salvador Allende as president of the republic in September 1970, with the huge support that he obtained from the popular and working-class sectors, symbolically expressed the desire for commitment and political participation by the so-called forward-thinking clergy of Santiago.

Allende's victory brought political participation with it, both from religious agents as well as some Catholic popular organizations that from the outset of his presidency chose to defend a government they believed was theirs. According to Father Pierre Dubois, advisor to the Movimiento Obrero de Acción Católica (MOAC, Workers' Movement for Catholic Action), "[There was] a desire to help consolidate a worker reality, a will to cooperate in the construction of socialism. It appeared to be a Christian necessity."[29] One female resident from La Victoria recalls that many Christians were "doubly militant," both Christian and leftist. Even the parish priest for the slum's parish, the Dutchman Santiago Thijssen, began to speak not only of syndicalism, as he normally had, but also to "make comparisons between Christianity and socialism." Thijssen mobilized residents from the neighborhood Council in defense of the government and organized a sort of civil defense. Seminars on Marxism were organized in which participants opined that Marxism offered "better modes of analysis to interpret and understand the world" as compared to social Christianity.[30] During this same time period, the priests' founding of the clerical group Cristianos por el Socialismo (CpS, Christians for Socialism) impacted and divided Chilean Catholics despite its relatively small numbers.[31]

The Chilean Episcopal Conference reacted almost immediately to CpS and initiated an exchange of documents that was both encouraging and tense. The bishops allowed that the priests might have a political preference but argued that they should not publicly adopt partisan positions. First, they pointed out that if a priest's political position was presented as a consequence of his Christian faith, it condemned "any other option implicitly" and infringed on "the liberty of other Christians."[32] Second, the prelates criticized the actions of CpS for encouraging the participation of Christians and, more seriously, of the church, in Allende's revolutionary political process. As Cardinal Silva put it, CpS leaders were misinterpreting the Council and were making a "caricature of Christianity," stripping it down to the point of "reducing it to a socioeconomic and political system" divested of its great religious values.[33]

The CpS maintained that they were in line with Vatican II and Medellín. One of its principal leaders, the Jesuit Gonzalo Arroyo, made it clear that the objective was neither the defense of Marxism nor of Marxist political parties, nor even of Allende's government, but rather to respond to a "a demand of faith for a true liberation of the Chilean people." Liberation was a task in which Christians and Marxists should "walk together in a common political action toward a historic project of liberation." Therefore, proponents of Marxism and Christianity had to put aside their past differences in the face of the needs of the people who cried out for them to be united.[34]

For Sister Francisca Morales of the Chilean religious congregation Amor Misericordioso, who participated in CpS, relations with the hierarchy and Cardinal Silva were a "tug of war." The hierarchy could not be ignorant of the fact that the priests and nuns exercising their apostolate in the slums of Santiago were the same ones who belonged to CpS. They were "active Church militants" to whom "pastoral confidence" had been entrusted.[35]

But they had strayed from doctrine and constituted the ideal flank for attack by those who accused the church as a whole of being allied with communism.

These disagreements escalated in the years of Popular Unity. The church not only found itself in the middle of the political and social conflicts. Some of its members, such as those in the CpS, participated beginning in 1968 as active Christian agents who fostered in the name of their faith the changes Chilean society experienced. This participation was mainly reflected in their political and ideological discourse, which attracted the interest of the regional and national media, along with their explicit and strategic support of the Allende government.

The military coup of September 1973 formally dismantled all this politicization and specifically the movement of CpS. One month later, the hierarchy released the document *Fe cristiana y actuación política* (Christian Faith and Political Behavior), which condemned CpS and prohibited priests and nuns from membership.[36] This document ended a period of disputes and misunderstandings within the church. Old divisions were left behind as a new context challenged the church.

Defense of Human Rights

The coup d'état in Chile on the morning of September 11, 1973, initiated for the Catholic Church a period of uncertainty and trial that tested its institutional, pastoral, and theological structures. In this new stage of repression, massive human rights violations, and the destruction of the social fabric, the Catholic Church was one of the very few institutions left standing. For some pastoral agents and laity, the Catholic Church found evangelical meaning in its mission as defender of the persecuted and the dispossessed. In the words of Francisca Morales: "Had there not already been an established church with the presence of priests, nuns, and laypersons, it would have been very difficult to build everything that was built in the first moment."[37] Even early on during the Pinochet regime, the church was able to reorganize and consolidate its place and role in the new context of military dictatorship, which lasted until 1989.

The archdiocesan church and its local communities performed new tasks: being "a haven for the persecuted," "a voice for the voiceless," "a defender of those who suffer from persecution and hunger," and "a meeting place" for the organizational initiatives even of groups that were non-Catholic.[38] Civil society began to reengage and organize through gatherings inside the churches, chapels, and the surrounding offices and rooms. In this way, some of the most important responses emerged, such as the *comedores infantiles* (children's soup kitchens); *comprando juntos* (buying cooperatives); health teams; women's and human rights workshops; and committees on homelessness, debt, and unemployment.

The ecclesiastic hierarchy stood behind these organizations and took concrete steps in defense of human rights. In October 1973, Cardinal Silva and leaders from other churches created the Comité Ecuménico de Cooperación para la Paz en Chile (COPACHI, Ecumenical Committee of Cooperation for Peace in Chile), with the objective of tending to the families of victims of repression they encountered "knocking on the Church doors." They offered these victims legal aid and other assistance. This organization functioned until the end of 1975, when General Pinochet dissolved it with the accusation that it entailed church intervention in political matters and furnished aid to Marxist-Leninists with the aim of destabilizing the regime. Cardinal Silva followed these orders, but on January 1, 1976, he created the Vicaría de la Solidaridad (Vicariate of Solidarity). This was a dependent institution of the Catholic Church, defender of the human rights of those persecuted by the regime. The Vicariate of Solidarity also took responsibility for the organization, financing, and coordination of community initiatives that had sprung up spontaneously.[39]

One expression of the adaptation that the church displayed to confront the new context was the *comunidades eclesiales de base* (CEBs, base or basic ecclesial communities), which emerged at the beginning of the 1960s during the General Mission and were promoted in the conferences of Medellín and the 1979 Latin American bishops' conference in Puebla, Mexico. The CEBs were grassroots expressions of the church, and for some they were an "awakening of the laity" that proliferated in the seventies and eighties as organizations of solidarity and also pockets of opposition to the dictatorship.[40]

This new context also led the church to produce both a teaching and a ministry focused on human rights and solidarity with the people. Church leaders published many documents, organized meetings, and directed evangelical messages to the regime's authorities through Eucharistic and liturgical acts. The church declared 1978 the year of human rights, the same year the regime carried out a "national enquiry" to validate its continuity and set the institutional foundations through a new constitution. The Archdiocese of Santiago convened workshops and two national meetings in September and October in which participants devised conceptual and theological definitions surrounding human rights. It was in such gatherings that, five years after the coup, religious and laity reflected on the Chilean reality.[41]

On November 22, 1978, an international symposium was held: "La Iglesia y la dignidad del hombre, sus derechos y deberes en el mundo de hoy" (The Church and the Dignity of Man, Its Rights and Duties in the World Today). The Cathedral of Santiago received specialists in human rights from the U.S. and European churches, representatives of other Christian churches, international institutions, and other groups specializing in the topic. Participants composed and signed the *Carta de Santiago de Chile* (Letter from Santiago, Chile), in which they expressed global concern surrounding the topic of human rights in the country.[42] It was via a pastoral on human rights and through the Vicariate of Solidarity that the Chilean church was able to give meaning to its religious and political mission following the coup d'état. This response emerged completely unforeseen, but it also connected in a fundamental way with the expressions of the Second Vatican Council, with the episcopal conference of Medellín, and with the encyclicals of Pope John XXIII and Pope Paul VI on the subject of human rights.[43]

The majority position of the Chilean church surrounding human rights created unity within the church, a unity that had been under threat just a few years before, and determined the parameters and limits of a coordinated action. This stance, however, brought recrimination from the right and some conservative sectors of society, which reacted against what they decried as the "manipulation" of the church for political ends. Critics alleged the actions of church leaders distorted the meaning of Vatican II. The editors of the influential newspaper *El Mercurio* demonstrated their disdain for the international symposium, which they considered to be a source of division among Christians, and even said that "it can only be compared to the occupation of the Cathedral that occurred in August of 1968."[44]

The defense of human rights that marked the 1970s and the existing differences among Catholics were reflected in the Third General Conference of Latin American Bishops in Puebla at the end of that decade. Some of the main disagreements revolved around the concept of the poor, liberation theology, politics, and the role of the church in society. Some thought that erroneous interpretations from Medellín should be corrected. The "preferential option for the poor" articulated at Puebla encompassed the conviction of participants and observers alike that priests should be concerned with unity and relinquish all political party ideologies. Nevertheless, the Puebla conference also confirmed the unconditional defense of human rights and the need for the church to take on the role of human rights defender, confronting the military dictatorships that were spreading across Latin America. Citing that stance of the bishops at Puebla, Chilean church leaders called for a prophetic church in which the voices of the most forward thinking would formally unite with the Catholic hierarchy to denounce the military dictatorship in Chile.[45]

Paths of Reconciliation

A subsequent event that caused tension between the military regime and the church of Santiago was the death of the French priest André Jarlan. It happened on the night of September 4, 1984, in the slum of La Victoria after a protest day similar to many other such days that marked the national scene from 1983 to 1986. A bullet killed Jarlan while he was praying, and word of his demise spread rapidly through the slum. The new cardinal of Santiago, Juan Francisco Fresno, who was named on May 6, 1983, offered to give the last rites to Jarlan in the Cathedral of Santiago. There was a massive attendance and the consequences were much greater than what had been foreseen.

Within this new context of civil resistance, the church was once again put to the test. The death of André Jarlan made him into a martyr of repression, not only for the poor in the slums of La Victoria but also for all those opposed to the regime. His death represented "a tremor in the consciences of Chileans. A tremor that awoke with more strength than before, reflection, the desire for change, the unity of the residents."[46] The topic of institutio- nalized violence that had arisen out of Medellín returned with force along with the question of the legitimacy of the use of violence to overthrow the dictatorship. The church of the slums attempted to confront the regime's violence with "active nonviolence," understood as a "force of liberation." As the *Boletín Zona Sur (Southern Zone Bulletin)* put it, "One must be con- scious of the injustice that oppresses us, lose the fear, and overcome passivity in order to be capable of discovering the abuses and commit oneself to liberation."[47]

The case of parish priest Pierre Dubois of La Victoria was emblematic insofar as he committed himself to nonviolent action to ignite what he called "the strength of the organized settler." He worked to convince residents to use methods of nonviolent protest in creative ways. Sister María Inés Urrutia recalls a time when he bought hundreds of soccer balls and the settlers spent "the whole day playing so that the *pacos* [cops] couldn't come in." The authorities referred to Dubois as "the head of the opposition" and "the leader of the slum protests."[48] Their antagonism toward him culminated in his expulsion from the country, along with two other foreign missionaries.

Concurrent with such protests, some leaders of the church initiated a new phase: a commitment to democracy. First, it was considered essential to work on creating awareness of democracy and the ways the people could put it into practice. The document published by the Episcopal Conference in 1983, *Para una real Democracia* (In Order to Have a Real Democracy) laid out some definitions and lines of action.[49] At the same time, the ecclesial base communities from the Vicariate of Solidarity and the Southern Zone received political training, and many workshops were carried out related to faith and politics.[50]

Cardinal Fresno, who generated less contempt from the authorities of the dictatorship than did Cardinal Silva, sought out paths to reconciliation in a still fractured and fearful Chilean society. In 1985, he proposed the organization of an institution with the aim of reaching agreement between various political constituencies to achieve a peaceful transition to democracy. This generated a bilateral rejection both from supporters of the regime, who saw a threat to the regime's continuity under such an agreement, as well as from those who wanted an abrupt end to the dictatorship and the immediate removal of Pinochet. Fresno coordinated a series of meetings with political leaders from the right, the center, and the left. Thus was born the *Acuerdo Nacional para la transición a la plena democracia* (National Agreement for the Transition to a Full Democracy), which achieved some basic consensus with great difficulty, specifically concerning the rejection of violence and a willingness to have a dialogue between the regime and those with other political views.

Pinochet's government vehemently rejected the National Agreement. Nevertheless, it was the first instance of a meeting between political forces that had previously been scattered, and it opened the path toward a dialogue among the forces of the opposition and those on the right. The mere fact of having them sit at the same table was a feat of a magnitude that can only be fully appreciated from the standpoint of those who have lived within a country that suffered radical violence and profound mistrust. Following the National Agreement, and under the initial leadership of the church, the political forces took on the role appropriate to them to reach agreements and forge the alliances that finally allowed for a peaceful transition to democracy following the plebiscite of 1988.

Vatican II and Catholic Mobilization

Chilean Catholics' initial reaction to the Second Vatican Council was that it was an ecclesial conference in Rome primarily focused on internal matters of the church. The vast majority of the faithful, as some studies have shown, at first identified the Council with liturgical changes. But given its consequences in Chilean society, Vatican II came to be most identified with the sociopolitical changes that occurred in Chile during the years before and especially in the wake of the Council.

The Council found in the Archdiocese of Santiago a fertile terrain, especially with the 1950s' history of dialogue and practice between the church and society in which the role of the church moved from addressing the welfare needs of the poor to the organization of the poor for their own advancement of human rights and social progress. In this way, the Council came to legitimize that experience and brought new forms and a new language with which to participate in and in some cases enact the social and political transformations of Chilean society.

This situation produced tensions, differences, and conflicts within the Chilean church as church leaders brought their understanding of the Council to bear on the social problems and political conflicts of their society. The church thus developed its own responses in the spirit of the Council: land reform, the occupation of lands on the outskirts of Santiago, liturgical changes, grassroots organizations, ecclesial communities, social participation, the defense of human rights, the search for political dialogue, and the defense of democracy.

Conciliar teachings provided a basis for these changes and for the adaptation to rapidly changing contexts, which in less than a decade ranged from democratic reformism, to socialism, to a dictatorship. The Chilean church's early thinking and experience among the lower-class sectors of society facilitated its capacity to adapt to these changing contexts, demonstrated its commitment to the poor, and gave it the tools to act as well as grounds for respect, to some extent even from the new regime. Thus, a confluence of historical factors, among them the general norms established at Vatican II as articulated for Latin America in the Latin American episcopal conferences of Medellín and of Puebla, enabled the Chilean church to take on an active role in representing and empowering the poor and becoming a key agent of change in Chilean society.

NOTES

1. In 1952, the Asociación Sindical Chilena (ASICH), the first rural Catholic union, was founded by Father Hurtado, as was the Acción Católica Rural. The Instituto de Educación Rural was founded in 1954 for the purpose of training leaders. *Mensaje* 59 (1957), 182–192.

2. Tracey Lynn Jaffe, "In the Footsteps of *Cristo Obrero*: Chile's Young Catholic Workers Movement in the Neighborhood, Factory and Family, 1946–1976," unpublished PhD diss., University of Pittsburgh, 2009, p. 50.

3. Mensaje 90 (1960), 256.

4. Mario Garcés, *Tomando su sitio. El movimiento de pobladores de Santiago, 1957–1970* (Santiago: Lom Ediciones, 2002), pp. 338–348.

5. Archdiocese of Santiago archive (AAS), Fondo General (general collection), Legajo (file) 172, no. 10, Misión General.

6. Ascanio Cavallo, *Memorias: Cardenal Raúl Silva Henríquez* (Santiago: Ediciones Copygraph, 1991), vol. I, p. 218.

7. Asamblea Plenaria Conferencia Episcopal de Chile, "Mientras el mundo marcha, la Cruz permanece," August 8, 1961, accessed at documentos. http://documentos .iglesia.cl/documento.php?id=965 on January 18, 2014.

8. Cavallo, *Memorias*, p. 231.

9. *La Iglesia y el problema del campesinado chileno*, pastoral document, Obispos de la Conferencia Episcopal Chilena, March 1, 1962, accessed at documentos. http:// documentos.iglesia.cl/documento.php?id=968, on January 18, 2014.

10. *Mensaje* 114 (1962), 521.

11. *La Voz*, September 20, 1962.

12. *La Voz*, October 7, 1962, p. 7. *La Voz* was an official newspaper of the archdiocese, managed by the laity.

13. Brian H. Smith, *The Church and Politics in Chile: Challenges to Modern Catholicism* (Princeton, Princeton University Press, 1982), pp. 106–125.

14. *La Voz*, August 12, 1962.

15. *La Voz*, August 12, 1962.

16. Luis Antonio Díaz, *Concilio Vaticano II y las intervenciones del Cardenal Silva Henríquez* (Santiago: Ediciones Mensaje, 2007); Robert Pelton, "The Reception of Vatican II in Latin America: A North American Perspective," *Theological Studies* 74 (2013), 1–9.

17. Cavallo, Memorias, vol. I, p. 270.

18. Quoted in Jaffe, "In the Footsteps," p. 194.

19. AAS, Fondo General, Legajo (file) 172, no. 10, Misión General.

20. Initially the Southern Zone Vicariate consisted of the deaneries of San Eugenio, Gran Avenida, Cardenal Caro, Santa Rosa, San Bernardo, and Puente Alto, totaling 35 parishes and 77 chapels. Later a deanery of San Joaquín was formed, that of Puente Alto shifted to the Eastern Zone, and that of San Bernardo became an autonomous vicariate.

21. Esteban Gumucio, SSCC, remembered the history of the Southern Vicariate in the second zonal meeting of laypeople, on August 12, 1984. *Boletín Zona Sur*, III: 21 (1984).

22. Personal interview with Patricio Frías, September 13, 2012, Santiago de Chile.

23. David Fernández, *Historia Oral de la Iglesia Católica en Santiago de Chile. Desde el Concilio Vaticano II hasta el golpe militar* (Cadiz: Servicio de Publicaciones Universidad de Cádiz, 1966) p. 180.

24. Cristian Venegas and Enrique Moreno, *Conversaciones con Esteban Gumucio* (Santiago: Congregación de los Sagrados Corazones, 2004) pp. 189–222.

25. Comisión Arquidiocesana Postconciliar, *¿Iglesia de Santiago, qué dices de ti misma?* (Santiago: Ediciones Paulina, 1968).

26. "Cardenal califica de profanación la toma de la Iglesia Catedral," El Mercurio, August 13, 1968, p. 18.
27. Conferencia General del Episcopado Latinoamericano, "Documento sobre la Paz" in *La Iglesia en la actual trasformación de América Latina a la luz del Concilio* (Santiago: Ediciones Paulinas, 1969).
28. Disagreements exist surrounding the influence that liberation theology had at the Medellín conference. For some liberation theologians, such as Gustavo Gutiérrez, liberation theology was born in Medellín. For others, such as the general secretary of CELAM (Consejo Episcopal Latinoamericano, Latin American Episcopal Council), Alfonso López Trujillo, the Marxist political and ideological elements that later manifested in liberation theology were not present in Medellín.
29. Personal interview with Father Pierre Dubois, May 27, 2009, Santiago de Chile.
30. Personal interview with Alicia Cáceres, resident of La Victoria, September 7, 2012.
31. For a bibliography about the group Christians for Socialism, see Mario Amorós, "La Iglesia que nace del pueblo: relevancia histórica del movimiento Cristianos por el Socialismo" in Julio Pinto (ed.), *Cuando hicimos historia. La experiencia de la Unidad Popular* (Santiago: Lom Ediciones, 2005).
32. "Evangelio, política y socialismos," Conferencia Episcopal de Chile, May 27, 1971, in Carlos Oviedo Cavada (ed.), *Documentos del Episcopado: Chile, 1970–1973* (Santiago: Ediciones Mundo, 1974).
33. "Carta de S. Em. el Cardenal Raúl Silva Henríquez al P. Gonzalo Arroyo, s.j., en respuesta a la invitación al 'Primer Encuentro Latinoamericano de Cristianos por el Socialismo'" in *Cristianos latinoamericanos y socialismo* (Bogotá, Colombia: Centro de Estudios para el Desarrollo e Integración de América Latina, 1972), pp. 204–209.
34. *Carta de Gonzalo Arroyo por los Cristianos por el Socialismo al Cardenal Raúl Silva Henríquez*, March 17, 1972. Archivo Chile, accessed at www.archivochile.com /Mov_sociales/iglesia_popular/MSiglepopu0002.pdf, January 18, 2014.
35. Personal interviews with Sister Francisca Morales, October 22 and November 11, 2009, Santiago de Chile
36. "Fe cristiana y actuación política," Conferencia Episcopal de Chile, August 1, 1973, in Cavada (ed.), *Documentos del Episcopado*.
37. Personal interviews with Sister Francisca Morales, October 22 and November, 2009, Santiago de Chile.
38. Boletín Zona Sur, III:21 (1984). Quoted phrases from Esteban Gumucio, at the second zonal meeting of laypeople, on August 12, 1984, where he recalls the history of the Southern Vicariate.
39. The Vicariate of Solidarity disseminated its thoughts and works through numerous writings and in the magazine *Solidaridad*, published between May 1976 and October 1988. Most of this documentation can be found in the virtual archive of the Vicariate of Solidarity, at www.archivovicaria.cl.
40. Many articles were dedicated to the basic ecclesial communities in *Solidaridad*. Among them are articles in issue 78, in September 1979, and issue 91, in April 1980.
41. Most of the statements were published in *Solidaridad*, "Derechos Humanos: La gran tarea de nuestro tiempo," no. 59, November 1978.
42. *Solidaridad*, no. 61, December 1978, special issue dedicated to coverage of the International Symposium on Human Rights.

43. One of the documents that outline the topic of human rights was developed by the Vicariate of Solidarity for the Conference of Puebla, in Mexico in 1979. "La Vicaría de la Solidaridad: una experiencia de Iglesia," archive of the Vicariate of Solidarity, April 1978.

44. *Solidaridad*, no. 61, December 1978.

45. "Monseñor Fernando Ariztía: "Reafirmar liberación de los pobres," Solidaridad, no. 54, September 1978; "Desde el pueblo," preparatory document of the Chilean delegation for the Conference of Puebla, *Solidaridad*, no. 63, January 1979.

46. *Boletín Zona Sur* dedicated a complete edition to cover the death of André Jarlan, III:22, October 1984.

47. "Más allá de la protesta y la violencia," *Boletín Zona Sur*, no. 9, July 1983.

48. Personal interview with Sister María Inés Urrutia, September 7, 2012.

49. *Para una real Democracia*, Comité Permanente de la Conferencia Episcopal de Chile, October 14, 1983, accessed at documentos.iglesia.cl/conf/documentos_sini.ficha.php?mod=documentos_sini&id=267&sw_volver=yes&descripcion, January 18, 2014.

50. "Encuentro Zonal de C.E.B," *Boletín Zona Sur*, II: 13 (November 1983), "Noticias Zonales" section. Starting in 1985 the *Boletín Zona Sur* began to publish supplements inside each issue with the objective of instructing members of the CEBs on the role that they should have as agents of political formation. Some of the recurring topics were the political role of Catholics, the option for the poor as a political commitment, and the instructive role of the church in the new political context in Chile.

9

THE POLITICS OF THE LITURGY IN THE ARCHDIOCESE OF BANGALORE

Brandon Vaidyanathan

This chapter examines two attempts at renewal in the Archdiocese of Bangalore, India – the adaptation of liturgical language to the local vernacular and "inculturation" of the form of liturgical expression into the local cultural context. It highlights the unintended consequences of these efforts, including conflicts and violence that persist to this day.

ON APRIL 6, 1990, A GROUP OF ABOUT EIGHT MEN STORMED into the residence of Archbishop Alphonsus Mathias in Bangalore.[1] The archbishop was away at the time, but his secretary, Fr. S. Jayanathan,[2] was in the office. Several of the insurgents bolted the door from within and threw red chili powder into Fr. Jayanathan's eyes. Others marched into the office of Fr. D'Silva, the vicar general, picked up a chair and smashed it onto his glass table. D'Silva's driver tried to intervene but backed away when threatened with a knife. The group disconnected the phones and left the building, heaving stones through the windows and scattering pamphlets with their demands.

The archbishop's complaint to the police identified Fr. C. Fatiraj, the parish priest of a church in Adigondanahalli, as the prime antagonist behind the episode. Fatiraj, who had an alibi and was eventually acquitted, was one of twelve diocesan priests[3] who had formed an association to redress what they saw as the marginalization of the Kannada language and people in the Catholic Church. Over the decade before the attack on the archbishop's residence, the group had become increasingly vocal in its central demand: the implementation of Kannada, the official state language, as the main language of the liturgy in the archdiocese. The April 1990 incident was not the first act of violence associated with these demands, nor would it be the last. On the night of March 31, 2013, Fr. K. J. Thomas, the rector of the archdiocesan seminary, was murdered. After a year of investigation, the police arrested two nationalist priests and a seminarian; in November 2015, the charge sheet was expanded to include four additional priests and three laypersons.[4] Though the two arrested priests allegedly confessed to the murder, priests and laity who identify as nationalist "agitators" continue to insist they have no role to play in any of the violence precipitated by this issue. Rather, they see themselves as victims of symbolic violence that has been systemically perpetrated by church leaders against Kannada Catholics.

This chapter focuses on political conflicts surrounding the liturgy that erupted in the Archdiocese of Bangalore after the Second Vatican Council. With the aim of improving lay participation, the Council, notably in *Sacrosanctum Concilium*, proposed the use of the vernacular in the celebration of the liturgy and sacraments.[5] While some resisted the shift from Latin,[6] laypeople around the world largely welcomed these changes, which made the liturgy more accessible to them. But in some locales, including Bangalore, identifying which of several languages was *the* vernacular became a matter of dispute, even of violence.[7] While this chapter's primary focus is the violence surrounding the adaptation of the liturgy to local language, it also touches on important conflicts around initiatives pioneered in the archdiocese to make the *form* or *expression* of the liturgy more accessible in the local cultural context, what came to be known after the Council as "inculturation," or "the incarnation of the Gospel in autonomous cultures and at the same time the introduction of these cultures into the life of the church."[8] Both of these attempts at renewal, aimed at fostering the Council's vision of a "fully conscious and active participation"[9] of the laity by adapting to local language and culture, backfired in the Archdiocese of Bangalore.

Conflict over Liturgical Language

Bengaluru (anglicized as Bangalore)[10] is a relatively young city by Indian standards.[11] It is the capital of Karnataka, a linguistic state with Kannada as its official language.[12] The Roman Catholic Archdiocese of Bangalore, with its jurisdiction extending well beyond the boundaries of the city, was erected in 1953 and is presently the third largest in the country in terms of Catholic population. The history of the church here dates back at least to Jesuit missionary activity in the 1600s.[13] The clearest starting point is the establishment of the Mysore Mission in 1649 by the Italian Jesuit Fr. Leonardo Cinnami. Initially driven out as a *piranghi* (foreigner), Fr. Cinnami dressed as a Brahmin *sannyasi* (a world-renouncing ascetic), following the methods of predecessors such as Jesuit missionary Roberto de Nobili, and moved farther inland. In 1653, he gained permission from King Kanthirava Narasaraja Wodeyar of Mysore to preach throughout the kingdom to the Canarese or Kannadigas, as locals are called.[14] Cinnami appears to have composed a grammar and dictionary in Kannada,[15] although no trace remains of these books. It is plausible they were burned along with other Christian books by a later king, Chikka Deveraja Wodeyar.[16]

Jesuit letters suggest a steady growth of Kannada Christians in the region until the 1750s. But missionary activity slowed down considerably after the suppression of the Jesuits beginning in 1759. The reign of Tipu Sultan (1782–1799) saw a drastic reduction in the Christian population through deportation, captivity, and the destruction of churches.[17] After the British army defeated Tipu, the colonial administration incorporated Bangalore into the Madras Presidency, an administrative region that covered much of southern India. The British restored the Wodeyars to the throne as subsidiaries of the British Raj and moved their garrison to what became the Cantonment area in the heart of Bangalore city. To cater to its needs, the army drew in migrants from the southern state of Tamil Nadu, who were then given important positions in railway stations, post offices, and other modern institutions as the city developed.[18]

In 1831, Bangalore became the capital of the Kingdom of Mysore, and Tamils came to comprise the majority of its Christian population. The Mysore Mission by this time became the province of the French Société des Missions Etrangères de Paris (MEP) priests, who began to develop schools, colleges, and churches for the new economic migrants. While they had assimilated to the local language, the Tamils still maintained their mother tongue, even though they would read and write it in Kannada script. At the time of the Second Vatican Council, it is estimated that at least 65 percent of Catholics in the archdiocese were Tamil speakers.[19]

The Council Years

Representing the archdiocese at the Council was Archbishop D. S. Lourdusamy, a Tamilian.[20] "He was very enthusiastic about implementing whatever the Council had said," recounted a former vicar general of the archdiocese, who preferred to remain anonymous.[21] Lourdusamy was especially keen on liturgical renewal. As texts of Council documents became available, Lourdusamy ordered translations to be made into local vernaculars – English, Kannada, and Tamil – and to be read at Mass in lieu of homilies. In 1964, Lourdusamy decreed that to faithfully implement the Council, the language of the liturgy ought to reflect that of the people.

This was interpreted to mean their mother tongue rather than regional language.[22] Kannada translations were in preparation and would soon be sent to the Vatican for approval; they would become available in 1967. Meanwhile, English and Tamil booklets were already in use.[23] Eager to implement changes, Lourdusamy introduced the Tamil liturgy even before the bishops of Tamil Nadu did, a step that upset them.[24] Tamil, the mother tongue of most Catholics in Bangalore, gained new prominence.

The significance of this shift cannot be appreciated without taking into account the tensions between Kannada and Tamil already simmering in Bangalore in the 1960s. Kannada nationalist movements, which began gaining momentum in these years, were both envious of and sympathetic to Tamil nationalism. Tamil films had become considerably more prominent in the city than Kannada ones, for instance, and following accusations that these movies depicted the Kannada people unfavorably, demands arose for cinemas showing Tamil movies to be shut down.[25] The dominance of Tamil was economic as well as cultural, evident in complaints about sought-after public sector jobs and unions being largely in the hands of Tamil speakers. For new Kannada-speaking migrants who flocked to the city from rural areas after the formation of the linguistic state, the humiliation of being a "local refugee" made unions and workers' organizations prominent sites of nationalist contestation.[26] In the decades that followed, tensions would worsen over issues including the sharing of the waters of the river Cauvery between the states of Karnataka and Tamil Nadu.[27]

In the church, the ethnic question was bubbling under the surface, and Lourdusamy played a key role in stoking the tension. First, he encouraged and supported urban Tamils to the neglect of rural Kannadigas. A Jesuit priest, Fr. Ronnie Prabhu, who was a seminarian at the time, remembers that "the ascendency of Tamil priests" began with Lourdusamy.[28] Diocesan historian Anthony Simo notes that Lourdusamy started a "Tamil academy" in the seminary, in response to which his vicar general, Fr. I. Anthappa (who was among the priests charged with Fr. Thomas's murder), introduced a rival "Kannada academy."[29] Lourdusamy's approach was seen at the time and since as an attempt to distance himself from his predecessor. Another Jesuit priest (a Kannadiga but not a supporter of the nationalists), also a seminarian during Lourdusamy's time, explained, "Lourdusamy was a votary of Tamil. [The p]revious bishop, Pothacamury, was for Kannada, and therefore since he got an auxiliary bishop who was a Tamilan, he disregarded him ... And when [Lourdusamy] became first Co-Agitur and afterwards he became Archbishop, he had his fit of anger against Kannada."[30] Fr. Anthappa, one of the most prominent Kannadiga agitators, was personally encouraged to go into the seminary by Archbishop Pothacamury. He recalls that the latter "took great interest in villages and in Kannada, even though he was not a Kannada man and didn't learn the language. He wanted all the priests to learn Kannada. He would deliberately send educated priests to villages." Another elderly priest, who preferred to remain anonymous, explained that Pothacamury's policy was "My priests should know both the languages. He should know Kannada, he should know Tamil, and he should be prepared to go anywhere in the diocese." Priests fluent in Tamil were sent in their early years to Kannada parishes to learn Kannada, and vice versa. As a result, the pre–Vatican II generation of priests was bilingual. But with Lourdusamy's policy, "new Tamil priests only knew Tamil; they did not know Kannada," the priest continued, "And the Kannada priests refused to learn Tamil. And that rivalry came. It was a very wrong policy. The previous archbishop's policy was the right one I felt." Anthappa expressed his frustration at working with Lourdusamy. "I was there every day to teach him," he says of the archbishop, "but he was not interested in learning, in Kannada people, or in the villages."

Another priest, Fr. Lawrence Noronha, observed that Tamil-speaking seminarians were mostly from the city and had been educated in schools in which English was the medium of instruction, whereas Kannada seminarians were from villages and studied in Kannada-medium public schools, since neither Catholic schooling nor English-language education was available to them. "So there was a bit of a tussle and many were sent back because they were not able to keep up with the studies," he recalls, "Grumbling started in the major seminary. Here they started getting this consciousness that 'We are Kannada,' 'We are Tamil.' So each group – rightly, I would say – started fighting for their rights."[31]

Despite these tensions, the conflict did not come to the fore while Lourdusamy was archbishop. Priests and laypeople who recall those days share the opinion that although he favored Tamils, Lourdusamy commanded enough authority to be respected even by Kannadiga priests. The problem erupted in a public way with his successor.

Casualties in a Language Tangle

In 1971, Archbishop Lourdusamy was appointed the joint secretary of the Sacred Congregation for the Evangelisation of Peoples, the wing of the Roman Curia responsible for the missionary efforts of the church.[32] He was whisked off to Rome and elevated a cardinal, becoming the first Asian member of the curia.[33] His successor, installed about a year later, was Packiam Arockiaswamy.

The first strike against Arockiaswamy in The first strike against the Arockiaswamy was that he was Tamilian, brought in from Tamil Nadu where he was bishop of Ooty. Ignatius Pinto, archbishop of Bangalore from 1998 to 2004, says that Arockiaswamy's installation considerably irked many. "The feeling of resentment was already there when Lourdusamy was appointed Auxiliary," Bishop Pinto recalled, and intensified with Arockiaswamy's installation. The short biography introducing Arockiaswamy to the archdiocese, however, mentions him as hailing "from an ancient Kannadiga family which migrated from Mysore." In his letter accepting this new position, he noted, "Though I am coming from outside the Archdiocese, I am not a complete stranger to you," since he underwent his clerical training in Bangalore.[34] This background seemed irrelevant; people perceived him as a Tamilian.

The spark that set off the public conflict in the church occurred in 1973[35] at Christ the King parish, where Fr. Fernando, a former soldier, was parish priest. As one priest recounts:

> [Fr. Fernando] was very stiff, and said that Mass would be only in Tamil, whereas there were so many people who were Kannada-speaking. He did not give them their due; he was not prepared to dialogue with them. Then it became very violent in that parish, all hammering and all that. And Mass itself they would disrupt. They would start shouting! In the end the priest was fed up. Then he had to be transferred. He got into the vehicle and he removed his slippers and dusted off and cursed the parish and went. *[laughs]* And ever since then this parish had a lot of trouble with language issues.[36]

Another priest recalls conflicts that would occur in this parish and several others: "There are people who will sing in one language in the church, and when they start the hymn, another group will start singing in another language loudly!" A retired laywoman, who also asked not to be named, explained that members of the laity were was affected by these conflicts: "We did experience in indirect ways remarks, conversations, the setup of committees, the organization of church services, scheduling of Masses, when was the important Mass to be said and in which language, who is in charge, who is the chairman of the committee." Archbishop Arockiaswamy became infamous for his wavering and indecisive behavior in response to the language issue. One priest called him "a man with no vision." Another said he had "no spine." Arockiaswamy was unable to command the sense of authority that his predecessor did. Under pressure from competing groups, he would "tilt this way and that just to accommodate [these] demands," Simo writes. "And once this hesitation was realized as a part of the man, the pressure became the stronger."[37] Under pressure from Kannada priests, Arockiaswamy decreed that Kannada would be "progressively given more prominence."[38] But Tamil priests pushed back, leaving the issue effectively at a stalemate.

The late 1970s and early 1980s saw the emergence of a more "fear-centered nationalism" in comparison with earlier forms of "spiritual nationalism" in Karnataka.[39] Agitation arose in response to concerns about the devaluing of Kannada education in schools and about the lack of jobs for Kannadigas. Nationalist associations of Catholic priests and laity were organized, notably the Kannada Catholic Christhara Sangha, which began to voice complaints about the neglect of the Kannada community. The group's dissatisfactions included the lack of catechists and priests and the absence of representation among bishops in the archdiocese. Less than one-half of the parishes in the city at that time had Kannada Masses available, whereas daily Tamil and English services were a staple in most parishes.[40] Some claimed that Kannada-speaking seminarians and aspiring religious were discriminated against in the selection process. Feeling that they lacked sufficient voice, some Catholic nationalists were co-opted by the broader fundamentalist wing of the Kannada movement, which was gaining ground.[41] The concerns of Kannada Catholics were amplified in local newspapers by prominent Kannada activist writers such as V. K. Gokak, who attacked the church for its imposition of Tamil.[42] A vocal Tamil faction of priests and laity expressed their outrage at these demands, in turn, and refused compromise, insisting instead on an increase in Tamil Masses for parishes with Tamil majority.

Mounting tensions eventually gave way to violence. In 1981, members of the Kannada nationalist coalition disrupted the Chrism Mass at the St. Francis Xavier Cathedral in Bangalore, a Tamil-majority parish and the archbishop's seat, and they attacked Arockiaswamy.[43] The Chrism Mass is a liturgy that takes place on the morning of the Thursday before Easter, during which the priests of the diocese gather together with the bishop for the blessing of the oils that will be used during sacraments in the coming year. "In the Cathedral, during Maundy Thursday service, they took the chairs and broke the chairs and broke one another's heads," one priest who was present remembers it, "Even the police had to come. Bloodshed there was! So we could not have the Chrism Mass for the next few years in the cathedral. We had it secretly in the bishop's house, only with the priests." Activists targeted the Chrism Mass, this priest said, because it "is supposed to be the Mass of the unity of the church," and they insisted that it be held only in Kannada. "That Mass used to be in English usually," explained F. T. Colaco, who was deputy general of police at the time, "I had gone there to be present at that Mass, and we tried our best to ensure that it was not disrupted. Even then, there were some of the laypeople who came and shouted slogans and tried to disrupt the service."[44] Kannada activists maintained that their attacks were provoked by Tamils who assaulted them first. Not long after, these activists attacked a parish with a Tamil-majority congregation, demanding the liturgy to be celebrated only in Kannada.[45] For a few years thereafter, some parishes went so far as to refuse to celebrate liturgies during the Easter *triduum* in protest. Fr. Prabhu recalls one occasion when he was asked by the archbishop's office to see if he might celebrate Mass at one of those parishes. "I contacted the parish priest. He warned me: 'Don't step in here!'"[46]

Despite occasional violence when laity were involved, the standard tactic of nationalist priests was to stage a *dharna* – a nonviolent sit-in protest, usually involving fasting – in front of the archbishop's house. The aims of these protests, organized by the Sangha, were to demonstrate the sense of injustice felt and to persuade the archbishop to make firm decisions to prioritize Kannada in the archdiocese. At times, the protesters even provoked opposition from Tamil supporters. One Kannadiga Jesuit vividly recalls how he helped defuse a conflict:

> In 1981, I saw, right in front of the [arch]bishop's house, Kannada priests of the diocese, with the people, held a *dharna* . . . Kannada group were all with Kannada; Tamil group were all with Tamil . . . And one of the leaders [of the agitation] was my classmate, so they wouldn't do anything to me or hammer me *[laughs]*. They brought hatchets and everything kept under their clothes, the people! I spoke to him. He said, "See, I am from a labor background. We put a hundred demands; if we get 2 demands or 3 demands, we are satisfied!" . . . And finally a truce was made. Otherwise if Jesuits had not intervened, it would have gone on some more days! *[laughs]*[47]

Arockiaswamy, severely shaken by the 1981 attacks, appealed to Rome for help. In the interim, he issued a circular declaring that "Kannada being the regional language of the State, there shall be a Mass said in Kannada in every church."[48] For occasions that required Mass to be celebrated in more than one language, the archbishop proposed a three-language formula of Kannada, Tamil, and English, with Kannada given prominence.

The Vatican's response was to form an episcopal commission composed of three other Indian bishops from North India to address the issue. The commission's concluding report, published in December 1982, recognized that Kannada Catholics saw themselves as a suppressed minority in their own state, but it emphasized that the criterion to determine language use was "the fuller and more active participation by all the people." "In such a cosmopolitan city like Bangalore," the bishops asserted, this would require "a sense of realism and fair-play."[49] The commission's verdict failed to satisfy the nationalists. A few months later, Arockiaswamy, likely under pressure, declared in another circular, "The policy of the Archdiocese of Bangalore is to make Kannada the principal language of its liturgical worship within five years or even earlier." This was to be regardless of the mother tongue of the majority.[50] Several Tamil Catholics, angered, took the issue to court. "Asking me to get rid of my mother tongue is like asking me to kill my mother," says one Tamil priest.[51] A year later, Arockiaswamy announced that "in view of the situation prevailing in the Archdiocese and for the good of the Church," he was going on indefinite leave.[52]

In 1986, Arockiaswamy was appointed bishop of Tanjore in Tamil Nadu, and Alphonsus Mathias took over as archbishop of Bangalore. Mathias was born in what is now the Udupi district in northern Karnataka and completed his seminary studies in Mangalore. He was ordained in Sri Lanka and studied for his doctorate in canon law and international civil law in Rome. Upon his return in 1964, he was appointed bishop of the new diocese of Chikmagalur, to the west of Bangalore. Later that year, he attended the third session of the Second Vatican Council, which he considered "absolutely an unique privilege which I treasure with deep faith and attachment."[53]

Attempting to resolve the language problem, Archbishop Mathias issued a circular in 1988 declaring that canon law gave him the prerogative to lay down "liturgical regulations which are binding to all."[54] Because of the diversity in the archdiocese, he explained, "uniformity in the matter of liturgical worship cannot be enforced in respect of language without detriment to the peace, unity, and spiritual growth of the people of God." It was in this light that his predecessor's circular setting a five-year goal to make Kannada the diocese's principal language of worship "ha[d] to be read and interpreted." Mathias reaffirmed the "three-language formula" that Arockiaswamy and the Liturgical Committee had proposed for all Masses celebrated by the archbishop at the diocesan level. Soon after Mathias's circular was issued, around 1,500 religious priests and nuns assembled in the compound of the archbishop's house in demonstration of their support. A headline in *The New Leader* announced in July 1989 that the "Row over Liturgical Language comes to an end in Bangalore church." But this announcement turned out to be premature. The nationalists could not abide such wavering and compromise, and they eventually attacked the archbishop's house in 1990.

Language and Symbolic Violence

The group that ransacked the archbishop's house on April 6 that year scattered leaflets that bore a printed manifesto.[55] The first two of their demands were for the implementation of Arockiaswamy's plan, and for all Good Friday and Easter Masses to be celebrated only in Kannada. The next two points in their agenda, however, reveal that the issue was not simply about language. The authors of the manifesto demanded that more Kannada Christians be ordained priests and that churches in villages be renovated. Nationalist agitators saw (and continue to see) the denigration of their language as responsible for the inequalities they experience vis-à-vis important roles in church and society. They believe that other language groups – Tamils, Konkanis, and Malayalees – have deprived them of social and economic opportunities, even in church-run organizations.[56] Although the group understood their actions as "agitation for . . . language inculturation,"[57] the conflict was never purely a matter of language.

As Fr. Chowrappa Selvaraj, a prominent agitator who passed away in 2016 and was among those charged with the murder of Fr. Thomas, explained, "Behind [the agitation over language] are things like development, education, and social empowerment."[58] In the eyes of Kannada activists, the church since the time of the British Raj consistently privileged urban migrants while systematically marginalizing Kannada natives. Fr. Anthappa insists that the early Jesuits' focus on evangelizing rural peoples and villages was lost when the French MEP fathers took over; it resumed under Pothacamury, but it died once Lourdusamy took over. Activists believe that church leaders have no interest in evangelizing or serving the needs of Kannadigas. "They feel they are only here to serve the immigrants," said Selvaraj, "The Church is not Bangalore city. But for them, church means only city."

Consistent in the narratives of agitators is a sense of marginalization, of being dismissed as unimportant. Anthappa spearheaded the process of translating the Bible into Kannada but received little support from the bishops. When he finally released his translation, none of the (Konkani) bishops in the state attended the release, although he had invited them. "It was the saddest thing in my life," he recalled with tears in his eyes.[59] The absence of the hierarchy signaled to him their disinterest in the Kannada people. Other activists felt a similar sense of marginalization. "Even though I was altar server, I had no attachment to church, because it was not in my language – the parish had only Tamil and English Mass," recounts Selvaraj, "How did we get a [Kannada] Mass in our parish? Throwing stones and breaking windows. Then they gave us evening mass at 5 p.m."

With the shift of the liturgical language from Latin to the vernacular of the majority of every parish, Tamil-speaking priests began to enjoy prime (urban) postings, while Kannada-speaking priests were relegated to rural areas. More than a slight to nationalist pride in their language, it felt to these priests like salt in their wounds. They were denied the privileges of city life and assigned to "backward" areas where roads and electricity were often lacking. This sense of humiliation echoed what nationalists in the city keenly felt at the time: they saw themselves as minorities deprived of opportunities in their own land.[60] For many priests, being sent to villages was an exile. Fr. Selvaraj talked about being thus "expelled" from 1983 to 2006. But he eventually decided this was also "a blessing in disguise," as he was able to build up local social and economic institutions, as well as strengthen agitation in rural areas.

The nationalists' story is complicated by the pervasive complaint among laity that many so-called Kannada priests apparently do not speak Kannada as their mother tongue, but rather, Telugu, which is the official language of another neighboring state, Andhra Pradesh.[61] This makes their insistence on the primacy of Kannada all the more peculiar. Their criterion for status is neither fluency in the language nor having been born and raised in the state of Karnataka, but instead having Kannada as a mother tongue and ethnicity.

The marginalization felt by Kannadiga Catholics was not restricted to the clergy. Rita Rini, a journalist who dedicated her life to Kannada activism, and who is among those charged with aiding in Fr. Thomas's murder (the Karnataka high court rejected the charges), recounts her childhood in a Catholic village: "We didn't have Bible, hymnbooks, or way of the cross for holy week . . . Now we have organized it ourselves as laypeople." She proudly remembers being part of the Kannada agitation from her childhood. She found a "sense of identity" in being part of the group in her parish that sang hymns in Kannada to disrupt those singing Tamil hymns. For Rita and many others, agitation was a means of asserting their identity and dignity as Kannada people.

While the target of Kannada nationalist agitation within the church was initially Tamil, since the 1990s they have increasingly turned against Konkani speakers (from regions such as Mangalore, also in Karnataka state), who increasingly came to enjoy positions of prominence in the archdiocese. As one Kannada activist, Fr. A. Thomas, complained in 1990, "The church at present is dominated by Konkani-speaking priests. All positions have been taken by them. You can see for yourself who is after power."[62] Nationalists resent the fact that the current archbishop, Bernard Moras, attends meetings of Konkani associations and that he has petitioned the government for land on their behalf: "He doesn't ask for land for the evangelization of local people."[63] Nationalists see the appointment of Konkani-origin bishops in recent decades (Mathias, Pinto, and Moras) as a "new colonization" that recalls the divide-and-conquer strategy of the British. "They express the preference for Kannada but in practice they favor Tamils," while they "build up their Konkani kingdom," argued Fr. Selvaraj. "When a language dominates, then the group that speaks the language dominates." For this reason, the agitators have set their hopes on a new bishop, a Kannada bishop. "Already the feeling of being colonized has come deep down," sighed Rini, "Another man with the same identity will not be acceptable."

Language, a real issue in itself, has many other implications. "We fight not for our language, but our identity," explained Fr. Selvaraj. Rita Rini talked about how the church's neglect to develop Kannada Catholics left her with "the feeling of being lost," of not mattering. This is compounded by interactions outside the church: "When I say I am a Catholic from Bangalore, people ask me if I speak Tamil or Konkani. 'Even Kannada-speaking Catholics are there?' they ask!" The frustrations of this conflict at times drove Rini to ask herself why she remains in the church: "But for us to detach from the church is suicidal to the rest of the community who remain powerless. They will not give up their faith for anything." Agitators thus see their defense of a Kannada Catholic identity as vital for the amelioration of their community.

Five decades after the Council, the issue of liturgical language in the Archdiocese of Bangalore is clearly far from resolved. Konkani and Malayalee groups have recently petitioned for Masses in their own languages. Nor has the violence completely abated.[64] With the murder of seminary rector Fr. K. J. Thomas in 2013, many see no resolution in sight to the conflict. As mentioned earlier, two nationalist priests, William Patrick and Elias Daniel, along with Peter, an altar boy in the latter's parish, were charged with the crime in March 2014.[65] According to the police, the suspects resented the Malayalee rector (who spent many years as a priest in Tamil Nadu) and were trying to break into the seminary to obtain documents pertaining to land granted to the seminary that would defend the privileging of Kannadigas in the seminary.[66] The police claim that the accused, along with confederates yet to be apprehended, marched to the seminary "armed with rods and other deadly weapons" late on the night of March 31; during the burglary, they were confronted by Fr. Thomas and murdered him.[67] Though the priests allegedly confessed to the crime, other Kannada activists insisted on their innocence.[68] They claimed that Kannada priests were being framed by the archbishop and continued to stage protests against what they saw as mounting injustice.[69]

Thus, conflicts of the past and ongoing tensions around the language issue have generated a climate of mistrust within the archdiocese – between priests and bishops, among priests, and between priests and laity. The language question, as Fr. Prabhu described it, "colors everything here and therefore nothing really can take place, because of this demon called the language problem."[70] But disputes concerning the local adaptation of the liturgy were not restricted simply to the language question.

Conflict over Liturgical Inculturation

New concern arose after the Council on updating the Westernized form of liturgical expression to better suit the Indian cultural context. Efforts at inculturation began in India as early as Jesuit missionaries such as de Nobili.[71] Later in history, developments such as the Ashram Movement of Henri le Saux and Bede Griffiths aimed to syncretize Christian monasticism with the *vedanta* and *sannyasa* traditions of Hinduism.[72] Yet focused attempts at liturgical renewal based on the principle of inculturation were pioneered only after the Council.[73] In Bangalore, while Archbishop Lourdusamy introduced the change in liturgical language, the principal architect of innovation in liturgical *expression* was his younger brother, Fr. D. S. Amalorpavadass.

Born in Kallery, Tamil Nadu, in 1932, Amalorpavadass attended St. Peter's Seminary in Bangalore. After ordination, he completed doctoral studies at the Institut Catholique de Paris, then returned to India in 1965 and served for a year as parish priest in central Tamil Nadu. Amalorpavadass had considerable influence on the Catholic Bishops' Conference of India (CBCI) as secretary of its Commission for Liturgy, the Commission for Catechetics, and Commission for the Bible. He was the first Indian to establish a chair and department of Christian studies at a secular university (Mysore University). In 1982, Amalorpavadass moved to Anjali Ashram in Mysore, which he founded in 1979 for spiritual seekers of all traditions. Here he remained as *acharya-guru* or spiritual guide until his death in a car accident in May 1990.

Amalorpavadass, like his brother, was profoundly dedicated to translating the meanings and aims of the Council into the local context, as his prolific theological writings attest.[74] Aside from his literary output, two innovations in particular marked the history of the archdiocese: the founding of the National Biblical, Cathechetical and Liturgical Centre in 1966 and the implementation of the Indian Rite Liturgy in 1969. These initiatives reflect the heart of Amalorpavadass's vision for the Church in India, and for an "an authentic Indian Christian Spirituality."[75] Yet, like the change in liturgical language, these attempts at inculturation also generated unintended consequences.

Inculturation of Space: The NBCLC

The National Biblical, Catechetical and Liturgical Centre (NBCLC), founded by Amalorpavadass in 1966, was envisaged by the Catholic Bishops' Conference of India as its key vehicle of the liturgical renewal of the church in India.[76] The center became an active hub for seminars, conferences, workshops, and retreats, drawing thousands from around the country to its events. At the heart of its campus sits a chapel that embodies Amalorpavadass's "artistic synthesis of spirituality." Its name, *Saccidananda*, is a compound Sanskrit word meaning "Reality, Awareness, and Bliss."[77] In Vedanta philosophy, the term refers to Brahman; Amalorpavadass intended it as a reference to the Trinity. The chapel is designed as a (Hindu) temple to represent "the archetype of man's deep spiritual quest and psychic longing for fulfillment." Consistent with South Indian temple architecture, at its top sits a *gopuram* – a seven-layered tower symbolizing "earth, water, fire, air, super mind and finally God Himself" – topped with a *kalasam*, an inverted pot representing "the nectar of immortality." This vessel was a meaningful symbol of Christ, Amalorpavadass argued, so that the temple did not need additional symbols such as a cross, which would violate "the laws of architecture and art."[78] Wrought iron window grills designed as an Indian equivalent of European stained glass windows were meant to function "as a living Catechesis." Images on the grills include the yogic prayer posture, the Orante posture, the four Gospels, the four *ashramas* or stages of life, the *upanayana* (Brahmin sacred thread ceremony), the Buddha begging, Abraham and Sarah, and more.[79] Overall, the campus and its architecture aimed to depict "a coherent synthesis of Indian Christian Spirituality."[80]

Reactions to these innovations were swift and harsh. Many Catholics were upset by what they saw as "paganization" or "Hinduization" of the church.[81] A campaign gathered thousands of signatures in protest. Members of the Charismatic Renewal were "up in arms against it," according to one of the renewal's leaders in Bangalore: "We were very, very, very anti. We didn't want to have anything to do with all this inculturation business. We just felt strongly it was just Hinduism and we were just averse to it."[82] Most upsetting for Catholic groups were the temple-like structure of the chapel and the grill windows depicting the Hindu *Trimurti (*Brahma, Vishnu, and Shiva) and the *Nataraja* (dancing Shiva), which they denounced as idolatry. Some Hindu groups also took offense to what they saw as unwarranted appropriations. A traditionalist Catholic association, the All India Laity Congress, and then later a Hindu association, Astikha Sabha, launched court cases against Amalorpavadass and the NBCLC and succeeded in removing these panels.[83] Though additional backlash threatened to tear down the chapel because of its use of brahminical religious symbols,[84] the chapel still stands.

Inculturation of Ritual

Amalorpavadass also pioneered experimentation to develop a form of the liturgy more suitable, in his view, to the Indian context. In January 1969, the second All-India Liturgical Meeting approved a twelve-point schema of adaptations to liturgical worship, which was approved by the CBCI in March and by the Consilium in April.[85] This new "Indian Rite" Mass was prominently featured in the "All India Seminar: Church in India Today" in May 1969, the first national event to discuss the Council and establish priorities for implementing renewal.

Benny Aguiar, former president of the Indian Catholic Press Association, provided a description:

> A hundred priests walked barefoot to the altar, the chief celebrant vested in a saffron shawl wrapped round his shoulders. Nuns and lay people squatted on the floor. As the priests came in, they made an "Anjali hasta" (a profound bow with hands joined) to the crucifix. Instead of kissing the altar, they touched it with their fingers, which they then brought to their foreheads. Then followed the lighting of the seven wicks of a tall, slender brass lamp, which signified Christ the light of the world. At the offertory there was the "aarti," the waving around of a thali or brass platter filled with fruits, a broken coconut, some joss sticks and the bread and wine.[86]

The reception was mixed. Again there was resentment against what many saw as the "conversion of the liturgy into a poor imitation of Hindu temple worship." Many observers objected that the symbols privileged Hindu expressions over other equally important aspects of Indian culture, including Islam. Some also argued that the symbols could not be extricated from underlying beliefs – or superstitions in their view – attached to them.[87] The Indian Rite Liturgy was better accepted in dioceses in the North than in South India; better received in villages than in urban areas; more welcome in religious houses than in parishes. Some archdioceses forbade the schema completely; others implemented the twelve points partially after surveying clergy and laity; still others in Muslim-majority and tribal-majority regions rejected them as unsuitable.[88] More recently, the NBCLC has started to phase out its Indian Rite Mass because of a lack of interest from the laity.[89]

In explaining its failure to generate lay interest, Fr. Noronha suggested they were insufficiently communicated to non-elites. "A lot of catechesis, information, education is necessary to accept it," he says, "It was more intellectual. You may be educated, you may be taught over there well. But ordinary people do not know and understand." In Fr. Prabhu's assessment, "Amalor . . . tried to promote the beauty of non-Christian scriptures and what is good in them . . . But it didn't catch on. That way, Amalor was too early for his time. Too early!" Amalorpavadass's liturgical experimentation generated neither the impact nor receptivity he envisioned. He strenuously denied the claim that he was "borrowing" from Hinduism[90] and saw "nothing specifically Hindu about the controversial adaptations," arguing that "they belong to the social customs and cultural traditions of India." The reason adaptation was a challenge, he maintained, was that the Catholic Church in India was still trapped in its sectarian, parochial ways, and out of step with its surrounding context.[91] Others think the opposition to inculturation efforts stems from "the anxiety of a minority community to preserve its social identity as a separate group,"[92] in the words of theologian Michael Amaladoss. But these efforts were also plagued by a deeper failure.

As religion scholar Mathew Schmalz notes, "One striking aspect of Amalorpavadass's writings, and indeed of nearly all Indian Catholic writings on inculturation, is the consistent refusal to engage any discipline beyond the confines of theology."[93] As a result, these inculturation efforts remain obtuse with regard to their essentialist and orientalist conceptions of Hinduism and "Indian culture." While focusing on the internal meanings of symbols, which they saw no problem interpreting with a Christian hermeneutic, proponents of such syntheses neglected to even imagine that these efforts would themselves become symbolic and "be interpreted fluidly and idiosyncratically" by others, as filtered through "Christianity's colonial history and its exclusive claims to truth."[94]

Efforts at Christian inculturation in India, from the time of Jesuit missionary Roberto de Nobili, assumed a "primacy of Brahmanism as a general social model of Indian civilization [which] became axiomatic in the centuries to follow."[95] While the indigenization undertaken by de Nobili and other early Jesuits backfired in the long run, they left a lasting imprint, inspiring not only future models of inculturation (such as Bede Griffiths) but also the suspicion with which many Hindus would view such attempts (i.e., as underhanded means of securing conversions).[96] Blind to their orientalist assumptions, such pioneering inculturation efforts neglected to include Dalit/untouchable Catholics, by incorporating, for instance, theologies or symbols of Kabir, Periyar, Ambedkar, or other figures with which Dalits identify. Schmalz cites a Catholic untouchable he spoke to outside a Catholic ashram who not only was unable to understand the talk (in English) on "Indian Christian Spiritual Experience" that preceded the Indian Rite Mass but was also offended by what he saw as capitulation to Brahminism, "something that he believed had oppressed his caste fellows for generations."[97] As Jesuit scholar George Soares-Prabhu argues, Brahminicized efforts at inculturation reproduce complicity with the exploitation of not only Dalits but also of women and tribal peoples.[98]

In fairness to Amalorpavadass, his experiments were intended to be simply one step toward further experimentation. He also aspired to integrate social justice commitments into the vision and central aims of the NBCLC. Nevertheless, these intentions were lost to a public in confrontation with the forms his innovations took.

Lived History beyond the Conflicts

It is important to keep in mind that the tensions I have tracked in this chapter preoccupied primarily diocesan priests and a small contingent of laity. Most laypeople remained significantly uninvolved; they may have been troubled by the innovations, certainly, but not enough to be debilitated. So these conflicts ought not to sideline the fact that for most people the shift away from Latin to the vernacular was a welcome change. "By and large people have been very happy with all the reforms that were introduced after Vatican II, particularly the Mass being said in the vernacular," F. T. Colaco, the former police deputy general, tells me. Rhoda D'Souza, a retired professor, recalls that some older people, "parents, aunts, uncles, that level," complained about "newfangled innovation" and a loss of the "beautiful Latin prayers and hymns," but the younger generation at the time liked it: "We knew what we were saying now."[99] Clergy likewise talked about the changes of the Council as mostly liberating. "The novitiate also moved from that regimentation to a relaxed kind of atmosphere," said one Jesuit. "All that *clausura* thing was slowly relaxed."[100] Priests and nuns appreciated the church's new emphasis on social change and development.

While intentional efforts to adapt to local Indian languages and culture generated heated conflict among institutional leaders, Bangalore increasingly became a cosmopolitan hub. By the late 1990s, the city was India's high-tech capital, drawing skilled migrants from around the country. The rising neo-liberalism made "global" competences such as familiarity with Western culture and the English language key assets for success. These factors would not leave the church untouched; they tapped into cultural capacities it had inherited from its colonial past.

The growing, educated, English-speaking middle class in Bangalore was not the audience envisaged by proponents of inculturation, either of language or liturgical expression. But as laity, the newcomers would become prominent in parish Councils, being nominated by virtue of their status as successful professionals. As D'Souza noted: "Irrespective of what caste, community, region they come from, the English-speaking educated class has a very inordinate influence on the management, decision-making, administrating, in every sphere. And the same applies to the church Councils. That's the way India is!"[101]

Many laypersons and some priests, however, complained that the clericalism in the archdiocese rendered parish Councils impotent coteries of yes-men and -women ingratiating themselves to pastors, without real decision-making power. According to one laywoman: "The priests made the point to have these Councils going. But it was perceived as gracious permission of the clergy to allow the laity to come and sit with them. But you know who's holding the reins. It was *dhikhava* [window dressing] . . . There's more show than substance." But one unexpected development after the Council would marshal the participation of many of the laity and would go on to become the fastest-growing lay Catholic movement in the country. The irony is that while the architects of the post-conciliar church in Bangalore sought the inspiration of the Holy Spirit in adaptation to the "local," many of the more active and influential (educated middle-class) laity found themselves drawn to winds blowing from elsewhere – American Pentecostalism, to be precise.

The Catholic Charismatic Renewal, originating in the United States in 1967, came to Bangalore in 1972 when a Merchant Navy officer from Bangalore, Fritz Mascarenhas, met a group of Pentecostals in Bombay and "had an experience of the Baptism in the Holy Spirit." Mascarenhas traveled to Japan, where he "had a further experience through some beautiful American nondenominational full-Gospel Christians." Growing up Catholic in Bangalore, he recalls, "we had no concept of evangelization. We grew up in our Catholic schools, with non-Christians all around us, and it never dawned on me even for a moment that I had to tell them about Jesus. So with this experience in Japan, my spiritual eyes were opened to this reality that Jesus is the only savior." While he appreciated the experience of growing up Catholic, "no priest could tell me how to meet You, no nun could tell me how to meet You," Mascarenhas said, referring to Jesus. The Pentecostal experience, on the other hand, "was so life-changing: Jesus came alive. Scriptures came alive. A thirst for prayer. A hunger for God."[102] He decided to "throw away [his] job and just go out and evangelize."

The first meetings of the Renewal in the city were held at the Mascarenhas home. Early on, the evangelist's worried mother complained to then-archbishop Arockiaswamy about her son, concerned he was ruining his life and soul. Mascarenhas describes his meeting with the archbishop in 1974:

> He just asked me one question, "What's happened to you?" The next 45 minutes I spoke to him and told him all that had happened. Finally when I ended, he said to me, "Son, I don't have this life that you have. Will you lay hands and pray for me for the Holy Spirit?" I was simply shocked. I couldn't believe the Archbishop asking me to pray for him![103]

Arockiaswamy, reviled for his incompetence in handling the language conflict, became the darling of the Renewal. Mascarenhas, with the bishop's full backing and blessing, saw God calling him into full-time evangelization. Arockiaswamy encouraged Mascarenhas to work closely with a Jesuit priest who had also experienced the baptism in the Holy Spirit, Francis Rebello, who was founder-director of the elite St. Joseph's College of Business Administration in the heart of Bangalore city. Charismatic groups proliferated rapidly in parishes and colleges in the city. Mascarenhas is clear that the Renewal owes its success in large part to the strong support of the archbishop and influential clergy. "Here in the Catholic Church," he says, "without the support of a priest and their encouragement, we laity couldn't do anything." The endorsement of the bishop and influential Jesuits "opened *all* the doors for me!" With diocesan priests absorbed in the language conflict and priests and nuns caught up in either inculturation initiatives or administration of the church's various institutions, the Renewal drew many of the laity who felt left on their own. While it generated problems of its own, including conflicts with church authority and rivalries among "splinter groups," some of which broke away from the church, the Renewal gave many laypeople opportunities for empowerment and leadership. Focused on its own language of tongues, it drew people of different vernaculars and remained distant from liturgical conflicts.

Legacy of Unintended Consequences

Attempts at adapting liturgical language and form to the local context in the Archdiocese of Bangalore generated unexpected conflicts that soured people's lived experience of the Council. Both these efforts at reform were motivated by a similar concern, a fuller participation of the laity, as envisioned by the Council. Yet both were based on faulty but widespread assumptions at the time. Just as Lourdusamy's linguistic inculturation assumed a nonproblematic notion of the vernacular, the attempt at cultural indigenization assumed an essentialist notion of "Indian culture" unproblematically distinct from Brahmanism.

Certainly the Council did not *cause* the language conflict. Rather, it intersected with simmering tensions on the ground, generating new situations that amplified the intensity of the conflict. Before the Council, the use of Latin prevented any particular vernacular from gaining prominence. Liturgies were not identified with languages (i.e., "Tamil Mass," "Kannada Mass"), and priests were encouraged to be fluent in all three languages. The role of bishops such as Lourdusamy and Arockiaswamy in fueling or mismanaging the conflict cannot be denied either. But nobody on either side of the conflict claims that retaining the Latin status quo would have been ideal. They recognize that were it not for the language conflict, other deeper tensions would have come to the fore, tensions surrounding caste, for example, which are rife in many other states in India. Identification with language, on both sides, brought together people from across diverse castes. "You can solve the language problem in Karnataka," Fr. Selvaraj insists, "But you can never solve the caste problem in Tamil Nadu."

People on both sides of the language conflict drew on the Council to justify their commitments to a "local church." For Kannada speakers, this phrase referred to rural Kannadiga Catholics, while for other groups it meant local parishes in which they spoke their respective mother tongues. People on both sides also understood the Council's central aim as being evangelization. Kannada activists claimed that the neglect of their language demonstrated church leaders' disinterest in evangelizing Kannada Catholics, while their opponents argued that privileging Kannada made little sense when the majority of parishioners could be more effectively evangelized in their mother tongues. Kannada activists also credit the Council for their very existence. When I asked Fr. Selvaraj what the Council meant to him, he replied, "It gave us an identity. A local identity. We should thank Rome for that."

The Council can also be credited for motivating Amalorpavadass's liturgical innovations. While there were some modes of syncretistic inculturation before the Council, it is unlikely that the liturgy could otherwise have become such a (contested) site for experimentation. But there was no appeal to the Council among opponents of inculturation to justify their criticisms. As for the Charismatic Renewal, the impact of the Council is more indirect: it created the context for the emergence and spread of the Renewal, with its emphasis on ecumenism and the role of the Holy Spirit.[104] But the Council as such holds little place in the memories of members and leaders of the

Renewal in Bangalore. The history of Vatican II in the Archdiocese of Bangalore illustrates the contradictions and tensions inherent in the project of modernity, to which the church is far from immune. Certain readings of the Council share the conceit of modernization theory of the sort developed by Talcott Parsons and others in the 1950s. The pervasive assumption among these social theorists was that modernization and urbanization would produce emotionally restrained and self-interested individuals who would simply be unaffected by racial or ethnic concerns. The various forms of ethnic and national revivals that emerged in the second half of the twentieth century have proved to be one of the more formidable challenges to modernization theory.[105]

NOTES

1. Details of the incident are found in Ravi Sharma, "Kannada and the Church: Unholy Conflict," *Blossom City*, 1 (1990). The full text of Sharma's story is reproduced in Anthony Simo, *The History of the Archdiocese of Bangalore, Volume II, 1971–1990* (Bangalore: Fr. Anthony Simo, printed by St. Paul's, 1997), pp. 491–503.
2. Sharma incorrectly reports his name as Jeganather.
3. Simo lists the "rebel priests" as Frs. I. Anthappa, T. S. Amruthraj (elsewhere spelled Amirthraj), A. Thomas, Stany Baptist, Fathiraj (also spelled Fatiraj), I. Joseph, C. Francis, Chowrappa Selvaraj, I. Chinappan, S. Mariappa, T. Bernard, and R. Savarimuthu.
4. "Additional charge sheet filed in Fr. Thomas murder case," *Deccan Herald*, December 2, 2015. Accessed at www.deccanherald.com/content/515105/additional-charge-sheet-filed-fr.html. The case continues to evolve, but as of this writing, the Supreme Court of Karnataka has rejected criminal proceedings against those named on a second charge sheet. Two priests, Fr. Elias and Fr. Patrick, await trial. See "Priest murder: Karnataka HC quashes proceedings against 6 accused," *Indian Express*, September 2, 2016. Accessed at indianexpress.com/article/india/india-news-india/priest-murder-karnataka-hc-quashes-proceedings-against-6-accused-k-j-thomas-3009083/.
5. *Sacrosanctum Concilium*, promulgated by Pope Paul VI, December 4, 1963, 22.2, 36, 63.
6. See Alana Harris, Chapter 12, this volume.
7. Many people I interviewed in researching this chapter were hesitant to speak about this issue openly and asked to remain anonymous. This is understandable in light of stories of nationalists attacking individuals and families who challenged them. Simo's historical volumes, intended primarily to make historical records of diocesan communications available to the people, were forcibly confiscated from bookstores and libraries and publicly burned because of his criticism of activist priests voiced at the end of the second volume, so I have been careful in respecting sources' requests for anonymity.
8. John Paul II, *Slavorum Apostoli*, June 2, 1985, 21.

9. *Sacrosanctum Concilium*, 14.

10. The state government changed the city's official name to its Kannada pronunciation in 2006 ("Good morning, Bengaluru," *Times of India*, Dec. 12, 2005). The archdiocese, however, retains "Bangalore."

11. Kempe Gowda I formally inaugurated it in 1537. However, research suggests human settlements in the area dating as far back as 2000 BCE. The earliest mention of the word "Bengaluru" appears in an inscription dating to 890 CE ("The City of Boiled Beans," *The Hindu*, July 25, 2002).

12. Indian states and territories were reorganized along linguistic lines in 1956. The majority Kannada-speaking region, initially named Mysore State, was renamed Karnataka in 1973.

13. Some records suggest an earlier Christian presence in the area from visits of Dominican friars in the tenth and fourteenth centuries, though there is little consensus among sources.

14. See Domenico Ferroli, *The Jesuits in Mysore* (Kozhikode: Xavier Press, 1955); Jean Castets, *La mission du Maduré* (Trinchinopoly: St. Joseph's Industrial School Press, 1924); Sanjay Subrahmanyam, "Warfare and State Finance in Wodeyar Mysore, 1724–25: A Missionary Perspective," *Indian Economic Social History Review* 26:2 (1989), 203–33; Anthony Simo, *The History of the Archdiocese of Bangalore*, vol. 1. (Bangalore: Fr. Anthony Simo, printed by St. Paul's, 1993), pp. 1–15; I. Anthappa, Shree Swamy, trans., *The Origin of Christianity in and around Srirangapattana* (Bangalore: St. Joseph's College, 2007), pp. 37–38.

15. Simo, *History*, p. 14; Ferroli, *Jesuits*, 86–7; Anthappa, *Origin*, p. 144–45.

16. Anthappa, *Origin*, p. 160

17. Lewin Bowring, *Haidar Alí and Tipú Sultán and the Struggle with the Musalmán Powers of the South* (Oxford: Clarendon Press, 1899), p. 126; Alan Machado Prabhu, *Sarasvati's Children: A History of the Mangalorean Christians* (Bangalore: I.J.A. Publications, 1999). Some, however, argue that Tipu was much more tolerant of Christians than most accounts indicate. See Praxy Fernandes, *The Tigers of Mysore—A Biography of Tipu Sultan and Hyder Ali* (New Delhi: Viking, 1991).

18. Muthaiah D. Appavoo, *The Effect of Migration on the Churches of Bangalore* (Bangalore: Christian Institute for the Study of Religion and Society, 1965), pp. 2, 10, 17; I. Anthappa, personal interview, March 15, 2014.

19. Personal interview with former archbishop Ignatius Pinto, February 6, 2012.

20. At the time of the Council, he was bishop auxiliary. Archbishop Pothacamury had taken seriously ill, and Lourdusamy would soon take over as archbishop.

21. Personal interview, February 2, 2012.

22. "The expression 'lingua vernacularis,' in the original Latin text of the Constitution [on the sacred liturgy] has been rendered into 'mother tongue' in all recognized English translations of that text ... and not the 'regions language' [*sic*] as understood in political terminology, unless it is also mother tongue of local Catholics." Report of the Proceedings of meetings of the Newman Association of India, December 7, 1980, and January 11, 1981, reproduced in Simo, *History*, 1997, p. 508.

23. Further, he added that indults for "the administration of the Sacraments and Sacramentals" were available for English and Tamil only, and all priests were "required to make full use of them," Simo, *History*, 1993, p. 460.

24. Personal interview, February 2, 2012. See also circular of Bishop Auxiliary, dated August 8, 1964.

25. Janaki Nair, *The Promise of the Metropolis: Bangalore's Twentieth Century* (New Delhi: Oxford University Press, 2005), p. 249.

26. Nair, The Promise of the Metropolis, p. 278.

27. Nair, *The Promise of the Metropolis*, p. 245.

28. Personal interview, April 22, 2012.

29. Simo, *History*, 1997, p. 490.

30. Personal interview, January 24, 2012.

31. Personal interview, April 23, 2012

32. I borrow the term "language tangle" from a Simo chapter title, *History*, 1997, p. 471.
   Founded in 1622 by Pope Gregory XV, it was known until 1982 as the Sacred Congregation for the Propagation of the Faith (Sacra Congregatio de Propaganda Fide).

33. A priest suggested that the reason may be in part complaints that came from Tamil Nadu bishops because he neglected to consult with them about activities in the Tamil vernacular. "There's a normal saying in Latin, '*Promoveatur ut amoveatur,*' which means, let him be promoted so that he is removed."

34. Circular letter 11/71, December 31, 1971.

35. As this is the year in which the state of Karnataka took its official name, nationalist sentiments must have been especially strong.

36. Personal interview, February 2, 2012.

37. Personal interview, February 2, 2012.

38. Circular letter 6/78, May 23, 1978.

39. Nair, *Promise*, p. 243.

40. Nair, *Promise*, p. 253

41. Sharma quotes one Fr. Thomas who expresses this coalition as a result of a lack of choice: "We have no platform to speak, [as] all channels within the Church have been closed to us . . . Like the good Samaritan, these organizations have come to our aid when no one in the Church cared" (in Simo, *History*, 1997, p. 500). Janaki Nair notes that throughout the various riots of the 1980s and 1990s, several other prominent Kannada intellectuals, representing a more secular stance, condemned the violent actions of their counterparts (p. 398, note 39). The Catholic agitators I spoke to claimed that they kept their distance from Hindu nationalists because they feared they would be used merely for political ends. Kannada nationalists should therefore not be seen as a monolithic group.

42. Nair, *Promise*, p. 253.

43. "Clash in Cathedral: Archbishop Gheraoed," *Deccan Herald*, April 17, 1981.

44. Personal interview, February 7, 2012.

45. "33 Held After Disturbance in Church," *Deccan Herald*, May 4, 1981.

46. Personal interview, April 22, 2012.

47. Personal interview, January 24, 2012.

48. Circular letter 4/31, April 21, 1981.

49. Circular letter 9/82, December 8, 1982.

50. Circular letter 3/83, March 24 1983.

51. Personal interview, March 24, 2014.

52. Circular letter 7/84, December 8, 1984.

53. Anil Alva, "M'lore: Most Rev. Dr. Alphonsus Mathias – Leading by Example!" mangalorean.com, August 11, 2009. Accessed at www.mangalorean.com/news.php? newstype=broadcast&broadcastid=138570

54. Circular letter 2/88, February 29, 1988.

55. A translation of the text of the manifesto is reproduced in Simo, *History*, 1997, p. 506.

56. In 1992, the president of the Kannada Catholic Christhara Sangha, J. R. Pereira, argued that Kannada Catholics were being refused jobs in Christian institutions, notably St. John's Medical College, Christ College, and Dharmaram College, and these jobs were being given instead to non-Kannadigas, at the archbishop's behest ("Jobs: Kannada Christians Allege Discrimination," *Indian Express*, Aug. 13, 1992).

57. Simo, *History*, 1997, p. 505.

58. Personal interview, March 15, 2014.

59. Personal interview, March 15, 2014.

60. See Nair, *Promise*, p. 246.

61. Several people I talked to echoed the following claim articulated by one priest, who preferred not to be named in this regard: "Of the Kannadigas also, *real* Kannadiga hardly anybody! They are more Telugus! They are Telugus whose education was in Kannada, that's all. At home they spoke Telugu, but they took up the cudgel for Kannada, that's all."

62. Quoted by Sharma (Simo, *History*, 1997, p. 497). Their grievances would intensify over the years. The three most recent archbishops, starting with Alphonsus Mathias, are of Konkani origin. However, many Konkani natives also consider themselves Kannadigas, since they are natives of the state of Karnataka and are usually fluent in Kannada, yet they want to retain their mother tongues as well.

63. Fr. Selvaraj, personal interview, March 15, 2014.

64. Some suggest that economic changes have helped temper the situation overall. "The encroaching of urban into rural areas reduces the base of people who can be marshaled for such protest," notes Fr. Francis Guntipilly. As a result, "the very children of the Kannada-movement people are in either English-medium and not with Kannada as a first language. So things have changed and their interests are changed." Personal interview, January 24, 2012. Even activists such as Fr. Selvaraj complained that most Kannada Catholics had become "commercialized" – fixated more on individual economic advancement than the welfare of their community.

65. "Rivalry Drove 2 Priests, Altar Boy to Murder Fr Thomas." *The Times of India*, March 21, 2014. Accessed at timesofindia.indiatimes.com/city/bangalore/Rivalry-drove-2-priests-altar-boy-to-murder-Fr-Thomas/articleshow/32438076.cms; "More Persons involved in Rector Murder" *The Hindu*, March 21, 2014, accessed at www .thehindu.com/news/cities/bangalore/more-persons-involved-in-rector-murder /article5815899.ece.

66. *Times of India*, March 21, 2014.

67. "Bangalore: Police Crack Fr K J Thomas Murder Case: 3 Arrested, More Likely." *Daiji World*, March 21, 2014. Accessed at www.daijiworld.com/news/news_disp .asp?n_id=224344.

68. "Fr K J Thomas Murder: Kannada Priests Claim Aarrested Are 'Innocent,'" *Daiji World*, March 22, 2014. Accessed at www.daijiworld.com/news/news_disp.asp? n_id=224575. Statements by the accused priests confessing to the crime are posted

on a publicly accessible Facebook page dedicated to the murdered rector: www
.facebook.com/permalink.php?story_fbid=860957397259448&id=563947853627072;
www.facebook.com/permalink.php?story_fbid=864951816860006&id=5639478536
27072

69. "Arrests in Priest Murder Case Divide Catholic Church," *Indian Express*, April 21,
    2014, accessed at indianexpress.com/article/cities/bangalore/arrests-in-priest-
    murder-case-divide-catholic-church/; "Rector Murder Case," *Indian Christian
    Activist Network*, March 24, 2015, accessed at www.persecutedchurch.info/2015/
    03/26/rector-murder-case/.

70. Personal interview, April 22, 2012.

71. Ines G. Zupanov, *Disputed Mission: Jesuit Experiments and Brahmanical Knowledge in
    Seventeenth-Century India* (New Delhi: Oxford University Press, 1999).

72. Helen Ralston, *Christian Ashrams: A New Religious Movement in Contemporary India*
    (Lewiston, NY: Edwin Mellen Press, 1987).

73. The term itself appears in official documents only starting in 1977 ("Message to the
    People of God," Oct 29, 1977) and then only sees a definition in 1985: "the intimate
    transformation of authentic cultural values through their integration in Christianity
    and the insertion of Christianity in the various human cultures" (Extraordinary
    Synod of Bishops, 1985: II, D.4; *Redemptoris Missio* 52).

74. For an exhaustive bibliography and exposition of his corpus, see Gerwin van
    Leeuwen, *Fully Indian – Authentically Christian: A study of the Ffirst Fifteen Years of
    the NBCLC (1967–1982), Bangalore, India, in the Light of the Theology of Its Founder,
    D. S. Amalorpavadass* (Kampen, Netherlands: J. H. Kok, 1990), and John
    Berchmans Barla, *Christian Theological Understanding of Other Religions according to
    D. S. Amalorpavadass*, Documenta Missionalia, 26 (Rome: Editrice Pontificia
    Universita Gregoriana, 1999).

75. D. S. Amalorpavadass, *Towards Indigenisation in the Liturgy: Theological Reflection, Policy,
    Programme, and Texts* (Bangalore: NBCLC, 1972), pp. 165–66; D. S. Amalorpavadass,
    NBCLC Campus: Milieu of God-Experience: An Artistic Synthesis of Spirituality, rev. ed.
    (Bangalore: NBCLC, 2005), p. 2.

76. The land was obtained and earmarked by Lourdusamy, who in a letter to the CBCI
    defends the choice of Bangalore as the ideal site for this all-India Center, found in
    D. S. Amalorpavadass, *Post Vatican Liturgical Renewal in India: 1963 December–1968*
    (Bangalore: NBCLC, 1977).

77. Amalorpavadass, NBCLC Campus, p. 12.

78. Amalorpavadass, NBCLC Campus, pp. 15–16.

79. Amalorpavadass, NBCLC Campus, pp. 18–34.

80. Amalorpavadass, NBCLC Campus, p. 18.

81. See, e.g., Victor J. F. Kulanday, *The Paganized Catholic Church in India* (Madras:
    The Laity, 1985).

82. Fritz Mascarenhas, personal interview, April 2, 2012.

83. Benny Aguiar, "Decolonizing the Church," in Teotónio R. de Souza (ed.),
    Discoveries, Missionary Expansion And Asian Cultures (New Delhi: Concept
    Publishing, 1994), pp. 139–150, at 142; Michael Davies, "On This and That," *The
    Angelus*, October 1984.

84. Michelle Voss Roberts, "Tasting the Divine: The Aesthetics of Religious Emotion
    in Indian Christianity," *Religion* 42: 4 (2012), 575–95.

85. Letter 851/1971/50, April 25, 1969, from the Consilium ad Exsequendam Constitutionem De Sacra Liturgia to Most Rev. D. Simon Lourdusamy, chairman, CBCI Commission for Liturgy. Prot. n. 802/69.

86. Benny Aguiar, "Impact of Vatican II on India and Sri Lanka," in *Down the Arches of the Years* (Mumbai: St. Paul's, 2002) pp.124–25. Published earlier as a chapter in Adrian Hastings (ed.), *Modern Catholicism, Vatican II and After* (Oxford University Press, 1991).

87. Aguiar, "Impact of Vatican II on India and Sri Lanka," p. 125.

88. Julian Saldanha, S.J. *Inculturation*, 2nd ed. (Mumbai: St. Paul's, 1996), p. 61.

89. Interview with current NBCLC director Cleophas Fernandes, cited in Roberts, "Tasting the Divine," p. 590.

90. "As Indians we can claim all that is Hindu and Indian as our own; as Christians we can state that whatever belongs to Christ [i.e., anything true in Hinduism] belongs to us. So we borrow nothing." D. S. Amalorpavadass, *Gospel and Culture* (Bangalore: NBCLC, 1978), pp. 40–41.

91. Saldanha, *Inculturation*, pp. 62–63; Amalorpavadass, *Gospel and Culture*, chap. 4.

92. Cited in Saldanha, *Inculturation*, p. 63.

93. Mathew N. Schmalz, "Ad Experimentum: The Paradoxes of Indian Catholic Inculturation" in Michael H. Barnes (ed.), *Theology and the Social Sciences* (Maryknoll, NY: Orbis, 2001), pp. 161–80.

94. Schmalz, "Ad Experimentum," p. 172.

95. Zupanov, *Disputed Mission*, p. 27.

96. This is very evident in the vicious debate between Bede Griffiths and Swami Devananda, published in Sita Ram Goel, *Catholic Ashrams: Sannyasins or Swindlers?* (New Delhi: Voice of India, 1994), chap. 12.

97. Schmalz, "Ad Experimentum," p. 175

98. George Soares-Prabhu, S.J., "A Letter from George Soares-Prabhu to Vandana Mataji" in *Christian Ashrams: A Movement with a Future?* (New Delhi: ISPCK, 1993), pp. 153–60.

99. Personal interview, April 15, 2012.

100. Fr. Guntipilly, S.J., personal interview.

101. Personal interview, April 15, 2012.

102. Personal interview, April 2, 2012.

103. Personal interview. Arockiaswamy also went on a foreign tour of the United States and Canada, and in a circular, mentions having spent time that year studying the Charismatic Renewal and participating in many Charismatic prayer meetings. He spoke with approval and admiration of this movement (Circular letter 9/76, September 15, 1976).

104. The influence of Cardinal Suenens as a proponent of this movement is especially important. See Leon Joseph Suenens, *A New Pentecost?* (New York: Seabury Press, 1975).

105. Vilho Harle, *The Enemy With a Thousand Faces: The Tradition of the Other in Western Political Thought and History* (Harcourt: Greenwood, 2000), p. 2.

10

DEBATING THE COUNCIL ON THE
AIR: MEDIA, PERSONALITY,
AND THE TRANSFORMATION
OF THE DUTCH CHURCH

MARJET DERKS

The diocese of 's-Hertogenbosch, the Netherlands, was the epitome of rapid religious transformation. Liberal episcopal policy apparently led to egalitarianism but actually endorsed specific groups: social scientists, progressive theologians, and liturgically experimental priests. Contributing to the confusing, sometimes chaotic consequences, was the Dutch media, itself fully in line with the liberal Catholic agenda.

ON MAY 9, 1966, THE NEARLY TWENTY-MILE ROAD BETWEEN the towns of 's-Hertogenbosch and Sint-Oedenrode, the Netherlands, was lined with people of all ages and occupations, silently, reverently watching the passage of the hearse bearing the last remains of Monsignor Rinie Bekkers. The immensely popular bishop of 's-Hertogenbosch had died at the age of 58 after a short illness. Following the funeral Mass in the diocesan cathedral of Saint John, Bekkers's body was brought to his hometown to be buried. His final journey was epic. It was the first time that the funeral of a Dutch bishop was broadcast on national television and radio. Viewers and listeners heard prominent Catholic politicians as well as the well-known Nijmegen Dominican theologian Edward Schillebeeckx give their recollections of Bekkers. Those who missed the funeral could follow it in the country's newspapers, which reported extensively on the "day of national mourning."[1]

The event of Bekkers's requiem and interment is in striking contrast to the visit of a more prominent member of the hierarchy just twenty years later. The streets were almost empty on the day in 1985 that Pope John Paul II began his visit to the Netherlands in 's-Hertogenbosch, usually known as Den Bosch. This did not surprise the secretary-general of the Dutch episcopate, Hans van Munster. "Given the mental climate in the Netherlands,"

206

Bishop van Munster told the press, "such an invitation was bound to fail." Only a few months before the pope's arrival, the overtly traditional Bishop Jan ter Schure was installed in the diocese, after his predecessor Jan Bluyssen (Bekkers's successor in 1966) had stepped down. The official reason given for Bluyssen's resignation was ill health, but it was an open secret that the bishop was increasingly troubled by the Vatican's policy of appointing conservative bishops as a way of reasserting ecclesiastical authority over the overly liberal Dutch church. The post-conciliar era definitely seemed to have come to an end in 's-Hertogenbosch by the time of the pope's visit. Cardinal Simonis, himself a conservative bishop, saw the lack of an audience for the pope as a protest. "It was very uneasy, a demonstrative emptiness," he said afterward.[2]

The Diocese of 's-Hertogenbosch (named after its capital city) was the central locus of changing church life in the Netherlands in the aftermath of Vatican II. Bishops Bekkers and Bluyssen along with the Dutch clergy vigorously supported a vision of the church as the people of God; the national media, taken with the idea of an up-to-date Catholicism, reported on their efforts at renewal with enthusiastic approval. But the public image of a more democratic church belied the persistence of old hierarchies and obscured the formation of new ones. Behind the enthusiastic press reports of *aggiornamento*, a clerical avant-garde together with an educated lay elite took over authoritative positions, molding the sacral and sacramental church into a shape that suited them but estranged many average Catholics in the diocese.

A Rural Diocese in Transformation

The Diocese of 's-Hertogenbosch, located in southern Netherlands, covers a large part of the province of Brabant and several smaller parts of Gelderland, all predominantly Catholic (85 percent). On the eve of the Second Vatican Council, with 1,129,714 baptized Catholics (more than 25 percent of the country's Catholic population), it was the largest diocese in the nation.[3] The culture of the large diocese was Catholic and rural; its fields were dotted with churches and with chapels of the Virgin Mary and statues of the Sacred Heart. There were just a few large cities in the diocese ('s-Hertogenbosch, Tilburg, Eindhoven, Nijmegen). In his popular books of regional imagery, local photographer Martien Coppens captured the small-scale, rural, and traditional context in which the church had once flourished. Its architecture, as well as its spirit, was identified as "Brabantine" Gothic.[4] Historians, however, have begun to question this image, pointing out that the vision of harmonious Catholic rural life emerged as opposition to regional emancipation in the first half of the twentieth century. Underlying tensions were effaced; they would surface later in the century.[5]

The transformations in the region during the 1960s and 1970s were not so much a break with the past as fully consistent with the diocese's historically ambiguous character. New churches were being built well into the 1950s to keep pace with the growing population; at the same time, religious and sociocultural circumstances had begun to change around them. As in other Dutch dioceses, the growth in the number of practicing Catholics was declining; then the number of Catholics dropped. From the middle of the 1960s onward, church attendance in the diocese went down significantly, from 70.8 percent in 1965 to 17.6 percent in 1985. Consequently, many city parishes were compelled to merge; churches in the smaller cities and villages followed. Consolidation efforts resulted eventually in the closing of 24 percent of all parishes, the highest number among dioceses in the Netherlands. A mass exodus from the priesthood and from religious life and a large fall in clerical and religious recruitment were also underway. All of these changes had already begun to cause concern in the diocese during the Vatican Council.[6]

Developments within the church after the Council must be seen against the wider background of profound social and cultural change. Prosperity and with it leisure time increased in the postwar economic boom and the rise of the welfare state. The year 1962 saw the introduction of the five-day workweek; weekend trips began to compete with Mass attendance. The state began to provide for social welfare for all Dutch citizens, assuming almost entire control of the vast network of church-based care institutions and charity.[7] People no longer depended on the church as a safety net. This was a time of radical change in Dutch education as well. Schools that had been in the care of religious orders since the nineteenth century were turned over to laypeople, further diminishing the public presence of religion. At the same time, levels of schooling increased. Children of farmers and laborers had begun to attend high school and then one of the two Dutch Catholic universities in Nijmegen or Tilburg, being often the first ones in families to do so. While the number of seminarians steadily decreased, that of regular students in Nijmegen increased from 2,000 in 1960 to 9,000 in 1970 and 15,000 in 1980.

In the cities largely, but throughout the diocese too, young people began to question authority as they demanded the right to shape their own understandings of their world. The generation of the 1960s and 1970s protested not only against capitalism or right-wing politics but also against the authority of the church. Illustrative of these shifts was the formation of a national leftist student union by a laborer's son and former seminarian in Nijmegen and the student magazine *NUB*'s transition from a Catholic periodical into a medium of social and religious protest. A satirical pornographic article in *NUB* (1969) led to accusations of public indecency and a lawsuit.[8] All of this had far-reaching consequences in the diocese, often leading to deep inner-family conflicts that came to center on church matters.[9]

Spreading *Aggiornamento*: Media Bishop

For a while, the Second Vatican Council and particularly the new bishop seemed a powerful antidote to these disturbing social transformations. The aforementioned Rinie Bekkers was appointed bishop of 's-Hertogenbosch in 1960. A farmer's son from a small village, Bekkers presented himself as an occasionally authoritative eminence on the one hand, but also as a man of the people. He was a good-natured and approachable communicator, the opposite of his predecessor, the aloof and conservative Willem Mutsaerts, who was the son of a wealthy factory owner from Tilburg. Bekkers was associated with the simplicity and harmony of rural and pastoral Brabant – an image that he deliberately cultivated – yet he also sympathized with modern currents. For many people, clerical and lay, who were confused by the ongoing upheavals of late modernity within and outside the church, Bekkers embodied the hope of preserving "tradition" without its sharp socially divisive edges.[10]

Bekkers personified the Second Vatican Council for many Dutch Catholics. He was even known as "the Dutch Pope John." To a large extent, the *aggiornamento* owed its acceptability to his advocacy. Bekkers represented the Council to his diocese as the beginnings of a new, more communal church that would be attentive to the needs of contemporaries. In this, he was in full accord with the Council's proclamations.

Bekkers's promotion of *aggiornamento* on television contributed to the Council's positive reception in the Netherlands. Manufactured by Philips in Eindhoven, television sets in the era of the Council were becoming a mass medium (11 percent of the households nationwide owned a television set, in 1958; in 1966, it was 80 percent). The nation's one channel had a monopoly of viewers' attention. Bekkers was on good terms with journalists, particularly with the new generation of young reporters from middle-class backgrounds who were keen on renewal.[11] Mediagenic, capable of attracting viewers, Bekkers became a regular guest in the nation's living rooms, just at the time the church was becoming less of a place of public gathering.

The successful courtship between bishop and television began to blossom during the Council and was in full bloom from 1963 onward. Bekkers made his first appearance on a Catholic news show called *Brandpunt* (*Focus*) in 1961. The program was scheduled on Saturday evening right after the eight o'clock news and drew a large audience. Once a month, at the end of the show, Bekkers delivered a short speech. Initially, his performance was what one might expect of a European bishop – in contrast, for example, to the suave and ebullient self-presentation of America's Bishop Fulton J. Sheen – but at the suggestion of the producers of *Brandpunt*, Bekkers changed his style. He began appearing in a simple priest's suit, speaking conversationally, and to address topical issues, including political ones. The new format was a hit, but it also led to confusion. Was this the bishop speaking *ex officio* or was the bishop speaking as a public figure, like others that appeared on television?[12]

This blurring of identity was reinforced by media coverage of the Vatican Council in the Netherlands, which relied on Bekkers to communicate news of the meeting in Rome to audiences at home. Contrary to official conciliar policy, the bishop actively sought out the press every day to present his version of *aggiornamento*, either after the morning sessions or in the evenings, when he frequently dined out in the Eternal City with Dutch journalists. In one interview, for example, Bekkers expressed his view that it was absolutely crucial for the church to identify with modern ways of life to be better able to Christianize them. City dwellers and young people, he said, no longer felt any connection to traditional devotional life (of the sort that was still flourishing in the Brabant). He concluded by calling for more sociological analysis of people's needs and expectations, together with more communication within the church, between clergy and laity. Communication became his watchword.[13]

After the first Council session in 1963, Bekkers, who had become quite accustomed to media attention, believed it was time to tackle one of the most urgent but also most complex questions of the time: contraception. Throughout the rural diocese of 's-Hertogenbosch, the powerful clergy had long emphasized the sin of contraception, and large families were presented as eminently Catholic and Brabantine, something to be proud of. The reality, of course, was more complex. Letters written in the 1980s in which mothers looked back on this period show that this was a profoundly stressful time, when women believed their whole existence was valued as "only someone who bears children." Some of the letter writers referred to the warmth of close-knit family life, but the large majority emphasized the monthly tensions and the anxiety this caused in married life, as well as the poverty that came with bringing up a large family.[14]

During his numerous trips through his diocese, Bekkers heard many such stories and was touched by them, as he told his own family members on several occasions.[15] By the time of his unprecedented television talk on the topic, the contraceptive pill had just become available on the Dutch market. Its manufacturer, Organon, was located within the diocese, and by the night of Bekkers's appearance on television to speak of contraception, many Catholics (particularly many family doctors) were anxiously awaiting the formal response of their church to the question. Convinced that official church policy was about to change, Bekkers took up the subject of family planning. Although he did not promote the use of the pill, Bekkers made an unexpected statement: the decision about the number of children to have, he said, was the responsibility of the married couple "and theirs only." It was a matter of conscience, he said, "in which no-one may intervene." Communication would show the way.[16]

Communication did not show the way. Bekkers's solo performance provoked an avalanche of reaction, more confused than outraged. What exactly had the bishop been saying, with his appealing accent and friendly demeanor? Was he stating official church policy? For weeks, comments and letters flowed in to Dutch newspapers and hundreds of letters were sent directly to Bekkers. The letters varied from enthusiastic approval to rejection, with much confusion in between. "For people with lax morals it's permission; for those who are serious there's too little to go on," one priest wrote. Many law abiding laypeople felt betrayed by Bekkers's position. Had their pain and suffering in the past been all gratuitous? Physicians, in particular, were at a loss. They suddenly found their waiting rooms full of women demanding the pill. Although he had rightfully sensed the urgency of the topic, Bekkers believed he had been misunderstood; he had not been advocating the pill, he insisted. But he had appropriated the Council's language of *aggiornamento* to discuss the issue, while underestimating the difficulty of its practical implementation. He had also failed to understand the power of television.[17]

A Diocese in Discussion

To the educated laity and several priests in Bekkers's diocese, renewal was not an unfamiliar concept. On the eve of the Vatican Council, they had already begun to be more forthright about their criticisms of the traditional church, in particular of the dominance of the "Italian" curia, the superficiality of devotional practices, and the underacknowledged role of the laity.[18] They expressed themselves at conferences; in the diocesan journal; and in so-called Ecclesia groups, loosely organized small parish debating societies made up in each case of laypeople and a priest. There were 305 of these groups in 68 parishes in the diocese in 1961. More than 2,800 people participated, particularly middle-class married couples, often newcomers to the larger cities who used the Ecclesia groups to meet people. The Ecclesia circles began to function as loci of new Catholic ideals.[19] From early 1962 onward, priests had also been meeting in discussion groups among themselves, to talk about the pastoral problems they were facing. In particular, they felt overburdened with the unfamiliar responsibilities of a dialogic, participatory church of the people of God, while having to face the fact that their old authority was diminishing.[20]

Inspired both by the Council and the discussion groups, Bekkers initiated what he called the "Bossche Council," an ongoing movement of discussion groups in his diocese to maintain the spirit of Vatican II ("communication") and to work on building a sustainable bottom-up church. In October 1963, a letter was sent to all households in the diocese, inviting people to participate in parish discussion groups to work on continuing the effect of Vatican II. Every year, a central topic would be announced; first up was the subject of confession. The fact that so many young people no longer went to confession was one reason to put this topic forward; another was the increasing discomfort of priests about having to hear it.[21]

Although at first there was some disapproval that questions were decided by the diocesan staff, Bekkers managed to disarm the critics.[22] More than 600 discussion groups were formed, meeting four times a year. Most consisted solely of laypeople (and some were only for youth), while others brought together laity and priests, still others were for priests only, for nuns only, or for male religious. The following year, tens of thousands of parishioners took up the theme "Liturgy and Eucharist." In the Dutch media as well as in international outlets, Bekkers's discussion movement was seen as the epitome of true post-conciliar spirit. A socialist newspaper praised this unprecedented progressiveness on the part of the Catholic hierarchy.[23] A German television documentary labeled it as "a landmark in the making of church history," with Bekkers cast in the role of the "reformer."[24]

It was quite astonishing to have more than 2,500 people discussing topics that hitherto had been taboo. However, contrary to what was sometimes suggested, this was not an unequivocally "popular" movement. Although everyone was invited, in practice only the most engaged and educated responded, along with leading local social and political figures, leaving out the less educated and the less eloquent, as well as those less involved with church affairs. The discussion movement also triggered the involvement of academically trained "social experts," priests and laity, who preferred well-organized discussions of readings and lectures. They generated a huge quantity of response papers. A newly installed secretariat in Eindhoven assisted all new groups by sending out written material and a set of questions. After every round of discussions, written reports were sent back to the secretariat, which was immediately overloaded by all the paperwork. These reports were digested by the now-expanded secretariat and then handed over to expert committees of sociologists and psychologists, who culled from them outcomes to serve as guidelines for the following round of discussions, as well as, eventually, for new diocesan policy. A chairperson trained in discussion techniques led all of the groups.[25]

"This is the beginning of a genuine Church, with three elements as its Fundamentals: God's mercy; science to figure it out; and the input of believers, priests, religious, and laypeople together," Bekkers told a journalist. In the meantime, while the bishop left "science to figure it out," language and practice had changed in the diocese: personal faith and dialogue were emphasized, devotional practices discouraged or even abolished. In the village of Groesbeek, for instance, in the eastern part of the diocese, six popular devotions were abolished during and after the Vatican Council. The procession of the Blessed Sacrament, held yearly since 1935, was halted after 1963; the practice of weekly benediction came to an end. The interior of the parish church was simplified. A newly built church in the diocese was designed as a square building with a modern interior, and with chairs arranged in a circle around the altar instead of pews. Whereas once upon a time, which is to say, as recently as 1955, the celebration of a priestly jubilee attracted as many as thirty-five parish societies, only ten attended the installation of two new priests in 1965. And whereas more than 600 families had purchased statues of the Sacred Heart between 1949 and 1959, this number dropped off dramatically after 1960. This steady elimination of the old devotions – by priests as well as by the bishop himself – added to the growing alienation and polarization in the diocese. It profoundly saddened some, who silently continued observing the older devotions in the privacy of their homes; others (and not only younger people) welcomed the changes, calling what had come before merely a kind of empty performance. For still others, it proved that the church leadership could not be trusted.[26]

Meanwhile, Bekkers extolled the contribution of the discussion method, within but increasingly also outside his diocese. In January 1966, the bishop held a nationally televised conversation with seven representatives of the discussion groups: a housewife, a nurse, a nun, an electrician, a chaplain, a schoolteacher, and a civil servant. In this "Talk with the Bishop," another first for Dutch television, it became apparent what had made the discussion group approach so successful. People associated it with the popular and approachable bishop who had instituted it. The representatives spoke freely, although the men were more frank than the women. The schoolteacher even commented to Bekkers, "it may be funny to say this to a bishop, but the Church will have to withdraw more in order to give lay people the chance to become more conscious as Christians." This was how seemingly egalitarian Dutch Catholic culture had become, at least in the diocese of 's-Hertogenbosch. Such things could be said to Bekkers, who replied with a witty remark and gave everyone present in the studio and those tuning in from outside the feeling that all would work out just fine.[27]

But confusion was mounting. In a lengthy reflective letter to the editor of a national Catholic newspaper, a woman from Eindhoven expressed her quandary. Did the bishop and many of his priests really think that the discussions would lead to a better type of Catholicism? Was the bishop at all aware of the confusion he had caused in so many families? The bishop was always talking about love and communication, the writer accused, but with the Catholic devotional past now held in such contempt, good people who had been acting out of love for God and the church were simply put aside.[28] From this and other letters, it becomes clear that Bekkers's interpretation of the Council did not appeal to all his flock, despite his own growing legend as "friend of us all," to which his untimely death added substantially.[29]

Social Sciences Enter the Sermon

The growing impact of discussion and the role that social scientists had begun to play can also be illustrated by sermon experiments in Eindhoven. The poor quality of sermons had become a familiar theme among the more articulate and educated in the diocese, even if from the clergy's perspective this meant more weekly work for them.[30] In 1963, the dean of Eindhoven came to the conclusion that it was becoming increasingly difficult to reach all believers through the traditional Mass. He concluded that the traditional Mass no longer held sufficient appeal, since more and more believers no longer felt inspired by it and threatened to skip Sunday Mass. He decided that a makeover was necessary. He called in a church-related consulting group, De Horstink, to provide consultancy advice.[31]

Members of the Horstink staff were trained as social scientists; church communications was their business. From March 1963 onward, they met on a regular basis with the dean, four priests, and two laypeople, a man and a woman. Earlier experiments in other dioceses allegedly had shown that within a couple of hours, two-thirds of the congregation in attendance had forgotten what the sermon they had just listened to was about. The view was taking shape among reformers that sermons could only reach people if they touched their emotions and addressed issues of people's everyday experience.[32] To improve the way that sermons communicated their message, the Horstink staff suggested a joint consultation involving priests from thirty parishes within the city and its immediate surroundings. It was proposed that for several weeks these priests all focus their sermons on the same themes. Churchgoers would be interviewed afterward at all the parishes simultaneously to find out how the sermon had been received. The feedback would serve both to improve the preaching and to stimulate communication between priests and believers.[33]

Not only did the proposal result in the usual mass of paperwork; it also put on public display how selection criteria were being used to include or exclude people from active participation in the changing life of the church. The Horstink staff stipulated that a working committee of priests and lay-people be installed to set the themes for the sermons. The laypeople were to be "professionals," preferably psychologists and sociologists, who were trained by their profession "to understand all that is going on within modern man regarding religion." The interviewers likewise had to be "intelligent and sensible people," whose religious views ought not to be outspoken, because this would prevent interviewees from speaking up. Horstink staff insisted that interviewers be between twenty-five and forty-five years old, because those older than forty-five were seen as "clinging too much to older views on religion and Church," which would put off younger respondents. The interviewers might be assisted and trained by "students of social sciences, social services, and experts in psychology, sociology and the like." To select these assistants, another committee was created.[34]

During the summer and early fall of 1963, the committee identified three themes: religious attitudes, interactions between believers and church, and the relationship between Christianity and humanism. More than 500 interviews were conducted. The results were predictable. A survey conducted early in 1964 showed that "a relatively high percentage of respondents had not returned the question sheets." Furthermore, the number of vague and roughly filled-in questions was also rather high. However, 45 percent of the priests were found to prefer sermons centered on the key dogmas of the Catholic faith, whereas younger chaplains expressed a preference for a prophetic sermon that addressed human relationships. It also emerged that since many of the priests were already overloaded with work, the majority did not have time for adequate sermon preparation, let alone for consultation with colleagues or laypeople.[35]

There is doubt as to whether this experiment in empirical research had any lasting effect. At least one letter to a Council postbox, the medium established for gathering opinions on church renewal, came from an Eindhoven parish priest who was still complaining in 1966 about the devastating effect of poor sermons on church attendance.[36] Another letter, by a teacher, accused the Eindhoven clergy of merely throwing questions at their flock instead of providing them with certainties and answers. A young man admitted to having left the church altogether because of what a priest had said during a sermon.[37] And a mother wrote that her adolescent children still were totally uninspired by the Sunday sermons.[38]

A Discursive Transformation

In hindsight, it becomes obvious that Bishop Bekkers's emphasis on communication and discussion produced equivocal results. Both the dialogue project reflecting his own direct approach to people and the sermon experiments were carried out with his authority. The identification of the dialogue project with the bishop was both its strongest and its weakest aspects. This became clear after Bekkers's death. In keeping with the egalitarianism and culture of dialogue in the diocese, the vicars gave the people a voice in drawing up the list of nominees for Bekkers's succession, another first in Dutch Catholic Church history. It was evident in the framing of the questions that it was expected Bekkers's successor would be someone like the beloved bishop: "What do you think about Msgr. Bekkers's policy and what were his most significant qualities?" The primary task of the man who succeeded him would be to continue Bekkers's policies. A large majority of the responses pointed to Bekkers's co-adjustor Jan Bluyssen (1926) and his appointment by the pope was met with great enthusiasm.[39]

Bluyssen was perhaps even more committed to the Vatican Council (at which he had been present) than his predecessor; he firmly upheld the conciliar ideal of the church as the people of God. Bluyssen had in fact been the organizer of many of Bekkers's casually introduced but never thoroughly worked out ideas, and so it was perhaps fitting that he bore the brunt of the backlash against Bekkers's renewal policy.[40] Bluyssen was a professor of spirituality, somewhat shy, with roots in the city of Nijmegen in the province of Gelderland, instead of rural Brabant. He left all of Bekkers's initiatives intact, but he also made it clear that there would be no more television broadcasts featuring the bishop of 's-Hertogenbosch. Yet, Bluyssen, too, believed in the power of words and the usefulness of pastoral talks. Already in his first letter to the diocese, he referred to himself as "an ordinary human being with his qualities and shortcomings." People who disagreed with him were invited to share their criticism.[41]

Perhaps for this reason, Bluyssen's pastoral letters grew ever longer over time, as he felt compelled to offer more extensive explanations of diocesan policy. The new bishop also found himself in the position of having to explain the meaning of rapidly introduced practices of renewal whose rationales were not immediately apparent to the clergy or the laity. More than once, the message was that further discussion was needed before the issue became clear. The flock began to send mixed signals back. In 1968, an evaluation report on the parish discussion groups revealed that although people did want a communicative clergy, more than 89 percent of the participants did not want priests to show their own personal uncertainties.[42]

Bluyssen freely offered social scientists, progressive theologians, and liturgically experimental priests room to have their way, even while the tumult in the church province grew in the second half of the 1960s and backlash became increasingly vociferous. The bishop believed that allowing dissident voices to speak was in accordance with the Vatican Council, which allowed for experimentation and dissent in the search for renewal and emphasized the importance of accepting "some temporality" in the quest for "authenticity."[43] However, the Curia decided that the Dutch were overstretching the approved bandwidth for experimenting. In 1967, Bluyssen was called to Rome to explain controversies that had risen, both in the Netherlands and elsewhere, about liturgical experiments.

The National Pastoral Council

The atmosphre at the National Pastoral Council of the Dutch Church Province in 1968 was tense and charged. A thoroughly renewal-oriented agenda prevailed. Allegedly the outcome of lengthy surveys and polling, the agenda allowed a long-simmering issue to boil over – the proposal to abolish clerical celibacy. Bluyssen and the other bishops were unable to prevent the issue from being voted on. A majority of young priests and educated laypeople accepted the proposal and urged Cardinal Bernard Alfrink to send their rejection of mandatory celibacy to Rome. This time, dialogue failed: Rome intervened, halting the Dutch interpretation of renewal by appointing conservative bishops. What had led to this outcome, which was quite unexpected by those who directed the renewal process?

During Bluyssen's episcopate, the Dutch bishops had decided to organize a National Pastoral Council to implement the decrees of Vatican II in a consistent way. Walter Goddijn, the influential Franciscan sociologist, had first suggested the idea for such a meeting. Inspired by the example of the diocese of 's-Hertogenbosch, Goddijn proposed involving as many Catholics as possible in the preparations for each year's meeting. In every diocese, Catholics were invited to take part in groups to talk about the changes they deemed necessary. New topics were put on the agenda each year, although renewal was the overall theme: "Working on the Church" (1966–1967), "Togetherness" (1967–1968), and "Tomorrow's Church" (1968–1969).[44] Those who did not want to or could not engage in such discussion groups were offered postboxes where they could send letters. The Catholic broadcasting company KRO also opened a postbox and, in addition, aired a weekly radio program, "Council Postbox," to discuss current Church affairs.[45]

Employees of the Diocesan Pastoral Centers (DPC) were assigned the task of sorting through the letters. Most were priests, although several who had left the priesthood remained employed by the centers; Bishop Bluyssen had spoken publicly more than once of his support for ex-priests and their difficulties in finding suitable work. After the DPC had sorted and separated the letters into categories, sociologists from the Institute of Applied Sociology in Nijmegen would further organize the results. Then a working group was tasked to interpret the documents. This process brought together all of the leading actors in renewal in the Netherlands: social scientists, educated and well-informed laity, priests, and members of the media (some of whom were priests). Several of those involved in the National Pastoral Council preparations were also involved in the analysis of two nationwide surveys on the priesthood (1967) and celibacy (1966–1968). The results of all these surveys and discussions, including their interpretation by the experts, served as the foundation for the debates on these subjects at the Pastoral Council, presented as the outcome of a democratic input by "the people."[46]

Between 1966 and 1968, a total of 2,200 letters on the 1968 meeting were sent to the Council postbox, 1,640 of which were analyzed. People of various social backgrounds, both men and women (the majority), mostly city based, expressed their worries and aspirations for church policy. Of these, 179 came directly from the diocese of Den Bosch; some of these were the result of group talks. The process of interpreting the information was remarkable. Although the official report that presented the results in 1968 made some preliminary remarks about the limits of representativeness, the outcomes were summarized to suggest that there were basically three viewpoints in all of the Netherlands. Dutch Catholics were either in favor of further renewal (20 percent), rejected it (40 percent) or in favor yet doubtful about certain consequences (40 percent). This outcome was obviously disappointing to the interpreters, who responded by downplaying the overall significance of the outcomes (contrary to the high expectations that had preceded the surveys). They maintained that in general, reactions were "more positive than negative" and were careful to point out that responses came from "plain *and* cultured people." The media likewise assisted in this work of reframing the results, editorializing that it was wrong to conclude that most of the letter writers were conservative because in relation to the touchy subject of celibacy, they expressed the same openness as "the Dutch Catholic population as a whole."[47]

A close reading of the letters from the diocese of Den Bosch shows something else, however. Rather than unequivocally expressing either sympathy or antipathy toward renewal, writers displayed a range of emotions, concerns, and doubts. But this range of views had been left out of the classifications arrived at by the diocesan DPC. Of a sample of ninety-seven letters classified by the DPC in 1968, each was labeled "conservative," "accommodating," or "progressive."[48] A mere fourteen letters were labeled "conservative"; eight were regarded as "progressive" (mostly from inhabitants of cities); the rest were "accommodating." However, a significant range of issues raised by the accommodating writers was lost in this labeling. Some of the accommodating expressed worries about the fading quality of the liturgy, referring to the poor quality of texts, the introduction of beat masses, and the rolling experimentation in various parishes (30). Others felt utterly confused, sometimes also betrayed, about what was described as the "desacralized role of priests" and the casual disposal of cherished traditions (26). Others expressed their problems with faith education for their children (14).

One feeling common to all letter writers, wherever they were on the ecclesial spectrum, was significantly underplayed in the analysis, namely, a sense of unease that the church had been "captured" by highly educated advocates of renewal, whose voices were being amplified as well by sympathetic media. "Renewal" was the dominant narrative of the Dutch church, but whose preference was it really? "The discussions in our community," a male teacher from the city of Eindhoven wrote, "are riddled with confusion because of all the articles and commentaries in the press and the opinions of those who know it all, but the mass of the people don't understand a word and just let it happen."[49] In the opinion of an older man from the village of Boxmeer, "It's such a pity that all that we get from the newspapers, radio and television are the voices of liberal Catholics."[50] "I get the impression that many publicists, both priests and lay people, are terrified that their writing isn't progressive enough," a small-town lawyer complained, "and this kills every possibility of an open discussion."[51] In the words of a married couple from Nijmegen, "In the past, the Catholic media hardly had any time for renewers ... Now, every daring proposition gets full attention. Shouldn't this be a sobering thought for all renewers, since the coverage is more about the spectacular than anything else?"[52] A shopkeeper from Eindhoven believed that "the whole discussion is being monopolized by a small number of academics who think they know it all and possess the media."[53] A married couple from Tilburg wrote, "What is really hurtful is the great intolerance towards everyone who still sees some value in 'the old' . . . This is done in the name of 'the humane' and 'God's people.'"[54] A man from Nijmegen raised objections to a new student church that was being built; a nearby church was already half empty during Mass. He believed that in his town, parish churches were even beginning to compete with one another by upgrading their Masses to attract more churchgoers.[55] Taken together, these letters speak of people's chaotic and bewildering experiences of the renewal, interlarded with deep-felt grief. But this was missing in the DPC categorization and in the final report. The prevailing tone of the preliminary surveys and reports presented at the Pastoral Council pointed at a type of renewal that permitted priests their human feelings and an educated lay elite its authoritative position.

In 1985, when to a large extent pre-conciliar structures had been restored, the National Pastoral Council was reevaluated. A poll of participants at the time, led (again) by Goddijn who by then had been appointed as professor of sociology at the Catholic University in Tilburg, showed that in hindsight they believed that highly educated men had been overrepresented in the Council. Unsurprisingly, those polled went on to say that in any case, the opinions of these highly educated men could be taken as representative of Dutch Catholics.[56]

From Childhood: Generational Effects

Although many of the letters to the postboxes gave a glimpse of the average Catholic's worries, they were still representative of a selective group. The majority of Dutch Catholics did not write in at all but found other ways of dealing with the changes in their church and lives. In the beginning of the 1990s, journalist Marga Kerklaan decided to examine the lived religion of ordinary people. In the first study of its kind, Kerklaan was interested in men and women who belonged neither to the clergy nor to the elite of scholars and its attendant circles. The voice of the Catholics in the pews, Kerklaan said, "has seldom been heard." She wanted to investigate the impact of secularization on three generations: people between ages sixty and seventy, their children, and their grandchildren. She put a notice inviting participation in her study in two popular magazines. The response entailed more than a hundred lengthy letters. Of these, Kerklaan interviewed sixty people at length, all from different social and geographical backgrounds. How had the changes brought about by church renewal influenced perceptions of religion, family, and sexuality?[57] Although the respondents represented various positions within the church (liberal, orthodox, moderate, Christian-yet-no-longer Catholic), a thread of disappointment ran through the narratives. Most of the stories depicted an intergenerational struggle between parents, who had been raised within the certainties of traditional religion, and their children, who were caught up in the experimental spirit of the Dutch renewal but then eventually drifted away from the church in the 1960s and 1970s. This second generation did not baptize their children. This narrative was widely accurate for Brabantine Catholics, although not all letters specified the geographical roots of the interviewees.

These were stories told in hindsight by people troubled enough by change to write, but nevertheless they represent a telling account. Never before had detailed testimonies been published explaining how religious practice itself had become a crucial site and cause of intergenerational estrangement during the era of *aggiornamento*, of renewal, and of the friendly and permissive bishops Bekkers and Bluyssen. Ordinary Catholics found their faith – once so firm, yet often unarticulated – being challenged, sometimes by their priests or the media, but also by their children, particularly as they went to high school and then off to university. Better educated than their parents and exposed to progressive teachers and professors, the middle generation swiftly adopted an anti-authority attitude, interlaced with radical critical and political language, and used it to protest against their parents' positions. A typical story is that of the widow of a laborer from a small village, mother of seven children who all were born between 1952 and 1961:

> As long as the children were going to primary school, everything went well. They all made their First Communion. The two eldest girls still accompanied us to Mass when they were teenagers. But as soon as the eldest boys went to high school, the misery began. They came home with stories we could not understand. We had never heard of evolution. Now they started saying that the Bible contained stories that were just not true. "Don't let them fool you," they argued. Within a short while, they became vehement adversaries of the Church, particularly because of its wealth while there was so much poverty in the world. Soon, faith, which meant so much to us, became meaningless to them ... It has caused us enormous grief. Was our own faith not strong enough to pass on?[58]

The mother's dejected resignation was in contrast to her late husband's anger, a gendered thread that appeared in many narratives. Fathers often expressed irritation at priests or teachers.[59] A man from a Tilburg working-class family who, thanks to a good Catholic school, had climbed the social ladder and become a teacher, believed that he and his wife had really tried to embrace renewal and be open minded, until they came upon their children's progressive teachers of religion: "There was a lot of door slamming in our house."[60]

This second generation, who were adolescents in the 1960s, vividly remembered its childhood faith. Often enough, the men had been altar boys. Their earliest ambitions were to become priests and missionaries (female respondents did not mention wanting to be nuns). Education and the media contributed to the change in their attitudes. One man reflected on the way in which religion gradually lost its significance in his life: "What I lost first was not faith itself, but faith in the Catholic Church as an institution. I felt it was just an authoritative suppression machine that took advantage of the credulousness and loyalty of ordinary, kind and simple people. Later I also started putting question marks against religion itself. "[61]

The numerous and often bitter discussions in the media both reflected and contributed to the growing generational gap in the families. On the contrary, interviewees mentioned an alarming discrepancy between the lengthy articles by priests in newspapers and magazines and their own daily anxieties. It was as if different languages had come into use, with priests and intellectual laypeople fighting verbal battles in technical theological language over renewal, celibacy, or democracy, while many ordinary people literally could not understand what they were talking about. A telling remark was made by someone identifying himself as just such "an ordinary reader" who complained to the magazine *De Nieuwe Linie* that its journalists – priests and former priests – were writing in a secret language and practicing self-pollination.[62]

Kerklaan concluded that despite all the grief and anger, the older generation had usually remained within the church, although they tended to be more involved with local parish life and its many social functions than with the universal church. A smaller group had adopted modern theological views and strategically sought out similar priests and parishes, labeling themselves as "Catholic but not Roman" or "believing but not belonging." The largest group of people, consisting of both the oldest and the middle generation, had gradually or radically drifted out of the church. A reason repeatedly given was its "implausibility."

Epilogue

Between 1960 and 1985, the diocese of 's-Hertogenbosch underwent a complicated transformation, religiously and culturally. The Second Vatican Council coincided with far-reaching societal changes. The two bishops Bekkers and Bluyssen eagerly spread the gospel of *aggiornamento*, which was appropriated by those in favor of an all-embracing renewal. This resulted in a quest for egalitarianism with confusing, sometimes chaotic consequences, to which the Dutch media, itself fully in line with the liberal Catholic agenda, contributed. The one thing that did not change in the diocese of 's-Hertogenbosch was the cultural memory of Bishop Bekkers, which has remained untouched. When photographer Toon Michiels in 1973 shot the interior of the home belonging to a traditional farming couple in Best, near 's-Hertogenbosch, he found that old-time devotions were still part of their daily life. The walls in their small farm home were hung with paintings of the saints. There was one remarkable addition: among the saints was a portrait of Msgr. Bekkers.[63] About thirty years later, in 2000, Bekkers was declared "Catholic of the century" by the Catholic broadcasting company that owed so much to its former co-worker. Two years later, a statue of the bishop was erected in his hometown, Sint-Oedenrode, and in 2010 another one in his old parish in Tilburg. Bekkers began to appear more and more often in exhibitions and photo books. His grave has become a popular pilgrimage site. Bishop Bekkers's human kindness and pastoral nearness are cherished. Perhaps it is forgotten that he, along with Bluyssen, presided over an *aggiornamento* that accelerated out of control, to the confusion and sorrow of the people who today lay flowers at his grave.

NOTES

1. "Beide zenders herdachten 'televisiebisschop,'" *Nieuwsblad van het Noorden*, May 10, 1966.
2. All parties involved expressed their views in a lengthy documentary in 2003: www.geschiedenis24.nl/andere-tijden/afleveringen/2002-2003/De-paus-in-Nederland-1985.html.
3. Joris Kregting, Theo Schepens, and Leo Spruit, *De Rooms-katholieke kerk in Nederland, 1960–2000*, Kaski Memorandum no. 326, The Hague, 2002, pp. 11–13; Kees Schuyt and Ed Taverne, *Welvaart in zwart-wit* (The Hague, the Netherlands: Sdu Uitgevers, 2000), pp. 355–378.
4. A. F. Manning, "Martien Coppens: een historisch fotograaf" in Manning, *Mensen en situaties* (Baarn, the Netherlands: Arbor, 1990), pp. 110–114.
5. Gerard Rooijakkers, "Bekkers en Brabant" in Kees Hakvoort, Peter Steffen, and Jan Walravens (eds.), *Bisschop Bekkers 1908–1966. Een hartstochtelijk priesterleven*

(Alphen aan de Maas: Veerhuis, 2007) pp. 44–59, at p. 48; *Noordbrabants Historisch Jaarboek*, Historische Vereniging Brabant, pp. 22–23, 2005–2006.

6. Kregting et al., *De Rooms-katholieke kerk*, pp. 11–18, 35–36.

7. Hans Righart, *De eindeloze jaren zestig: Geschiedenis van een generatieconflict* (Amsterdam University Press, 1995) pp. 16–17.

8. "Redactieleden Nijmeegs Universiteitsblad gedagvaard," *Nieuwsblad van het Noorden*, February 25, 1969.

9. Jan Brabers, "Cultuur in de twintigste eeuw" in Brabers, *Nijmegen: Geschiedenis van de oudste stad van Nederland* (Wormer, the Netherlands: Inmerc, 2005), pp. 376–466, at p. 450.

10. Rooijakkers, "Bekkers en Brabant."

11. Marjet Derks, "Media, Gender, and the Invisible Conservative Dutch Catholic," *Schweizerische Zeitschrift für Religions-und Kulturgeschichte* 104 (2010), 135–154, at 141–142.

12. Jan Bank and Theo Potma, "De macht van televisie. Bisschop Bekkers' optreden in Brandpunt," *Jaarboek van het Katholiek Documentatie Centrum* 14 (1984), 55–87.

13. Koen Piket, "Concilie moet brug slaan tussen kerk en wereld," *Bisdomblad* 39:2049 (1962), 2.

14. Marga Kerklaan, "*Zodoende was de vrouw maar een mens om kinderen te krijgen*": *300 brieven over het roomse huwelijksleven* (Baarn, the Netherlands: Ambo, 1987).

15. Interview with Joke Zwanikken-Leenders (Bekkers was her mother's cousin), July 9, 2012.

16. Bank and Potma, "De macht van televisie."

17. Eugène van Deutekom, lecture, April 20, 2010. Because the diocese's episcopal archives were closed down in April 2012, the original letters could not be consulted. Former archivist Van Deutekom was able to consult them and partly based his paper on them.

18. Koen Piket, "Onze wensen en het Concilie," *Bisdomblad* 39: 2018 (1962), 1–2.

19. *Bisdomblad* 39: 2032 (1962), 2.

20. "Huisbezoek of niet," *Bisdomblad* 39: 2007 (1962), 8.

21. "Diocesaan concilie over de biecht: Tweehonderdvijftig gespreksgroepen," *Limburgs Dagblad*, September 21, 1963.

22. "Diocesane gespreksgroepen," *De Tijd/De Maasbode*, January 27, 1964.

23. Joost van Roon, "In gesprek met bisschop Bekkers," *Het vrije volk*, February 16, 1962.

24. Erwin Kleine, manuscript of "Bischof Bekkers – Reformator aus Brabant," National Center of Catholic Action archive, no. 4130.

25. "'Concilie' in het Bossche diocees over de biecht," *De Tijd*, September 21, 1963.

26. G.G. Driessen, *Het Rijke Roomse Leven van de Groesbeekse parochie 'Cosmas en Damianus'* (Nijmegen, the Netherlands: Uitgeverij Heemkunde, 2004).

27. "Leken 'praten met de bisschop' voor K.R.O.-t.v.," *De Tijd*, January 8, 1966.

28. "Zorg voor het Rijk Gods," *De Tijd/De Maasbode*, July 1, 1964.

29. Nico van Hees, *Bisschop Bekkers, vriend van ons allen* (Leiden/Amsterdam: H. J. W. Becht, 1966).

30. "Nut of onnut van de preek?" *Bisdomblad* 39:2009 (1962), 3.

31. Peter De Haan, *Van volgzame elitestrijder tot kritische gelovige*, pp. 262–263.

32. Report of meeting between Dean Kaal and the Horstink staff, March 11, 1963, National Center of Catholic Action archive, no. 4193.

33. Note on sermon experiments, November 1963, National Center of Catholic Action archive.
34. Note on sermon experiments, November 1963, National Center of Catholic Action archive.
35. Report on Pastoral Practices in the Deanship of Eindhoven, 1965, National Center of Catholic Action archive.
36. Letter no. 14, August 12, 1966, Pastoral Council of the Dutch Church Province (PCDCP) archive.
37. Letter no. 28, April 4, 1966, PCDCP archive.
38. Letter no. 16, August 22, 1966 and letter no. 20, September 1966, PCDCP archive.
39. "Diocesanen beraden zich over bisschopskeuze," *De Tijd*, April 4, 1966.
40. Marc van Dijk, "Bekkers was de bisschop van Brabant. Interview met Jan Bluyssen," *Trouw*, December 15, 2006.
41. Letter from Bishop Bluyssen, read in all churches on November 20, *De Tijd*, December 10, 1966.
42. "Pastorale gesprekken," *Bisdomblad* 45:2349 (1968), 3.
43. "Gesprek met vicaris Thuis," *Bisdomblad* 45:2312 (1968), 1–3.
44. Discussion groups of the Den Bosch diocese, 1962–1969, no. 243, PCDCP archive.
45. "Conciliepostbus van de KRO," *De Tijd*, August 9, 1966.
46. Marjet Derks and Chris Dols, "Sprekende cijfers. Katholiek sociaalingenieurs en de enscenering van de celibaatcrisis, 1963–1972," *Tijdschrift voor Geschiedenis* 123 (2010), 414–429.
47. Instituut voor Toegepaste Sociologie, *Brieven aan het Pastoraal Concilie*, pp. 8–11, 27.
48. Council postboxes of Den Bosch, nos. 296 and 297, PCDCP archive.
49. Letter no. 16 to the Council postbox, August 22, 1966, no. 297, PCDCP archive.
50. Letter no. 17, August 26, 1966, PCDCP archive.
51. Letter no. 30, October 7, 1966, PCDCP archive.
52. Letter no. 31, October 10, 1966, PCDCP archive.
53. Letter no. 74, February 12, 1967, PCDCP archive.
54. Letter no. 62, December 29, 1967, PCDCP archive.
55. Letter no. 25, July 29, 1966, PCDCP archive.
56. Walter Goddijn, Hans Wewerinke, and Fons Mommers, *Pastoraal Concilie (1965–1970). Een experiment in kerkelijk leiderschap* (Baarn, the Netherlands: Nelissen, 1986).
57. Marga Kerklaan, *Van huis uit. Drie generaties katholieken over de invloed van de secularisatie op hun beleving van seksualiteit, gezin en geloof* (Baarn, the Netherlands: Ambo, 1994); Letter from Kerklaan to Böckert, March 30, 1995, no. 3, Ben Böckert archives.
58. Kerklaan, *Van huis uit*, pp. 11–12.
59. Kerklaan, *Van huis uit*, pp. 11–12.
60. Kerklaan, *Van huis uit*, p. 26.
61. Kerklaan, *Van huis uit*, p. 89.
62. Kerklaan, *Van huis uit*, p. 263.
63. Toon Michiels, *Zeldzame mensen* (Zaltbommel, the Netherlands: Kempen, 2004), p. 60.

VATICAN II AND THE GOVERNANCE
OF THE LOCAL CHURCH: THE DIOCESE
OF FERRARA, 1959–1976

MASSIMO FAGGIOLI

This chapter analyzes the first decade of the post–Vatican II period in the diocese of Ferrara in northern Italy. The growing role of a number of actors in the local church (lay Catholic intellectuals, priests, and members of the religious orders) casts a light on the isolation of the bishop and his leadership in the local church.

V ATICAN II WAS ABOUT CHANGE OR, IN THE TERMINOLOGY that emphasizes the continuity of the Council with the previous tradition, *reform*: "Vatican II falls under the rubric of a reform council."[1] Much of what the Council accomplished can be measured against the reform of ecclesial institutions in its wake, including changes in matters of church governance and decision making.[2] Institutional reforms that transpired in local churches far away from Rome reveal the extent of change Vatican II set in motion. One such church was in Ferrara, a mid-sized European diocese that underwent a tumultuous decade following the conclusion of Vatican II.

Part of the Papal States between 1598 and 1861, the city of Ferrara, located in northeast Italy between Bologna and Venice, was one of the many peripheries of Italian Catholicism. It was a border city between Rome-controlled central Italy (Rome is 280 miles away) and the powerful Republic of Venice (which was also independent from the pope, especially from the standpoint of church government and ecclesiastical appointments). Until World War II, a strong Jewish community added to Ferrara's importance. During the decades before and after Vatican II, the Ferrara diocese included 220,000 to 250,000 Catholics, 220 priests (150 diocesan and 70 religious), 120 parishes, and a territory that was urban, industrial, and rural. It was

I would like to thank Elisabetta Antonioni, Alessandra Chiappini, Francesco Lavezzi, Carlo Pagnoni, Pier Paolo Pedriali, Miriam Turrini, and Andrea Zerbini for their help in retrieving the archival sources and the interviews they agreed to give me. I owe them for many of the insights coming from this research.

the least prosperous province of the flourishing region of Emilia-Romagna. Nonetheless, between the 1950s and the mid-1980s, the diocese of Ferrara experienced a period of institutional and political stability; the 1950s–1960s was a period of greater activity, with the construction of many new churches and of a new diocesan seminary. The political landscape of Ferrara in the post–World War II period paralleled that of many European dioceses in which the Catholic Church was active in a political environment split between a strong Communist Party and an equally strong and Catholic Church–backed Christian Democratic Party.[3]

A Polycentric Diocese and Its Bishop

Msgr. Natale Mosconi (1904–1988) was bishop of Ferrara between 1954 and 1976 and participated in the sessions of Vatican II. Just like most of his fellow Italian bishops, he was not active in the theological exchanges on the floor of St. Peter's during the Council. Yet during his tenure as bishop, a new seminary was built and the diocese experienced the flourishing of new venues and media of theological and pastoral reflection: the center "Casa Cini" for conferences and symposia, which the Jesuits ran until the 1980s; the creation of a new journal for the history of the local church, *Analecta Pomposiana*; the calling of "weeks of pastoral-theological renewal" for the local clergy starting in 1966; and the Centro Studi Charles de Foucauld, an important study center for the laity, run by the historian Luciano Chiappini (1922–2002). These developments illustrate that although Bishop Mosconi closely controlled the diocese for more than 20 years with a monarchical style of leadership, the impact of Vatican II on the governance of the diocese in the decades after Vatican II was substantial. Vatican II changed the situation and enabled lay leaders, diocesan clergy, and the Jesuits to have a voice in the local church of Ferrara. Those who had been relatively quiet before Vatican II became more active during and after the Council, despite what they perceived as reluctance on the part of the bishop to reform the diocese along the lines of the conciliar decrees.

Bishop Mosconi did not exhibit much enthusiasm during the diocesan preparation for the Council. The *Bollettino Ecclesiastico* of the diocese for the year 1959 has only a brief, formal announcement of the Council, which Pope John XXIII called on January 25 of that year. On August 25, Bishop Mosconi replied in writing, as most bishops did, to the official invitation that he offer his insights to the preparation of Vatican II with the submission of his *votum*. Mosconi stated he did not see the need to change, develop, or reform anything. He flatly avowed that "no new definition is necessary in the present circumstances" and recommended a more careful catechetical effort to teach Christian doctrine, as well as a more attentive promotion of "modesty" and "chastity."[4]

From 1960 to 1961, Bishop Mosconi held to the notion that Vatican II would not substantially change the church.[5] In his pastoral letter to the diocese for Lent 1961, *Verso il Concilio* (To the Council), Mosconi quoted authors who would be of great importance for the theology of Vatican II, such as Johann Adam Möhler, Romano Guardini, Daniel Rops, and Émile Guerry. But the tone of the letter was consistent with the pastoral letters of Italian bishops in the first half of the twentieth century, as it emphasized anti-Marxism and anti-liberalism, with a deep suspicion of the ethos of modern democracy.[6] In the conclusion of the letter, the only preparatory document Mosconi issued to his diocese before the Council, the prelate warned: "We live in extraordinary times of scientific progress and social change, of promotion of peoples and of wealth that seem to benefit all. But before these positive social changes in our times and in humanity there are very painful realities and awfully negative aspects."[7]

Nevertheless, changes were already afoot that facilitated transformations in the life of the diocese following Vatican II. A very active group of lay Catholics created a study center named after the French priest and missionary Charles de Foucauld. Under the foundational leadership of the left-leaning Christian Democrat and historian Luciano Chiappini, the center was inaugurated on April 13, 1962, six months before the opening of the Council. The Centro Studi Charles de Foucauld enabled center-leftist lay Catholics to express their perspectives in the local church, especially on the relationship between Catholicism and politics in an area that a strong Communist Party had shaped historically. Their aspiration was not a reactive, anti-communist Catholicism, but a Catholicism able to engage and dialogue with Marxism on an intellectual level and to cooperate with communists locally to address social issues in a region Rome had seemingly forgotten.

This was not the first initiative of lay Catholics gathered around Luciano Chiappini, who came from a bourgeois family that rallied around the fascist regime and was connected with Fernando Tambroni, the leader of the most reactionary faction of the Christian Democratic Party in Italy during the early years after World War II. Chiappini took a stance quite divergent from that of his parents and decided to make a different contribution to the life of Catholics in Ferrara, which after 1945 was politically and socially dominated by the Partito Comunista Italiano together with the Socialist Party (Partito Socialista Italiano).[8] Chiappini soon became the most prominent Catholic intellectual in the communist- and socialist-run city of

Ferrara, respected by Catholics and non-Catholics alike, with many contacts among media observers in postwar Italy. Even before the pontificate of John XXIII, Chiappini had been in contact with one of the most important liberal-leaning leaders of Italian Catholicism in the post–World War II years, Fr. Primo Mazzolari.

Before leaving the Christian Democratic Party in 1959, Chiappini founded the short-lived journal *Prospettive Ferraresi*. The journal initiative involved organizing conferences and talks with prominent Italian lay theologians and priests such as Emilio Guano, Mario Gozzini, Ernesto Balducci, and Giorgio La Pira. Participants also included authors and editors of the Florence-based journal *Testimonianze* who were enmeshed in the new wave of progressive Catholicism in Italy at the end of the pontificate of Pius XII.[9] These early efforts set the stage for the Centro Studi Charles de Foucauld, which remained active between 1962 and 1974, the first decade following the close of the Council. Centro leaders organized events featuring prominent and progressive Italian Catholics, as well as internationally known figures such as Elémire Zolla and Abbé Pierre. In the second issue of the Centro's newsletter, Chiappini wrote the following:

> Our program is very simple, though not easy to implement: Catholicism, not conformism; ideological coherence, not strict and disturbing fundamentalism; openness to all sincere and vital human experiences in today's world, not easygoing and shallow avant-gardism; an attempt to interpret realistically and in depth historical, religious, spiritual, political phenomena, such as that of Communism.[10]

The Centro soon began to organize a library, along with study groups and public talks, and to engage in social and political issues such as youth culture, labor conditions, and worker unions. In a short period of time, the activities of the Centro stirred the waters of the quiet diocese of Ferrara: the Centro featured public talks on communism, on the "new theology" from France, on social justice and the Third World. It represented, in the very same years of the early 1960s when Italy tried the political experiment of the so-called center-left (Christian Democratic Party allied with the Socialist Party), an attempt to build a bridge between what its leaders perceived as the lethargic Catholicism of the diocese and the powerful structures of the Communist Party throughout the province of Ferrara. In a letter to a member of the Centro, Chiappini acknowledged in December 1962 that just a few short months after the opening of the Vatican Council, some "fresh air" was coming in: "We can feel already the fruits of our labor in spite of the proverbial apathy of the citizens of Ferrara (and among them especially the Catholics) and the lack of understanding of the most conservative sectors of the same Catholic milieu and the archbishop's curia."[11]

The Centro Studi Charles de Foucauld was not the only new vehicle for public Catholic expression in the diocese of Ferrara. Since 1954 the Jesuit study center was also active just a few blocks from the cathedral in the city center. The Jesuit-run center was nicknamed "Casa Cini" after the building it occupied, the medieval palace of the famous patron of Italian arts Vittorio Cini. It was active between 1954 and the early 1980s. Especially during the Council and the immediate post-Council years, the Jesuits of Casa Cini offered the city and the local church a series of activities and opportunities that took advantage of the "fresh air" of Vatican II. Members approved a document in October 1969 that affirmed the openness of the conciliar spirit, declaring that "the community feels itself part of a church that is responsive to the worries and to the progress of the Christian community and that wants to present the Christ of the Gospel in response to the needs of our places and our times."[12] Those frequenting Casa Cini also gathered for talks on theological issues debated by the Council. As the Council was nearing its concluding session during the 1964–1965 academic year, for example, the Jesuits hosted talks on Judaism, religious liberty, the laity, and the church and the modern world.

These different groups of center-left lay Catholics in Ferrara sought to create a Catholic environment different from the one Luigi Gedda, the crusader of Catholic anti-communism in Italy, fostered following World War II.[13] As a result of such efforts, many Catholics in Ferrara saw Vatican II as an opening for reconciliation not only between church and modernity but also between church and democracy and the various social and political cultures at the heart of modernity in Europe. This comprises one important way a number of lay Catholics were more receptive than the very bishops who participated in Vatican II. Significantly for the case of Ferrara, Bishop Mosconi attended all four Council sessions but skipped between one-quarter and one-third of the "general congregations" of each Council period between 1962 and 1965. Moreover, he was not a member of any Vatican II commission, nor did he speak on the floor of the Council in St. Peter's, sign petitions, or participate in the many informal groups of bishops active at the Council. Only a few months before the conclusion of Vatican II, at the end of September 1965, he began writing his "conciliar letters" to the diocese.[14] Once back in Ferrara after December 1965, Mosconi pushed for an interpretation of Vatican II that was marked by a lack of urgency and centered on the power of the bishop:

Not inaction or adventure, it is time for action. But do not hurry, do not bustle, no fever, as we have seen recently in statements, interpretations, illegitimate avant-gardes and genuine errors.

. . . There is no time for debates, they took place already. There is no time for adventurous projects.[15]

First Signs of Unrest, 1966–1969

Mosconi's Catholic flock in Ferrara did not unilaterally share the cautious approach that the bishop showed toward Vatican II.[16] Some saw it as indifference. With the growing influence of the mass media, Vatican II entered the homes of millions of Catholics through TV, radio, and newspapers, ensuring that the local reception of Vatican II did not depend entirely on the initiative of the local bishop. On the other hand, as with other Councils in the history of Catholicism, the perception of the impact of the Council came through ensuing institutional reforms. At the time many thought that the primary expression of such reforms would be the institution of new collegial church bodies such as diocesan Councils and parish Councils, which the Council decrees *Christus Dominus* and *Presbyterorum Ordinis* prescribed.[17]

For Lent of the year 1966, Bishop Mosconi published a pastoral letter in which he acknowledged the importance of the Council for the diocese.[18] The letter testified to the bishop's intellectual grasp of Vatican II and its importance. He even quoted figures whom progressives admired, such as Emmanuel Mounier, Jacques Maritain, Jean Guitton, Pierre Teilhard de Chardin, the famous Italian Catholic-communist Felice Balbo, and Dag Hammarskjöld. Nonetheless, this letter revealed the bishop's interpretation of Vatican II not in terms of structural changes and a more pastoral and ecumenical church, but as a confirmation and clarification of the doctrinal patrimony of the church.

During the pontificate of Pope Paul VI, leadership for structural ecclesial reforms in dioceses such as Ferrara did not come primarily from the local bishop, but from Rome. Paul VI's August 6, 1966, motu proprio *Ecclesiae Sanctae* set in motion the creation of new consultative bodies in the local churches all over the world. These bodies increased the participation of priests in the governance of dioceses and the participation of laymen and laywomen in the oversight of parishes, though members of these new bodies had only a consultative vote, not a deliberative one. The diocese of Ferrara, like many others, went through a period of transition: Between 1966 and 1969, these new governing bodies worked *ad experimentum*.

Controversy ensued during this period of experimentation with the issuance of anonymous letters attacking the episcopal curia and the inner circle of priests serving in it. The response to the first letter came in September 1966 from the inner circle of the diocesan administration, a clerical group that included the diocesan vicar general, the *camerlengo* of the chapter of the cathedral, the rector of the seminary, and the bishop's delegate to Catholic Action. These priests tried to defend the authority of the bishop and the process of receiving Vatican II he was leading in the diocese:

> We invite all the clergy to rally around our bishop. Renovated in our spiritual life and decided in the will and in the apostolate, in the hands of Him [Jesus Christ], the only one responsible for our salvation and that of our faithful, we want to become instruments of determined and well-ordered cooperation for the battles of faith, grace, and morality, to which Council Vatican II has called.[19]

The contestation of the Vatican II reforms was illuminated in a lively yet relatively invisible debate. Already in 1966, Luciano Chiappini had published an article in the important Florence-based journal *Testimonianze* that related the state of the Council's reception in the diocese of Ferrara. Chiappini noted the "many expressions of enthusiasm and no real nostalgia for going back" to a pre–Vatican II era. But he also contended that, despite the initiatives of "private" centers of Catholic culture in the diocese, "there is a lack of initiative" from the institutional church.[20]

Behind Chiappini's article there was certainly another notable figure in the diocese, Fr. Elios Giuseppe Mori, a leader of a group of priests that was formed in 1966 and engaged in a "Vatican II–style" priestly formation.[21] In that same year, Fr. Mori was asked to lead a diocesan commission for priestly formation; in November 1966, the commission organized a seminar for the clergy of the diocese on the constitution *Lumen Gentium* and the ecclesiology of Vatican II. Joseph Lécuyer, an important *peritus* at the Council, led the seminar. Soon thereafter a smaller group of more progressive priests gathered around Mori for a more intense continuation of their discussions. The focus of the group was a collegial and informal engagement of *aggiornamento* in the church. Participants held a summer seminar every year between 1966 and 1976 and during this decade offered formation to approximately 60 priests of the diocese.

The impact of the year 1968 on the post–Vatican II church reform was complex and is still difficult to evaluate, but there is no doubt that it was felt globally as well as locally. In a politically tense year for Italy, Catholics going through the Vatican II transition in Ferrara raised a new issue, namely the possibility of pursing an electoral option beyond the Catholic status quo. Echoing a plea for Catholic voter unity they had pressed for two decades, the general assembly of the Italian Bishops Conference sent a spring 1968 pre-election message to Italian Catholics, *I cristiani e la vita pubblica*, in which the bishops invited Catholics to vote once again for the Christian Democratic Party. Many Italian Catholics perceived this message as fundamentally incoherent with the new ecclesiology of Vatican II. A group of forty-five lay Catholics in Ferrara challenged the authority of the bishops to determine the political orientations of the faithful. In a public statement published on April 29, they declared the following:

In principle it is a legitimate right of the Church to issue statements on non-political, non-cultural, but rather authentically evangelical issues that affect the lives of people and communities. However, because on the eve of the elections the Italian episcopate expressed its views with statements that for a careful observer are clear about their resolve to urgently seek the Catholic vote for the Christian Democratic Party, we here say that we do not accept the call for a "political unity" of Catholics that is not built on the basis of actual political convergence because it would not be proof of Christian consistency but rather of confusion or ambiguity. We also believe that this kind of statement, issued in very specific circumstances, regardless of the intentions of the promoters, runs the dangerous risk of covering political and economic forces that will manipulate the authority of the Catholic Church for their goals of hegemony and conservation and that, perhaps even worse, will cause the rejection of religion in those who do not accept a particular political line and see it as an imposition coming from a religious belief.[22]

A lively debate began in the diocese in 1968 about the new shape the local church was supposed to take. In a document drafted by the Centro Studi Charles de Foucauld, its founder took a strong position on impending reforms in the diocese:

Now more than ever – and according to the instructions of Vatican II – there is an urgent need for the religious authority not to isolate itself because of a strong mandate that none of us puts in doubt, but to exercise its ministry in constant communion with his children ... Our proposal is that the two bodies provided by Vatican II, the Diocesan Pastoral Council and the Diocesan Presbyteral Council, work with constant regularity ... It is also our proposal that the Diocesan Consultative body meets frequently, as an expression of the various Catholic organizations, to create a true community and to study the implementation of the conciliar documents, in order to overcome separatism, selfishness, and lack of mutual understanding of the different groups active in the diocesan territory, the overlap of similar initiatives, and the difficulty to synergize the activities undertaken by various organizations.[23]

Yet concurrently with this pronouncement, at the end of summer 1968 the diocese proceeded with the renewal and updating of the formation of its clergy through a three-day seminar on "the foundations of moral theology." In this and other diocesan efforts to implement the Council, the demands for more involvement of the laity in the shaping of the future of the local church were scarcely acknowledged.

Lay Catholics and Secularization, 1969–1971

Catholics hopeful for fruitful cooperation between the bishop and the laity in Ferrara were disappointed in the spring of 1969, when the Centro Studi Charles de Foucauld invited as a speaker Fr. Ernesto Balducci, a left-leaning priest from Florence and the most outspoken advocate in Italy for a "progressive" interpretation of Vatican II. Balducci was particularly outspoken about social and political issues such as world peace, militarism, and equal access to education in a social system that in Italy was still very much class based.[24] In March 1969, Mosconi replied negatively to a request for his approval of this invitation: "The present time does not call for manifestations that then increase the disorientation and confusion of ideas, but demands firmness of principles, methods loyal with the Church, and especially the humble subjection to the Church, which alone is the Mother and Teacher of all children of God, redeemed by Christ."[25] The study center did not withdraw its invitation to the prominent speaker from Florence. On March 9, Fr. Balducci gave his talk on the topic "People of God and Local Church" based on the famous experience of the base ecclesial community of "L'Isolotto" in Florence.[26] A similar quest for a more progressive theological and cultural grasp of the shift of Vatican II was visible in the activities at Casa Cini, where Jesuits sponsored a series of talks between 1969 and 1970 addressing the responsibility of laity in the church, religious freedom and ecumenism, and Catholicism and political power in Italy.[27]

Leaders seeking to enact the reforms of Vatican II seemed more and more divided into two parallel paths in the diocese of Ferrara. On one side was the "institutional reception" through new governing bodies that seemingly sought to domesticate the enthusiasm of laity and clergy for the alleged novelty Vatican II initiated. On the other side were informal groups of lay

Catholics and Jesuits organizing debates and pushing proposals that the bishop and those allied with him met with skepticism.

The formation of the Pastoral Council and the Presbyteral Council in Ferrara began in spring 1969. Just like the other dioceses in Italy, it followed the model the Congregations of the Roman Curia offered, with only a few exceptions. The idea was to have seven commissions and a coordinating commission or secretary.[28]

By the fall of 1969, these new consultative bodies took shape thanks to elections. Those for the diocesan pastoral council resulted in three-year terms for twenty priests, two religious men, two religious women, and twenty-three lay persons. The lay members were all elected on the basis of their belonging to Catholic associations and movements active in the diocese, but they included some local notable Catholic intellectuals such as Luciano Chiappini.[29] The Presbyteral Council organized the election of new members in September. However, the new governing bodies never became key players in the life of the diocese: in early 1969 the Pastoral Council and the Presbyteral Council had planned the establishment of commissions and study groups, but in all of 1969 the Presbyteral Council met only three times.[30] In November the secretary of the Presbyteral Council was not even able to report on the work done by its subcommissions during the previous months of 1969.[31] Hopes for the substantive involvement of the councils in diocesan governance and renewal diminished.

The new governing bodies faced strong headwinds in terms of the tensions running deep in the local church, especially among priests of different generations, and between some priests and the bishop. In this state of discomfort, an unprecedented dissent exploded: a few priests sent anonymous letters to express their discontent with the bishop and some of his colleagues, which resulted in a further hardening of positions. On Christmas Day 1969, a group of priests of the "Gruppo di studio sacerdotale" advocated for more dialogue and more co-responsibility in the diocese. Though they also blamed some anonymous letter writers for poisoning the climate of the local church, they forcefully stated the following:

> In the local church of Ferrara, in the priests and the laity, in people and structures, we see difficulties, sufferings, and shortcomings, which are common to all other communities and to the universal Church. The whole church is growing and seeking new and more appropriate ways. At the same time in Ferrara we must achieve a greater unity, a shared responsibility at all levels, to the shared management of the goods of the community. But the tone and manner of your speeches leave us very perplexed, often in pain, and sometimes averse.[32]

Between 1968 and 1970, the situation in Ferrara worsened as a result of the mounting tensions in the neighboring dioceses of Bologna and especially Ravenna, where Bishop Salvatore Baldassarri (1907–1982) became one of the leaders of the small but influential "radical-progressive" party within the Italian episcopate. In 1975, Vatican officials forced Baldassarri to resign, a few years after the same predicament had touched the cardinal of Bologna, Giacomo Lercaro in 1968.[33] But already in 1970, many Catholics in Ferrara were questioning the difference in the way Vatican II was being received in the two similar and geographically neighboring dioceses of Ferrara and Ravenna. Bishop Mosconi and Bishop Baldassarri were two opposing examples of the approach to Vatican II among Italian bishops, and many lay Catholics in Ferrara were clearly taking sides with the model the more progressive bishop of Ravenna offered. As the leaders of the Centro Studi Charles de Foucauld put it:

> To realize this plan, the Church must be articulated in particular faces and the Christian people must differentiate rituals and theologies in the disciplines, not – of course – but for surface velleitarism but to answer more appropriately God's call. In this context, the role of leadership is essential and providential as protector of diversity and as a guarantor of the unity of the universal Church. Precisely from these premises and at the same time by inserting this perspective, we feel solidarity with the pastoral action conducted by Msgr. Salvatore Baldassarri, as there we recognize a positive, solid, original contribution to the promotion of free and conscious expressions of witness of the Christian faith and a building up of the one Church.[34]

In a few years, both Mosconi and Baldassarri would resign, but for opposite reasons. In Ferrara, the reason was ultimately the tensions between the bishop and the rest of the diocese, which had surfaced already in early 1970 in this letter Mosconi penned to lay Catholic leader Luciano Chiappini:

> Dear Luciano, I read the document prepared by the Center De Foucauld and I feel compelled to underscore something. It's a duty for me: "Vae mihi quia tacui!" and "Woe to the dumb dog." About the venerable Archbishop of Ravenna [Baldassarri], I have nothing to say. I do not understand the issue. I have always worshiped my confreres knowing that I am the least of them and have always been close to all suffering, avoiding vain curiosity and speeches which were unnecessary or unfounded. Instead, some of the wording of the document on basic issues does not seem clear. How can we speak of "repression" of the Church? It is necessary to clarify what is meant by this term and wonder if the sanctions are not necessary in the Church. The Acts of the Apostles and the letters of St. Paul are illuminating.

The problem of the relationship between charismatic Church and institutional Church has always been there.

However, the charisms can be inauthentic, and judgment on the charisms is up to the hierarchy of the Church, as it is attested by the letters of Princes of the Apostles, St. Peter and St. Paul. Recently too, the Successor of Peter, Paul VI spoke on the subject of charisma with clarity and authority. His teaching must be accepted in full and ever. There is full ecclesial communion if there is communion with the Successor of Peter and Vicar of Christ, now Pope Paul VI. This is the Catholic faith. This is the faith of the Roman Catholic Church, the Church to which I belong as a Christian priest and bishop, to which I want to be faithful, willing, with God's help, to give my life for her. I pray that the young people of the De Foucauld Center are always in communion with the Roman Catholic Church and with your head, the Supreme Pontiff and Vicar of Christ today Paul VI.[35]

A Long Episcopate's End, 1971–1976

The anonymous letters clergy wrote attacking the episcopal curia at the end of 1970 coincided with a paralysis of activities from the new diocesan government bodies. Promoters of these bodies contended that from 1970 on, they never fulfilled the hopes they had for collective diocesan pastoral leadership and renewal. The tensions in the diocese were not just personal. They also stemmed from the growing gap between the cultural and spiritual insights of many Catholics trying to implement Vatican II according to a multidisciplinary method involving the insights of sociology, psychology, and political science, and the simultaneous choice of the bishop to proceed according to a traditional, curia-centered, top-down way to teach Vatican II. Already in December 1970, a questionnaire was sent to the priests of the dioceses on behalf of the Presbyteral Council, only to be disavowed by the same Presbyteral Council just a few days later.[36]

Between 1971 and 1972, Italy experienced a wave of new legislation on divorce and contraception that many Catholics perceived as the end of Catholic Christianity in Italy. Catholics were split on the issues, but most were at least tacitly on the side of the legislation and rejected the call for a new crusade coming from many bishops and from the Christian Democratic Party. In the dioceses of Ferrara, groups of lay Catholics expressed skepticism about the "modernity" of these new laws, but at the same time they refused to be part of the crusade for the restoration of the former laws.[37]

In early 1972, the Pastoral Council proposed the formation of a new commission for the study of "the sociology of religion" in the diocese. The bishop never accepted this proposal.[38] Opponents construed his reluctance to accept more modern methods of propagating the gospel as a rejection of a bottom-up mentality, of an inductive method, and of a more collegial local church. They also saw his stance as a refusal of the "anthropological turn" they saw operative in Vatican II, which for them meant the value of personal experience and the sovereignty of individual conscience, freedom, and responsibility.

In this respect, the differences in theological cultures between the bishop and his curia and other centers of Catholic culture in Ferrara were more than evident. Much of the resentment of lay Catholics toward their bishop was based on the fact that Mosconi never allowed the new governing bodies of the dioceses to function:

> Why, instead of continuing in that sort of pitiful compromise that has so far been the Diocesan Pastoral Council (in which you never put any faith, and all of its components know it – whether they tell you or not), don't we gather where and how you want, even in the Pastoral Council (but in a new, serious, credible Diocesan Pastoral Council) or without the Pastoral Council, and we say everything we say and we face the issues with trust, love, without suspicion, without unnecessary fears?[39]

Under the pressure of secularizing tendencies in Italy, and especially in northern Italy in the early 1970s, the Catholic Church reacted with attempts to rally Catholics around the bishops and their moral teaching about marriage and sexuality. Italian bishops sent strong messages warning Catholics about the impending catastrophic moral decay of the country. The bishop of Ferrara published in July 1973 the notification "Tempo di cedimenti" (time of failures):

> The public dissent that has attacked and shaken confidence in the souls of the faithful in the Roman Catholic Church has led to the rejection of the Magisterium of the Church, the rejection of marriage according to the Concordat, and the celebration of civil marriage wanting to ignore the serious obligation with which the Church binds Italian Catholics. The rejection of the Magisterium of the Church has made more serious the refusal of ecclesiastical discipline and of the moral law, so the norm . . . is more and more autonomous, situation-based, subjective, and thus arbitrary and unrealistic. Immoral behavior becomes normal and, worse, becomes desecrating and aggressive. I am calling my fellow Christians to reconsider in the light of Christ their behavior. I am calling the priests to carefully review the laws of the Church that must be masters to guide the faithful. I am calling all to respect the innocence of children, their own and others' person, the moral law, the Christian way of life, for themselves and for others.[40]

The reaction of lay Catholics to these "political" messages from the hierarchy was lukewarm, to say the least, in Ferrara as well as in other locales of Italian Catholicism. In Ferrara, the Catholic lay faithful could not help but notice the growing sense of isolation in a magisterial authority unable to set in motion the new diocesan governing bodies Vatican II had mandated.[41] The Presbyteral Council, and especially the commission for the clergy, was criticized in 1973 for a lack of transparency in the management of financial resources of the diocese.[42] Between 1973 and 1974, the bishop rejected new appeals for a renewal of these governing bodies and the lay organizations openly accused the bishop of sabotaging them:

> The diocese must address with extreme urgency the serious social and pastoral problems ... These problems can be addressed only by the Bishop or by the Bishop and the people of God together. If the Bishop believes he can address them by himself – without, that is, consulting his people – that can be done, but he has the duty, human and Christian at the same time, to say that openly and officially ... A Pastoral Council restored just to silence annoying and intrusive people but essentially designed not to work in a serious way would be objectively a serious impropriety against the Church our Mother and our brothers in the faith.[43]

Supremacy Battles post-Vatican II

In September 1975, a large conference in Ferrara celebrated the history of the Catholic social movement in Italy, one of whose founders was a celebrated local figure from Ferrara, Giovanni Grosoli. Also in Ferrara, the local conference on "Evangelization and Human Promotion" (Evangelizzazione e promozione umana, or EPU) took place in March 1976 – a part of the national evangelizing effort of the Italian Bishops Conference aimed at engaging lay Catholics and secular culture for a renewed dialogue with the Catholic Church. As it happened in many other dioceses in Italy, Bishop Mosconi remained largely untouched by these new initiatives.

Just a few days after the EPU conference, Mosconi resigned at the age of 72, three years before he was required to do so by canon law. A growing sense of isolation of the episcopal curia from the rest of the local church, both clergy and lay faithful, marked the last two years of Bishop Mosconi's twenty-two-year episcopate. It is important to note that Mosconi was the last bishop in the history of the Ferrara diocese who spent all of his life as a bishop in a single diocese; subsequently, episcopal turnover became more commonplace. Vatican II was the beginning of the redefinition of the "job description" for Catholic bishops all over the world: a job increasingly complicated, demanding skills typical of a leader, of a mediator, of a media savvy communicator, and of a CEO – but always subject to the Vatican and with a mandate that ends at age seventy-five. But Mosconi's early retirement came at the end of a stable record of leadership over more than two decades.

A member of a cohort of clergy trained in the 1920s, Bishop Mosconi's tenure in Ferrara showed a significant gap in the enthusiasm for the reforms of Vatican II among lay and clergy leaders in his diocese. This lack of enthusiasm was not exceptional in bishops of small dioceses in Italy, and it was part of the post-conciliar experience of many local churches whose bishops were not key players at Vatican II. In many cases, reforms and teachings emanating from Vatican II were promoted – paradoxically, if we consider the more "localist" ecclesiology of Vatican II in comparison to the ecclesiology of Vatican I – much more by the centralized body of church government (the papacy, the national bishops conferences) than by local bishops. The application of Vatican II locally had to overcome the hurdle of a cohort of bishops who, in many cases, had little part in shaping the documents of the Council.[44] These bishops were surprised by what they perceived as waves of novelties resulting from the Council. Their surprise came not only from the reception of these reforms among the laity but also the reformist agenda of Paul VI in liturgy and various other areas of church life. A significant difference between the application of earlier church councils such as Trent was the speed and pace of the reforms of Vatican II in the first few years after the Council.

Notwithstanding the reluctance of Bishop Mosconi, a significant change occurred in the diocese of Ferrara between the late 1950s and the mid-1970s. In just a few years, a clerically controlled local church met the challenges of a significant network of lay Catholics participating in Vatican II-mandated governing bodies. The church authorities (the bishop and the clergy) also confronted centers of debate connected to the church like Casa Cini and the Centro Charles de Foucauld. The center of gravity for the reception of Vatican II in the diocese did not come solely from the bishop's curia, but also from independent initiatives of priests and laity. Whether these bottom-up initiatives began with Vatican II or predated Vatican II, the sources of their access to the Council were not limited to the teaching of their bishop and his curial priests. Lay leaders, independent organizations, and even the media shaped local reception and attempts to enact the conciliar reform.

It is thus clear from the example of Ferrara that Vatican II gave way to a post–Vatican II period marked by a fight for supremacy in the local church, often between older clerical elites, younger priests, and lay leaders usually headed by upper-middle-class leftist Catholic intellectuals.[45] Moreover, this clash within the local church of Ferrara shows the potential for conflict in the shift from a church government based, at least since the Council of Trent, on a mixed "charismatic-traditional-legal" kind of leadership (to use Max Weber's ideal types for the classification of authority) to a church government less influenced by the "charismatic" and the "traditional" element and more shaped by "rational-legal-collegial" bodies.[46] The struggles in the government of the local churches after Vatican II happened, in different forms, in the government of global Catholicism, with the shift from a papal-episcopal-clerical leadership to a mixed kind of leadership, with more movements and institutions trying to forge more rational ecclesial structures.[47]

In the short run, the balance of power in the local churches shifted toward a less clerical church, a shift abetted by the quick turnover in the bishops' ranks Paul VI fostered. The role of the religious orders active in the diocese (in this case, the Jesuits) speaks of a leadership role in reorganizing the pastoral activities toward a more socially and politically aware Catholicism, more engaging toward secular culture, even able to build bridges with socialists and communists.

What came from Rome with Vatican II was an unsolved power struggle between bishops and priests – unsolved theologically by the Council – with much more time spent debating the power of the bishops vis-à-vis the papacy than time devoted to the debate of collegiality in the churches at the local level. This tension needed to be resolved locally as the balance of power among bishops, local clergy, and laity shifted in the years after Vatican II. As this chapter demonstrates, only a lived history of Vatican II can begin to assess what happened as a result of this aspect of the Vatican II reform Council.[48]

NOTES

1. John W. O'Malley, *What Happened at Vatican II?* (Cambridge, MA: Harvard University Press, 2008), pp. 30.

2. See Giuseppe Alberigo, *History of Vatican II*, 5 vols. Joseph A. Komonchak edited the English version (Maryknoll, NY: Orbis, 1995–2006).

3. On the Italian dioceses between John XXIII and Paul VI, see Alberto Melloni, "Da Giovanni XXIII alle chiese italiane del Vaticano II" in Giuseppe De Rosa, Tullio Gregory and André Vauchez (eds.), *Storia religiosa dell'Italia contemporanea* (Rome-Bari: Laterza, 1995), pp. 361–403. For the case of the Archdiocese of Milan, see Luca Bressan, Gilles Routhier, Luciano Vaccaro (eds.), *Da Montini a Martini: il Vaticano II a Milano, vol. 1, Le figure* (Brescia: Morcelliana, 2012); in the case of Bologna, see the old but still useful volume by Giampiero Forcesi, *Il Vaticano II a Bologna. La riforma conciliare nella città di Lercaro e Dossetti* (Bologna: Il Mulino, 2011, first edition 1985).

4. *Acta et documenta concilio oecumenico Vaticano II apparando*, series 1, *Antepraeparatoria*, vol. II, *Consilia et vota episcoporum ac praelatorum, part III: Europa, Italia* (Vatican City:

Typis Polyglottis Vaticanis, 1960), p. 261. For a comparison with other *vota* during the preparation of Vatican II, see Mauro Velati, "I 'consilia et vota' dei vescovi italiani" in Mathijs Lamberigts and Claude Soetens (eds.), *A la veille du Concile Vatican II. Vota et réactions en Europe et dans le catholicisme oriental* (Leuven: Peeters, 1992), pp. 83–97.

5. See Francesco Lavezzi, "La partecipazione di mons. Natale Mosconi al Concilio Vaticano II (1959–1965)," dissertation, University of Bologna (1990), p. 11.

6. See Daniele Menozzi (ed.), *Lettere pastorali dei vescovi dell'Emilia Romagna* (Genoa: Marietti, 1986).

7. Bishop Natale Mosconi, pastoral letter "Seguite la Chiesa," *Bollettino Diocesano della diocesi di Ferrara*, LI:2 (1961), p. 38.

8. About Luciano Chiappini see Carlo Pagnoni, "Introduzione" in Carlo Pagnoni (ed.), *Una voce fedele e libera: 'Il taccuino' di Luciano Chiappini* (Ferrara: Corbo, 2000), pp. 28–33.

9. On this progressive Catholic milieu in Italy, see Daniela Saresella, *Dal Concilio alla contestazione. Riviste cattoliche negli anni del cambiamento (1958–1968)* (Brescia: Morcelliana, 2005); Daniela Saresella, *Cattolici a sinistra. Dal modernismo ai giorni nostri* (Rome-Bari: Laterza, 2011).

10. Luciano Chiappini, "Riflessioni," *Bollettino del Centro Studi Charles de Foucauld*, June 2, 1962, p. 2.

11. Luciano Chiappini, letter to a member of the center, December 21, 1962, personal archives of Prof. Luciano Chiappini.

12. From "Lo spirito del Circolo" (of "Casa Cini"), approved on October 3, 1969, quoted in Miriam Turrini, "Casa Cini a Ferrara negli anni conciliari e postconciliari (1962–1976)" in *Miscellanea di studi per il sessantesimo sacerdotale di mons. Antonio Samaritani. Analecta pomposiana. Studi di storia religiosa delle diocesi di Ferrara e Comacchio* 34 (2009), 710.

13. Luciano Chiappini's letter to the editor of the weekly of the dioceses, La Voce Cattolica, Fr. Giulio Zerbini, February 2, 1963.

14. See Natale Mosconi, *Lettere dal Concilio* (Ferrara: Industrie Grafiche, 1965).

15. Bishop Natale Mosconi, "Dopo il concilio," *Bollettino Ecclesiastico*, 11–12 (1965), pp. 260–263.

16. Bishop Mosconi spent much of his time in Rome during Vatican II researching and working in the Vatican Library on books of "ecclesiastical history" that he published during and immediately after the Council: *Francesco Spinelli Servo del Signore* (Cremona: Pizzorni, 1963); *Il Vescovo Paolo Rota* (Rome: Sales, 1964); *La nunziatura di Praga di Cesare Speciano (1592–1598) nelle carte inedite vaticane e ambrosiane*, 5 vols. (Brescia: Morcelliana, 1966–1967).

17. See Massimo Faggioli, *Il vescovo e il concilio. Modello episcopale e aggiornamento al Vaticano II* (Bologna: Il Mulino, 2005), pp. 448–455.

18. See Natale Mosconi, "Realizzare il concilio," *Bollettino Ecclesiastico*, Diocesi di Ferrara, no. 1–2 (1966) pp. 1–17.

19. Letter of September 6, 1966, in the archives of the Cancelleria Arcivescovile di Ferrara.

20. Luciano Chiappini, "Resistenze alla dinamica conciliare," *Testimonianze* 81–2 (1966), 132.

21. See Andrea Zerbini, "La diocesi di Ferrara (1954–1976)" in Maurizio Tagliaferri (ed.), *Il Vaticano II in Emilia-Romagna. Apporti e ricezioni* (Bologna: EDB, 2007), pp. 321–366, at pp. 336–339.

22. Personal archives of Prof. Luciano Chiappini (Ferrara), April 29, 1968.
23. Personal archives of Prof. Luciano Chiappini (Ferrara), June 1968.
24. See Bruna Bocchini Camaiani (ed.), *Ernesto Balducci. La Chiesa, la società, la pace* (Morcelliana: Brescia, 2006).
25. Letter of Bishop Mosconi, March 29, 1969, in the archives of the Cancelleria Arcivescovile di Ferrara.
26. On the history of L'Isolotto in Florence, see Comunità dell'Isolotto (ed.), *Il processo dell'Isolotto* (Rome: Manifesto Libri, 2011).
27. Miriam Turrini, "Casa Cini a Ferrara negli anni conciliari e postconciliari (1962–1976)" in *Miscellanea di studi per il sessantesimo sacerdotale di mons. Antonio Samaritani. Analecta pomposiana. Studi di storia religiosa delle diocesi di Ferrara e Comacchio* 34 (2009), 665–715, at 688.
28. *La Voce di Ferrara*, April 26, 1969.
29. Msgr. Giuseppe Cenacchi (secretary of the diocesan pastoral Council), "Attività del Consiglio Pastorale Diocesano nell'anno 1969–1970," in the archives of the Cancelleria Arcivescovile di Ferrara.
30. *La Voce di Ferrara*, April, 26, 1969, and October 26, 1969.
31. Report of Msgr. Carlo Borgatti, November 3, 1969, to the newly elected Presbyteral Council, in the archives of the Cancelleria Arcivescovile di Ferrara.
32. Letter "To the brothers in priesthood who write anonymous letters," Ferrara, Christmas 1969, in the archives of the Cancelleria Arcivescovile di Ferrara.
33. About Bishop Baldassarri, see Andrea Riccardi, *Vescovi d'Italia. Storie e profili del Novecento* (Cinisello Balsamo: San Paolo, 2000), pp. 155–173.
34. Bulletin of the Charles de Foucauld center, March 10, 1970.
35. Letter of Bishop Mosconi to Luciano Chiappini and the Charles de Foucauld center, March 24, 1970, in the personal archive of Luciano Chiappini.
36. Letter of the secretary of the Presbyteral Council, Fr. Pietro Tosi, December 29, 1970, in the archives of the Cancelleria Arcivescovile di Ferrara.
37. See Luciano Chiappini's letter in the bulletin of the Charles de Foucauld center, March 22, 1971.
38. Minutes of the meeting of the pastoral Council of June 12, 1972, in the archives of the Cancelleria Arcivescovile di Ferrara.
39. Luciano Chiappini's letter to Bishop Mosconi, June 9, 1972.
40. "Tempo di cedimenti," *Bollettino Ecclesiastico*, July 15, 1973.
41. See Luciano Chiappini's letter to Bishop Mosconi, August 1, 1973, in the personal archives of Luciano Chiappini.
42. *La Voce di Ferrara*, May 26, 1973.
43. Letter of the Charles de Foucauld center to the bishop of Ferrara and all the priests of the dioceses, January 21, 1974.
44. An interesting comparison would be the study of the reception of Vatican II in dioceses whose bishops were top leaders of the conciliar majority at Vatican II. Thus far we have only the first few steps, for example, the cases of Cardinal Lercaro (in Bologna) and Cardinal Döpfner (in Munich). See Giampiero Forcesi, *Il Vaticano II a Bologna. La riforma conciliare nella città di Lercaro e Dossetti* (Bologna: Il Mulino, 2011), MA dissertation of 1985, republished in 2011, edited by Enrico Galavotti and Giovanni Turbanti); Julius Döpfner, *Tagebücher, Briefe und Notizen zum Zweiten Vatikanischen Konzil*, edited by Guido Treffler (Regensburg: Schnell & Steiner, 2006).

45. See Wolfgang Reinhard, "Kirche als Mobilitätskanal in der frühneuzeitlichen Gesellschaft" in Winfried Schulze (ed.), *Ständische Gesellschaft und soziale Mobilität* (Oldenbourg: München, 1982) pp. 333–351.

46. See Max Weber, *Wirtschaft und Gesellschaft* (Mohr: Tübingen, 1922).

47. See Massimo Faggioli, "The Roman Curia at and after Vatican II: Legal-Rational or Theological Reform?" *Theological Studies* 76:3 (2015), 550–571.

48. Other sources used in research for this chapter include Archive Centro di Documentazione Santa Francesca Romana (Ferrara); Natale Mosconi, *Sermoni conciliari* (Rovigo: Istituto Padano per le Arti Grafiche, 1966); Mosconi, *Commento storico-dottrinale-mistico-ascetico del Concilio Vaticano II* (unpublished); Carlo Pagnoni, *Don Alberto Dioli da Ferrara a Kamituga* (Ferrara: Corbo, 1998); Lorenzo Paliotto, *Il Seminario di Ferrara: notizie e documenti* (Ferrara: Sate, 1998); Sergio Vincenzi, *Ricezione ed attuazione del Concilio Ecumenico Vaticano II nell'opera dell'Arcivescovo di Ferrara Mons. Natale Mosconi*, dissertation (Lagosanto: Grafiche Riunite, 2003); Andrea Zerbini, *Ambiti, figure e tappe della ricezione conciliare nella chiesa di Ferrara 1954–1976* (Ferrara: Cedoc SFR, 2007).

A FRESH STRIPPING OF THE ALTARS? LITURGICAL LANGUAGE AND THE LEGACY OF THE REFORMATION IN ENGLAND, 1964–1984

ALANA HARRIS

Analyzing the often acrimonious debates over the language of the liturgy communicated in a vast correspondence to the Archbishop of Westminster, England, this chapter argues that a "rhetoric of the Reformation" was mobilized by both critics and champions of the vernacular to interrogate the rapid changes to the rite and rote of the Catholic Mass.

I N AN INTENSELY PERSONAL AND HIGHLY EMOTIVE LETTER WRIT- ten in 1967 to his bishop, layman Peter Hutton reluctantly confessed the following:

> I am no longer able to recognise the Church of today as being the same as that to which I pledged my loyalty [37] years ago [and] developments have now reached a point where it is no longer possible for me any longer to silence the criticisms of my conscience, my reason and my judgment.[1]

This founder-member of the London-based Latin Mass Society (LMS) was writing to express, in terms that ironically foregrounded conciliar precepts such as the *sensus fidelium* and the "primacy of conscience", his objections to the changes in Roman Catholicism inaugurated following the promulgation of the *Constitution on the Sacred Liturgy, Sacrosanctum Concilium,* on December 4, 1963.[2] In evaluating these transformations in the Roman Rite, including the substitution of English for Latin as the language of the Mass, Hutton concluded:

> It is further all too evident that the Reformers in their iconoclastic enthusiasm would gladly actually physically destroy the glorious monuments of the Catholic tradition and past . . . In exchange they would like to substitute erections in the debased modern idiom representative of their new religion.[3]

Such strongly expressed sentiments self-consciously evoked historical precedent and the specter of the English Protestant Reformation, analogously linking the present transformations in rite and rote to the upheavals experienced by the sixteenth-century English Catholic community and remembered as a "stripping of the altars."[4]

In analyzing the frequently heated and often acrimonious debates over the language of the liturgy occasioned in the wake of the Second Vatican Council, this chapter foregrounds the particularity of the English Catholic context (centered on the Diocese of Westminster) in its reception of these changes.[i] This lived religious history identifies the centrality of a latent but potent narrative of English history, which foregrounded the Council of Trent and a history of penal persecution. English Catholics across the ecclesiological and political spectrum were engaged in a reflexive recollection of the Reformation and a politicized and presentist invocation of the legacy of the recusant martyrs as contemporaneous resources to integrate or interrogate "the vernacular." In this employment of freighted constructions of their history and collective memory, English Catholics struggled with concepts of tradition and development – a process also polemically encapsulated in the present-day debates surrounding Vatican II and a so-called hermeneutic of continuity[5] – to find mechanisms to cope with these profound shifts in religious practice and the reformulation of a "modern" English Catholic identity. As the Council Fathers, drawing on the legacy of the liturgical movement, mobilized concepts of *ressourcement and rapprochement* in drafting the *Constitution on the Sacred Liturgy*,[6] so too did English Catholics – those supportive or equally those despairing of the changes. They thereby utilized understandings of "history"[7] and "ecumenical receptivity" in reaching their own conclusions about the "doings in Rome."

Utilizing a rich seam of correspondence to the archbishop of Westminster, the archival records of the London-based Latin Mass Society and the Jesuit archives in Farm Street (West London), as well as the editorials and letters that dominated diverse strands of the English Catholic press until the 1980s, this chapter explores the ways in which England's largest religious minority employed a "rhetoric of the Reformation" and differing configurations of "historical continuity" not only to deal with the implementation of *Sacrosanctum Concilium* but also the decree on ecumenism, *Unitatis Redintegratio* (1964). It argues that the debates of English Catholics about their history, religious memories, and ultimately their Catholic identity as a minority in "Protestant Britain"[8] – a religious landscape that was simultaneously shifting through decolonization and increasing (non-Christian) immigration – properly centered on the changes to the liturgy, given the pivotal significance of the Mass as a reenactment/recreation of the historical events at the heart of Christianity. Intrinsic to Christ's command to "do this in remembrance of me" is the recognition of the power of the past, interpreted and adapted to the needs of the present. A close examination of the vocabularies and tropes of ordinary English Catholics when discussing the movement to the vernacular not only exhibits the range of positions adopted on linguistic, liturgical, and ultimately ecclesiological questions in the years following the Council but also illuminates the broader perspectives of English Catholics on class identity and social mobility, integration into British society, and their relationships with their non-Catholic (and particularly Church of England) compatriots. At the heart of these debates, which pivoted around the altar and the liturgy, are fundamental issues about the spirituality and social identity of English Catholics negotiating a period in Britain, as elsewhere in the Western European world, of widespread change and transition.[9]

Liturgical Change

The *Constitution on the Sacred Liturgy*, known by its opening words, *Sacrosanctum Concilium*, was the first of the Council's documents and was endorsed by an overwhelming majority of bishops but not, tellingly, by the then archbishop of Westminster, Cardinal William Godfrey.[10] While stressing that "the use of the Latin language is to be maintained in the Latin rites,"[11] the constitution also expressed its strong desire for "all believers to be led to take a full, conscious and active part in liturgical celebration."[12] To this end: "In the mass, the administration of the sacraments, and in other parts of the liturgy, there cannot at all infrequently exist a practice of using the local language, a practice which is really helpful among the people."[13] The constitution advocated that "it should therefore become possible for more scope to be given for such practices"[14] and provided general guidance as to the parts of the Mass and other sacraments in which the local language could be incorporated.[15] It also recommended a "revision of the way the mass is structured . . . so that it becomes easier for the people to take a proper and active part."[16] Implementation of these principles commenced with the motu proprio *Sacram Liturgiam*, issued by Pope Paul VI on January 25, 1964, which provided guidance "for the preservation, the improvement and – where needed – the reform of the liturgy."[17] A spate of further instructions followed throughout the decade, extending the role of the vernacular and introducing other changes to the liturgical setting and devotional practices. These developments culminated in the much-debated

apostolic constitution *Missale Romanum* on April 3, 1969, which ushered in
a new order of Mass replacing the Tridentine Rite promulgated by Pope
Pius V in 1570 (and refined in subsequent years) in response to many of the
challenges of the Protestant Reformation.[18] In issuing his subsequent *General
Instruction* on the adapted Roman Missal, Pope Paul described it as contin-
uous with the tradition of Trent, through the preservation of "the deposit of
faith handed down to us through the more recent Councils [but nevertheless
constituting] a very important step forward in the liturgical tradition."[19]
Reflecting on the changes from a distance of four decades, the English priest
and well-respected church historian Adrian Hastings acutely observed the
following:

> When one considered that the Latin mass had remained almost unchanged
> for more than five hundred years, that its revision constituted one of the
> most burning issues of the Reformation and one which Rome had been
> adamant in refusing, then the speed and decisiveness of liturgical reform in
> the 1960s becomes really amazing.[20]

Described by Reformation historian (and Catholic commentator) Eamon
Duffy as the "unfreezing of a liturgical tradition, which had seemed to many
as sacrosanct and immemorial, beyond question or change,"[21] the changes in
the Mass were met with particular consternation by many English Catholics.
The English church, with the notable exception of liturgists such as Clifford
Howell, SJ, and those promoting dialogue masses within the Young
Christian Workers' movement,[22] was theologically unprepared for the developments foreshadowed decades before by the Continental liturgical
movement.[23] The English Church had based much of its self-understanding
and public identity around a distinctiveness vested in Romanism, ultramontane practices, Latin, and (in the 1960s, rapidly disappearing) endogamy.[24]
As the English Catholic hierarchy acknowledged in 1964, the implementation of the liturgical decree "had launched a movement which will uproot
all kinds of age-old habits, cut psychological and emotional ties [and] shake
to the foundation the ways of thought of three to four million Catholics."[25]
The Diocese of Westminster was at the epicenter of these debates, not only
because of its size and profile – encompassing "swinging Sixties" central
London[26] and the See of the Primate of England and Wales – but also
because it was at the heart of debates about Vatican II. Much of the conciliar
dynamism (and dissension), epitomized within the diocese by entities such
as the ill-fated Corpus Christi theological college (the English Lumen
Vitae)[27] and the Latin Mass Society headquarters, played out through the
increasingly well-educated, metropolitan, and ethnically diverse parishes

north of the Thames, including Middlesex and the suburban, middle-class commuter zones of Hertfordshire. With a population of nearly half a million Catholics in 1960,[28] which made it slightly smaller but nevertheless institutionally more powerful than the still very Irish diocese of Liverpool in the north of England,[29] the Diocese of Westminster was recognized as the flagship of English Catholicism. Moreover its archbishop functioned as the primary point of contact, as leader of the English hierarchy, for those disillusioned, despairing, or disgruntled about the course of liturgical change throughout the country.

Setting the Scene

In his opinion piece on the reception of the liturgical constitution within the Manchester-based *Universe and Catholic Times* – the largest-selling religious weekly in the world with a circulation in the 1960s that remained near 200,000 copies[30] – the Benedictine monk Benet Innes wryly observed: "'How are you getting along with the new liturgy?' is as common an opening for a conversation among Catholics nowadays as a remark about the weather. The liturgical changes must have struck deep to have rivalled the weather as a topic for conversation!"[31]

The first Sunday of Advent in 1964 marked the introduction of some vernacular into limited parts of the liturgy within England and Wales and was dubbed "E-day" by one columnist.[32] These reforms were soon surpassed by further changes in early 1965, which resulted in English being used for most of the Mass except for the Canon and some specific, well-known prayers.[33] While other changes were occasioned by these liturgical reforms, it was this wholesale movement from Latin to English that excited the most controversy in England and that forms the focus of this study.[34] Resistance to liturgical change began with small, personal advertisements in mainstream British press, with readers of *The Times* and *The Guardian* newspapers asking: "Will anyone wishing to preserve the ancient Latin liturgy in England and who wishes to join me in an appeal please write to..."[35] Lay Catholics Cathleen Hindmarsh from Manchester[36] and Geoffrey Houghton-Brown in London initiated these advertisements. Houghton-Brown (who was to serve as LMS chairman between 1969 and1970 and London diocesan representative from 1965–1972), in his rich, unpublished history of the LMS, recounted that the idea for *The Times* "appeal" came to him on the feast day of St. Edward the Confessor in 1964, while praying at his tomb in Westminster Abbey.[37] Other rallying calls followed, from Gillian Edwards and Ruth McQuillan of Cambridge[38] and Mary Teresa Parnell of Sussex, who used the correspondence columns in papers such as the *Daily Telegraph* as a spokesperson for "the many Roman Catholics who do not express their views outwardly, [but] who are filled with sorrow at the passing of the Latin in the liturgy and look forward to the coming changes with real dismay."[39]

This lay-led agitation led to the formation of the Latin Mass Society in January 1965, under the impetus of Hugh Byrne,[40] as "an association of Catholic Faithful dedicated to the preservation of the traditional Latin Mass as one of the legitimate forms of the Church's liturgy."[41] In 1969, the society boasted 2,417 members,[42] rising to around 5,000 in 1971[43] – with a preponderance of women taking active organizational roles[44] and financial support for office premises, secretarial support, and publications funded by Lady Claude Kinnoull.[45] The LMS became the focal point for such traditionalist dissent, presenting arguments for the retention of the Latin Mass in each diocese and the minimization of liturgical change to the English bishops, particularly Cardinal John Carmel Heenan, who was personally sympathetic to their arguments and ecclesiastically cautious, if slightly more media savvy than his predecessor.[46] The promulgation of the revised order of the Mass in 1969, the so-called *Novus Ordo*, caused considerable internal dissension within the LMS, centered on differing interpretations of the association's relationship to the pope and understandings of "orthodoxy," which were interrogated through the membership's commitment to Latin as a liturgical language as opposed to the old Latin rite itself. The result was a split in the membership and the formation by Dr. R. Richens of an alternative, smaller Association for Latin Liturgy (1969), which advocated the use of Latin within the New Rite.[47]

Following this schism, the LMS unequivocally refocused its attention on the restoration of the Tridentine Mass (1570) and the promotion of this cause through a variety of innovative mechanisms. In 1971, with much publicity, it coordinated a petition to the pope signed by many distinguished scholars, writers, historians, and musicians who "call[ed] to the attention of the Holy See the appalling responsibility it would incur in the history of the human spirit were it to refuse to allow the traditional Mass to survive."[48] The impact of this so-called Agatha Christie indult, to which the famous crime writer was a signatory, added weight to the formal request of Cardinal Heenan to Rome for a dispensation for English Catholics to use the Tridentine Mass "on special occasions."[49] This dispensation, which was exceptional in the context of international Catholicism (excepting Poland),[50] was granted on November 5, 1971. As such, this compromise "helped to contain what could have developed into a nasty and difficult case of open defiance"[51] and illustrates the passion and concerted opposition to these changes within a section of the English Catholic community (and beyond),[52] in contrast to their mostly favorable reception in Scotland and Ireland,[53] and other parts of the English-speaking world, including Britain's former colonies.[54] Consternation and controversy continued throughout the 1970s and was a feature of the wider discussions surrounding the National Pastoral Congress in Liverpool in 1980 – an unprecedented (and unrepeated) gathering of more than 2,000 clerical and lay representatives who assembled in a synod-like forum to evaluate the state of the contemporary church. The dispensation granted to English Catholics to use the Tridentine Mass "on special occasions" was interpreted relatively liberally – though not uniformly – in English dioceses throughout the 1970s,[55] and this policy was given further centralized Roman endorsement in 1984, when Pope John Paul II granted a universal dispensation and then emphatically commended the Latin liturgical tradition in his motu proprio *Ecclesia Dei*, in 1988.[56]

Remembrance of Times Past

In the introduction to his 1969 study of the modern Mass, dedicated to LMS members whom he called "defenders of the Faith," the Reformation historian Hugh Ross Williamson acknowledged that "An English historian is apt, by the nature of things to be suspicious of liturgical change. He knows that in his country it has happened before and that the consequences of it have moulded his religious background."[57] This inherent tendency to resist present liturgical innovation through reference to the Reformation was also noted by advocates of reform such as Michael Richards, who emphasized in 1966 that:

> The memory of penal times is still an active influence in the approach of the English Catholic to the style of his public worship ... It has been given a particular form by our life as a small minority ... conscious of being authentic representatives of a past whose achievements others have inherited and now transformed.[58]

This constant invocation of the legacy of the Reformation was not confined to academic critiques of the liturgical changes, but it attained a currency within more popular commentaries, voluminous correspondence within the Catholic press, and agonized letters from the laity to the archbishop of Westminster. Such tendencies were initially manifest in the frequent denunciations of liturgical progressives as "reformers," perhaps most caustically expressed in 1965 *The Tablet* correspondence columns by Evelyn Waugh, who bewailed the loss of the Latin Mass and decried the vernacularists as "cranks" pursuing a schismatic, modern-day Reformation.[59] The iconic convert novelist called on historical memories of Reformation devastation when speaking for "suffering Catholics who have for many years now seen their public devotions stripped of more and more which they valued."[60] His extended commentary blazed combatively:

> To history let us turn. You will find that there have been a few inspired geniuses who have revived the Church and, in doing so, changed it. For every one of these there have been hundreds of presumptuous and misguided men . . . All the tongues of Babel are to be employed save only Latin, the language of the Church since the mission of St Augustine. That is forbidden to us.[61]

Early English missionary and Reformation history, the antiquity of the Latin Mass, and the authority of the Old Testament were employed to give legitimacy to his obduracy. Seeking relative anonymity rather than public notoriety, a self-styled "Very Ordinary Catholic" wrote in a similar vein a year earlier to the archbishop of Westminster. Communicating his distress as a "convert of 33 years" about the "liturgical shambles" and the distracting "proceedings in the Sanctuary" within his London-based parish, this layman fumed that "'mystery' has become a dirty word among the reformers, they want to strip it out of our Churches [and] are in fact following the steps of the Protestant reformers so long ago."[62]

The potent trope of the English Catholic penal past was frequently employed by public polemists and correspondents resistant both to liturgical change and, what was seen as its corollary, ecumenical rapprochement. In yet another critique of "the invalidity of the New Mass," provocatively entitled *The Great Betrayal* (1970), Hugh Ross Williamson drew on the hagiography of the scholar, cardinal, and martyr St. John Fisher, canonized in 1935 alongside Thomas More, to chastise the current English hierarchy for its complicity and capitulation in the replacement of the 1570 Mass.[63] A few years earlier in 1967, the bishop of Clifton was rebuked in congruent terms by Peter Hutton, who contested: "The Church down the ages has scorned to make an 'aggiornamento' with the world; the Cross, the Colosseum and Tyburn are witness of it."[64] In Hutton's historical analogy, the trials for traditional Catholics presented by the Council mirrored the tribulations of the martyrs of the past, and their sufferings even resembled those of the rejected Messiah. The explicit recollection of the Elizabethan martyr-priests at Tyburn (the historic site of the penal executions by hanging, near Mable Arch in London) was also mobilized by Ella Collier, writing to Cardinal Heenan in 1964, to remind him that "It was the Protestant ministers who shrieked at Blessed Robert Johnson 'Pray in English!' . . . It was the Latin which the Reformers hated, because it bound the Church in England to Rome and that Pope . . . This polyglot Mass will have exactly the reverse effect."[65] The precedent of martyrdoms past offered a potent and emotive metaphor and was often redeployed, as reflected in the correspondence of Rev. H. E. G. Rope in *The Universe* in 1964: "Some of us owe our conversion, under God, to the splendid army of martyrs who are, if she only knew it, the true glory of our country. To Erasmus and his like we owe nothing whatever . . . 'So the Faith was planted. So it must be restored.'"[66]

For Father Rope, as Tertullian, "the blood of the martyrs is seed," and this comingling of the patristic and penal was also adopted by *The Tablet* contributor Rosalind Scott: "Our progressives presumably dismiss the very unaccommodating English martyrs as products of the later Middle Ages or of the Council of Trent – yet they are fond of extolling the early Church, many of whose members chose the arena, or other forms of torture, rather than take a broadminded view of the Roman gods."[67] Through such appeals to tradition, resistance to social accommodation and recollection of the sacrifices of the sixteenth century, those opposed to the post-conciliar reforms employed a "Reformation rhetoric" to convince their coreligionists of the dangers of this present-day restripping of the altars. Their aim was to rally English Catholics to resistance, drawing on historically acknowledged constructions of denominational differentiation and Catholic isolation from the wider English society.

As the traditionalist opposition to the translation of the Mass was formulated in historical terms, it is not surprising that some arguments in favor of the changes, voiced by Catholics from across the social spectrum writing to *The Tablet* and *The Universe* as well as their pastors, were similarly premised on various constructions of English Catholic history. These approaches sometimes took the form of rejection of the need for continuity altogether but more often appealed to the priority of the early church or sought to reconcile Reformation references with contemporary ecumenical concerns. The more radical stance of acknowledging innovation and disparaging conservation was generally adopted by those enthusiastically embracing the vernacular, such as the radically progressive (but marginal) pro-Marxist *Slant* group centered in Cambridge[68] or the noted English liturgist J. D. Crichton, who frankly surmised that "we are starting out on a venture similar to that of the reformers of the sixteenth century."[69] Joyce Carey, a Yorkshire laywoman, was also playfully dismissive of conservative appeals to history in opposition to the vernacular, ironically parodying those who say: "What was good enough for our fathers (chained in prison dark, etc.) should be good for us ... We might equally argue that it is quite wicked to install central heating and electric lights in church, since these too were unknown to our forefathers."[70] In a more scholarly vein, a group of mostly clerical and academic commentators writing in 1964 directly contested the use of Reformation history and the insistence on the Latin Mass, rhetorically asking: "Is England's history all that unique? It is those very countries which shared the Reformation with her that have pioneered the liturgical movement and inspired the Council's Constitution."[71] In the assessment of these correspondents, English Catholics had "long resisted worship in our mother tongue, simply *because* it was promoted by the Protestants."[72]

Another tactic for defusing such criticisms was to link the vernacular to a common English nationalism, evidenced in *The Tablet*'s contemporaneous advocacy of a historically minded translation modeled on "the vernacular liturgy of the English peoples which has stood the test of four centuries [and] earned the soubriquet 'incomparable.'"[73] Similarly, C. R. A. Cunliffe, the president of the Vernacular Society of Great Britain, noted the aptness of the change to the vernacular with the "quartercentenary of the birth of Shakespeare" and the legacy of English as "a *lingua franca* for the modern world as ever Latin was for Christendom."[74] In place of recollecting the anniversary of Trent, recourse was made to the common, cross-denominational history of the English tongue. The debates in modern scholarship about the supposed recusant Catholic background of this quintessentially "English" poet perhaps also recommended Shakespeare's invocation to illustrate the compatibility of English nationalism with Catholicism and the Mass rendered in (poetic) English.

It was to avoid such charges of the "Protestantization" of the liturgy, and undue Anglican accommodation, that commentators and correspondents also drew on an alternative patristic history highlighted by the liturgical movement itself[75] to stress the continuity of the English language with the earliest Christian traditions. Conservative MP, Catholic convert, and prolific author Christopher Hollis[76] typified such tactics: "I was very interested the other day to discover from some tolerably well, if not excessively well instructed Catholics, how many of them believed that the use of Latin in the Mass dated back to the first origins of the Church."[77] This former Notre Dame visiting professor invited his current readership of ordinary, mostly Northern Catholics to "stop and think" whether "Our Lord had instituted the Sacrament in Latin words,"[78] whereas layman Randle Lunt bluntly challenged his audience of converts and literati: "did Jesus Christ at the Last Supper say '*hoc est enim Corpus meum*'?"[79] Following the introduction of the New Rite in 1970, Dr. Anthony Roberts wrote to Cardinal Heenan to assert his preference for the new liturgy (despite his own fluency in Latin) and to air his frustrations with "many ignorant criticisms," such as "The wording of the Our Father is 'Protestant.' So what? It is quite orthodox. I gently point out that this ending is in the third century liturgy of St. Chrysostom and St. Basil also."[80]

Most correspondents, however, urged a "return to the sources" in ways that strategically muted the congruity between this enterprise and any Protestant resonances, best evidenced in a letter from seven ordinary (though well-informed) laymen to *The Tablet* in 1964 tackling the "traditionalism" of the Latin Mass Society directly:

> As for its being "traditional" there are traditions and traditions, some good, some bad, and by no means all belonging to the tradition of the Church. As a matter of historical fact the Latin low Mass is an impoverished and truncated version of an ancient corporate celebration of the Eucharist … ultimately in contradiction with the central teaching of the Gospel.[81]

In these references to ancient practices and the Gospel, these Catholics were stressing a common Christian foundation, but one that effectively circumvented charges of denominational compromise or capitulation. However, such arguments, and those advocating a dispensation altogether from historical continuity, failed to persuade people such as J. A. Green, writing to *The Universe* in 1965 to articulate his puzzlement at those "very keen to return to some primitive rite and thereby completely ignore 2000 years of Catholic development and 'growing up in Christ.'"[82] Predictably, Evelyn Waugh, anticipating just such rhetorical tactics in 1962 when writing in *The Spectator* (a conservative weekly of long-standing influence), remained unconvinced by "the strange alliance between archaeologists absorbed in their speculations on the rites of the second century, and modernists who wish to give the Church the character of our own deplorable epoch. In combination they call themselves 'liturgists.'"[83] For Waugh and Green, laymen from quite different backgrounds, yet exhibiting similar ecclesiological temperaments, these developments were denounced as diminishing Catholics' liturgical inheritance and disregarding the history of that church in England.

History and Priorities of the Present

Between the previously canvassed perspectives of the "traditionalists" and the "liturgists," the correspondence of many Catholic laity and clergy within the press and to their bishops revealed an attempt to reconcile the sustaining historical narratives of the past with the social priorities of the present – chiefly articulated as English Catholics' increasing educational and socioeconomic mobility, integration in British society (through "mixed marriages"), and a greater ecumenical orientation in the postwar period.[84] As *The Tablet* editor Douglas Woodruff recognized, writing sympathetically of the apprehensions of cradle Catholics and the fears of converts: "The Latin Mass has been in some sense a symbol of our faith. It will take time for us to adapt ourselves to these distinctions between doctrine and discipline which are much more clearly evident to other people.[85] This negotiation of doctrine and discipline, and implicitly the distinctiveness of the English Catholic community deprived of such symbols – part of a raft of disappearing semiotics such as bells and smells and fish on Fridays that now rendered Catholics "just like other people," to paraphrase English Catholic anthropologist Mary Douglas[86] – took the form of a reconsideration of Catholic history and identity, rather than the heated (and more explicitly) theological debates on the continent. Symptomatic of these troubled reconceptualizations of Catholicity is a report in *The Universe* on a conference in early 1964 at Campion Hall, the Jesuit residence in Oxford, which sought to "discuss the ecumenical movement as it affects the man on the street."[87] The staff reporter for the newspaper continued: "One after another a don's wife, a psychologist, a medical student and a young covert voiced their fears. Conversions would drop. The faith would be 'watered down.' We would 'betray' the English Martyrs if we 'gave way' now."[88]

The conference spokesmen, LMS pamphleteer (and later chairman) and administrator at Oxford's Radcliffe Infirmary Jerome Burrough, concluded that a lack of self-confidence and ignorance of the facts were the source of most difficulties. In reality, the problems for ordinary Catholics lay in reconciling the often-contradictory conclusions to be drawn from these "facts" within the context of post-conciliar Catholicism and a rapidly trans-forming British society.

A prominent example of this complex reconceptualization of English Catholic history is evident in the troubled correspondence within the press, to the archbishop of Westminster, and indeed in the archives of and public communications to the Office of Vice Postulation (OVP) (coordinated out of the Jesuit headquarters at Farm Street, London) to canonize the Forty Martyrs of England and Wales. This clerically coordi-nated campaign for Vatican recognition of those men and women exe-cuted during the years of the Henrician and Elizabethan Reformations commenced unproblematically in 1960 but became intensely contested in the years surrounding the Council until what came to be called the Cause's successful conclusion with their canonization in 1970.[89] As well as provid-ing scope for popular devotions (and countless "favors"), particularly in the recusant heartland of the north of England,[90] the Cause appealed to an indigenous recusant tradition stressing "ties of blood, environment and nationality."[91] Such sentiments were encapsulated in a 1963 commission from the OVP to Daphne Pollen to paint a collective illustration of the Forty Martyrs, with the Tower of London, gallows of Tyburn, and a makeshift altar center stage. Within this historically inflected revisioning of a group of highly diverse saints, virtue is presented in romanticized and typologized terms – demure Margaret Clitherow in the foreground, aristocratic Philip Howard painted with his hound, and surrounding ranks of male sanctity spanning the priesthood, scholarship (with Jesuit Edward Campion clasping a manuscript) and the virile martyrdom of teacher Richard Gwyn, with hat and quill.

The remembrance of penal persecution and continuing Catholic dissension began to be acknowledged as potentially incompatible with the new emphasis on ecumenism following *Unitatis Redintegratio* (1964), reinforced by the historic meeting in Rome in 1966 of Pope Paul VI and Archbishop of Canterbury Michael Ramsey – thereby initiating an unprecedented series of bilateral ecumenical conversations. The fear of "betraying" the faith for which the martyrs died, through the countenance of ecumenical conversation, collaboration (or emulation), played through many articles and letters and was the subject of an extended, emotive discussion in *The Tablet* in 1965 about whether the martyrs "died for ecumenism." Joan Eland opened the debate when she reflected: "All of this is old history, and no-one wants to drag up old bitterness, but it does seem to me ridiculous to say that the martyrs died for anything but that one true faith, as it was in the beginning, is now, and ever shall be. Amen."[92]

A laywoman working on the canonization campaign, Margaret FitzHerbert, agreed with Eland's purported near-credal statement, herself affirming that "anyone who has read the lives and utterances of the martyrs knows that, rightly or wrongly, they regarded Protestantism as the enemy and themselves as soldiers in the fight against it."[93] Father Rope also weighed into this forum, facetiously observing that the martyrs "were not forerunners of the Abbé Portal or Fr Kung" (evoking Catholic theologians spanning a century of ecumenical conversations from Malines to the pages of *Concilium*), but "they were reactionary enough to die for that denomination against which the gates of hell have not prevailed, either before or after 1962."[94] He concluded that the "only ecumenism" those executed knew was the "*unconditional* submission to the *one unchanging uncompromising* Church" (original emphasis).[95] Numerous correspondents to Cardinal Heenan from 1964 onward agreed,[96] and representative of such correspondence (especially in the wake of the New Rite) was an irate letter penned by Roger de Wever (from Outer Broad, Suffolk) denouncing as "hippies" those who appealed to "relevance" with a preference for "an instant Mass ... in the language of the supermarket."[97] Rebuking the archbishop for indifference, he claimed to cleave for intercessory intervention to "our Blessed Lady, St Pius V, St Thomas More, St John Fisher and the Blessed English martyrs who generously gave their lives rather than forgo the very Mass which has now been thrown into the ecumenical hotpot."[98] As Jerome Burrough wrote in a letter to *The Tablet* in 1971, "I accept the validity of the New Rite, as indeed I must, but what are my grandchildren going to believe that Cranmer, Latimer and Ridley did not believe?"[99]

Promoters of the Cause also recognized these difficulties, and in a devastating report in 1966 to the hierarchy reflecting on his first year as sole vice-postulator of the Cause, James Walsh, SJ, was disarmingly direct. He wrote in unequivocal terms of the "unpalatable truth of dwindling devotion" and the attitudes of the Catholic laity "ranging from minority support to majority indifference."[100] In his opening gambit, he charted the difficulties he confronted in fulfilling his brief, as follows: "In many quarters, it has become the fashion to see devotion to the saints as démodé; the cult of the Martyrs as a sign of the state of siege, and the Cause as inopportune to the ecumenical movement."[101] Despite some genuine strains of popular devotion,[102] invocation of the Forty Martyrs (and appeal to the tactics of recusancy) did seem to recommend itself chiefly to those concertedly opposed both to the vernacular and the new missal. Traditionalist campaigner (and frequent correspondent within the pro-reform pages of the *Catholic Herald*) D. G. Galvin wrote to his cardinal in 1970 to share his conviction that "the historic Latin Mass was all things to all men" and that the emerging trend for the celebration of the Tridentine Rite in some London churches (and indeed Catholic houses) had "shades of the old Catholic recusants!"[103] Indeed an illicit parish was set up in south London, with funding from many members of the LMS, for the regular provision of the Tridentine rite by a Lefebvrist priest.[104] St. John's Wood correspondent Barbara Mitchell Cots directly invoked this legacy when writing to her bishop, claiming her lineage as "a member of a Catholic family (Throckmorton) who have never lost their faith" and asked his eminence plaintively if he could "hold out a crumb of hope that the Mass we know and love will not be suppressed."[105]

Yet while such accounts strategically evoked an English Catholic aristocratic past, LMS advocates – in the vein of other conservative moral campaigners such as Mary Whitehouse, who utilized 1960s counterculture ideals (and methods) for traditionalist ends[106] – also presented their campaign as "democratic" and a cross-class, broad-based protest movement. President Sir Arnold Lunn was at pains to point out that "it is untrue to suggest that the [Latin] Mass only appeals to a particular class."[107] In a letter to Cardinal Heenan in late 1965 written in his capacity as LMS chairman, Peter Kenworthy-Browne assured his archbishop that the "large number[s] … suffering greatly … are by no means confined to the well-educated" and, drawing on conciliar notions of "active participation," these principled rebels find within the Latin Mass "a source of spiritual strength, refreshment and repose [that] promotes for them the true participation in the Holy Sacrifice."[108] Echoing remarkably similar debates within the Church of England with its near contemporaneous reform of the Book of Common Prayer through the 1960s, appeals to liturgical "authenticity," the "numinous" and true engagement in the Mass were mobilized by liturgical conservationists and innovators alike.[109] Yet within the archbishop's correspondence and letter columns in the Catholic press, there are some traces of working-class, grassroots discontent with the abandonment of Latin, ranging from recounted bus-stop conversations between a grandee and an immigrant "domestic <u>servant</u>, no clever degrees for her!"[110] and the correspondence of Mrs. F. Coupe from Lancashire, who wrote to *The Tablet* on behalf of "busy mothers" who missed the opportunity to stop and "lapse into quiet acquiescence, into the sublime peace of the Mass."[111] Father Anthony Hayes of Silvertown (in East London's Docklands) spoke of the devotion of his working-class parish to the Latin Mass and its appreciation of "a little 'elegance' and 'refinement' whenever possible – something 'special' on Sundays."[112] Perhaps the most arresting plea to Cardinal Heenan was a heart-rending appeal from an Irish Catholic woman on behalf of her twenty-four-year-old motor mechanic son who "would be most upset if he knew I had written to you."[113] Chronicling the devastating impact of these "liturgical infidelities" and contesting the justification of this "suffering [as] going to benefit future generations," Mrs. Pegge closed by reflecting: "He values Latin intensely as being so ancient, so loved and suffered for in the past, and so apart from the coarse everyday English that surrounds him at work. Also he values silence."[114]

Explicitly reworking (and democratizing) notions of a recusant past through implicit evocation of conciliar concepts of *aggiornamento* and the evolution of radical base communities, LMS member Mary Prendergast wrote in justificatory terms about a Tridentine Mass held after the promulgation of the New Missal at the Carmelite Church in Kensington:

> This was not an end, a nostalgic "harking back," but a beginning, a real
> "renewal." There are thousands of loyal Catholics only waiting and praying
> for the restoration of the true and only acceptable, because unambiguous,
> form of Mass ... [Please support us] so that we are not driven to the
> makeshift of house-Masses.[115]

Cardinal Heenan's response to much of this correspondence was an ambiva-
lent mixture of support and perplexity, torn by his contrasting constructions
of what ultramontane Catholic loyalty (then and now) required, and the
curious mixture of appeals to conscience and renewal by traditionalists who,
for him, sometimes echoed the excesses of progressives.[116] His exasperation
was articulated in correspondence to Dr. J. B. Robinson (from Hartlepool,
County Durham), who wrote in 1970 to vent about the Lutheran concepts of
the Eucharist seemingly embodied in the various words of consecration[117]
and announcing his intention to leave the church as a "form of protest ... in
clear conscience."[118] Heenan's revealing reply retorted:

> I sympathise with you but I cannot agree with you. To cut ourselves off
> from the sacraments because we do not agree with the teaching of the Pope
> is a very Protestant thing to do. Some have left the Church because of the
> Pope's teaching on contraception and now priests are leaving because of his
> teaching on the vow of chastity.[119]

In the context of large-scale revolt among English Catholics over issues of
contraception and celibacy – which itself still awaits a thorough historical
examination[120] – and the inauguration of formal ecumenical activities
between the Church of England and the Church of Rome (with the
establishment of the Anglican-Roman Catholic International
Commission [ARCIC] in 1969), the archbishop of Westminster sought
a mechanism to calm this vocal, vociferous, and intractable minority.
In a telling piece of internal correspondence in February 1970 between
Cardinal Heenan and the episcopal chairman of the National Liturgical
Commission for England and Wales, the archbishop acknowledged the
impact of these "fresh shocks to the poor old faithful" and asked "can nothing
be done for the Tridentine Mass non-cranks who would like a little peaceful
co-existence for the old Mass?"[121] The solution this reluctant innovator
adopted was to write to Pope Paul VI on October 30, 1971, to seek permission
for "certain groups of the faithful ... on special occasions ... to participate in
the Mass celebrated according to the Rites and texts of the former Roman
Missal."[122] Yet even this was not enough for some, as the so-called Heenan
Indult granted on November 5, 1971, added a caveat that "at all regular
parish and other community Masses, the Order of the Mass in the new

Roman Missal should be used" lest more regular practice "become a sign or cause of disunity in the Catholic community."[123] Alongside regular celebrations of the Tridentine Rite at the Brompton Oratory (Kensington),[124] Notre Dame de France (off Leicester Square), Our Lady and St. Simon (Carmelite church, Kensington) and indeed Westminster Cathedral (where four of the eight representatives elected to the parish Council and staff such as Fr. Ware and organist Colin Mawby were LMS members),[125] a small village church in Norfolk became the scene of national attention. This followed an article in the *Sunday Observer* newspaper in 1975 reporting the decision of the bishop of East Anglia (and Roman Catholic co-chair of ARCIC) to close Downham Market parish and therefore remove its incumbent, Father Oswald Baker (1915–2004) – a figurehead for traditionalists in his intransigent refusal to offer the *Novus Ordo* in this rural area. Denounced even within the then mostly progressive pages of *The Tablet* as an "unnecessary confrontation,"[126] the incident was gently parodied by John Ryan (1921–2009), creator of the well-loved English children's cartoon character Captain Pugwash and *Catholic Herald* chronicler of the post-Vatican II church. Above the caption "*You can come out, Father . . . His Lordship's gone,*" Ryan sketched a wry, sympathetic picture of an altar *ad orientem*, a packed congregation of mostly older people (including women wearing mantillas) that spilled outside the church, and the vested deacon communicating his message of reassurance through a trapdoor, reminiscent of the priest-holes of penal times.

Yet the majority of items within Cardinal Heenan's mailbag, and indeed the majority of articles within the Catholic press, eschewed the resurrection of an English Catholic past modeled on *Brideshead Revisited*, penal defiance, and the persecution of the ghetto. Not all agreed with the assessment of Fr. Bryan Houghton – a parish priest from Bury St. Edmunds in Suffolk who retired on the introduction of the New Order – who in his witty novel *Mitre and Crook* (1979) charted the (re)conversion of the fictional Bishop Forester with the reintroduction of the Old Mass and recognition of his (and other bishops') arrogant disregard of their flock.[127] Indeed as the pages of David Lodge's novel illustrated, published for a British audience under the title *How Far Can You Go?* (1980) and set in London from the 1950 to the 1970s, it is traditionalist Miles who is out of step with his friends Michael and Miriam, who are at the forefront of the *agape* house-masses presided over by Fr. Austin Brierley.[128] In the archbishop of Westminster's reply to a complaint in 1964 about the lack of lay consultation surrounding the liturgical changes, Cardinal Heenan referred to the "hundreds of letters . . . awaiting my return [from Rome] . . . deal[ing] with the

vernacular," and that "almost all of those from the less well educated are
expressions of thanks."[129] As Hennan's private secretary Monsignor
F. A. Miles also acknowledged in a letter five years later to Mrs. Olive
Scott (and clearly contrary to his own sympathies), the results of a diocesan
questionnaire distributed to churches across London seemed to indicate
that "it was undeniable that the great majority in these parishes welcomed
what has been done."[130] This assessment was confirmed in an oral history
interview with Monsignor Canon Tom Egan (b. 1942, County Mayo),
who was a newly ordained parish priest from 1967 to 1972 in a Hiberno-
English, upper-working-class parish in Hanwell (north London).
The parish of Our Lady and St. Joseph also hosted a growing community
of postwar Asian migrants and, as the space provided by the Victorian Pugin
church was outgrown, in 1967 a new concrete modernist building was
erected.[131] Speaking about the liturgical changes during these years,
Fr. Egan stressed that the majority of his congregation were unfazed by
the liturgical changes, accustomed as they were to clerical deference and
passive acceptance of episcopal direction.[132] Self-confessedly "typical" (but
vociferous) Liverpudlian Catholic Bernard Jubb agreed, denouncing the
LMS as out of touch with working-class parishes to assert:

> I find the current liturgy quite as dignified as the Latin . . . Catholicism is not
> a game for the elite, it must include everybody, and you aren't going to get
> in the harlots by telling them to educate themselves first. I think everybody
> must be sorry to lose Latin . . . but it is ridiculous to act as if the Pope and the
> Council were turning us over to the Bishop of Woolwich or worse.[133]

In his reference to the notorious Anglican bishop of dockland South
London, John A. T. Robinson, who had appeared as an expert defense
witness in the *Lady Chatterley's Lover* obscenity trial and established his
reputation as a "radical" theologian through his 1963 internationally best-
selling book *Honest to God*, which synthesized the work of Paul Tillich,
Dietrich Bonhoeffer, and Rudolf Bultmann,[134] Jubb dismissed as paranoia
the fears of those who asserted English Catholicism's capitulation to modernism or Protestantism. For one youthful correspondent to Cardinal
Heenan in 1969, sixteen-year-old David Power, the liturgical changes
had increased both his personalized and corporate involvement:

> I can truly say that I have never experienced such a great sense of commu-
> nion and participation as with the Normative Mass . . . [and] the greater
> emphasis on being Christian than Catholic, all enhance the meaning of
> Mass . . . I really get quite a "kick" out of . . . [the] experience [of] this
> calming and relaxing union with the ground of our being.[135]

Scarcely making allowances for youthful fervor, Cardinal Heenan expressed some pleasure that his youthful charge from Hertfordshire found the changes "attractive" but sternly chastised him for using "agnostic" expressions such as "ground of our being"[136] made popular through the pages of *Honest to God.*

By the 1970s – following the semi-regular provision of the Tridentine Mass under the terms of the Indult and the implosion of the LMS over critiques of the "validity" of the New Rite (and support of Archbishop Lefebvre)[137] – the furor over liturgical form and language had dissipated as an issue within mainstream parishes. Most Catholics, such as Mrs. Pantcheff from Watford writing to the *Catholic Herald* in 1974, dismissed as eccentrics those who "think [Catholicism] was invented in 1570."[138] As the editor of *The Universe* reported in a special "ballot of issues" ahead of the National Pastoral Congress in 1980, to which 3,500 readers replied:

> The revised liturgy is very much on the readers' minds. The heaviest correspondence I have ever had came on the question of the translation of the New Rite of Mass. Most of the readers who wrote [in 1969] said they would prefer a better translation, but most of those who voted in the ballot [now] say the present translation is a good one.[139]

This level of equanimity among a sample the editor described as "Mass-going Catholics whose commitment to the Church and the Faith is strong enough to lead them ... to buy a Catholic paper [and] post their ballot forms" should be contextualized against their balloted strong opposition to birth control, against married or female priests, and overwhelmingly against "recognition of the validity of Anglican Orders."[140] Against these markers of moral and ecclesiological conservatism, the fact that there was general satisfaction with the New Rite (and only 50 percent support for allowance of the Tridentine Mass occasionally),[141] and that the New Missal did not excite any great controversy among the National Pastoral Congress delegates generally,[142] illustrates an accepting consensus by 1980. Two decades after the Council, most English Catholics, across a generational and theological spectrum, no longer interpreted the post-conciliar liturgical reforms within a historical continuum characterized by Catholic dissent and Reformation iconoclasm. It was the issue of contraception, and the representations of Cardinal Basil Hume and Archbishop Derek Worlock of Liverpool in favor of a reexamination of *Humanae Vitae* at the 1980 Synod of Bishops on the Family in Rome, that now represented the site of long-standing mainstream English Catholic "recusancy."[143]

Conclusion

Writing in 1965 as the chairman of the Liturgical Commission for England and Wales, and drawing on his pastoral experience as bishop of Leeds (and then Birmingham), Archbishop George Dwyer rightly acknowledged, "the Mass is the most intimate and personal act of our religion [and] associations of a lifetime have gathered around it."[144] The ambivalence implicit within this statement, from the prelate responsible for the implementation of *Sacrosanctum Concilium* and the liturgical instructions that followed, epitomized the stance of his fellow bishops – and indeed many of the laity – who were mostly unprepared for the conciliar liturgical developments but passively dutiful in their adherence to Vatican directives.[145] While there were some Westminster parishes renowned for their liturgical experimentation and an enthusiastic embrace of reform (such as St. John the Evangelist in Islington under Fr. Vincent Rochford), and certain religious orders (such as the Olivetan Benedictines under Dom Edmund Jones at Christ the King, Cockfosters,[146] and the Dominican Priory in North London),[147] the vast majority introduced the post-conciliar changes to rite, rote, architectural setting, and devotional practice gradually and cautiously. Paradoxically, something of the conciliar dynamism in seeking to encourage active participation and the "priesthood of the laity," a recognition of the "primacy of conscience" and greater engagement with and reflexive understanding of the Mass were instead exhibited in the articulate protests (in the secular press) and the proactive pressure group maneuvers of Catholic traditionalists and the Latin Mass Society. In the debates around the appropriate liturgical language for English Catholics, and the implications of the reforms to the Mass chiefly interrogated in terms of "orthodoxy" and denominational distinctiveness, there was clearly a "rhetoric of the Reformation" operational. And differing configurations of "historical continuity" were mobilized by both advocates and critics alike.[148] Nevertheless as this chapter has also shown, profoundly "modern" conciliar considerations and the preoccupations of British society negotiating the postwar period were also at play. In these differing interpretations of loyalty and lay autonomy, the devotional needs of the contemporary church and the status and standing of English Catholics especially in relationship to the established Church of England, there was, indeed, a reorientation (if not quite a reformation) underway.

NOTES

1. Letter from Peter Hutton to Bishop Joseph E. Rudderham, bishop of Clifton, December 15, 1967, pp. 1–2, London Mass Society (LMS), miscellaneous correspondence file.

2. For an in-depth theological consideration of the constitution and its legacy, see Massimo Faggioli, *True Reform: Liturgy and Ecclesiology in Sacrosanctum Concilium* (Collegeville, MN: Liturgical Press, 2012).

3. Letter from Peter Hutton to Bishop Joseph E. Rudderham, December 15, 1967, p. 4, LMS, miscellaneous correspondence file.

4. Cambridge historian Eamon Duffy popularized the phrase "the stripping of the altars" as a description of the English Reformation in his highly controversial but influential study *The Stripping of the Altars: Traditional Religion in England c.1400– c.1580,* 2nd ed. (New Haven: Yale University Press, 2005). Duffy is an outspoken critic of the liturgical reforms following the Second Vatican Council. See Eamon Duffy, "The Stripping of the Liturgy," *The Tablet,* July 6, 1996, p. 882 and *Faith of Fathers: Reflections on Catholic Tradition* (London: Continuum, 2004).

5. Pope Benedict XVI's Christmas Address to the Roman Curia, December 22, 2005, www.vatican.va/holy_father/benedict_xvi/speeches/2005/december/documents/ hf_be n_xvi_spe_20051222_roman-curia_en.html, accessed June 30, 2012, and N. Ormerod, "Vatican II – Continuity or Discontinuity? Towards an Ontology of Meaning," *Theological Studies* 71:3 (2010), 609–636.

6. Faggioli, *True Reform,* cf. Aidan Nichols*, Looking at the Liturgy: A Critical View of Its Contemporary Form* (San Francisco: Ignatius Press, 1996); Alcuin Reid, *The Organic Development of the Liturgy: The Principles of Liturgical Reform and Their Relation to the Twentieth Century Liturgical Movement Prior to the Second Vatican Council* (Farnborough: St Michael's Abbey Press, 2004).

7. See John W. O'Malley, *Tradition and Transition: Historical Perspectives on Vatican II* (Wilmington, DE: Michael Glazier, 1989), p. 174; J. Komonchak, J. O'Malley, Neil J. Ormerod, Steven Schloesser, *Vatican II: Did Anything Happen?* (London: Continuum, 2008).

8. See Simon Green, *The Passing of Protestant Britain: Secularisation and Social Change c. 1920–1960* (Cambridge University Press, 2011) and Matthew Grimley, "The Church of England, Race and Multiculturalism, 1962–2012" in Jane Garnett and Alana Harris (eds.), *Re-scripting Religion in the City: Migration and Religious Identity in the Modern Metropolis* (Farnham: Ashgate, 2013), pp. 207–221.

9. See Hugh McLeod, *The Religious Crisis of the 1960s* (Oxford University Press, 2007); Callum Brown, *The Death of Christian Britain: Understanding Secularisation 1800–2000,* 2nd ed. (London: Routledge, 2009) and *Religion and the Demographic Revolution: Women and Secularisation in Canada, Ireland, UK and USA since the 1960s* (London: Boydell and Brewer, 2012).

10. Giuseppe Alberigo and Joseph A. Komonchak (eds.), *History of Vatican II,* vol. 1, *Announcing and Preparing Vatican Council II: Toward a new era in Catholicism* (Leuven, Belgium: Peeters, 1995), pp. 117, 214, 259.

11. Norman P. Tanner (ed.), *Decrees of the Ecumenical Councils,* volume 2, *Trent to Vatican II* (London: Sheed and Ward, 1990), SC36.1, p. 828.

12. Tanner, *Decrees of the Ecumenical Council*, SC14, p. 824. For more about "active participation," see also the noted English liturgist J. B. O'Connell, *Active Sharing in Public Worship: A Commentary on the Chief Purposes of the Second Vatican Council's Constitution on the Sacred Liturgy* (London: Burns and Oates, 1964).

13. Tanner, *Decrees of the Ecumenical Council*, SC36.2, p. 828.

14. Tanner, *Decrees of the Ecumenical Council*.

15. Tanner, *Decrees of the Ecumenical Council*. See SC54 (readings and common prayer), 63 (sacraments and sacramental) and 101 (Divine Office).

16. Tanner, *Decrees of the Ecumenical Council*, SC50, pp. 830–1.

17. Austin Flannery (ed.), *Vatican Council II: vol. 2, The Conciliar and Postconciliar Documents* (New York: Costello Publications, 1996), p. 41.

18. Joseph Cardinal Cordiero, "The Liturgy Constitution: *Sacrosanctum Concilium*" in Alberic Stacpole (ed.), *Vatican II by Those Who Were There* (London: Geoffrey Chapman, 1986), p. 187.

19. Flannery (ed.), *Vatican Council II*, p. 158.

20. Adrian Hastings, *A History of English Christianity 1920–2000* (London: SCM Press, 2001), p. 526 and Keith Robbins, *England, Ireland, Scotland, Wales: The Christian Church 1900–2000* (Oxford University Press, 2008), pp. 350–355.

21. Eamon Duffy "Rewriting the Liturgy: The Theological Implications of Translation" in Stratford Caldecott (ed.), *Beyond the Prosaic: Renewing the Liturgical Movement* (Edinburgh: T&T Clark, 1998), p. 97.

22. See Clifford Howell, *The Work of Our Redemption* (Oxford: Catholic Social Guild, 1955) and Charles Walker, *Worker Apostles: the YCW Movement in Britain* (London: Catholic Truth Society, 1994).

23. E.g. "We have been made to feel a dull, unimaginative lot, content with old routine, while others adventurously cast off the stranglehold of rubrics in search of new, more meaningful modes of expression," in Michael Richards, *The Liturgy in England* (London: Geoffrey Chapman, 1966), p. 3. See also the admission of Cardinal Heenan, *A Crown of Thorns: An Autobiography 1951–1963* (London: Hodder and Stoughton, 1974), p. 339.

24. See Michael P. Hornsby-Smith, *Roman Catholics in England: Studies in Social Structure since the Second World War* (Cambridge University Press, 1987); *The Changing Parish: A Study of Parishes, Priests and Parishioners after Vatican II* (London: Routledge, 1989); *Roman Catholic Beliefs in England: Customary Catholicism and Transformations of Religious Authority* (Cambridge University Press, 1991).

25. Statement of Bishop Dwyer of Leeds, British Representative on the Liturgical Commission, reported in "The English Bishops on Scheme 13," *The Tablet*, October 31, 1964, pp. 1244–1245.

26. On London in the 1960s, see Jerry White, *London in the Twentieth Century: A City and Its People* (London: Viking, 2001) and Mark Donnelly, *Sixties Britain: Culture, Society and Politics* (Harlow: Pearson Longman, 2005).

27. V. A. McClelland, "John Carmel Heenan, The Second Vatican Council and the Rise and Fall of an English *Lumen Vitae*" in A. Seery (ed.), *Essays in Tribute to J. Valentine Rice, 1935–2006* (Dublin: Lilliput Press, 2010), pp. 69–97.

28. The Diocese of Westminster reported a Catholic population of 470,000 (compared with 497,000 in Liverpool) – see *The Catholic Directory, 1960* (London: Burns Oates and Washbourne, 1960), p. 723.

29. For details on Liverpool, see Frank Boyce, "Catholicism in Liverpool's Docklands: 1950s–1990s" in M. P. Hornsby-Smith (ed.), *Catholics in England 1950–2000: Historical and Sociological Perspectives* (London: Continuum 1999), pp. 46–66; and Peter Doyle, *Mitres and Missions in Lancashire: the Roman Catholic Diocese of Liverpool, 1850–2000* (Liverpool: Blue Coat Press, 2005).

30. George Andrew Beck (ed.), *The English Catholics 1850–1950: Essays to Commemorate the Restoration of the Hierarchy of England and Wales* (London: Burns and Oates, 1950), pp. 506ff; Peter G. McCaffrey, "Catholic Radicalism and Counter-Radicalism: A Comparative Study of England and the Netherlands" (unpublished University of Oxford DPhil thesis, 1979), p. 134 (n. 128); Peter Stanford, *Cardinal Hume and the Changing Face of English Catholicism* (London: G. Chapman, 1993), p. 11.

31. Dom Benet Innes, "Most People Are Good-Tempered about It but – How Are YOU Liking the New Liturgy?," *The Universe and Catholic Times*, July 30, 1965, p. 6. (hereafter *The Universe*).

32. See "E-day Is November 29th," *The Universe*, July 31, 1964, p. 1 and "E-day and an Enthusiastic Response: Mass in English Gets off to a Good Start," *The Universe*, December 4, 1964, p. 22.

33. For further discussion of the specifics of these changes, see J. R. Ainslie, J. D. Crichton, and H. E. Winstone, *English Catholic Worship: Liturgical Renewal in England since 1990* (London: Geoffrey Chapman, 1979), pp. 79ff.

34. For a discussion of other elements of liturgical change, see Adrian Hastings (ed.), *Modern Catholicism: Vatican II and After* (Oxford University Press, 1991) and Michael P. Hornsby-Smith, *The Changing Parish: A Study of Parishes, Priests and Parishioners after Vatican II* (London: Routledge, 1989).

35. Personal advertisement, *The Times*, November 30, 1964. See also "... And for Those Who Still Want Latin," *The Universe*, January 22, 1965, p. 1.

36. For further information on Cathleen Hindmarsh and her motivations, see Clement Dane, "Housewife Leads the Fight to Save Latin," *The Universe*, April 23, 1965, p. 3. Geoffrey Houghton-Brown recounts that his advertisement was the stimulus to Mrs. Hindmarsh's notice in *The Guardian*, generating 3,000 signatures and her appearance on BBC Radio 4's *Today Programme*. See Houghton-Brown, *Notes*, p. 6 (1964).

37. Houghton-Brown, *Notes*, p. 5.

38. Houghton-Brown, *Notes*.

39. *Daily Telegraph*, November 12, 1964, p. 16, and follow-up correspondence from Douglass Woodruff, "Latin Liturgy,' *Daily Telegraph*, November 17, 1964, p. 16.

40. Houghton-Brown, *Notes*, p. 1 (1965). Founding members were Hugh Byrne, Peter Kenworthy-Browne, Jean Le Clercq, Kathleen Hindmarsh, Gillian Edwards, Ruth McQuillan, Mrs. Mary Teresa Parnell, Barbara Witty, Anthony Couldery, and Miss Lowe. Sir Arnold Lunn was appointed president shortly thereafter (pp. 4–5).

41. Carol Byrne, *A Guide to the Latin Mass Society: Its Purpose and Functions* (London: Latin Mass Society, 1997).

42. Houghton-Brown *Notes*, p. 2 (1969).

43. Houghton-Brown *Notes*, p. 14 (1971) – although some put the figure at 3,500, with 1,300 paying subscriptions.

44. The group district leaders in 1966 in the Diocese of Westminster were Mr. R. L. Travers, Miss Sheila Johnson, Mrs. Mary Teresa Parnell, Miss Joan Williams, Miss Moltene, Mrs. Cloudesley Seddon, Mrs. Hughes-Smith, Mr. A. J. Booker, Mrs. Ursula Carr, Lady Mitchell Cotts (sister of Nicholas Throckmorton), and Mrs. Stigell acting as accountant/treasurer. See Houghton-Brown, *Notes*, pp. 4–6 (1966). Cf. Jay P. Corrin, *Catholic Progressives in England After Vatican II* (University of Notre Dame Press, 2013), pp. 157–158 who described the LMS as an organization of converts, "Old Catholic families" and (citing Robert Nowell) "old men."

45. Houghton-Brown, *Notes*, pp. 4–5 (1966) and p. 13 (1969).

46. See John Carmel Heenan, *Not the Whole Truth: An Autobiography* (London: Hodder and Stoughton, 1971) and *A Crown of Thorns*; Scott M. P. Reid, *A Bitter Trail: Evelyn Waugh and John Carmel Cardinal Heenan on the Liturgical Changes* (London: Saint Austin Press, 2000); and James Hagerty, *Cardinal John Heenan* (Leominster: Gracewing, 2013).

47. See Houghton-Brown, *Notes* (1969), p. 6, and an associated survey of LMS members in which 66 percent expressed commitment to the Tridentine Mass (rather than Latin itself). For a flavor of these discussions, see Mrs. R. Richards, *Latin Mass Society Bulletin*, no. 15, July 1969, pp. 3–4.

48. Published with great debate and publicity, "Appeal to Reserve Mass Sent to the Vatican," *The Times*, July 6, 1971, p. 5. The well-known and mostly non-Catholic signatories included Kenneth Clark, Robert Graves, Graham Greene, F. R. Leavis, Cecil Day Lewis, Yehudi Menuhin, Nancy Mitford, Iris Murdoch, William Rees-Mogg (editor of *The Times*), Anglican Bishop John Ripon, and Joan Sutherland.

49. Letter from A. Bugnini, secretary of the Sacra Congregation Pro Culta Divino, November 5, 1971, see Houghton-Brown, *Notes*, p. 13 (1972).

50. Houghton-Brown, *Notes*, p. 14 (1972). Polish Catholics in London also seemed to support the retention of the Latin Mass. See the election of Miss Ewa Csaykowska to the LMS committee on May 8, 1971, Houghton-Brown, *Notes*, p. 5 (1971).

51. Hastings (ed.), *Modern Catholicism*, p. 368.

52. See the article in the *Sunday Telegraph*, November 30, 1969, lamenting the loss of the mass of Palestrina and Bach to be "replaced by a ritual hotch potch," and *Daily Telegraph*, January 2, 1970, discussing the substitution of "the noble and traditional language of the old Mass [with] the language of a public notice of a government advertisement about the joys of Post Office life," cited in Houghton-Brown, *Notes*, p. 14 (1969) and p. 1 (1970).

53. Corrin, *Catholic Progressives*, pp. 159–160.

54. Contrast, for example, the uncontroversial acceptance of the changes in Ireland recounted in Hastings (ed.), *Modern Catholicism*, p. 366, and the speed with which Australian bishops introduced the vernacular, as reported in "English in the Australian Mass," *The Tablet*, June 27, 1964, pp. 731–732; On "They Already Have Breviary in English," *The Universe*, January 21, 1964, p. 7 and "English in the Mass: All Are 'Enthusiastic,'" *The Universe*, July 31, 1964, p. 2. Note however that there were Maltese, Australian, and Canadian members of the LMS, Houghton-Brown, *Notes*, p. 9 (1965).

55. Rural areas posed particular difficulties, and Mr. and Mrs. Kenworthy-Browne reported considerable episcopal opposition in Portsmouth and Clifton, see

Houghton-Brown, *Notes*, p. 11 (1972). Other areas in which the LMS had difficulty utilizing the Indult included Southwark, Hexham, and Newcastle. See the extensive and fraught correspondence between Mrs. S. Coote and Bishop Lindsay from December 1980 to April 1981, LMS, miscellaneous correspondence file.

56. See *The Most Beautiful Thing This Side of Heaven* (Glenview: Coalition in Support of Ecclesia Dei, 2002), pp. 46–48.

57. Hugh Ross Williamson, *The Modern Mass: A Reversion to the Reforms of Cranmer* (Devon: Britons Publishing Company, 1969), p. 7.

58. Richards, *The Liturgy in England*, p. 7.

59. Evelyn Waugh, "Sweetness of Temper," *The Tablet*, August 14, 1965, p. 914. See also Auberon Herbert, "National Liturgies and Catholic Unity," *The Tablet*, July 11, 1964, p. 784.

60. Evelyn Waugh, "Fides Quaetenen Intellectum," *The Tablet*, July 31, 1965, p. 864.

61. Waugh, "Fides Quaetenen Intellectum."

62. Anonymous letter to Cardinal Heenan headed "The Observations of a Very Ordinary Catholic on the New Liturgy," 1964, Archive of the Archdiocese of Westminster (hereafter AAW), Heenan, HE1/L6(a) Letters from the Laity 1964–8.

63. Hugh Ross Williamson, *The Great Betrayal: Some Thoughts on the Invalidity of the New Mass* (Devon: Britons Publishing Company, 1969).

64. Letter from Peter Hutton to Bishop Rudderham, December 15, 1967, p. 7, LMS, miscellaneous correspondence file.

65. Letter from Ella Collier to Cardinal Heenan, December 15, 1964, AAW, Heenan, HE1/L6(a).

66. Rev. H. E. G. Rope, "The Martyrs," *The Universe*, May 15, 1964, p. 3.

67. Rosalind H. A. Scott, "Ecclesia Semper Reformanda," *The Tablet*, November 14, 1964, p. 1296.

68. Corrin, *Catholic Progressives*, pp. 187, 216–250.

69. J. D. Crichton, *The Church's Worship: Considerations on the Liturgical Constitution of the Second Vatican Council* (London: Geoffrey Chapman, 1964), p. 121.

70. Joyce Carey, "Dragging our Feet over the Vernacular," *The Tablet*, March 18, 1964, p. 361.

71. James Burtchaell, Edmund King, Peter Morgan, John Rawsthorne, Paul Racey, Harry Stratton, "Tarda Celeriter," *The Tablet*, February 8, 1964, p. 164.

72. Burtchaell et al., "Tarda Celeriter."

73. Douglas Woodruff, "Festina Lente," *The Tablet*, February 1, 1964, p. 121.

74. C. R. A. Cunliffe, "The New English Liturgy," *The Tablet*, July 11, 1964, pp. 784–785.

75. See J. A. Jungmann, *The Mass of the Roman Rite: Its Origins and Development* (New York: Benziger, 1951–1955) and, critically, Reid, *The Organic Development of the Liturgy*, pp. 153ff.

76. See T. F. Burns, "Hollis (Maurice) Christopher (1902–77)," www.oxforddnb.com /view/article/31248, accessed February 12, 2014.

77. Christopher Hollis, "Let Christians Worship in Their Own Languages of Love," *The Universe*, June 12, 1964, p. 9.

78. Hollis, "Let Christians Worship in Their Own Languages of Love."

79. Randle Lunt, "Language, Truth and Liturgy," *The Tablet*, April 4, 1964, p. 387.
80. Letter from Dr. Anthony Roberts to Cardinal Heenan, February 12, 1970, AAW, Heenan, HE1/L6(b) Liturgy, Letters from the Laity 1969–2970.
81. A. Manson (et. al.), "National Liturgies and Catholic Unity," *The Tablet*, July 18, 1964, pp. 811–812.
82. J. A. Green, "Correspondence," *The Universe*, January 29, 1965, p. 3.
83. Evelyn Waugh, "The Same Again, Please," *The Spectator*, November 23, 1962, pp. 785–788. See also letter from Mrs. Winifred Jackson (Reading) to Cardinal Heenan, October 23, 1964, AAW, Heenan, HE1/L6(a), who bewailed "expert liturgists, PhD monks and blue stockinged nuns, with computers where their hearts should be."
84. George Scott, *The R.C.s: A Report on Roman Catholics in Britain Today* (London: Hutchinson, 1967); Kester Aspden, *Fortress Church: the English Roman Catholic Bishops and Politics, 1903–1963* (Leominster: Gracewing, 2002); Dennis Sewell, *Catholics: Britain's Largest Minority* (London: Viking, 2001); James Lothian, *The Making and Unmaking of the English Catholic Intellectual Community, 1910–1950* (University of Notre Dame Press, 2009).
85. Douglas Woodruff, "Festina Lente," *The Tablet*, February 1, 1964, p. 120.
86. Mary Douglas, *Natural Symbols: Explorations in Cosmology* (London: Harmond, 1973), p. 67.
87. "Mention Unity and Out Comes Hidden Fears," *The Universe*, January 24, 1964, p. 10.
88. "Mention Unity and Out Comes Hidden Fears."
89. See Andrew Atherstone, "The Canonisation of the Forty English Martyrs: An Ecumenical Dilemma," *Recusant History* 30:4 (2011), 573–587.
90. See Alana Harris, *Faith in the Family: A Lived Religious History of English Catholicism, 1945–82* (Manchester University Press, 2013), pp. 233–250.
91. Office of the Vice Postulator, "Notes for Short Sermons on the English and Welsh Martyrs, c. 1960," Birmingham Archdiocese archives, hereafter BAA, AP/M6 Cause of the English and Welsh Martyrs 1955–1962, folders 1–4.
92. Joan Eland, "The Martyrs and Ecumenism," *The Tablet*, August 14, 1965, p. 914. See also her reply to Fr. Walsh in *The Tablet*, August 28, 1965, p. 963.
93. Margaret FitzHerbert, "The Martyrs and Ecumenism," *The Tablet*, September 4, 1965, p. 985.
94. Rev. H. E. G. Rope, "The Martyrs and Ecumenism," *The Tablet*, October 2, 1965, p. 1098.
95. Rope, "The Martyrs and Ecumenism."
96. For a selection of correspondence to Cardinal Heenan making reference to the "martyrs," see J. B. P. Hastie, November 21, 1965, AAW, Heenan, HE1/L6(a), and Adrian Bush, September 14, 1970; Giles Swayne, February 2, 1970 and Audrey Krynski, February 3, 1970, AAW, Heenan, HE1/L6(b).
97. Letter from Roger de Wever to Cardinal Heenan, March 2, 1970, AAW, Heenan, HE1/L6(b).
98. Letter from Roger de Wever to Cardinal Heenan, March 2, 1970.
99. Jerome Burrough, "The Mass That Matters," *The Tablet*, August 7, 1971, p. 773.
100. J. Walsh, "Vice-Postulator's Report to the Hierarchy of England and Wales on the State of the Cause of the Forty Martyrs," 1966 (BAA GPD/P/A1).

101. Walsh, "Vice-Postulator's Report to the Hierarchy of England and Wales."

102. See Archivum Britannicum Societatis Ieus (ABSI), Cause of the English Martyrs, filing cabinet 34 "Lists of Favours and Petitions," as discussed in Harris, *Faith in the Family*, pp. 243–247.

103. Letter D. G. Galvin to Cardinal Heenan, November 11, 1970, AAW, Heenan, HE1/L6(b).

104. See Houghton-Brown, *Notes*, pp. 3 and 14 (1971) under SSPX priest Fr. Morgan and for a discussion of the real tensions within the LMS over whether officially to support Archbishop Lefebvre's seminary, see Houghton-Brown, *Notes*, p. 8 (1972). Plans for LMS parishes (and provision of Latin masses) were mooted as early as 1969 by Maria Stigwell and Miss Pond, who had identified a disused church in Oxford, see Houghton-Brown, *Notes*, p. 7 (1969). In February 1970, a parish in Sanderstead (Surrey) was established by Major Hurst under Rev. Dr. Duffy, an Irish priest, whose salary was provided by assembly contributions, Houghton-Brown, *Notes*, p. 4 (1970). Other sites contemplated included Norwich, Houghton-Brown, *Notes*, p. 8 (1971).

105. Letter from Barbara Mitchell Cots to Cardinal Heenan, January 28, 1970, AAW, Heenan, HE1/L6(b).

106. E.g. Lawrence Black, "There Was Something about Mary: The National Viewers' and Listeners Association and Social Movement History" in N. J. Crowson, Matthew Hilton, and Kames McKay (eds.), *NGOs in Contemporary Britain: Non-State Actors in Society and Politics Since 1945* (Basingstoke: Palgrave, 2009), pp. 182–200.

107. Letter from Sir Arnold Lunn to Cardinal Heenan, September 11, 1965, reproduced in Houghton-Brown, *Notes* p. 9 (1965).

108. Letter from Peter Kenworthy-Browne to Cardinal Heenan, November 12, 1965, AAW, Heenan, HE1/L6(a).

109. For an extended discussion and cross-denominational comparison, see Alana Harris, "'The Prayer in the Syntax?': The Roman Missal, the Book of Common Prayer and Changes in Liturgical Language, 1945–80" in Jane Garnett, Matthew Grimley, Alana Harris, Sarah Williams, and William Whyte (eds.), *Redefining Christian Britain: Post–1945 Perspectives* (London: SCM Press, 2006), pp. 36–49.

110. Letter from Margaret Peckham to Cardinal Heenan, February 11, 1964, AAW, Heenan, HE1/L6(b). *Miss Peckham undertook clerical work for the LMS from 1965 onwards*, see Houghton-Brown, *Notes*, p. 7 (1965).

111. Mrs. F. Coupe, "The Dialogue Mass," *The Tablet*, December 29, 1962, p. 1282.

112. Houghton-Brown, *Notes*, p. 8 (1968).

113. Letter from Mary Pegge to Cardinal Heenan, December 8, 1964, AAW, Heenan, HE1/L6(a).

114. Ibid. Contrast however James Mulligan, who praised the vernacular as providing for his children "a Liturgy they will see and understand, learn from and help to perform" and thus "survive as Christians in a society which is too clearly the antithesis of what we believe to be right." Letter from James Mulligan to Cardinal Heenan, December 7, 1964, AAW HE1/L6(a).

115. Letter from Mary Prendergast to Cardinal Heenan, September 20, 1970, AAW, Heenan, HE1/L6(b). For discussion of this Mass and its media coverage in the *Catholic Herald* and on the BBC, see Houghton-Brown, *Notes*, p. 19 (1970).

116. See e.g. his sermon in Westminster Cathedral on January 21, 1968, in which he praised "our forefathers [who were] ready to die for the Latin Mass" but contrasted the present in which "No Catholic in his sense would go to the stake to-day for the sake of any language. For the Mass, yes . . . but not for customs and devotions, however cherished, which are not essential to the faith." Cited in Houghton-Brown, *Notes*, p. 5 (1968).

117. Much debate within this correspondence turned on the new canon and fears about a diminished priority given to transubstantiation and the Real Presence. This was especially heighted in view of the first ARCIC-agreed statement on *Eucharistic Doctrine* (1972) and the shifting Eucharistic emphasis within Catholic ecclesiology of the latter twentieth century generally. Space has not permitted a further elaboration here, but see Harris, *Faith in the Family*, chap. 3.

118. Letter from Dr. J. B. Robinson to Cardinal Heenan, February 11, 1970, AAW, Heenan, HE1/L6(b).

119. Letter from Dr. J. B. Robinson to Cardinal Heenan, February 11, 1970, annexed response. See also letter from Cardinal Heenan to J. B. P. Hastie, November 21, 1965, AAW, Heenan, HE1/L6(a), which chastises the correspondent's sarcastic celebration of the first anniversary of his forced separation from the sacraments with the opening line "Your letter makes me feel thoroughly ashamed of you. I did not know an intelligent Catholic could be so lacking in humility."

120. For a beginning, situating Britain within the American context, see Robert Lair Kaiser, *The Politics of Sex and Religion: A Case Study in the Development of Doctrine 1962–1984*, 2nd ed. (Smashwords.com, 2012). With a specific focus on the English case, see Alana Harris, "Love Divine and Love Sublime: The Catholic Marriage Advisory Council, the National Marriage Guidance Movement and the State" in Alana Harris and Timothy Jones (eds.), *Love and Romance in Britain 1918– 1970* (London: Palgrave, 2014), pp. 188–224 and Alana Harris, "'The Writings of Querulous Women': Contraception, Conscience and Clerical Authority in 1960s Britain," *British Catholic Studies*, 34:2 (2015), 557–585.

121. Cardinal J. Heenan to Bishop G. P. Dwyer, February 28, 1970, BAA GPD/H/B5 Liturgy: General 1970–1.

122. Clifford Longley, "Keeping the Tridentine Tradition: A Plea for the Latin Mass," *The Times*, July 9, 1971, p. 2.

123. See www.lms.org.uk/resources/documents/heenan-indult, accessed February 28, 2013, and Clifford Longley, "Pope Sanctions Traditional Latin Mass in Britain," *The Times*, December 2, 1971, p. 2.

124. E.g. requiem masses for deceased LMS members, Houghton-Brown, *Notes*, p. 8 (1966), pp. 8 and p. 11 (1968), with the support of London Oratory priests such as Fr. Michael Crowdy and Fr. Mark Taylor. LMS prayer cards were also commissioned, featuring a drawing of the statue of Pope Pius V from the altar of Our Lady at the Brompton Oratory, Houghton-Brown, *Notes*, p. 2 (1969).

125. Houghton-Brown, *Notes*, pp. 3 and 6 (1969). One mass a month was celebrated in Latin, Houghton-Brown, *Notes*, p. 14 (1970).

126. Editorial, "Order of the Mass," *The Tablet*, September 6, 1975, p. 849.

127. Bryan Houghton, *Mitre and Crook* (Plymouth: Roman Catholic Books, 1979) pp. 33–34.

128. David Lodge, *How Far Can You Go?* (London: Penguin, 1980), pp. 81, 83, 42–43. See also Dorothy Spencer, "The Second Vatican Council and the English Catholic Novel," unpublished PhD thesis, University of Liverpool, 1996.

129. Letter from Cardinal Heenan to Mr. J. Moroney, December 17, 1964, AAW, Heenan, HE1/L6(a).

130. Letter from Monsignor Miles to Mrs. Olive Scott, May 22, 1969, AAW, Heenan, HE1/L6(b).

131. For a fascinating, contextualized discussion of these architectural innovations and transformations, see Robert Proctor, *Building the Modern Church: Roman Catholic Church Architecture in Britain, 1955 to 1975* (Farnham: Ashgate, 2014).

132. Oral history interview with Monsignor Canon Tom Egan, May 19, 2014 (typed transcribed notes).

133. Bernard Jubb, "Less Sweetness of Temper," *The Tablet*, August 21, 1965, p. 939.

134. Mark Chapman, "Theology in the Public Arena: The Case of South Bank Religion" in Jane Garnett, *et. al.* (eds.), *Redefining Christian Britain* (London: SCM Press, 2007), pp. 92–105.

135. Letter from David Power to Cardinal Heenan, November 14, 1969, AAW, Heenan, HE1/L6(b).

136. Letter from David Power to Cardinal Heenan, November 14, 1969.

137. Houghton-Brown, *Notes*, pp. 7–10 (1972).

138. Mrs. P. Pantcheff, Correspondence, *Catholic Herald*, March 22, 1974, p. 5.

139. "Congress 1980," *The Universe*, May 2, 1980, pp. 14, 18–19.

140. "Congress 1980."

141. "Congress 1980."

142. For a discussion of the written communications made to the NPC organizers by the Latin Mass Society, see Liverpool Diocesan Archives, S6 XXXVIIIa/23 Criticism in Press, Apos Delegate, Minority Report. Mrs. Sue Coote and David Crane wrote reports of their experience of being treated with "derision, animosity and hostility" (p. 3) by NPC delegates and their "minority interests" being likened to those of the Catholic Lesbian Sisterhood (p. 9), asserting that the proceedings were manipulated to sideline discussion of the Tridentine Mass, which was deemed a "hot potato." See "Latin Mass Society: Reports from Delegates to the National Pastoral Congress – May 1980," LMS, miscellaneous correspondence file. There is minimal coverage of liturgical issues; see *Congress Report: The Principal Documents of the 1980 National Pastoral Congress of England and Wales* (London: Catholic Truth Society, 1980), Sector A, p. 16, which advocates "the greatest possible variety of celebration of the one eucharist (within the limits laid down by the present rite) to meet the needs of different conditions and ages; children, teenagers, ethnic groups and others."

143. For a discussion of the reception of *Humanae Vitae*, and increasing radicalism among clergy and laity, see Corrin, *Catholic Progressives*, pp. 162–164, 168.

144. Bishop Dwyer, cited in "More English: The Second Stage of Liturgical Reform," *The Tablet*, March 20, 1965, p. 33.

145. This is indeed asserted by the traditionalist priest (of the Diocese of Southwark) and NPC delegate (and author of the "Minority Report") Michael Clifton in his *Before and After Vatican II: The English Scene* (Surbiton: Real Press, 1996). My thanks to Alan Whaits for this reference.

146. Oral history interview with Monsignor Canon Tom Egan, May 19, 2014 (typed transcribed notes). See also www.praytellblog.com/index.php/2012/02/02/liturgi cal-pioneers-pull-out/, accessed May 31, 2014.

147. Corrin, *Catholic Progressives*, pp. 190–193.

148. As Auberon Waugh reflected in his article "Martyrs in Vain," *The Times*, May 2, 1970, p. 9, the "peculiar spirit of English Catholicism" in its attachment to the Tridentine Mass meant that the liturgical changes were felt "more acutely among England's five million Catholic than among the 545 million Catholics who live elsewhere." There was some agitation within wider Europe also – the European Centre of Traditionalist Catholics collected 100,000 signatures in 1971 to protest the disappearance of the Tridentine Rite – see Geoffrey Houghton-Brown, *Notes on the Struggle to Retain the Roman Liturgy 1964–1972*, unpublished manuscript, 1975, p. 6, LMS, miscellaneous correspondence file. Contrast "Behind the Scenes: English Liturgy in Australia," *Search*, May 1964, 19–22.

AFTERWORD: THE COUNCIL
AND THE CHURCHES

JOSEPH A. KOMONCHAK

This chapter explores the multiple meanings of "Vatican II," noting that different actors, at different times, refer to the council as its texts; as the experience of those who attended, covered, and otherwise participated in the council from 1959 to 1965; and as an event whose significance and interpretation are still unfolding, with final results yet to be determined but looked for in the lives of Catholics around the world.

C ATHOLICS IN THE VATICAN II ERA: LOCAL HISTORIES OF A Global Event explores how Vatican II was lived in the social, political, religious, and existential circumstances in local churches around the world. It raises the important question of what local histories contribute to the understanding of Vatican II, a question whose answer will depend in large part in what is meant by the phrase "Vatican II." I have found three meanings for the term: Vatican II as texts, as experience, and as event, and I would like to say a word about each of them.

Vatican II as Texts

As texts, "Vatican II" refers to the sixteen documents composed during four sessions held in the autumns of 1962 to 1965. A modest-sized book contains the four constitutions, nine decrees, and three declarations in which the bishops of the Second Vatican Council expressed what they had to say to and about the church and the world at the beginning of the last third of the twentieth century. The bishops met in order to speak, and these sixteen documents are what they decided to say. There is an objectivity to these texts in the sense that they provide the answer to certain questions that arise, a certain control over what may and may not be considered to be the teaching of the Second Vatican Council.

I want to stress this meaning of "Vatican II," because there is a danger of neglecting what the council actually said in favor of either or both of the other two meanings. Theologians, at least, work largely with authoritative texts, biblical or traditional, and they will make use of all the historical and hermeneutical tools available for interpreting them. They know that texts do not speak unless they are spoken to, unless, that is, a reader brings certain questions to them, and even in the case of texts composed relatively recently, they will be interested in knowing how and why they were written as they were, with this history bearing more or less greatly on what the final texts mean. The history of the elaboration of the conciliar texts, then, is an intrinsic element in the determination and interpretation of the council's teaching. But the legitimate aim is to know what was intended and said in the promulgated texts, which are authoritative for Catholics. Later developments and documents claiming to be applications or implementations of Vatican II need to be assessed by the criterion of the final texts of the council.

Vatican II as Experience

By Vatican II as experience, I am referring to what happened between January 25, 1959, when Pope John XXIII announced his intention to convoke an ecumenical council, and December 8, 1965, when Pope Paul VI presided over the solemn close of the Second Vatican Council. Under the general heading of "experience," I mean the intentions and decisions and actions of the protagonists of Vatican II: two popes and 2,500 bishops, of course. But I also mean the hundreds, if not thousands, of theologians and other experts who took part in the conciliar process, and the observers from other Christian churches and communities and the auditors invited to the last three sessions. And I mean as well the hundreds of journalists who covered the council and were the principal means by which not only did most Catholics learn of what was happening in Rome but often enough the bishops themselves learned what was happening! There is even a sense in which one could legitimately include in the experience of Vatican II the responses and reactions of Catholics throughout the world as they watched this remarkable event unfold.

In terms of what was happening in Rome, one could quote from an essay by the young theologian Joseph Ratzinger at the end of the council's third session. Noting that in the course of the three sessions, the bishops had become more open-minded, less timid and tentative, more frank and bold, he saw that as the main achievement of the council:

This spiritual awakening, which the bishops accomplished in full view of the Church, or, rather, accomplished *as* the Church, was the great and irrevocable event of the Council. It was more important in many respects than the texts it passed, for these texts could only voice a part of the new life that had been awakened in this encounter of the Church with its inner self. Progress may at times have seemed difficult and slow, entangled as it often was in the political devices and disputes, both large and small, which to a considerable degree marked the public image of the Council and often enough its daily routine. But all of this seems trivial and transitory in comparison with the true event – the awakening of the Church.[1]

I think that this is a valid point, apart from his identifying the bishops with the church and their awakening to that of the church. Among the many things happening in Rome at the time – part of the experience of the council – was the very fact that a council was being held, that the exercise of supreme authority in the church was collegial and not monarchical, that movements of renewal that had been stifled in the decades before were being allowed to breathe, that a system of control was being challenged, that possibilities of renewal and even reform were being entertained that would have been unthinkable not very long before. And this was not only being felt in Rome; it was being communicated to the larger world, not least of all by the secular media for which all this was genuinely "news," so much did it depart from what everyone had come to expect from Rome. Much of this experience, as Ratzinger noted, could not be expressed in the final documents, which necessarily were compromise texts drawn up in such a way as to elicit consensus among the bishops.[2]

In addition, there were topics of conversation that were poorly represented in the texts but were to develop and mature in the years after the council. I think, first, of the themes of poverty and inculturation. At the end of the first session, Cardinal Giacomo Lercaro of Bologna proposed that the entire agenda of the council focus on the church as of the poor and for the poor, and a relatively small group of bishops met regularly in Rome to urge the matter. But it has to be said that they had only slight effect on the conciliar documents. There is a brief reference to the poor in *Lumen Gentium* and the problem of economic inequality is noted in *Gaudium et Spes*, but this is rather small pickings when compared to what the Group of the Poor wanted done. As the great Italian historian of the council Giuseppe Alberigo wrote, "References to evangelical poverty remained peripheral and embryonic."[3] "Was this," he wondered, "because poverty was considered a problem for other continents? Or perhaps because of the impenetrability of the optimistic anthropology then prevalent in European culture?"[4]

As for inculturation, although they do not use the word, several conciliar texts encourage what would become known under that word in the decades after the council. But there was a moment in the first session's debate over the draft on the sources of revelation that has not perhaps been given enough attention. Criticisms of that text included that it did not meet Pope John's insistence in his opening speech that the council's exercise of its teaching role be "pastoral in character." To this, defenders of the draft replied that the role of ecumenical councils was to be dogmatic; pastoral applications could be left to bishops and priests. When it was insisted that one did not have to choose between being doctrinal and being pastoral, but that the council, like a good preacher, should always have in mind the audience to which it was bringing the truths of the faith, Cardinal Rufino Santos made a valid point:

> Since we're all shepherds of souls, we write pastoral letters for our sheep. But in our many and diverse circumstances, don't we write different letters or the same letters differently? It's not fitting, then, or prudent for this Council to decide with one stroke, as it were, on some pastoral action, precisely because of the diversity of circumstances in different regions or nations. We should instead solemnly set out only the doctrinal principles from which each of us can, as local circumstances require, offer appropriate food for our sheep.[5]

In other words, how could a text be "pastoral" for the entire world in all its diverse and even contrasting circumstances?

The two examples point out a feature of the council that is quite pertinent to the chapters in this volume. Vatican II was largely the work of bishops and theologians from the developed world, that is, from the industrialized, pluralistic, and democratic countries of the North Atlantic. It is difficult to find a bishop or theologian from behind the Iron Curtain or from the Southern Hemisphere who was as much a presence or protagonist of the council as were its many leaders from Western Europe and from North America. Jan Grootaers, of KU Leuven (Katholieke Universiteit Leuven), Belgium, published a large book entitled *Acts and Actors of Vatican II* in which he makes the comment, "Examining Vatican II retrospectively, we are struck by the hegemony that the Western episcopates and theologians exercised there, not only with regard to the basic tendencies but also over the very choice of questions that would be placed on the agenda."[6] Grootaers included chapters on two Polish bishops, Cardinal Stefan Wyszynski and Archbishop Karol Wojtyla, but one wonders if the chapter on Wojtyla would have been written had he not later become pope; and Grootaers had to report their efforts to remind the assembled bishops that there is more than one "modern world." From Latin America perhaps the two best-known bishops were Dom Hélder Câmara and Archbishop Marcos McGrath, with the latter far more effective than the former, and influential within the commission that wrote *Gaudium et Spes*. From Asia the only significant figure one can point to is Patriarch Maximos IV. Alberigo comments:

> One of the tensions at Vatican II was due precisely to the presence in large numbers of third-world episcopates, which, however, had quite limited influence on the work and decisions of the Council. The African, Latin American, and Asian bishops acted rather as supporters of the Central European leadership and were unable effectively to influence it, much less go beyond it. This does not mean that they participated passively; on the contrary, the experience of these bishops at the Council was the basis for the role that they and their churches are now playing in the final decades of the twentieth century.[7]

It surely was because of their experience of the council that the Latin American, African, and Asian episcopates were able to take up the challenges of poverty and inculturation in the decades after. But Vatican II addressed itself to "modern man" and to the "modern world" (in the singular), and, in the eyes of Europeans and North Americans, the world of "modern man" was not Africa, Asia, or Latin America.

A history of the dynamic experience of Vatican II as it unfolded in Rome is what was attempted by the international team under the direction of Giuseppe Alberigo in their five-volume *History of Vatican II*. As the leader of the project, Alberigo insisted that it was not to be a history of the production of texts. The council, he said, was not a publishing house or a printing office. Instead he and his colleagues would try to set out the character, the dynamics, the drama of the conciliar event, as he called it, distinguishing it from the final texts. I think that he came close at times to counterposing the event (in his sense) and the final documents, in which he did not have a great deal of interest.[8] Even at the time of planning the history, I did not think that this distinction should be pressed, since I contended that the drama of the council lies in the contest over what the council should say to the church and to the world on the various topics of its agenda. And where else can one find what the council decided to say, that is, the result of the conflict, if not in the final texts? This remains, I believe, the most serious limitation of the *History*.

The two meanings of "Vatican II" identified so far are obviously interrelated and should, in any adequate hermeneutic, illuminate each other. The final texts can cast light on the experience – for example, providing a focus, even a plot-line, that determines the questions that need to be asked to explain their genesis, the protagonists who need to be consulted, the decisions that ought to be highlighted. In turn, the reconstructed experience can cast light on texts whose meanings and purpose in many cases cannot be ascertained, understood, or evaluated without knowledge of the history of their redaction. Why does the text say this? Why does it say nothing about that? Three more or less famous examples: Why instead of saying what was said in all earlier drafts of the *Constitution on the Church*, that the Church of Christ *is* the Roman Catholic Church, does *Lumen Gentium* say that Christ's Church *subsists in* the Catholic Church? Why does *Dei Verbum* describe the inerrancy of the Bible in the way it does? Why in the *Decree Concerning the Pastoral Office of Bishops* are episcopal conferences not said to be instances of episcopal collegiality? None of these questions can be answered without studying the dynamic and often conflicted dynamics of their elaboration.

On the other hand, the conciliar texts were intended and written to illuminate and guide the church's self-realization in the years and decades after the council. In addition, they serve as reference points in contemporary ecclesial debates, which often turn on what "fidelity to the council" means. Some are using some of the texts in a way that other people believe betrays not only the council's intentions but what it actually said. Appeals simply to the "event" of the council will not be an adequate reply to such claims. Close analysis of the texts is necessary.[9]

After all, was not the drama of the council in large part a conflict over what the council should say and about how to say it? This question is crucial not only because an ecumenical council is one of the supreme organs of the church's teaching office but also because for a community constituted by meaning what such an authoritative council says is self-defining, indeed self-constituting. To appeal to the texts need not imply that the council was simply a "machine" for producing documents; it certainly was a process for determining what the leaders of the Catholic Church wished to say to that church and to the world as the twentieth century began to move toward its close. Not to attend to the texts is to focus on dynamics while ignoring what the dynamics produced. The struggles at the council had some result, and what was it but the conciliar texts?

Attention to the texts is one way to grasp the event-character of the council. The official texts prepared for the council's consideration proposed that it say certain things; the texts finally promulgated say some of those things, fail to say some of them, say many other things, and almost always say what they say differently than did the prepared texts. In some cases, on some issues, the difference between what some hoped the council would say and what the council ended by saying is so dramatic as to entitle the use of words such as "break" and "discontinuity." In this respect, Ratzinger is correct that the final texts help one understand the event of the council.

Vatican II as Event

There is, however, I believe, a third meaning of the council – Vatican II as "event." I mean this in a sense different from that of Professor Alberigo, who uses "event" to describe what I have called the "experience" of the council. By "event" I mean something like what is at stake when Zhou Enlai was asked what he thought of the French Revolution and he is said to have replied: "It's too soon to tell!" One could invoke the Council of Trent. A history of Trent similar in method and aim to our *History of Vatican II* would attempt to reconstruct the experience of that council as intended and lived by its protagonists. But would one really have completed the task of a historian if one ended there? Would not one writing even such a history today have in mind also the effect, the impact, of Trent on the subsequent history of the Catholic Church and, indeed, of Western religious history? Fifty years after the close of the Council of Trent, it certainly was too soon to tell what its effect would be because its *Wirkungsgeschichte* had by then scarcely begun to reveal the consequences of that council. That is where we are, of course, with regard to the Second Vatican Council.

What is meant by speaking of Vatican II as an "event"? I mean the term in the sense used by historians who speak of events as occurrences or sets of occurrences that do not leave persons or institutions or things what they were before. Events, in other words, represent difference, and the difference may mean a rupture or break from what went before. It was perhaps my reference to this historiographical meaning of the word that led people to criticize the idea that Vatican II represented a rupture or break or discontinuity in the life of the Catholic Church. The denial by then Cardinal Ratzinger of any leaps or fractures or breaks in continuity in the life of the church[10] was somewhat nuanced when as Pope Benedict XVI, in a speech to the Roman Curia on December 22, 2005, he addressed the issue of rival interpretations of the council. Here, he said again that the church is "a single subject ... that grows in time and develops, while always remaining the same." But now he counterposed to a hermeneutic of rupture or discontinuity, not a hermeneutics of continuity, but a hermeneutics of reform, and he defined reform as "continuity and discontinuity at different levels."

Simply contrasting continuity and discontinuity in the interpretation of the council, as Catholics on both the left and the right are wont to do, is a dead end. I agree with the Italian historian Paolo Prodi, who commented, "There can't be an attitude more anti-historical than to counterpose continuity and discontinuity."[11] After all, discontinuities can only be discerned or identified against a backdrop of continuity. An event only makes sense when located in a series of occurrences and as an episode in a plot. In the case of Vatican II, this means placing the council in a broad historical context that includes the postwar years, the economic recovery of Western Europe, the beginnings of decolonization, and an incipient technological revolution. It also includes locating it in the context of earlier church history. How far back that history has to be taken is a good question. But as the authors and editors of this volume argue, the lived histories of Vatican II can only be plotted against the varied backdrops of the local churches and communities.

The most important thing to note about this event-character is that it cannot be reduced to or measured by the intentions of the protagonists. An analogous case is the effect of Mikhail Gorbachev's *glasnost* (openness, transparency) and *perestroika* (restructuring). It seems he thought these goals could be pursued without the dismantling of the Soviet empire, an outcome he most likely had not intended. If the thoughts and intentions of the protagonists of a historical event enter into and indeed constitute the experience of the event, the rounded view that a historian pursues goes beyond what any or even all of them thought or intended. As Paul Veyne remarked, the event as it comes from the hands of a historian is not identical to the event as experienced by the protagonists. Historians seek to understand what contemporaries mostly did not know and even could not have known.

I do not think the popes and bishops of the Second Vatican Council intended revolution in the church. They spoke instead of "reform" and "renewal." But this does not necessarily mean that the revolutions that occurred in certain areas of Catholic church life must be regarded simply as betrayals of the "true" council, illegitimate consequences of a "hermeneutic of rupture," in the words of Pope Benedict XVI. Decisions made by the council in its pursuit of renewal and reform had the potential to result in, and did in fact result in, quite revolutionary consequences. There is a well-known "law of unintended consequences" that applies to the life of the church also and some of the apparent consequences of Vatican II were certainly not intended – for example, mass exodus from the priesthood and religious life, plummeting vocations, decline in Mass attendance and in use of the sacrament of reconciliation, and widespread dissent.[12]

How much of the change that authors in this volume describe is to be attributed to the council and how much to movements and events in the larger society and culture? Denis Pelletier noted at the beginning of his book

La crise catholique that even before the major documents on the church-world relationship were being finalized at the council, movements were already underway that would undercut the logic of modernity and usher in what became known as "post-modernism."[13] The irony, then, is that at the very moment that the council was urging an accommodation of Christian practice and even teaching to modern society and culture, deep and broad challenges to modernity were about to be posed to the whole modern project. The council occurred in the sixties, and the sixties, as we know, were not just another ordinary decade in the twentieth century. I have clear memories of the power and excitement created by the coincidence of a church at last freed from the suffocating system described by Yves Congar, Henri de Lubac, and the young Joseph Ratzinger and the antiestablishment movements of the time. The Catholic Church was reforming itself at the very moment when much of the logic of modernity was coming under attack.

Examples of transformative events in the sixties include the trauma of the assassinations of 1963 and 1968; the civil rights movement; the free speech movement; the hippies and flower power; the drug culture; the arrival of the Beatles; the sexual revolution; the gay rights movement after Stonewall (1969); Charles A. Reich's *The Greening of America* (1970) with its championing of "Consciousness III"; protests against the war in Vietnam; Woodstock (1969); the rise of the New Left, with its critique of capitalism and fascination with Marxism; the violence at the 1968 political conventions in Chicago and Miami; May 1968 in France; the Prague Spring and the Soviet crushing of it; *Humanae vitae* (1968); the Christmas bombing of Cambodia; the shootings at Kent State; the political crisis of Watergate; and so on. I have often used this metaphor: many people became Catholics in the decades before Vatican II to find a firm place, a rock, on which to stand amid the storms of modern life; in the 1960s, those storms became more common, larger, and more violent, but at that very moment it seemed that the Catholic Church had ceased to be a rock and was now more like a raft, which went up and down with the latest waves, making many people very seasick.

What Was (Is) the "Event"?

If one takes "event" in the historian's or sociologist's sense of an occurrence or sequence of occurrences that constitutes or brings about difference, perhaps even breaks and discontinuity, one has to be able to say what was the former state disrupted by the event. In other words, one has to be able to identify a "before" and an "after."

It was not uncommon during the council to hear talk about "the end of the Constantinian era" or about "the end of the Counter-Reformation." Various historians and sociologists have spoken of "Catholicism" (a word coined in English and French in the early seventeenth century); of "Tridentinism," the system devised against the Reformation; the Enlightenment; and modernism. Within the post-Tridentine era, I have proposed that a distinctively modern Roman Catholicism was constructed in the nineteenth century in opposition to new and even revolutionary economic, social, political, and cultural developments.[14] Joseph Ratzinger described it as a little Catholic *Sonderwelt*. The church before the council, he said, was

> in the late phases of a culture that looks no longer forwards but backwards . . . Theology seemed to have thought its way through everything, piety to have practiced and crystallized everything that could possibly be done and formulated; every space had been filled up with the data of tradition, just like a church-building that is packed with altars, pictures, and testimonies to the piety of former generations.[15]

The great achievement of Vatican II, French Dominican theologian Yves Congar argued, was its departure from that Tridentine "system."

Even more decisive, Congar maintained, were developments occurring in the world at large. The council met in a world that no longer understood itself in terms of a "metaphysics of fixed and hierarchically ordered natures." The world had been historicized; it was now what human beings have made, are making, and will make of themselves. "Humanity," he wrote, "has taken charge of itself." The old hardened distinction between a sacred sphere for which the church is responsible and a secular or temporal sphere for which the state is responsible was no longer adequate. The world is now history, and "man is the subject of the process by which he constructs himself."[16]

The council met, Congar said, at the beginning of "a socio-cultural change whose breadth, radicalness, rapidity, and cosmic character have no equivalent in any other age of history."[17] He summarized the result of all these developments:

> The substructure, not of the faith itself, but its classical cultural expression, has collapsed. "The present crisis is not a crisis of faith, but a crisis of the metaphysics behind which the Church believed it could take refuge in order to confront modern culture – a metaphysics also linked to social systems that the Church agreed to sacralize." Even if one can debate so massive a statement, the diagnosis, in general, is accurate.[18]

Even before the council had ended, Canadian theologian Bernard Lonergan was offering a nearly identical analysis. The crisis, he said, "is a crisis not of faith but of culture."[19] What Lonergan called "the massive breakthrough" effected at Vatican II was part of "a disengagement from the forms of classicist culture and a transposition into the forms of modern culture."[20] By classicist culture Lonergan meant an ideal that developed in the early modern era but remained dominant in Catholic circles well into the twentieth century. It was a normative notion of culture, content with the universal and the abstract in its notions of individual and collective human life. But the scientific revolution and the Enlightenment; the rise of historical consciousness; the development of the human sciences (*Geisteswissenschaften*); and the economic, social, political, and cultural revolutions of the past two centuries elaborated and made dominant a modern notion of culture that is impatient with the abstract and the universal, glories in the particular and concrete, and makes few if any normative claims.[21] Most distinctively, it is historically conscious, that is, self-aware:

> Modern culture is the culture that knows about itself and other cultures. It is aware that they are man-made. It is aware that the cultural may sustain or destroy or refashion the social. So it is that modern man not only individually is responsible for the life he leads but also collectively is responsible for the world in which he leads it.[22]

This is the characteristic of modernity that Lonergan stresses most: the awareness of the humanly constructed character of economies, societies, polities, even religions, and the accompanying sense of responsibility for what we are making or will make of all these. (This is the equivalent of the existential moment when an individual discovers that it is up to himself to decide for himself what to make of himself.) To describe the historical and cultural moment, Lonergan adopted and adapted Georg Simmel's notion of *die Wendung zur Idee*, which he took to refer to "the tendency and even the necessity of every large social, cultural, or religious movement, to reflect on itself, to define its goals, to scrutinize the means it employs or might employ, to keep in mind its origins, its past achievements, its failures."[23] Such an "axial shift" he goes on, will vary from one cultural or historical setting to another, and as these change so will the idea of the movement if it is to be in harmony with the mentality or horizon of the new context.

This recognition of humanity's individual and collective self-responsibility is one of the most important constituents of the cultural context in which Vatican II met, but surprisingly it does not often appear in interpretations of the event of the council. Ever since the French Revolution, the church had resisted this notion, regularly counterposing the rights of God to the rights of man, as if agreeing with Ludwig Feuerbach's stark alternative: "To enrich

God, man must become poor; that God may be all, man must become nothing."[24] The growing sense of human self-responsibility was even made equivalent to the New Testament description of "the son of perdition and adversary who exalts himself above every so-called god proposed for worship, he who seats himself in God's temple and even declares himself to be God" (2 Thess 2:4).[25] Among the "prophets of doom" from whom Pope John distanced himself in his opening speech to the council, a number of his predecessors on Peter's chair would have to be included. The church had to travel a long and difficult journey before it could accept the validity of this defining aspect of modernity.

The council did so, first, in the section of *Gaudium et Spes* devoted to human activity in the world (33–39), which denies that human activity must be set in opposition to divine sovereignty and vindicates a legitimate autonomy of earthly activities. In the (40– 45), the council explains not only what the church can offer to individuals and societies today but also what it can learn from them. Yet perhaps clearest is the later chapter on "Culture" (53–62), particularly the description of the factors that have produced the modern world and its distinctive culture (54), whose chief characteristic is described in section 55:

> In every group or nation, there is an ever-increasing number of men and women who are aware that they themselves are the artisans and originators of the culture of their community. Throughout the world a sense of both autonomy and responsibility is constantly growing that is of the greatest importance for the spiritual and moral maturity of the human race. This becomes clearer if we consider how the world is becoming more unified and how we have the duty to build a better world in truth and righteousness. In this way we are witnessing the birth of a new humanism, one in which man is defined first of all by his responsibility toward his brothers and toward history.[26]

But the council's recognition of human self-responsibility did not end here. Rather, the council may be seen as the particular moment when the Catholic Church became more conscious of its responsibility *for its own self-realization* and eagerly accepted the challenge. Lonergan's description of the *Wendung zur Idee* reads almost like a description of what the church in council undertook to do: "to reflect on itself, to define its goals, to scrutinize the means it employs or might employ, to keep in mind its origins, its past achievements, its failures." Perhaps this is what Christoph Theobald meant when he spoke of "*une sorte de retour sur soi de la conscience ecclésiale*" realized at the council, a greater awareness of its responsibility for itself. It was an important moment in the process by which in a historically conscious age the church too had to become "a fully conscious process of self-constitution."[27]

Here is my interpretation of "what happened at Vatican II":

Under the comparatively innocuous banner of *aggiornamento*, Vatican II represented a long-overdue effort by the Catholic Church to deal seriously and discriminatingly with the culture created in the West by the Enlightenment, the economic and political revolutions of the last two centuries, the development of the natural and human sciences, and the secularization and pluralization of society. The Church undertook this effort at what now appears to have been the term of one stage of that cultural transformation, when it had reached a moment of supreme self-confidence . . . Even apart from its documents and the specific reforms to which it gave rise, Vatican II must be seen as a cultural turning point for Roman Catholicism. It sanctioned with the highest authority movements for institutional, liturgical, and theological reform that had been resisted if not repudiated for two centuries. It substantively altered the way in which the Church responded to the modern world and the fashion in which it was to deal with political problems and powers. It relativized the normative character of the language and habits of thought with which the Church had legitimized its teachings and activities. It called Catholics out of their cultural alienation to assume new and more positive relationships with Protestants, members of other religions, and the bearers of modern social, political, and cultural movements. It abandoned the idea of a single normative culture, identified with Western "Christian civilization," and called for an incarnation of Catholic Christianity in the variety of the world's cultures.[28]

The conciliar texts can be read as so many efforts to lead the church to take fuller and more conscious responsibility for its own self-realization. Some of these efforts were more successful than others; some of them were implemented more fully and consistently than others; some of them are more relevant to today's changed circumstances than others. The interpretation of Vatican II is now unavoidably linked with the interpretation of its aftermath. What began more than fifty years ago with the announcement of Vatican II did not end with the solemn close of the council, and the decades that followed the council must enter as much as do the intentions and texts of the popes and bishops into a determination of whether and in what sense Vatican II may be considered an "event."[29]

If the council, as experience and in its texts, was an effort by the church to take fully conscious responsibility for its own self-realization, then this great assumption of ecclesial self-responsibility was made by the leaders of the entire church, that is, by the leaders of the churches, the bishops, and popes of Vatican II. But if there were decisions with implications for the whole church, the unfolding of these implications would be the responsibility of the individual churches and of Catholic women and men. And the assumption and undertaking of that self-responsibility would involve the same sort of process of discernment and decision that constituted the essential event of Vatican II. Now the local churches would have to reflect on themselves, acknowledge their achievements and their failures, consider their cultural circumstances and historical challenges, and determine what they must be and do to meet those challenges in those circumstances. The most striking example of such an undertaking was the one carried out at the Medellín meeting of CELAM (Consejo Episcopal Latinoamericano) devoted to "The Church in the Present-day Transformation of Latin America in the Light of the Council." Medellín attempted to do for the church in Latin America what Vatican II had attempted for the entire church.

More than fifty years later, when the question arises, "What was the impact of Vatican II on the Catholic Church?" we recognize that it cannot be answered by appeal to some "single subject." It can only be answered by looking at the life, or lives, of the churches, of Catholics, to how the church here, and the church there, and the church over there received the council and how it affected their lives. Just as there is no church apart from the churches, so how the council was received by the church can only be studied by how the council was received by the churches, that is, as the lived history, or histories, of Vatican II. This volume offers studies of how this process was undertaken in various places and times by various groups. Of the Second Vatican Council is true what is true of all great historical events: they can only be understood, indeed only be identified, in the light of their consequences, intended or not. In that respect what the Second Vatican Council was as an event is still being determined. And it is being determined in and as the lived histories of the churches.

NOTES

1. Joseph Ratzinger, *Theological Highlights of Vatican II* (New York: Paulist Press, 1966), p. 132.
2. To reconstruct this experience of the council was the primary goal of a project directed by Giuseppe Alberigo that resulted in the five-volume *History of Vatican II*.
3. "The Christian Situation after Vatican II" in [Giuseppe Alberigo, Jean-Pierre Jossua, and Joseph A. Komonchak (eds.), *The Reception of Vatican II* (Washington, DC: The Catholic University of America Press, 1987), p. 11, fn. 32.

4. Alberigo, "Transition to a New Age" in *History of Vatican II*, V, p. 622. In another essay he commented on the reception of Cardinal Lercaro's speech at the end of the first session: "The Latin American and African bishops recognized themselves in it with the unheard of awareness that at the Council their churches might not simply be present but might be real protagonists: *res nostra agitur*." "Giuseppe Dossetti al Concilio Vaticano II" in *Transizione epocale: Studi sul Concilio Vaticano II* (Bologna: Il Mulino, 2009), p. 414; see also further comments on p. 705, where he admits that "the two poles of 'the Church's poverty' and 'the evangelization of the poor' were not adequately treated." He wonders there whether, nevertheless, the theme did not seep into ecclesial consciousness, despite its scarce influence on the final texts.

5. *Acta Synodalia*, I/III, pp. 76–79.

6. Jan Grootaers, *Actes et acteurs à Vatican II* (Leuven: Leuven University Press, 1998), pp. 131–132, where he notes: "Complaints about this were expressed with regard to the composition of the conciliar commissions."

7. Alberigo, "The Christian Situation after Vatican II" in *The Reception of Vatican II*, p. 11, fn. 33.

8. In one of his last essays on the council, Alberigo wrote: "I am convinced that no significant results are to be expected from a new period of commentaries on the various decisions – constitutions, decrees, and declarations – nor from a minute study of particular formulations." Alberigo, "L'Histoire du Convile Vatican II: Problèmes et perspectives" in Christophe Theobald (ed.), *Vatican II sous le regard des historiens* (Paris: Médiasèvres, 2006) pp. 26–48, at p. 43.

9. This is a point well made by Hervé Legrand, "Relecture et évaluation de l'*Histoire du Concile Vatican II* d'un point de vue ecclésiologique" in *Vatican II sous le regard des historiens*, pp. 49–82.

10. "There is no 'pre-' or 'post-' conciliar Church; there is but one, unique Church that walks the path toward the Lord, ever deepening and ever better understanding the treasure of faith that he himself entrusted to her. There are no leaps in this history, there are no fractures, and there is no break in continuity." *The Ratzinger Report: An Exclusive Report on the State of the Church* (San Francisco: Ignatius Press, 1985), p. 35.

11. Paolo Prodi, *Il paradigma tridentino: Un'epoca della storia della Chiesa* (Breccia: Morcelliana, 2010), p. 208 as quoted in Saverio Xeres, "La storiografia sul Vaticano II: Prospettive di lettura e questioni di metodo," *Teologia* 38 (2013), 59–84, at 81 n.

12. I described some of these changes in "The Local Realization of the Church" in *The Reception of Vatican II*, pp. 77–90.

13. See Denis Pelletier, *La crise catholique. Religion, société, politique en France (1965–1978)* (Paris: Payot, 2002).

14. Joseph A. Komonchak, "Modernity and the Construction of Roman Catholicism," *Cristianesimo nella Storia* 18 (1997), 353–385.

15. Joseph Ratzinger, *Faith and the Future* (Chicago: Franciscan Herald Press, 1971), pp. 78–79.

16. Yves Congar, *Église catholique et France moderne* (Paris: Hachette, 1978), pp. 57, 230.

17. Yves Congar, *Le Concile de Vatican II* (Paris: Beauchesne, 1984), p. 106.

18. Yves Congar, *Église catholique et France moderne*, p. 50. Congar quotes from Jacques-J. Natanson, in *Esprit*, November 1971, 600.

19. Bernard Lonergan, "Dimensions of Meaning" in *Collection, Collected Works*, IV (Toronto: University of Toronto Press, 1988), p. 244. This is the text of a talk given May 12, 1965.

20. Bernard Lonergan, "The Future of Christianity" in *Second Collection* (Philadelphia: Westminster, 1974), pp. 149–163.

21. Fuller descriptions of the impact on theology of these cultural transformations can be found in lectures delivered in the early 1970s and published in *Philosophical and Theological Papers 1965–1980 (Collected Works of Bernard Lonergan*, vol. XVII), ed. Robert C. Croken and Robert M. Doran (Toronto: University of Toronto Press, 2004), pp. 221–298.

22. Lonergan, "The Absence of God in Modern Culture" in *Second Collection*, p. 115.

23. Lonergan, "The Future of Christianity" in *Second Collection*, p. 159.

24. Ludwig Feuerbach, *The Essence of Christianity* (New York: Harper Torchbooks, 1957), p. 26.

25. Pius X's inaugural encyclical, *E supremi*, October 4, 1903, *ASS* 36, 131–132.

26. Forty years later, Pope Benedict XVI echoed this definition of a "new humanism": "Promoting a new humanism, in fact, requires a clear understanding of what this 'newness' actually embodies. Far from being the fruit of a superficial desire for novelty, the quest for a new humanism must take serious account of the fact that Europe today is experiencing a massive cultural shift, one in which men and women are increasingly conscious of their call to be actively engaged in shaping their own history." There is, however, no reference to *Gaudium et Spes* 55. (Speech to conference on the new humanism, June 2007.)

27. Lonergan, *Method in Theology*, p. 364.

28. Komonchak, "The Local Realization of the Church" in *The Reception of Vatican II*, pp. 79, 81.

29. In an essay entitled "Do We Miss Karl Rahner?" Johann Baptist Metz has some pertinent remarks. He points out that for an interpretation of Vatican II, it is not enough "to appeal to arbitrarily selected conciliar texts"; one has also to take into consideration "how the church has concretely appropriated this council in the intervening years, particularly how the regional churches have tried to make it bear fruit for their particular situations. In other words, this approach takes as the standard for an understanding of the council the history of its effects [*Wirkungsgeschichte*] within the church ... One might look at the documents of the Latin American bishops conferences at Medillín and Puebla, at the post-conciliar documents of the Asian bishops, at the episcopal synods in the Federal Republic [of Germany], or at other comparable events in France, Holland, and the United States." J. B. Metz, *A Passion for God: The Mystical-Political Dimension of Christianity* (Mahwah, NJ: Paulist Press, 1998), p. 93.

INDEX